# Lecture Notes in Computer Science 2949

Edited by G. Goos, J. Hartmanis, and J. van Leeuwen

# Springer

*Berlin*
*Heidelberg*
*New York*
*Hong Kong*
*London*
*Milan*
*Paris*
*Tokyo*

Rocco De Nicola   Gianluigi Ferrari
Greg Meredith (Eds.)

# Coordination Models and Languages

6th International Conference, COORDINATION 2004
Pisa Italy, February 24-27, 2004
Proceedings

Springer

Series Editors

Gerhard Goos, Karlsruhe University, Germany
Juris Hartmanis, Cornell University, NY, USA
Jan van Leeuwen, Utrecht University, The Netherlands

Volume Editors

Rocco De Nicola
Università. di Firenze, Dipartimento di Sistemi e Informatica
Via Lombroso 6/17, 50134 Firenze, Italy
E-mail: denicola@dsi.unifi.it

Gianluigi Ferrari
Università di Pisa, Dipartimento di Informatica
Via F. Buonarroti, 2, 56127 Pisa, Italy
E-mail: giangi@di.unipi.it

Greg Meredith
Microsoft Corporation
Redmont, WA 98052-6399, USA
E-mail: gregmer@microsoft.com

Cataloging-in-Publication Data applied for

A catalog record for this book is available from the Library of Congress.

Bibliographic information published by Die Deutsche Bibliothek
Die Deutsche Bibliothek lists this publication in the Deutsche Nationalbibliografie;
detailed bibliographic data is available in the Internet at <http://dnb.ddb.de>.

CR Subject Classification (1998): D.1.3, C.2.4, F.1.2, D.2.4, I.2.11

ISSN 0302-9743
ISBN 3-540-21044-X Springer-Verlag Berlin Heidelberg New York

Springer-Verlag is a part of Springer Science+Business Media

springeronline.com

© Springer-Verlag Berlin Heidelberg 2004
Printed in Germany

Typesetting: Camera-ready by author, data conversion by DA-TeX Gerd Blumenstein
Printed on acid-free paper     SPIN: 10986257     06/3142     5 4 3 2 1 0

# Preface

The 6th International Conference on Coordination Models and Languages (Coordination 2004) was held at the Computer Science Department of Pisa University, Italy, on February 24–27 2004. The previous conferences in this series took place in Cesena (Italy), Berlin (Germany), Amsterdam (Netherlands), Limasol (Cyprus), and York (UK). Building on the success of these events, the latest conference provided a forum for the growing community of researchers interested in models, languages, and implementation techniques for coordination and component-based software, as well as applications that exploit them.

The need for increasing programming productivity and rapid development of complex systems provides the pragmatic motivation for the development of coordination/orchestration languages and models. The intellectual excitement associated with such endeavors is rooted in the decades-old desire to leverage off increasingly higher levels of abstractions. Coordination-based methods provide a clean separation between individual software components and their interactions within their overall software organization. Coordination is relevant in design, development, debugging, maintenance, and reuse of all complex concurrent and distributed systems. Specifically, coordination becomes paramount in the context of open systems, systems with mobile entities, and dynamically reconfigurable evolving systems. Moreover, coordination models and languages focus on such key issues in component-based software engineering as specification, interaction, and dynamic compositions. More recently, market trends brought on by the commercialization of the World-Wide Web, have fuelled a new level of interest in coordination-based approaches in industry. Applications like BizTalk, standards like the Web services' WS-* family, and contending coordination standards like BEPL4WS and WSCI, are all examples of this phenomenon. This interest is opening up new opportunities both to apply coordination-based techniques to a broad class of applications as well as to grapple with potentially new kinds of requirements coming from Internet-scale scenarios.

The main topics of the conference included: theoretical models and foundations for coordination, coordination middleware, specification, refinement, and analysis of software architectures, architectural and interface definition languages, agent-oriented languages and models, dynamic software architectures, component programming, Web services, coordination in peer-to-peer and grid computing, tools and environments for the development of coordinated applications, industrial relevance of coordination and software architectures, domain-specific software coordination models, and case studies.

The Program Committee, consisting of 23 members, considered 72 papers and selected 20 for presentation. These papers were selected on the basis of originality, quality and relevance to the topic of the conference. These proceedings include the revised version of the 20 accepted papers, and the abstracts of the invited talks by Gérard Boudol (*Inria Sophia Antipolis, France*), Fabio Casati (*HP Labs, USA*) and Paola Inverardi (*Università dell'Aquila, Italy*).

Paper selection was a difficult and challenging task, and many good submissions had to be rejected. Each submission was refereed by at least four reviewers, and some had five reports or more. We are very grateful to all the program committee members, who devoted much effort and valuable time to read and select the papers. In addition, we gratefully acknowledge the help of a large number of colleagues who reviewed submissions in their area of expertise. They are all listed below. We apologize for any inadvertent omissions.

Following the example of previous editions, we encouraged authors to submit their contributions in electronic format. We handled the submissions with Conf-Man (http://confman.unik.no/~confman) a free Web-based paper submission and reviewing system. With reference to this, we would like to thank Antonio Cisternino who managed a lot at crucial steps of the whole process. His computer skill and the time and effort he invested were crucial ingredients in our running of the program committee. Moreover, we would like to thank Roberto Bruni and Emilio Tuosto who managed the activity of editing the proceedings.

Finally, we would like to thank all the authors who submitted their papers for making this conference possible, the Program Committee members, as well as all the conference participants.

February 2003

Rocco De Nicola
Gianluigi Ferrari
Greg Meredith

## Program Co-chair

Rocco De Nicola       Università di Firenze, Italy
Greg Meredith       Microsoft, USA

## Program Committee

Roberto Amadio       Univ. Marseilles, France
Farhad Arbab       CWI, The Netherlands
Marcelo Bonsangue       Leiden University, The Netherlands
Paolo Ciancarini       Univ. Bologna, Italy
Gianluigi Ferrari       Univ. Pisa, Italy
José Fiadeiro       Univ. Leicester, UK
Chris Hankin       Imperial College, UK
Jean-Marie Jacquet       Univ. Namur, Belgium
Antonia Lopes       Univ. Lisbon, Portugal
Jeff Magee       Imperial College, UK
George Papadopoulos       Univ. Cyprus, Cyprus
Gian Pietro Picco       Politecnico di Milano, Italy
Rosario Pugliese       Univ. Firenze, Italy
Gruia-Catalin Roman       Washington University in St. Louis, USA
Ant Rowstrom       Microsoft, Cambridge, UK
Vijay Saraswat       IBM Research, USA
Carolin Talcott       SRI, USA
Robert Tolksdorf       Free University of Berlin, Germany
Herbert Wiklicky       Imperial College, UK
Alan Wood       Univ. York, UK
Franco Zambonelli       Univ. Modena, Italy

## Sponsoring Organizations

Università di
Pisa

Dipartimento di Informatica
Università di Pisa

Polo Didattico *Fibonacci*
Università di Pisa

Dipartimento di Sistemi e Informatica
Università di Firenze

Microsoft Research
Microsoft Corporation USA

## Organizing Chair

Gianluigi Ferrari       Università di Pisa, Italy

## Organizing Committee

Andrea Bracciali, Roberto Bruni, Antonio Cisternino, Dan Hirsch, Laura Semini,
Emilio Tuosto

# Referees

Marco Aldinucci
Andreas Andreou
Pedro Antunes
Lorenzo Bettini
Michele Boreale
Pietro Braione
Antonio Brogi
Roberto Bruni
Marzia Buscemi
Nathan Caswell
Giorgos Chrysanthou
Silvano Dal Zilio
Vincent Danos
Giorgio Ghelli
Daniele Gorla
Juan Guillen-Scholten
Dan Hirsch
Cosimo Laneve

Alessandro Lapadula
Michele Loreti
Marco Mamei
Luis Moniz
Pavlos Moraitis
Amy L. Murphy
Anna Philippou
Darrell Reimer
Laura Semini
Simone Semprini
Leon van der Torre
Emilio Tuosto
Vincent Vanackere
Vasco Vasconcelos
M.J. Wiering
Gianluigi Zavattaro
Sarah Zennou
Peter Zoeteweij

# Table of Contents

## Invited Talks

## Contributed Papers

# A Reactive Programming Model for Global Computing

Gérard Boudol

*Inria Sophia Antipolis, France*

## Abstract

In this talk I introduce a programming model for the mobile code, and more generally for programming in a global computing perspective. I first present some requirements for this style of programming, arising from the features and new observables of the global computing context, and I briefly discuss some of the models and programming languages that have been proposed - Obliq, pi-based and Linda-based models, Ambients. I then present a model based on the ideas of "synchronous" programming, that is based on suspension and preemption primitives associated with locally broadcast events. This programming style, providing a notion of reaction and time-out, looks appropriate to address the unreliable character of accessing resources in a global computing context, and to deal with the various kinds of failures – such as unpredictable delays, transient disconnections, congestion, etc. – that arise in a global network.

The proposed model, called ULM, combines a standard imperative and functional style, such as the one of ML or Scheme, with some construct for "reactive" programming. The model also proposes constructs for programming mobile agents, that move together with their state, made of a control stack and a store. This makes the access to references also potentially suspensive, and this is one of the main novelties of the model. The focus of this work is on giving a precise semantics for a small, yet expressive core language. Some examples of this expressiveness are given in the talk.

R. de Nicola et al. (Eds.): COORDINATION 2004, LNCS 2949, p. 1, 2004.

# Open Issues and Opportunities in Web Services Modeling, Development, and Management

Fabio Casati

Hewlett-Packard
1501 Page Mill road, MS 1142
Palo Alto, CA, 94304, USA
fabio.casati@hp.com

## Extended Abstract

Despite the great interest and the enormous potential, Web services, and more in general service-oriented architectures (SOAs), are still in their infancy. The speed at which software vendors have released middleware and development tools for Web services is unprecedented, but their level of maturity is still far from their counterparts in conventional middleware. This is only natural and common to any novel technology, and will be corrected over time, as more users adopt this technology and provide feedback on what the actual needs are.

Aside from considerations related to the young age of the technology, the interesting aspect of Web services is that they have characteristics that differ from services in conventional middleware, and that can service development and management tools to a new dimension. For example, services in conventional middleware were often tightly coupled and developed by the same team. This means that it was difficult to combine services in different ways, and that service descriptions were rather poor. Web services are instead loosely-coupled and designed for B2B applications. This means that Web services are independent of each other and are invoked by clients who have no access to the service development team. Since service descriptions are all clients have available to understand the service behavior, they are richer than their counterpart in conventional middleware, going well beyond interface descriptions. This factor, along with the increased standardization and the loose coupling, makes *composition* technologies more applicable. The opportunity of composing Web services and of leveraging richer service descriptions are some of the factors that both create more requirements and enable a greater level of automated support from the middleware and from CASE-like development tools.

Other important aspects are related not so much to Web service technology, but to their intended applicability. For example, Web services are typically used to integrate complex systems and not to perform simple computations. Hence, manageability and ease of deployment become often more important than performance.

In this presentation I will elaborate on these and other key aspects of Web services, emphasizing the opportunities they provide and the unsolved challenges they present from a modeling and management perspective.

R. de Nicola et al. (Eds.): COORDINATION 2004, LNCS 2949, p. 2, 2004.

# Compositionality, Coordination and Software Architecture

Paola Inverardi

Dipartimento di Informatica
Universitá dell'Aquila

## Abstract

In the last decade the way software is produced has been radically changing. Software component technology has witnessed growing popularity with the advent and diffusion of effective component-based infrastructures like CORBA, .Net and Java Beans. Component Based Software Development allowed integration of heterogeneous and legacy components and their availability in innovative contexts like the Internet. At the same time Component Based Software (CBS) systems, often based on Components Off The Shelf (COTS), exhibit severe integration problems at execution time, due to component coordination and synchronization failures [2, 1].

Thus, on one side, component-based infrastructures made easier the assembling of heterogeneous COTS components by providing mechanisms to solve syntactic and static semantics mismatches among components. On the other side, they did not offer support to solve coordination and synchronization problems. This situation is made worse by insufficient component behavioral specifications that make it difficult to establish correct behavioral properties on component assembly.

There has been in the last years a growing interest in the specification and analysis of component assembly [3]. In this respect, CBS development poses old problems in a new context. From a verification point of view the interest is, as usual, in being able to prove behavioral properties of the assembled system. On the negative side we have that in general component behavior is underspecified or unknown, while on the positive side we have that the way components are put together is already known, since it is forced by the software architecture of the component-based infrastructure. As far as behavioral failure recovery is concerned, on the negative side we have that components can be black-box and thus unmodifiable, however on the positive side we can use the software architecture to regulate and control component interaction.

In our research we have identified three different but related research areas:

1. How components, including COTS, can be provided with a behavioral interface useful to prove behavioral properties at the system level.
2. How components are assembled together and what is the impact of the way components are assembled on the behavioral analysis.

R. de Nicola et al. (Eds.): COORDINATION 2004, LNCS 2949, pp. 3–4, 2004.

3. How an assembled system can be checked and made correct with respect to a certain set of behavioral properties.

In my talk I will analyse these three research areas, trying to put our own contribution in the more general perspective of the current research in these different fields and their relations with research in compositionality and coordination.

Our approach uses a specific software architecture as the logical skeleton to assemble components. The information on the software architecture , i.e., on the way components interact together via connectors, allows us to achieve the automatic enforcement of specific coordination policies on the interaction behavior of the components of an assembled system. In our approach, starting from a suitable (and simple) specification of the expected behavior of the assembled system and of its desired behavioral properties, we are able to automatically synthesize architectural connectors that allow only correct interaction (w.r.t. the behavioral properties) to occurr among components [4, 5, 7, 6, 8].

# References

[1] B. Boehm and C. Abts, COTS Integration: Plug and Pray?, IEEE Computer, Vol. 32, Num. 1, 1999. 3

[2] D. Garlan and R. Allen and J. Ockerbloom, Architectural mismatch: Why reuse is so hard. In *IEEE Software Journal, 1995, vol. 12, num. 6.* 3

[3] Proceeding Component Based Software Engineering Workshops. *CBSE series,* http://sei.cmu.edu. 3

[4] Paola Inverardi, Simone Scriboni, Connectors Synthesis for Deadlock-Free Component Based Architectures, *IEEE Proc. 16th ASE 2001.* 4

[5] Paola Inverardi, Massimo Tivoli, Automatic Synthesis of Deadlock free connectors for COM/DCOM Applications. *ACM Proc. FSE/ESEC 2001, Vienna 2001.* 4

[6] Paola Inverardi, Massimo Tivoli, Deadlock free Software Architectures for COM/DCOM Applications. *Journal of System and Software, CBSE Special Issue 2003.* 4

[7] A. Bucchiarone, P. Inverardi, M. Tivoli, Automatic synthesis of coordinators of COTS group-ware applications: an example. *DMC 2003, IEEE proceedings WET-ICE 2003.* 4

[8] P. Inverardi, M. Tivoli, Software Architecture for Correct Components Assembly. In *Formal Methods for the Design of Computer, Communication and Software Systems: Software Architecture, Springer, LNCS 2804.* 4

# Problem Frames:
# A Case for Coordination

L. Barroca[1], J.L. Fiadeiro[2], M. Jackson[1], R. Laney[1], and B.Nuseibeh[1]

[1] Department of Computing, The Open University
Milton Keynes MK7 6AA, UK
{l.barroca,r.c.laney,m.jackson}@open.ac.uk
[2] Department of Computer Science, University of Leicester
University Road, Leicester LE1 7RH, UK
jose@fiadeiro.org

**Abstract.** We show how principles of separation of *Coordination* from *Computation* can be used to endow the Problem Frames approach to problem analysis with representation schemes. These representation schemes facilitate the way evolution of requirements or of the application domain can be reflected in the decomposition structure, making it easier to change.

## 1 Introduction

Decomposition as an aid to tackle complexity has been used in software development for a long time; after all, software engineering is a human activity and problem solving through "divide-and-conquer" must be as old as humanity. Many approaches to decomposition can be found in the literature, some of which have got into day-to-day practice, from domain modelling down to design.

However, problem domains can change over time: changes in the application domain may require software solutions to be changed to maintain customers' expectations. Even when the application domain remains stable, customers come up with new requirements that often necessitate new solutions to be developed! This means that problem analysis and decomposition are essentially part of a continuous process. Indeed, even if a problem decomposition structure succeeds in breaking down the complexity of a problem and allows a suitable solution to be developed, such a structure may not be easy to evolve as the original problem and its requirements change.

Finding a problem decomposition that can evolve easily is often difficult – unfortunately, we do not need to go back very far in history to observe situations of "conquest" through "division" that have left in place structures that have evolved in undesirable ways ... A good knowledge of the problem domain, of the type of changes that are likely to occur, and of their frequency, is, again, fundamental for knowing the costs of evolution. Therefore, it is important that mechanisms be provided for changes to be reflected incrementally in the decomposition structure. This allows these changes to be tracked down to sub-problems, where they can be localised without affecting the rest of the structure, or through the addition of sub-

R. de Nicola, G. Ferrari, G. Meredith (Eds.): COORDINATION 2004, LNCS 2949, pp. 5–19, 2004.
© Springer-Verlag Berlin Heidelberg 2004

problems that reflect the new properties that need to be brought about and the way they relate to the existing ones.

In this paper, we report on the work through which we are addressing this problem by extending and combining the Problem Frames approach to problem analysis and description [13] with the *coordination*-based approach to run-time software evolution [3]. This extension endows Problem Frames with representation structures that allow for forms of problem decomposition that separate aspects related to the coordination of the interactions between solution (called the *Machine*) and problem domain, from the computational aspects that the machine implements. This principle of separation of concerns has been proposed for software design in the form of *Coordination Languages and Models* [10]. Our contribution in this paper is the application of this principle to problem analysis and requirements specification in order to control the complexity of managing evolution resulting from changes in customers' requirements or the application domain. We achieve this separation by the explicit externalisation of the coordination aspects, the *coordination interfaces*, and the explicit representation of the interactions with *coordination rules*.

The paper is structured as follows. Section 2 provides an overview of Problem Frames and presents the example that we use throughout the paper to illustrate our approach. In Section 3, we delimit the scope of our work and introduce the proposed application of coordination primitives and modelling techniques. Section 4 shows how assumptions about the domain can be captured through *coordination interfaces*. Section 5 takes these coordination interfaces and discusses the description of the behaviour of the Machine through *coordination rules*. In Section 6, we summarise the impact of our approach in the context of related work. Section 7 concludes the paper and discusses future work.

## 2    Problem Frames

The Problem Frames approach to problem analysis and description recognises that domain problems can usually be categorised as a set of commonly occurring patterns for which the same type of models can be used. The approach emphasises the relationships of systems to the real world domains where they live. Problem Frames encapsulate both real world and system objects, and describe the interactions between them.

A simple problem frame is represented typically by a context diagram (Figure 1) showing one machine, one domain, and the shared phenomena between them.

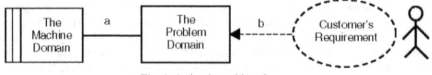

**Fig. 1.** A simple problem frame

The Machine Domain represents the piece of software that the customer requires and the platform on which it executes in order to bring about some desired effects. The Problem Domain is that part of the world in which those effects are perceived by the customer. The Requirements are the properties that the customer wants to observe, through the shared phenomena *b*, in the Problem Domain as a result of the effects brought about by the software as it executes and interacts with the domain via the shared phenomena *a*.

We illustrate this using a simple example of a sluice gate control introduced by Jackson [13]:

> *A rising and falling gate is used in an irrigation system. A computer system is needed to control the gate. The gate is opened and closed by rotating vertical screws controlled by clockwise and anticlockwise pulses. There are sensors at the top and bottom of the gate travel indicating when the gate is fully opened and fully shut.*

The sluice gate control we look at is a timed one:

> *A timed sluice gate is required to be in the fully opened position for ten minutes in every three hours and otherwise kept closed.*

Problem analysis is essentially concerned with the description of the relationships among the phenomena that are shared between these different domains: *a* for the phenomena shared between the Machine and the Problem Domain; *b* for the phenomena of the Problem Domain that the Customer can observe.

In the example, the Problem Domain is clearly concerned with the gate, its motor, and the way it can be observed and operated. The Machine, i.e. the computer system that is needed to control the gate, shares with the Problem Domain the two events that it controls – the commands for opening and closing the gate as made available through the motor – and the observations of the state of the gate as made available through the sensors – being fully up or down (altogether denoted *a2* in Figure 2). These two observations are also shared with the customer (denoted *b2* in Figure 2).

Because the sluice gate that we will be analysing is a timed one, a timer should also be made part of the problem domain. The machine observes and resets the timer (*a1* in Figure 2) and the timer can also be observed by the customer (*b1* in Figure 2). The machine observes and controls the sluice gate (*a2* in Figure 2) and the sluice gate can be observed by the customer (*b2* in Figure 2).

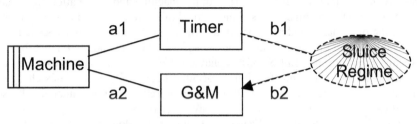

**Fig. 2.** Problem frame for a timed sluice gate

The separation that Problem Frames provide between the different domains is particularly important during evolution. The relationship between the Machine Domain and the Problem Domain is one that the software engineering activity targets and controls. As software does not degrade in a physical sense, the need for evolving the machine will result from changes occurring in the Customer's Requirements or the

Problem Domain. Changes in customer requirements are a fact of life, even an intrinsic characteristic of software systems according to Lehman [19]. It is often hard for the customer to foresee all the consequences that a Machine will have in the Problem Domain and, therefore, a newly installed machine may lead to new properties of the Problem Domain that, in turn, may lead to a revised set of customer requirements. On the other hand, the Problem Domain can change in ways that are not under the control of the Machine, which means that the behaviour of the Machine in the new domain no longer satisfies the customer requirements. Naturally, these two scenarios are not mutually exclusive; they just distil two simple situations that lead to the need to change the Machine.

This paper is concerned with the problem of finding representations of the interaction between the machine and the part of the domain that it observes and controls, in ways that allow for evolution to be managed or even programmed. These representations provide a means of ensuring that the machine can self-adapt to certain classes of change known to occur in the application domain. The principle of separating coordination from computation plays a fundamental role here.

## 3    The Scope for Coordination

Coordination is intrinsic to the way Problem Frames are used to decompose and analyse problems. The Machine is a computational device that is superposed on the domain so that, through the interaction between Machine and Domain, new behaviour can emerge to satisfy user requirements. The computations of the Machine are of interest only to the extent that, when interacting with the domain, they enable the required properties to emerge. Hence, the central concern for evolution must be the explicit representation of the mechanisms that are responsible for the coordination of the interaction between the Machine and the Domain.

In order to motivate the approach that we propose in this paper, let us refine the diagram in Figure 1. The purpose of the diagram was to note the need to distinguish between three domains and the relationships that concern them. Software engineering works on descriptions of the entities, phenomena, and properties that are involved in these domains and relationships [14]. So, the machine and the relationship $a$ have to be developed and established based on a model of the relevant part of the domain.

On the other hand, and perhaps not as obvious, the relationship $a$ does not need to be established on the basis of the concrete software system code (computation) that is executing, but of a description of its behaviour (specification) as it is executed on the chosen platform. The specification is essential because it encapsulates changes that do not have any bearing on the customer's requirements as formulated. These are modifications that software engineers may wish or be required to perform on the machine in order to take advantage of new technologies or to respond to IT infrastructure changes

Figure 3 depicts the wider software development context, in which the dashed line separates the domains and their descriptions:

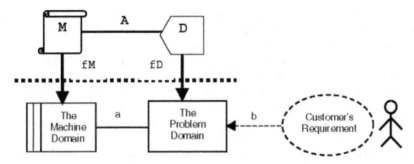

**Fig. 3.** Enriched problem frame diagram

By $M$ we mean the description of the behaviour of the execution of the software system on a particular platform. This description is based on the shared phenomena identified in $a$ and other parameters that relate to nature of the formalism that is being used for describing the behaviour. These additional parameters are not features of the code that lies in the Machine, but mere "prosthesis".

By $D$ we mean the model that abstracts the properties of the Problem Domain that concern the way the Machine can interact with it, and by $A$ we denote the way descriptions $M$ and $D$ are related. This is where we separate coordination from computation: in $A/D$ we wish to place all and only the aspects that concern the way the machine interacts with the domain. These include the phenomena through which this interaction takes place, and the assumptions on which it is based, i.e. the properties that are assumed of the domain in the way the computations taking place in the Machine are programmed. This explicit externalisation of the coordination aspects, which we call the *coordination interface* of the Machine, is the contribution that we claim and discuss in section 4 of the paper.

The vertical relationships between the description and the domain worlds also play a central rôle in our approach. By $fM$ we mean the *fit* that needs to exist between the description and the behaviour being described. This fit can be the object of formal verification once the description $M$ is translated to an acceptable semantics for the language/platform in which the Machine is coded. It is the responsibility of the software provider to ensure $fM$ throughout the life of the system. In contrast, customer satisfaction is established exclusively on the basis of the triple $M/A/D$ and therefore $fM$ is not within the scope of the kind of evolution that we are addressing. Therefore, we will not discuss $fM$ any further in this paper.

By $fD$ we mean the fit between the model and the Problem Domain. Depending on the nature of the domain that the software system is controlling, this fit may or not be of a formal nature. For instance, the Machine may be controlling another software system (e.g., monitoring some of its properties), in which case $fD$ can be cast in a semantic domain common to the two language/platform couples. Because, again, the satisfaction of the customer's requirements is established on basis of the triple $M/A/D$ alone, the customer can only observe the required properties in the Problem Domain if the fit is correct.

Maintaining the correctness of $fD$ is a hard problem as discussed in [15]. It is not part of the responsibility of the software engineer; otherwise it would be part of the Problem Domain. Rather, it is the responsibility of the problem analyst. Indeed, one of the reasons a given system may need to evolve is, precisely, because its boundary with the Problem Domain may be required to change in order for some parts of the environment to become under its control.    For instance, new sensors may be introduced that allow the software system to monitor part of the fit and react when deviations occur [14].  What is important is that the control of the correctness of $fD$ is an activity that may require a change of the original problem and, hence, of the frames that apply, bringing $fD$, or part of it, into the realm of the problem domain.  In any given state of the decomposition, the $fD$ in place is not under the control of the Machine and, hence, will remain outside the scope of the paper.

In summary, we are concerned with the representation of the triple $M/A/D$.  It is at this level that the satisfaction of the customer's requirements can be established. These requirements should be expressed in a logical formalism $(L, \vdash)$ as a sentence $R$.  On the other hand, a mapping $P(M/A/D,fD)$ into $L$ should be provided that is correct with respect to the semantics of $(L, \vdash)$ and the language in which $M$ is described, characterising customer satisfaction as:

$$P(M/A/D,fD), G \vdash R$$

where $G$ represents properties of the domain that can provide an adequate bridge between the phenomena at $a$ and the phenomena at $b$.  The truth of $G$ will be independent of the problem being analysed and hence used as an evolution invariant. Any formalisation of the properties of a physical domain is an approximation to the truth, and different approximations are appropriate for different problems, of course. One may very well need to evolve the triple due to changes in $G$ that arise from the realisation that the approximations being made are not good enough or valid anymore (e.g., relativistic considerations may become relevant in a domain previously described in purely Newtonian mechanics).  We leave a more detailed discussion of these issues to a future paper.

Our approach to the representation of the coordination aspects involved in Problem Frames is based on the *coordination technologies* presented in [3]: a set of principles and modelling techniques that were first proposed in [2] based on the notion of *coordination contract*, or *contract*, for short.  The purpose of coordination contracts is to make available in modelling languages, like the UML [5], the expressive power of *connectors* in the terminology of Software Architecture [23].  The overall goal is to provide a means for the interaction mechanisms that relate system components to be externalised from the code that implements these components.  It makes the relationships explicit in system models so that they can be evolved independently of the computations that the components perform.

Contracts prescribe certain coordination effects (the *glue* of architectural connectors in the sense of [1]) that can be superposed on a collection of partners (system components) when the occurrence of one of a set of specified *triggers* is detected in the system.  Contracts establish interactions at the instance level when superposed on a running system.  In the terminology that we used in the previous section, they sit in the Machine domain as part of the code.  At the level that concerns us in the paper, the triple $M/A/D$, the primitive that abstracts the properties of the coordination glue from the code that implements it in contracts, is called a *coordination law* as described in section 5.

A coordination law corresponds to a connector type as in Architecture Description Languages. In business modelling, coordination laws can be used to model the rules according to which organisations make available to the market the services that their core entities provide [16,17]. In control systems, they can be used to model the mechanisms that need to be superposed over the components of the target plant to monitor their behaviour, adapt them to new modes of operation, or interconnect them to ensure required emergent behaviour [4]. In the description of a coordination law, the nature of the components over which the law can be instantiated are identified as *coordination interfaces* (the *roles* of the connector type in the sense of [1]). Our approach is to capture each problem frame triple *M/A/D* as a coordination law for which *M* corresponds to the glue, *D* defines a coordination interface, and *A* is captured in the way the interface is used in the law.

## 4    Domain Assumptions as Coordination Interfaces

We now illustrate our approach by returning to the timed sluice gate example in section 2.

Let us deal first with the way the domain model is abstracted as a coordination interface. The idea is to declare what the Machine is expecting from the problem domain in the way it has been designed to control it. Two primitives are made available in coordination interfaces for that purpose: *services* and *events*.

- Services identify operations that the domain must provide for the Machine to invoke. In our example, these correspond to the actions that the motor makes available to operate the gate – *onClockw* for starting the motor clockwise, *onAnti* for starting it anticlockwise, and *off* for stopping it.

- Events identify state transitions that the Machine needs to be able to detect in the problem domain. These act as triggers for the contract that is being put in place to react and activate a *coordination rule* as discussed below. In our example, the events correspond to the states that the sensors of the gate make available – *top* and *bottom* – so that the Machine knows when the motor has to be stopped.

```
coordination interface sluice_gate
services      onClockw, onAnti, off
events        top, bottom
properties    (onClockw ∨ onAnti) ⊃ (¬(onClockw ∨ onAnti) before off)
              onClockw ⊃ (top unless off)
              onAnti ⊃ (bottom unless off)
end interface
```

This example also illustrates that coordination interfaces are not just declarations of features (signatures). They specify properties that must be proved upon instantiation, i.e. express requirements on the behaviour of the components that can come under the coordination of the machine. These properties capture semantic aspects of the roles that components play in the application domain. Such properties are defined so as to state *requirements* placed by the law on the entities that can be subjected to its coordination rules, not as a declaration of features or properties that entities offer to be coordinated. In our application to Problem Frames, these are assumptions made on the problem domain that determine the correctness of the fit *fD*.

Returning to our example, we chose three properties to illustrate the kinds of assumptions that can be made and the implications that they have.

- The first reads: "After an onClockw or an onAnti command is accepted, no more such commands will be accepted before an off command is accepted". In physical terms, this means that the domain couple Gate&Motor is being assumed to prevent these events from occurring. One may think, for instance, of a motor that provides three buttons, one for each operation, and that the onClockw and onAnti buttons become locked once pressed and will only be unlocked after the off button is pressed.
- The second reads: "After the onClockw button is pressed, the event top will be eventually observed unless the off button is pressed in the meanwhile". In other words, if the motor is started clockwise and left undisturbed for long enough, the event top will eventually be observed through the sensors.
- The third is similar to the second; it states that if the motor is started anti-clockwise and left undisturbed for long enough, the event bottom will be eventually observed through the sensors.

The language that we have used for specifying these properties is that of a temporal logic, the syntax and semantics of which we shall not discuss in the paper because they are not relevant for understanding our approach (see [21] for examples of temporal logics typically used in Computer Science). In [3], an alternate to temporal logic that uses pre/post conditions on services is illustrated.

The implications of including properties such as these in a coordination interface have to be understood in the context of the triple *M/A/D*. They are taken in conjunction with the properties of the Machine to ensure the satisfaction of the requirements. Hence, they provide the criteria for the fit *fD* to be judged. That is to say, these are properties that need to be checked when the machine is installed in the domain. They result from an agreement between the problem analyst and the customer as to the nature of the problem domain over which the machine is going to operate.

From the point of view of the software engineer, these are properties that can be assumed when designing the machine. Hence, in our example, the software engineer will not bear any responsibility for the behaviour of the machine if it is interconnected with a sluice-gate that allows for buttons to be pushed indiscriminately. A software engineer who builds a machine that relies on the observation of the top event to switch off the engine after having set it clockwise, cannot be blamed if the motor burns down because the sensor that should emit the top event is faulty.

Hence, the more properties are included in a coordination interface, the simpler the task of programming the computations on the machine will be, which can turn to the customer's advantage as reduced development costs. However, this comes at the cost of controlling that the fit *fD* is maintained correct which, as already argued, is to be born by the customer, not the software engineer. It is the customer's responsibility to make sure that the sensors are working properly and that only motors that do not allow for buttons to be pushed indiscriminately are used. If, for instance, this assumption on motors ceases to be sensible, for instance because motors of that kind are no longer available, then the problem analyst should be brought in to renegotiate the original problem frame, which may lead to a new triple *M/A/D* to be developed.

Because the operation of the sluice gate needs to be timed, we have to account for a timer as well. The timer needs to provide a service for being *reset* and events that report elapsed time – *tick(n:nat)*.

```
coordination interface timer
services     reset
events       tick(n:nat)
properties   tick(n) ⊃ (¬tick(m) before (tick(n+1) ∨ reset))
             reset ⊃ tick(0)
end interface
```

In this case, the properties are specifying that the ticking should be incremental and sequential until the timer is reset, starting with 0. Again, the software engineer will bear no responsibility for the outcome of a connection of the machine with a timer that decrements or is not sequential.

This example also illustrates how coordination interfaces can be used for identifying not only the features of the domain through which required forms of coordination are going to be superposed, but also components that need to be provided in addition to the Machine. Such components, like the timer, are not necessarily part of the original problem domain – the Gate&Motor does not necessarily come with an integrated timer or clock – nor of the solution domain – the timer is not to be realised by software. They need to be provided at configuration time, and they may be evolved independently of the Machine and changes operated in the application domain, provided that the fit to the coordination interface is maintained.

Coordination interfaces are named for the sake of reusability and simplification of the binding process that establishes the fit *fD*. Their actual names are not important. Our experience in using these coordination primitives in real projects has shown that it is useful to externalise coordination interfaces from the laws in the context of which they are defined, to establish a hierarchy between them that is consistent with the *fD* relationship in the sense that a fit to a given interface is also a fit to any ancestor of that interface. In business environments, this is useful because coordination interfaces fulfil the role of representations of abstract business entities and, hence, the hierarchy of interfaces will, ultimately, provide a taxonomy of all the business uses that are made of entities in the application domain. For control based systems, the hierarchy of interfaces can be mapped to an existing classification of the component types that can be found for the target plant, allowing a component to be replaced by a more specialised one without destroying the fit that binds it to the controller.

## 5   Describing Machine Behaviour through Coordination Rules

The effects that the software system is required to bring about are described through the *coordination rules* of the law that describes the behaviour of the Machine:

```
coordination law timed_sluice_gate_controller
interfaces  sg: sluice_gate; tm:timer
```

```
attributes  open: bool
rules       when sg.top
            do   sg.off ‖ open:=true ‖ tm.reset
            when tm.tick(10) ∧ open
            do   sg.onAnti
            when sg.bottom
            do   sg.off ‖ open:=false ‖ tm.reset
            when tm.tick(170) ∧ ¬open
            do   sg.onClockw
end law
```

Each coordination rule is of the form:

```
when trigger
with condition
do   set of operations
```

Under the "when" clause, the trigger to which the contracts that instantiate the law will react is specified as a Boolean condition defined over the events declared in the interface and conditions over the internal state of the law. Under the "with" clause we specify a guard, a Boolean condition defined over the internal state of the law that, if false, leads to a rejection of the trigger; this means that the reaction will not be executed and, depending on the nature of the trigger, failure will be reported back to the domain entity for suitable handling. The reaction to be performed is identified under the "do" clause as a set of operations, each of which is either a service declared in the interface or an update on the internal state of the law. The whole interaction is handled as a single transaction, i.e. its execution is atomic. In particular, multiple assignments are executed by using the values of the attributes before the occurrence of the trigger.

In our example, none of the rules are guarded. Intuitively, this is because the gate is not proactive: it does not invoke the controller; it is the controller that reacts to the observations it makes of the sensors and timer.

The example also shows that it is possible to declare features that are local to the law itself such as attributes that facilitate the definition of the scheduling of the different rules. As already mentioned, these are just a prosthesis that relates to the nature of the formalism that is being used for describing the behaviour of the Machine; they are not features that are required of the code that lies in the Machine and, therefore, can be ignored by the fit $fM$. In fact, we are also working on more abstract notions of machine that are more descriptive, less prescriptive, but this is not an essential aspect for understanding the approach that we are proposing. The value of the Boolean attribute *open* must not, of course, be confused with the Boolean value "Sluice Gate is fully open". The former is a tiny model domain constructed to act as a model or surrogate for the latter.

When more than one trigger is true, the guards ("with"-conditions) of the corresponding rules are evaluated and the trigger fails if any of them is false. If all the guards are true, the union of all reactions is performed, again as an atomic action. Notice that, in case of conflicting assignments being brought into the same synchronisation set, the reaction fails.

Finally, we must point out that nothing in the description of the law is intrinsic to the sluice-gate. Although we named services and events in a way that relates them directly to the problem domain, these names do not provide any binding to the entities of the domain that the Machine is intended to control: the connection to the problem domain always needs to be made explicit through the fit *fD*. This is strictly enforced by the semantics of the *coordination approach* [9], which is justified by the principle that all interactions should be made explicit. The fits are applied at configuration-time in what in [3] are called *coordination contexts*, as part of a process that manages the evolution of the global system. Our discussion of coordination laws addresses analysis-time, i.e. it concerns the modelling and analysis of machines for given problem frames but not the actual deployment of instances of such machines to control given domain entities.

This principle of explicit representation of interactions supports our use of coordination laws as generic descriptions of solutions that can be used for different problem frames. For instance, the coordination law above describes a simple two-cycle timer, which can be captured by a more neutral choice of names such as:

```
coordination interface two_action&sensor
services      up, down, off
events        top, bottom
properties    (up ∨ down) ⊃ (¬(up ∨ down) before off)
              up ⊃ (top unless off)
              down ⊃ (bottom unless off)
end interface

coordination law two_cycle_controller
interfaces   mc: two_action&sensor; tm: timer;
parameters   one,two:nat
attributes   open: bool
rules        when  mc.top
             do    mc.off ‖ open:=true ‖ tm.reset;

             when  tm.tick(one) ∧ open
             do    mc.down;

             when  mc.bottom
             do    mc.off ‖ open:=false ‖ tm.reset

             when  tm.tick(two) ∧ ¬open
             do    mc.up
end law
```

Its application to the sluice-gate problem consists of the instantiation of the parameters *one* and *two* with values *10* and *170*, respectively, the fit *fG&M*, which should map *up* to *onClockw, down* to *onAnti,* and *off* to *off,* and a fit *fT* to a physical timer.

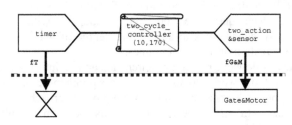

**Fig. 4.** Generic coordination law and its application to the sluice gate

This example was chosen to illustrate another feature of coordination laws. Besides the declaration of attributes for structuring an (abstract) internal state, parameters can also be defined that are controlled by the environment. These are just examples of services that the law can declare as part of its public interface: besides parameters that can be set, we may include operations that act on the internal state and some of the services that it gets from the components through the fits.

We should also stress the fact that a fit $fM$ needs to be established for each target platform. Each time a technological change is introduced, it makes it necessary for the Machine to be redeployed. The binding mechanism is also likely to have to change accordingly and, hence, the fit needs to be re-established.


# 6   Related Work

In the previous sections, we have discussed primitives for representing explicitly, in Problem Frames, the coordination aspects that concern the interaction  between the Machine and the Problem Domain.   The Machine can be evolved without compromising satisfaction of user requirements.  Also, changes in the application domain can be detected at the levels of the interface that connects the Machine with the domain and not at the level of the computations that implement the services offered by the Machine.  As far as we know, this is one of the first attempts at bringing together problem decomposition approaches to requirements specification and principles of separation of concerns that have been typically used for software design; this is an effort that, in our opinion, will allow us to contribute towards taming the complexity of evolving software applications according to the changes that occur in the problems that they are meant to solve.

Indeed, on the one hand, there are only a few other general approaches to decomposing problems rather than solutions.  Notable exceptions are the goal-based approaches of KAOS [18] and the NFR framework [7].   However these two approaches are not immediately suited to the separation of concerns that our coordination approach promotes, as they do not concentrate on domain properties in the same pervading manner as Problem Frames.

On the other hand, composition of software artefacts on the basis of separation of concerns has been addressed by a range of aspect-oriented techniques [8].  However with the notable exception of [11] and [24], aspect-based approaches, whilst good at addressing design and implementation issues, are weak with regards to requirements, and in particular their decomposition.  The approaches of [11] and [24] are mainly concerned with reconciling conflicts between a range of non-functional requirements and do not fully address decomposition of functional requirements.  Furthermore, aspect-oriented techniques are too tightly coupled with object-oriented and component-based technologies to sustain the degree of generality of approaches to problem decomposition of  Problem Frames.

There is also little work relating requirements and architecture, exceptions include [5,6].  However, those works do not fully address problem decomposition.  Ultimately we see our approach encompassing an iterative approach to requirements and architecture [22].  In this respect, our previous work on mapping solution space artifacts to the problem space complements the approach of this paper [12].

# 7    Conclusions and Further Work

We have shown the application of separation of concerns to problem analysis and requirements specification. Our contribution has been to add representation structures to Problem Frames in order to control the complexity of managing evolution.

The coordination primitives that we described fit well into the Problem Frames approach to decomposition, which itself is substantially different from what is normally found in traditional Software Engineering. Traditional decomposition assumes a pre-established structure or architecture into which the parts identified in the decomposition are fitted as they are successively identified. This means that each part needs to conform to the modes of interaction that this structure subsumes, say remote procedural calls of given services, or reading and writing of sequential data streams, which do not necessarily reflect requirements that derive from the problem domain and, therefore, introduce unnecessary bias. Our modelling primitives provide precise, means for the coordination of interactions to be separated from the way they get encoded in the computations by the Machine.

Although the paper focused on the relationship between the Problem Domain and the Machine, there are other levels at which coordination can be exploited to take advantage of the way requirements are captured and evolved with Problem Frames. One of the advantages is that different requirements, leading to different Problem Frames, can be represented through different coordination laws. Thus, a typical and-composition of requirements corresponds to a typical parallel composition of the machines that enforce them in ways that do not have to be pre-determined by earlier design decisions.

In Problem Frames, decomposition is carried out by making few or no explicit assumptions about the mechanisms by which each machine may interact with others. Because the coordination approach is based on the externalisation of interactions and the dynamic superposition of the connectors that coordinate them, each machine can be described and developed by assuming no more than that is a solution to a sub-problem. Composition concerns can be addressed at configuration time, i.e. when the different machines need to be brought together as a global solution to the top-level problem.

Deferring composition concerns until the different sub-problems have been well identified and understood is a key feature of Problem Frames. In our opinion, this is well justified given that we consider that composition is not a static, compile-time problem of linkage, but a dynamic process that needs to be subjected to its own rules. The coordination approach goes somewhat further by advocating an explicit separation between the two concerns and providing specific primitives to model configuration and evolution. Indeed, there is further added value of the application of coordination techniques to problem decomposition: dynamic assembly and integration of requirements can benefit from existing reconfiguration techniques [20].

The work described in this paper has opened up a variety of opportunities for further work. We are currently building on previous work on composition [25,26] to provide better control on the complexity of software evolution. On the other hand, the mathematical foundations of the coordination-based approach to architectures are pretty well established by now (see [9] for a summary). They make it possible to provide a uniform semantics for the notation that was presented for interfaces and laws. They also provide reasoning mechanisms that support the derivation of emergent properties arising from composition and correctness checking of realisations.

## Acknowledgements

The second author would like to thank his colleagues L.Andrade (ATX Software SA), A.Lopes (University of Lisbon), and M.Wermelinger (New University of Lisbon), with whom he developed much of the work around "Coordination" that was used in this paper.

## References

[1]     R.Allen and D.Garlan, "A Formal Basis for Architectural Connectors", *ACM TOSEM,* 6(3), 1997, 213-249.

[2]     L.F.Andrade and J.L.Fiadeiro, "Interconnecting Objects via Contracts", in R.France and B.Rumpe (eds), *UML'99 – Beyond the Standard*, LNCS 1723, Springer-Verlag 1999, 566-583.

[3]     L.F.Andrade and J.L.Fiadeiro, "Architecture Based Evolution of Software Systems", in M.Bernardo & P.Inverardi (eds), *Formal Methods for Software Architectures*, LNCS 2804, Springer Verlag 2003, 148-181.

[4]     L.F.Andrade, J.L.Fiadeiro, A.Lopes and M.Wermelinger, "Architectural Techniques for Evolving Control Systems", in *Formal Methods for Railway Operation and Control Systems*, G.Tarnai & E.Schnieder (eds), L'Harmattan Press 2003.

[5]     D.Berry, R.Kazman and R.Wieringa (eds), *Proceedings of Second International Workshop from Software Requirements to Architectures (STRAW'03)*, Portland, USA, 2003.

[6]     J.Castro and   J.Kramer (eds), *Proceedings of First International Workshop from Software Requirements to Architectures (STRAW'01)*, Toronto, Canada, 2001.

[7]     L.Chung, B.A.Nixon, E.Yu and J.Mylopoulos.   *Non-Functional Requirements in Software Engineering.*  Kluwer Academic Publishers, 2000.

[8]     T.Elrad, R.Filman and A.Bader (Guest editors).   Special Issue on Aspect Oriented Programming. *Communications of the ACM* 44(10) 2001.

[9]     J.L.Fiadeiro,   A.Lopes   and   M.Wermelinger,   "A   Mathematical   Semantics   for Architectural Connectors", in *Generic Programming*, R.Backhouse and J.Gibbons (eds), LNCS 2793, Springer-Verlag 2003, 190-234.

[10]     D.Gelernter and  N.Carriero, "Coordination Languages and their Significance", *Communications ACM* 35(2), 1992, 97-107.

[11]     J.Grundy, "Aspect-Oriented Requirements Engineering for Component-based software systems", in *Fourth IEEE International Symposium on Requirements Engineering (RE'99)*. IEEE Computer Society Press 1999.

[12]     J.G.Hall, M.Jackson, R.C.Laney, B.Nuseibeh, L.Rapanotti, "Relating Software Requirements and Architectures using Problem Frames", *IEEE Proceedings of RE 2002*, 2002.

[13]     M.Jackson, *Problem Frames: Analysing and Structuring Software Development Problems*, Addison Wesley 2000.

[14]     M.Jackson, "Some Basic Tenets of Description", *Software System Modelling* 1, 2002, 5–9.

[15] M.Jackson, "Why Software Writing is Difficult and Will Remain So", in J.Fiadeiro, J.Madey and A.Tarlecki (eds), *Information Processing Letters Special Issue in Honour of Wlad Turski* 88(1-2), 2003.

[16] G.Koutsoukos, J.Gouveia, L.Andrade and J.L.Fiadeiro, "Managing Evolution in Telecommunications Systems", in *New Developments on Distributed Applications and Interoperable Systems*, K.Zielinski, K.Geihs and A.Laurentowski (eds), Kluwer Academic Publishers 2001; 133-139.

[17] G.Koutsoukos, T.Kotridis, L.Andrade, J.L.Fiadeiro, J.Gouveia and M.Wermelinger, "Coordination technologies for business strategy support: a case study in stock-trading", in R.Corchuelo, A,Ruiz and M.Toro (eds), *Advances in Business Solutions*, Catedral Publicaciones 2002, 45-56.

[18] A. van Lamsweerde, "Goal-Oriented Requirements Engineering: A Guided Tour", in *Proceedings of the 5th International Symposium on Requirements Engineering (RE'01)*, IEEE Computer Society Press 2001, 249-261.

[19] M.Lehman, "Uncertainty in Computer Application", *Communications ACM* 33(5), 1990, 584 - 586

[20] J.Magee and J.Kramer, "Dynamic Structure in Software Architectures", in *4th Symp. on Foundations of Software Engineering*, ACM Press 1996, 3-14.

[21] Z.Manna and A.Pnueli, *The Temporal Logic of Reactive and Concurrent Systems*, Springer-Verlag 1991.

[22] B.A.Nuseibeh, "Weaving Together Requirements and Architecture", IEEE Computer 34 (3):115-117, March 2001.

[23] D.Perry and A.Wolf, "Foundations for the Study of Software Architectures", *ACM SIGSOFT Software Engineering Notes* 17(4), 1992, 40-52.

[24] A.Rashid, A.Moreira, and J.Araujo, "Modularisation and Composition of Aspectual Requirements", *Aspect Oriented Software Development* 2003.

[25] P.Zave, "Feature Interactions and Formal Specifications in Telecommunications", *IEEE Computer* XXVI(8), 1993, 20-30.

[26] P.Zave and M.Jackson, "Conjunction as Composition", *ACM TOSEM* 2(4), 1993, 371-411.

# O'Klaim: A Coordination Language with Mobile Mixins*

Lorenzo Bettini[1], Viviana Bono[2], and Betti Venneri[1]

[1] Dipartimento di Sistemi e Informatica, Università di Firenze
{bettini,venneri}@dsi.unifi.it
[2] Dipartimento di Informatica, Università di Torino
bono@di.unito.it

**Abstract.** This paper presents O'Klaim (Object-Oriented Klaim), a linguistic extension of the higher-order calculus for mobile processes Klaim with object-oriented features. Processes interact by an asynchronous communication model: they can distribute and retrieve resources, sometimes structured as incomplete classes, i.e., mixins, to and from distributed tuple spaces. This mechanism is coordinated by providing a subtyping relation on classes and mixins, which become polymorphic items during communication. We propose a static typing system for: (*i*) checking locally each process in its own locality; (*ii*) decorating object-oriented code that is sent to remote sites with its type. This way, tuples can be dynamically retrieved only if they match by subtyping with the expected type. If this pattern matching succeeds, the retrieved code can be composed with local code, dynamically and automatically, in a type-safe way. Thus a global safety condition is guaranteed without requiring any additional information on the local reconfiguration of local and foreign code, and, in particular, without any further type checking. Finally, we present main issues concerning the implementation of O'Klaim.

## 1 Introduction

Mixins [14, 22, 1] are (sub)class definitions parameterized over a superclass and were introduced as an alternative to standard class inheritance. A mixin could be seen as a function that, given one class as an argument, produces another class, by adding or overriding specific sets of methods. The same mixin can be used to produce a variety of classes with the same functionality and behavior, since they all have the same sets of methods added and/or redefined. The superclass definition is not needed at the time of writing the mixin definition, thus improving modularity. The uniform extension and modification of classes is instead absent from the classical class-based languages.

---

* This work has been partially supported by EU within the FET - Global Computing initiative, project MIKADO IST-2001-32222, DART project IST-2001-33477 and by MIUR project NAPOLI. The funding bodies are not responsible for any use that might be made of the results presented here.

R. de Nicola et al. (Eds.): COORDINATION 2004, LNCS 2949, pp. 20–38, 2004.
© Springer-Verlag Berlin Heidelberg 2004

Due to their dynamic nature, mixin inheritance can be fruitfully used in a *mobile code* setting [28, 17]. In [8], we introduced MOMI (Mobile Mixins), a coordination model for mobile processes that exchange object-oriented code. The underlying idea motivating MOMI is that standard class-based inheritance mechanisms, which are often used to implement distributed systems, do not appear to scale well to a distributed context with mobility. MOMI's approach consists in structuring mobile object-oriented code by using mixin-based inheritance, and this is shown to fit into the dynamic and open nature of a mobile code scenario. For example, a downloaded mixin, describing a mobile agent that must access some files, can be completed with a base class in order to provide access methods that are specific of the local file system. Conversely, critical operations of a mobile agent enclosed in a downloaded class can be redefined by applying a local mixin to it (e.g., in order to restrict the access to sensible resources, as in a *sand-box*). Therefore, MOMI is a combination of a core coordination calculus and an object-oriented mixin-based calculus.

MOMI highly relies on typing. The most important feature of MOMI's typing is the *subtyping* relation that guarantees safe, yet flexible, code communication. We assume that the code that is sent around has been successfully compiled in its own site (independently from the other sites), and it travels together with its static type. When the code is received on a site (whose code has been successfully compiled, too), it is accepted only if its type is compliant with respect to the one expected, where compliance is based on subtyping. Thus, dynamic type checking is performed only at communication time. This is a crucial matter for mobility, since mobile code and in particular mobile agents are expected to be autonomous: once the communication successfully occurred, transmitted code behaves remotely in a type safe way (no run-time errors due to type violations). This makes the code exchange an *atomic* action.

This paper presents the experimental language O'KLAIM that is obtained by applying MOMI's approach [8] to the language KLAIM [18, 4], which is specifically designed to program distributed systems where mobile components interact through multiple distributed tuple spaces and mobile code. A preliminary design that led to O'KLAIM was introduced in [7]. KLAIM offers a much more sophisticated, complete, and effective coordination mechanism of mobile processes than the toy language of MOMI, where the focus was mainly on the subtyping relation on classes and mixins. O'KLAIM integrates the mixin-based object-oriented features into a mobile code calculus with an asynchronous coordination mechanism. To this aim, the notion of "tuple" is extended to include object-oriented code, therefore KLAIM processes can retrieve from and insert into tuple spaces object-oriented components (in particular, classes, mixins and objects) as well as standard KLAIM processes. A type system is designed for checking statically the extended notion of processes, so that compiled processes contain some static type information which is used dynamically. Therefore, the tuples that are added to a tuple space are decorated with their type, and a process willing to retrieve a tuple from a tuple space will employ an extended pattern matching mechanism that uses also this tuple type information. This matching essentially consists in checking subtyping on object-oriented components. If the code is successfully accepted, it can interact with the local code in a safe way (i.e., no run-time errors) without requiring any further type checking of the whole code. Type safety of the communication results from the static type soundness of local and foreign code and a (global) subject reduction property. In particular, we show that the subject reduction property is based on a crucial property of substitutivity by subtyping. The underlying substitution operation requires specific methods renaming, in order to avoid name collision problems that arise when classes and mixins are used as first-class data in a mobile code setting where matching relies on subtyping. These new metatheoretical results about the precise concept of substitution to be used extend and improve the results presented for MoMi in [8].

Summarizing, O'Klaim aims at two complementary goals. Firstly, subtyping on classes and mixins (as designed for MoMi) is successfully experimented as a tractable mechanism to coordinate mobile code exchange within a process calculus with a more sophisticated communication mechanism. Secondly, the language Klaim is enriched with object-oriented code. This casts some light on how the same approach can be fruitfully used for extending other mobile code languages with safe object-oriented code exchange. Finally, the implementation of O'Klaim is presented. This consists in a Java package, momi, providing the run-time systems for classes and mixins that can be dynamically manipulated and composed. The programming language X-Klaim (that implements the basic concepts of Klaim) has been extended in order to be compiled into Java code exploiting the momi package.

## 2  O'Klaim: **An Object-Oriented** Klaim

O'Klaim is a linguistic integration of Klaim with object-oriented features, following the design of MoMi [8]. The coordination part and the object-oriented part are orthogonal, so that, in principle, such an integration would work for any extension/restriction of Klaim (as discussed in [4]) and also for other calculi for mobility and distribution, such as *DJoin* [23]. We first recall the main features of Klaim and MoMi and then we show how they are integrated in order to build O'Klaim.

### 2.1  **The Basics of** Klaim

Klaim (*Kernel Language for Agent Interaction and Mobility*) [18, 4] is a coordination language inspired by the Linda model [24], hence it relies on the concept of *tuple space*. A tuple space is a multiset of *tuples*; these are sequences of information items (called *fields*). There are two kinds of fields: *actual fields* (i.e., expressions, processes, localities, constants, identifiers) and *formal fields* (i.e., variables). Syntactically, a formal field is denoted with !*ide*, where *ide* is an identifier. Tuples are anonymous and content-addressable; *pattern-matching* is used to select tuples in a tuple space:

- two tuples match if they have the same number of fields and corresponding fields have matching values or formals;
- formal fields match any value of the same type, but two formals never match, and two actual fields match only if they are identical.

For instance, tuple ("foo", "bar", 300) matches with ("foo", "bar", !val). After matching, the variable of a formal field gets the value of the matched field: in the previous example, after matching, val (an integer variable) will contain the value 300.

Tuple spaces are placed on *nodes* (or *sites*), which are part of a *net*. Each node contains a single tuple space and processes in execution, and can be accessed through its *locality*. The distinction between logical and physical locality (and thus the concept of "allocation environment"), and the creation of new nodes and process definitions are not relevant in the O'Klaim context, thus, for the sake of simplicity, we omit them in the present formal presentation. Notice, however, that their integration, being orthogonal, is completely smooth.

Klaim processes may run concurrently, both at the same node or at different nodes, and can perform four basic operations over nodes. The **in**(t)@ℓ operation looks for tuple t′ that matches with t in the tuple space located at ℓ. Whenever the matching tuple t′ is found, it is removed from the tuple space. The corresponding values of t′ are then assigned to the formal fields of t and the operation terminates. If no matching tuple is found, the operation is suspended until one is available. The **read**(t)@ℓ operation differs from **in**(t)@ℓ only because the tuple t′, selected by pattern-matching, is not removed from the tuple space located at ℓ. The **out**(t)@ℓ operation adds the tuple t to the tuple space located at ℓ. The **eval**(P)@ℓ operation spawns process P for execution at node ℓ.

Klaim is higher-order in that processes can be exchanged as primary class data. While **eval**(P)@ℓ spawns a process for (remote) evaluation at ℓ, processes sent with an **out** must be retrieved explicitly at the destination site. The receiver can then execute the received process locally, as in the following process: **in**(!X)@**self**.**eval**(X)@**self**.

## 2.2 MoMi and O'Klaim

MoMi was introduced in [8], where mixin inheritance is shown to be more flexible than standard class inheritance to fit into the dynamic nature of a mobile code scenario. The key rôle in MoMi's typing is played by a *subtyping* relation that guarantees safe, yet flexible and scalable, code communication. MoMi's subtyping involves not only object subtyping, but also a form of class subtyping and mixin subtyping: therefore, subtyping hierarchies are provided along with the inheritance hierarchies. It is important to notice that we are not violating the design rule of keeping inheritance and subtyping separated, since mixin and class subtyping plays a pivotal role only during the communication, when classes and mixins become genuine run-time polymorphic values.

**Table 1.** Syntax of object-oriented terms

$$
\begin{array}{lr}
exp ::= v & \text{(value)}\\
\quad\mid\ \text{new } exp & \text{(object creation)}\\
\quad\mid\ exp \Leftarrow m & \text{(method call)}\\
\quad\mid\ exp_1 \diamond exp_2 & \text{(mixin appl.)}\\
v ::= \{m_i : \tau_{m_i} = b_i{}^{i \in I}\} & \text{(record)}\\
\quad\mid\ x & \text{(variable)}\\
\quad\mid\ \text{class } [m_i : \tau_{m_i} = b_i{}^{i \in I}] \text{ end} & \text{(class def)}\\
\quad\mid\ \text{mixin} & \text{(mixin def)}\\
\qquad \text{expect}[m_i : \tau_{m_i}{}^{i \in I}]\\
\qquad \text{redef}[m_k : \tau_{m_k} \text{ with } b_k{}^{k \in K}]\\
\qquad \text{def}[m_j : \tau_{m_j} = b_j{}^{j \in J}]\\
\qquad \text{end}
\end{array}
$$

In synthesis, MoMi consists of:

1. the definition of an object-oriented "surface calculus" containing essential features that an object-oriented language must have to write mixin-based code;
2. the definition of a new subtyping relation on class and mixin types to be exploited dynamically at communication time;
3. a very primitive coordination language consisting in a synchronous send/receive mechanism, to study the communication of the mixin-based code among different site.

O'Klaim integrates the object-oriented component of MoMi, in particular the subtyping relation on classes and mixins (both described in the next section), within Klaim, which offers a much more sophisticated, complete, and effective coordination mechanism than the toy one of MoMi.

## 2.3  O'Klaim: **Object-Oriented Expressions**

In this section we present the object-oriented part of O'Klaim, which is defined as a class-based object-oriented language supporting mixin-based class hierarchies via *mixin definition* and *mixin application* (see Table 1). It is important to notice that specific incarnations of most object-oriented notions (such as, e.g., functional or imperative nature of method bodies, object references, cloning, etc.) are irrelevant in this context, where the emphasis is on the structure of the object-oriented mobile code. Hence, we work here with a basic syntax of the kernel object-oriented calculus.

Object-oriented expressions offer object instantiation, method call and mixin application; $\diamond$ denotes the mixin application operator. An object-oriented value, to which an expression reduces, is either an object, which is a (recursive) record $\{m_i : \tau_{m_i} = b_i{}^{i \in I}\}$, or a class definition, or a mixin definition, where $[m_i : \tau_{m_i} =$

$b_i$ $^{i\in I}]$ denotes a sequence of method definitions, $[m_k : \tau_{m_k}$ with $b_k$ $^{k\in K}]$ denotes a sequence of method re-definitions, and $I$, $J$ and $K$ are sets of indexes. Method bodies, denoted here with $b$ (possibly with subscripts), are closed terms/programs and we ignore their actual structure. A mixin can be seen as an abstract class that is parameterized over a (super)class. Let us describe informally the mixin use through a tutorial example:

```
M = mixin
    expect [n : τ]                    C = class
    redef [m₂ : τ₂ with ... next ...]     [n = ... ˜m₂ = ...]     (new (M ◇ C)) ⟸ m₁()
    def [m₁ : τ₁ = ... n() ...]       end
end
```

Each mixin consists of three parts:

1. methods *defined* in the mixins, like $m_1$;
2. *expected methods*, like $n$, that must be provided by the superclass;
3. *redefined methods*, like $m_2$, where next can be used to access the implementation of $m_2$ in the superclass.

The application $M \diamond C$ constructs a class, which is a subclass of $C$.

The typing for the object-oriented code refines essentially the typing rules sketched in [8]. The set $\mathcal{T}$ of types is defined as follows.

$$\tau ::= \Sigma \mid \iota \mid \tau_1 \rightarrow \tau_2 \mid \text{class}\langle\Sigma\rangle \mid \text{mixin}\langle\Sigma_{new}, \Sigma_{red}, \Sigma_{exp}\rangle \qquad \Sigma ::= \{m_i : \tau_{m_i} \ ^{i\in I}\}$$

$\iota$ is a basic type and $\rightarrow$ is the functional type operator. $\Sigma$ (possibly with a subscript) denotes a record type of the form $\{m_i : \tau_{m_i} \ ^{i\in I}\}$. if $m_i : \tau_{m_i} \in \Sigma$ we say that the *subject* $m_i$ *occurs* in $\Sigma$ (with type $\tau_{m_i}$). $Subj(\Sigma)$ is the set of the *subjects* of $\Sigma$ and $Meth(\Sigma)$ is the set of all the method names occurring in $\Sigma$ (e.g., if $\Sigma = \{m : \{n : \tau\}\}$ then $Subj(\Sigma) = \{m\}$ while $Meth(\Sigma) = \{m, n\}$). As we left method bodies unspecified (see above), we must assume that there is an underlying system to type method bodies and records. We will denote this typing with $\Vdash$. Rules for $\Vdash$ are obviously not specified, but $\Vdash$-statements are used as assumptions in other typing rules. The typing rules for values are in Table 2.

Mixin types, in particular, encode the following information:

1. record types $\Sigma_{new}$ and $\Sigma_{red}$ contain the types of the mixin methods (new and redefined, respectively);
2. record type $\Sigma_{exp}$ contains the *expected* types, i.e., the types of the methods expected to be supported by the superclass;
3. well typed mixins are well formed, in the sense that name clashes among the different families of methods are absent (the last three clauses of the (*mixin*) rule).

**Table 2.** Typing rules for object-oriented values

$$\frac{}{\Gamma, x : \tau \vdash x : \tau} \ (proj) \qquad \frac{\Gamma \Vdash \{m_i : \tau_{m_i} = b_i{}^{i \in I}\} : \{m_i : \tau_{m_i}{}^{i \in I}\}}{\Gamma \vdash \{m_i : \tau_{m_i} = b_i{}^{i \in I}\} : \{m_i : \tau_{m_i}{}^{i \in I}\}} \ (rec)$$

$$\frac{\Gamma \vdash \{m_i : \tau_{m_i} = b_i{}^{i \in I}\} : \{m_i : \tau_{m_i}{}^{i \in I}\}}{\Gamma \vdash \mathsf{class}\,[m_i : \tau_{m_i} = b_i{}^{i \in I}]\,\mathsf{end} : \mathsf{class}\langle\{m_i : \tau_{m_i}{}^{i \in I}\}\rangle} \ (class)$$

$$\frac{\begin{array}{c} \Gamma, \bigcup_{i \in I} m_i : \tau_{m_i}, \bigcup_{k \in K} m_k : \tau_{m_k} \vdash \{m_j : \tau_{m_j} = b_j{}^{j \in J}\} : \{m_j : \tau_{m_j}{}^{j \in J}\} \\ \Gamma, \bigcup_{i \in I} m_i : \tau_{m_i}, \bigcup_{k \in K} m_k : \tau_{m_k}, \bigcup_{j \in J} m_j : \tau_{m_j}, \mathsf{next} : \tau_{m_r} \Vdash b_r : \tau'_{m_r} \quad \tau'_{m_r} <: \tau_{m_r} \quad \forall r \in K \\ Subj(\Sigma_{new}) \cap Subj(\Sigma_{exp}) = \emptyset \quad Subj(\Sigma_{new}) \cap Subj(\Sigma_{red}) = \emptyset \\ Subj(\Sigma_{red}) \cap Subj(\Sigma_{exp}) = \emptyset \end{array}}{\Gamma \vdash \begin{array}{l} \mathsf{mixin} \\ \quad \mathsf{expect}[m_i : \tau_{m_i}{}^{i \in I}] \\ \quad \mathsf{redef}[m_k : \tau_{m_k}\,\mathsf{with}\,b_k{}^{k \in K}] \\ \quad \mathsf{def}[m_j : \tau_{m_j} = b_j{}^{j \in J}] \\ \mathsf{end} \end{array} : \mathsf{mixin}\langle \Sigma_{new}, \Sigma_{red}, \Sigma_{exp}\rangle} \ (mixin)$$

where $\Sigma_{new} = \{m_j : \tau_{m_j}{}^{j \in J}\}, \Sigma_{red} = \{m_k : \tau_{m_k}{}^{k \in K}\}, \Sigma_{exp} = \{m_i : \tau_{m_i}{}^{i \in I}\}$

**Table 3.** Typing rules for object-oriented expressions

$$\frac{\Gamma \vdash exp : \{m_i : \tau_{m_i}{}^{i \in I}\} \qquad j \in I}{\Gamma \vdash exp \Leftarrow m_j : \tau_{m_j}} \ (lookup) \qquad \frac{\Gamma \vdash exp : \mathsf{class}\langle\{m_i : \tau_{m_i}{}^{i \in I}\}\rangle}{\Gamma \vdash \mathsf{new}\ exp : \{m_i : \tau_{m_i}{}^{i \in I}\}} \ (new)$$

$$\frac{\begin{array}{l} \Gamma \vdash exp_1 : \mathsf{mixin}\langle \Sigma_{new}, \Sigma_{red}, \Sigma_{exp}\rangle \\ \Gamma \vdash exp_2 : \mathsf{class}\langle \Sigma_b\rangle \\ \Sigma_b <: (\Sigma_{exp} \cup \Sigma_{red}) \\ Meth(\Sigma_b) \cap Meth(\Sigma_{new}) = \emptyset \end{array}}{\Gamma \vdash exp_1 \diamond exp_2 : \mathsf{class}\langle \Sigma_b \cup \Sigma_{new}\rangle} \ (mixin\ app)$$

The typing rules for expressions are in Table 3.

Rule (*mixin app*) relies strongly on a subtyping relation $<:$. The subtyping relation rules depend obviously on the nature of the object-oriented language we choose, but an essential constraint is that it must contain the *width subtyping* rule for record types: $\Sigma_2 \subseteq \Sigma_1 \Rightarrow \Sigma_1 <: \Sigma_2$.

We consider $m : \tau_1$ and $m : \tau_2$ ($\tau_1 \not\equiv \tau_2$) as distinct elements, and $\Sigma_1 \cup \Sigma_2$ is the standard record union. $\Sigma_1$ and $\Sigma_2$ are considered *equivalent*, denoted by $\Sigma_1 = \Sigma_2$, if they differ only for the order of their pairs $m_i : \tau_{m_i}$.

In the rule (*mixin app*), $\Sigma_b$ contains the type signatures of all methods supported by the superclass to which the mixin is applied. The premises of the rule (*mixin app*) are as follows:

**Table 4.** Subtype on class and mixin types

$$\frac{\Sigma' <: \Sigma}{\mathsf{class}\langle\Sigma'\rangle \sqsubseteq \mathsf{class}\langle\Sigma\rangle} \ (\sqsubseteq class)$$

$$\frac{\Sigma'_{new} <: \Sigma_{new} \qquad \Sigma_{exp} <: \Sigma'_{exp} \qquad \Sigma'_{red} = \Sigma_{red}}{\mathsf{mixin}\langle\Sigma'_{new}, \Sigma'_{red}, \Sigma'_{exp}\rangle \sqsubseteq \mathsf{mixin}\langle\Sigma_{new}, \Sigma_{red}, \Sigma_{exp}\rangle} \ (\sqsubseteq mixin)$$

**Table 5.** O'KLAIM syntax (see Table 1 for the syntax of $exp$ and $v$, and Section 2.5 for types $\sigma$)

| | | | | |
|---|---|---|---|---|
| $P ::= \mathbf{nil}$ | (null process) | $N ::= l :: p$ | | (single node) |
| $\mid act.P$ | (action prefixing) | $\mid N_1 \parallel N_2$ | | (net composition) |
| $\mid P_1 \mid P_2$ | (parallel composition) | $p ::= P \mid \langle t \rangle \mid p_1 \mid p_2$ | | (located item) |
| $\mid X$ | (process variable) | | | |
| $\mid \mathbf{let}\ x = exp\ \mathbf{in}\ P$ | (OO expression) | | | |
| $act ::= \mathbf{out}(t)@\ell \mid \mathbf{in}(t)@\ell \mid \mathbf{read}(t)@\ell \mid \mathbf{eval}(P)@\ell \qquad \ell ::= l \mid \chi \qquad t ::= f \mid f,t$ | | | | |
| $f ::= arg \mid !id : \sigma \qquad id ::= x \mid X \mid \chi \qquad arg ::= id \mid e \mid P \mid l \mid v$ | | | | |

 

i) $\Sigma_b <: (\Sigma_{exp} \cup \Sigma_{red})$ requires that the superclass provides all the methods that the mixin expects and redefines;

ii) $Meth(\Sigma_b) \cap Meth(\Sigma_{new}) = \emptyset$ guarantees that name clashes cannot occur during the mixin application.

Notice that the superclass may have more methods than those required by the mixin constraints. Thus, the type of the mixin application expression is a class type containing both the signatures of all the methods supplied by the superclass ($\Sigma_b$) and those of the new methods defined by the mixin ($\Sigma_{new}$).

The key point is the introduction of a novel subtyping relation, denoted by $\sqsubseteq$, defined on class and mixin types. This subtyping relation is used to match dynamically the actual parameter's types against the formal parameter's types during communication. The part of the operational semantics of O'KLAIM, which describes communication formally, is presented in Section 2.6. The subtyping relation $\sqsubseteq$ is defined in Table 4. Rule ($\sqsubseteq class$) is naturally induced by the (width) subtyping on record types, while rule ($\sqsubseteq mixin$): permits the subtype to define more 'new' methods; prohibits to override more methods; and enables a subtype to require less expected methods.

## 2.4 O'Klaim: Processes and Nets

O'KLAIM syntax is defined in Table 5. In order to obtain O'KLAIM, we extend the KLAIM syntax of tuples $t$ to include any object-oriented value $v$ (defined in Table 1). In particular, differently from KLAIM, formal fields are now

**Table 6.** Typing rules for processes

$$\frac{}{\Gamma, id : \sigma \vdash id : \sigma}\ (proj) \qquad \frac{}{\Gamma \vdash l : \mathsf{loc}}\ (loc) \qquad \frac{}{\Gamma \vdash \mathbf{nil} : \mathsf{proc}}\ (nil)$$

$$a \equiv \mathbf{in, read, out} \quad \frac{\begin{array}{l} \Gamma \vdash \ell : \mathsf{loc} \\ \Gamma \vdash f_i : \sigma_i \quad i = 1, \ldots, n \wedge f_i \equiv arg \\ \Gamma \cup \mathit{ftypes}(f_1, \ldots, f_n) \vdash P : \mathsf{proc} \end{array}}{\Gamma \vdash a(f_1, \ldots, f_n)@\ell.P : \mathsf{proc}}\ (action)$$

$$\mathit{ftypes}(f, t) = \begin{cases} \{id : \sigma\} \cup \mathit{ftypes}(t) & \text{if } f \equiv !id : \sigma \\ \mathit{ftypes}(t) & \text{otherwise} \end{cases}$$

$$\frac{\Gamma \vdash Q : \mathsf{proc} \qquad \Gamma \vdash \ell : \mathsf{loc}}{\Gamma \vdash \mathbf{eval}(Q)@\ell.P : \mathsf{proc}}\ (eval)$$

$$\frac{\Gamma \vdash P_1 : \mathsf{proc} \qquad \Gamma \vdash P_2 : \mathsf{proc}}{\Gamma \vdash (P_1 \mid P_2) : \mathsf{proc}}\ (comp) \qquad \frac{\Gamma \vdash exp : \tau \qquad \Gamma, x : \tau \vdash P : \mathsf{proc}}{\Gamma \vdash \mathbf{let}\ x = exp\ \mathbf{in}\ P : \mathsf{proc}}\ (let)$$

explicitly typed. Actions **in**$(t)@\ell$ (and **read**$(t)@\ell$) and **out**$(t)@\ell$ can be used to move object-oriented code (together with the other KLAIM items) from/to a locality $\ell$, respectively. Moreover, we add to KLAIM processes the construct **let** $x = exp$ **in** $P$ in order to pass to the sub-process $P$ the result of computing an object-oriented expression $exp$ (for $exp$ syntax see Table 1). We use the following syntactic convention: $x$, $X$ and $\chi$ are variables representing object-oriented values, processes and localities, respectively. A constant locality (e.g., IP:port) is denoted by $l$. Moreover, $e$ is a basic expression (i.e., not object-oriented).

A *Net* is a finite collection of *nodes*. A node is a pair where the first component is a (constant) locality and the second component is either a process $P$ or a tuple $\langle t \rangle$ or a composition of processes and tuples. Thus, a tuple space is represented by the parallel composition of located tuples. Notice that programmers write only located processes, while located tuples are produced at run-time by evaluating **out** actions (see Table 8).

## 2.5   Typing for O'KLAIM

In order to type processes and nets, we extend the set of types $\mathcal{T}$ to $\mathcal{T}^* = \mathcal{T} \cup \{\mathsf{proc}, \mathsf{loc}\}$. $\sigma$ will range over $\mathcal{T}^*$; in particular, loc is used to type localities and proc for well-typed processes. Typing rules for processes are defined in Table 6. O'KLAIM type system is not concerned with access rights and capabilities, as it is instead the type system for KLAIM presented in [19]. In the O'KLAIM setting, types serve the purpose of avoiding the "message-not-understood" error when merging local and foreign object-oriented code in a site. Thus, we are not interested in typing actions inside processes: from our perspective, an O'KLAIM process is well typed when it has type proc, which only means that the object-oriented code that the process may contain is well typed.

O'KLAIM requires that every process is statically type-checked separately on its site and annotated with its type. The annotation process, not formally presented here, can be performed by the compiler during type checking: namely, every tuple item $t_i$ that takes part in the information exchange (which may be an object-oriented value) must be decorated with its type information, denoted by $t_i^{\sigma_i}$. The types of the tuples are built statically by the compiler, while the types of tuple formal fields must be written explicitly by the programmer. In a process of the form $\mathbf{in}(!id : \sigma)@\ell.P$, the type $\sigma$ is used to statically type check the continuation $P$, where $id$ is possibly used. More generally, concerning (action) rule, in a process performing an operation with a tuple (i.e., $\mathbf{out}$, $\mathbf{read}$ and $\mathbf{in}$), the actual fields of the tuple are type checked, and the types of formal fields (collected by the function $ftypes$) are used to type check the continuation.

We observe that the typing rules for object-oriented expressions are syntax-driven and do not contain an explicit subsumption rule. Thus, they define an algorithm to assign a principal type to each expression, in a given environment $\Gamma$. Analogously, both subtyping and typing rules for processes are in an algorithmic shape.

## 2.6   Operational Semantics for O'KLAIM

The operational semantics of O'KLAIM involves two sets of rules. The first set of rules describes how object-oriented expressions reduce to values and is denoted by $\twoheadrightarrow$. We omit here most of the rules because they are quite standard; they can be found in [6, 3]. However, we want to discuss the rule concerning mixin application, that produces a new class containing all the methods which are added and redefined by the mixin and those defined by the superclass. The rule (mixinapp) is presented in Table 7. The function override, defined below and used by rule (mixinapp), takes care of introducing in the new class the overridden methods. In particular, in the body of a mixin's overridden method $m_i$, the reserved variable next can be used to denote $m_i$'s implementation in the superclass: this "old" implementation is given a fresh name $m_{i'}$. Dynamic binding is then implemented for redefined methods, and old implementations from the super class are basically hidden in the derived class, since they are given a fresh name.

**Definition 1.** *Given two method sets, $\varrho_1$ and $\varrho_2$, the result of* $override(\varrho_1, \varrho_2)$ *is the method set $\varrho_3$ defined as follows:*

- *for all $m_i : \tau_{m_i} = b_i \in \varrho_2$ such that  $m_i \neq m_j$ for all $m_j : \tau_{m_j} = b_j \in \varrho_1$, then $m_i : \tau_{m_i} = b_i \in \varrho_3$;*
- *for all $m_i : \tau_{m_i} = b_i \in \varrho_1$ such that $m_i : \tau_{m_i} = b'_i \in \varrho_2$, let $m_{i'}$ be a fresh method name: then $m_{i'} : \tau_{m_i} = b'_i \in \varrho_3$ and $m_i : \tau_{m_i} = b_i[m_{i'}/next] \in \varrho_3$.*

Notice that name clashes among methods during the application will never take place, since they have already been solved during the typing of mixin application.

**Table 7.** The (*mixinapp*) operational rule

$$
exp_1 \twoheadrightarrow \left( \begin{array}{l} \text{mixin} \\ \text{expect}[m_i : \tau_{m_i}{}^{i \in I}] \\ \text{redef}[m_k : \tau_{m_k} \text{ with } b_k{}^{k \in K}] \\ \text{def}[m_j : \tau_{m_j} = b_j{}^{j \in J}] \\ \text{end} \end{array} \right) \qquad exp_2 \twoheadrightarrow \text{class } [m_l : \tau_{m_l} = b_l{}^{l \in L}] \text{ end}
$$

$$
exp_1 \diamond exp_2 \twoheadrightarrow \left( \begin{array}{l} \text{class} \\ \quad [m_j : \tau_{m_j} = b_j{}^{j \in J}] \cup \\ \quad override([m_k : \tau_{m_k} = b_k{}^{k \in K}], [m_l : \tau_{m_l} = b_l{}^{l \in L}]) \\ \text{end} \end{array} \right)
$$

**Table 8.** O'KLAIM operational rules

$$
\frac{}{l :: \mathbf{out}(t)@l'.P \parallel l' :: P' \succ\!\!\longrightarrow l :: P \parallel l' :: P' \mid \langle t \rangle} \text{ (OUT)}
$$

$$
\frac{match(t,t')}{l :: \mathbf{in}(t)@l'.P \parallel l' :: \langle t' \rangle \succ\!\!\longrightarrow l :: P[t'/t] \parallel l' :: \mathbf{nil}} \text{ (IN)}
$$

$$
\frac{match(t,t')}{l :: \mathbf{read}(t)@l'.P \parallel l' :: \langle t' \rangle \succ\!\!\longrightarrow l :: P[t'/t] \parallel l' :: \langle t' \rangle} \text{ (READ)}
$$

$$
\frac{}{l :: \mathbf{eval}(P)@l'.P' \parallel l' :: P'' \succ\!\!\longrightarrow l :: P' \parallel l' :: P' \mid P} \text{ (EVAL)}
$$

$$
\frac{exp \twoheadrightarrow v}{l :: \mathbf{let}\, x = exp \text{ in } P \succ\!\!\longrightarrow l :: P[v/x]} \text{ (LET)} \qquad \frac{N \equiv N_1 \quad N_1 \succ\!\!\longrightarrow N_2 \quad N_2 \equiv N'}{N \succ\!\!\longrightarrow N'} \text{ (NET)}
$$

The second set of rules for O'KLAIM, shown in Table 8, concerns processes and it is an extension of the operational semantics of KLAIM. Notice that the O'KLAIM's operational semantics must be defined on typed *compiled* processes, i.e., processes where each object-oriented value and tuples are decorated with their types, as explained in Section 2.5, because the crucial point is the dynamic matching of types. In fact, an **out** operation adds a tuple decorated with a (static) type to a tuple space, and a process can perform an **in** action by synchronizing with a process which represents a matching typed tuple. The rule for let $x = exp$ in $P$ relies on the reduction relation for object-oriented expressions $\twoheadrightarrow$.

The predicate for tuples, *match*, is presented in Table 9. The matching rules exploit the static type information, delivered together with the tuple items, in order to dynamically check that the received item is correct with respect to the type of the formal field, say $\tau$. Therefore, an item is accepted if and only if it is subtyping-compliant with the expected type of the formal field. Informally

**Table 9.** Matching rules (with $\mathtt{proc} <: \mathtt{proc}$ and $\mathtt{bc} <: \mathtt{bc}$)

$$match(e,e) \qquad match(l,l) \qquad \frac{match(t_2,t_1)}{match(t_1,t_2)}$$

$$\frac{match(t_1,t_2) \quad match(t_3,t_4)}{match((t_1,t_3),(t_2,t_4))} \qquad \frac{match(\sigma,\sigma_i)}{match(!id:\sigma,t_i{}^{\sigma_i})}$$

$$match(\sigma_1,\sigma_2) = \begin{cases} \sigma_1 \sqsubseteq \sigma_2 & \text{if } \sigma_1 \text{ and } \sigma_2 \text{ are mixin or class types} \\ \sigma_1 <: \sigma_2 & \text{otherwise} \end{cases}$$

speaking, one can accept any class containing more resources than expected, and any mixin with weaker requests about methods expected from the superclass can be accepted. This subtyping checking is analogous to the one we would perform in a sequential language where mixins and classes could be passed as parameters to methods. In a sequential setting, this dynamic checking might look as a burden (for example, in [13], mixins and classes are first-order entities, i.e., they can be passed as parameters in methods, but the matching among formal and actual parameters is by syntactic equality on types and not by subtyping), but in a distributed mobile setting the burden seems well-compensated by the added flexibility in communications.

Finally, the semantics for the distributed part is based on structural congruence and reduction relations. Reduction represents individual computation steps, and is defined in terms of structural congruence. The structural congruence $\equiv$ allows the rearrangement of the syntactic structure of a term so that reduction rules may be applied. It is defined as the least congruence relation closed under the following rules.

$$N_1 \parallel N_2 = N_2 \parallel N_1 \quad (N_1 \parallel N_2) \parallel N_3 = N_1 \parallel (N_2 \parallel N_3) \quad l :: P = l :: P \mid \mathbf{nil}$$
$$l :: (P_1 \mid P_2) = l :: P_1 \parallel l :: P_2$$

As a final remark, let us observe that we do not define a matching predicate for actual fields containing object-oriented values and processes since this would require to decide equalities on classes, mixins and objects (e.g., equality on their interfaces) and on processes (e.g., a bisimulation). This issue is out of the scope of the present work, since matching between two actual fields does not involve any substitution and then does not cause problems w.r.t. typing.

## 3   Typing Issues and Subject-Reduction Property

The important point in O'KLAIM semantics is that if a process $P$ (statically well-typed) retrieves a tuple by the subtyping matching mechanism and the retrieved value is merged in the continuation of $P$, then the evaluation proceeds without any additional type-checking. Thus, in order to obtain the subject-reduction the-orem, we need to prove that substitution preserves well-typedness, in particular when classes and mixins are replaced to variables inside object-oriented expressions. In the following, we address this issue and we outline the main technical steps, skipping proofs and details for lack of space.

The crucial case concerns mixin application expressions; namely if class/mixin variables are replaced by classes/mixins having a subtype, accidental overrides can occur because of names of the new methods added by the replacing value (see the definition of $\sqsubseteq$). This matter is related to the "width subtyping versus method addition" problem (well known in the object-based setting, see for instance [21]), that in our case boils down to a careful management of these *dynamic name clashes*. Thus, we must define a suitable capture-avoid-substitution, [ ], requiring possible renaming of methods with fresh names.

**Definition 2 (Substitution by refresh).** *If $x$ is a class variable of type* $\mathsf{class}\langle \Sigma \rangle$ *and $C$ is a class value of type* $\mathsf{class}\langle \Sigma' \rangle$ *such that* $\mathsf{class}\langle \Sigma' \rangle \sqsubseteq \mathsf{class}\langle \Sigma \rangle$, *then $[C/x]$ denotes the replacement of $C'$ to $x$, where $C'$ is obtained from $C$ by renaming all methods belonging to* $Meth(\Sigma') - Meth(\Sigma)$ *with fresh names. For mixins variables and values, the renaming acts on all and only the methods belonging to* $Meth(\Sigma'_{new}) - Meth(\Sigma_{new})$.

With our solution, new methods added by a class or a mixin value during substitution are hidden by renaming, for each occurrence of the variable to be replaced (this is very similar to the "privacy via subsumption" of [27]). On the other hand, we only rename methods that do not appear in the type of the variable $x$. This second constraint ensures a basic property: the refreshed version $C'$ of $C$ has a type $\tau'$ such that $\tau' \sqsubseteq \mathsf{class}\langle \Sigma \rangle$. The same holds for refreshed mixins.

Now, using this definition, we can prove that substitution is type safe. For simplicity, in order to deal with $<:$ and $\sqsubseteq$ at the same time, we introduce the meta notation:

$$\tau_1 \preccurlyeq \tau_2 = \begin{cases} \tau_1 \sqsubseteq \tau_2 & \text{if } \tau_1 \text{ is a mixin or a class type} \\ \tau_1 <: \tau_2 & \text{otherwise} \end{cases}$$

**Lemma 1 (Substitution by narrowing).** *Let $v$, $exp$ and $P$ be an object-oriented value, an object-oriented expression and a process, respectively,*

1. *if $x : \tau_1 \vdash exp : \tau$ and $\Gamma \vdash v : \tau_2$ where $\tau_2 \preccurlyeq \tau_1$, then $\Gamma \vdash exp[v/x] : \tau'$ with $\tau' \preccurlyeq \tau$;*
2. *if $x : \tau_1 \vdash P : \mathsf{proc}$ and $\Gamma \vdash v : \tau_2$ where $\tau_2 \preccurlyeq \tau_1$, then $\Gamma \vdash P[v/x] : \mathsf{proc}$.*

**Sketch of proof:**

1. By induction on typing rules for expressions. The only crucial case is when $exp$ is a mixin application and $v$ is a class value or a mixin. Notice that, $exp$ is well-typed and no method occurring in the type $x$ is renamed; then the last condition in (*mixin app*) rule is preserved and ensures that no name clash can occur after substitution.

2. By induction on typing rules for processes using the previous point.

Summarizing, the type safety of the communication results from two main properties: (*i*) static type soundness of local and foreign code; (*ii*) the preservation of well-typedness under substitution by subtyping. It is standard to verify that all the other rules concerning $\rightarrow$ preserve well typedness and so we obtain the *subject-reduction theorem*. Thus, the local evaluation of a process cannot produce errors like "message-not-understood" even if it retrieves data from foreign sites and merges it in the local configuration. In other words, a *well-typed net* (i.e., a net where each process in each site is well-typed) remains well typed during its evolution (*global safety condition*).

We remark that, from the point of view of the implementation, the above treatment of "global" fresh names can be solved with static binding for the mentioned methods. The technique of using the static types of variables and the actual types of substituted mixin and class definitions may recall the approach of [22] of allowing overriding, i.e., dynamic binding, only for methods declared in the mixin's *inheritance interface*.

# 4    The Implementation

We recall that the implementation we present is based on X-KLAIM [10, 11] (extended with the proper object-oriented mixin-based primitives), used both as the "surface" object-oriented calculus and as the coordination language, with the added bonus of being able to write methods that can perform KLAIM actions, all the same guaranteeing absence of message-not-understood run-time errors, as shown in the previous section.

The implementation of the O'KLAIM object-oriented component in Java consists in a package momi presented in [2] and described in details in [3]. This package provides the run-time system, or the virtual machine, for classes, mixins and objects that can be downloaded from the network and dynamically composed (via the mixin application operation). It thus provides functionalities for checking subtyping among classes and among mixins and for building at run-time new subclasses. Since we abstract from the specific communication and mobility features, this package does not provide means for code mobility and network communication, so that momi can be smoothly integrated into existing Java mobility frameworks. We would like to stress that this package should be thought of as an "assembly" language that is the target of a compiler for a high-level language (in our case the language is X-KLAIM). If momi, as it is, was used for directly writing object-oriented expressions, the programmer would be left with the burden of writing methods containing Java statements dealing with momi objects, classes and mixins, and to check manually that they are well typed. Basically these are the same difficulties a programmer has to face when using an assembly language directly, instead of a high-level language. We could say that momi enhances the functionalities of the Java virtual machine: while the latter already provides useful mechanisms for dynamically loading new classes into a running application, the former supplies means for dynamically building class hierarchies (based on mixins) and for inserting new subclasses into existing hierarchies (which is not possible in Java).

In order to implement O'KLAIM we extended the KLAIM programming framework that consists in the programming language X-KLAIM [10, 11], which extends KLAIM with high-level programming constructs, and KLAVA [12] a Java package that implements the run-time system for X-KLAIM operations (X-KLAIM programs are compiled into Java programs that use KLAVA). The package KLAVA already provided all the primitives for network communication, through distributed tuple spaces, and, in particular, for code mobility, not supplied by momi. Thus the package has been modified in order to be able to exchange code that is based on momi, and for performing subtyping on momi elements during pattern matching by relying on the MoMiType classes and the associated subtyping. On the other hand, the X-KLAIM compiler generates code that uses both the KLAVA package and momi. Obviously, before generating code, it also performs type checking according to the type system defined by MoMi. All this software is freely available at http://music.dsi.unifi.it.

The programming example shown in this section involves mixin code mobility, and implements "dynamic inheritance" since the received mixin is applied to a local parent class at run-time. We assume that a site provides printing facilities for local and mobile agents. Access to the printer requires a driver that the site itself has to provide to those that want to print, since it highly depends on the system and on the printer. Thus, the agent that wants to print is designed as a mixin, that expects a method for actually printing, print_doc, and defines a method start_agent through which the site can start its execution. The actual instance of the printing agent is instantiated from a class dynamically generated by applying such mixin to a local superclass that provides the method print_doc acting as a wrapper for the printer driver. However the system is willing to accept any agent that has a compatible interface, i.e., any mixin that is a subtype of the one used for describing the printing agent. Thus any client wishing to print on this site can send a mixin that is subtyping compliant with the one expected. In particular such a mixin can implement finer printing formatting capabilities.

Listing 1, where rec is the X-KLAIM keyword for defining a process, presents a possible implementation of the printing client node (on the left) and of the printer server node (on the right). The printer client sends to the server a mixin MyPrinterAgent that complies with (it is a subtype of) the mixin that the server expects to receive, PrinterAgent. In particular MyPrinterAgent mixin will print a document on the printer of the server after preprocessing it (method preprocess). On the server, once the mixin is received, it is applied to the local (super)class LocalPrinter, and an object (the agent) is instantiated from the resulting class, and started so that it can actually print its document. The result of the printing task is then retrieved and sent back to the client.

We observe that the sender does not actually know the mixin name PrinterAgent: it only has to be aware of the mixin type expected by the server. Furthermore, the sent mixin can also define more methods than those specified in the receiving site, thanks to the mixin subtyping relation. This adds a great

```
mixin MyPrinterAgent
  expect print_doc(doc : str) : str;
  def start_agent() : str
  begin
    return
      this.print_doc
      (this.preprocess("my document"))
  end;
  def preprocess(doc : str) : str
  begin
    return "preprocessed(" | doc | ")"
  end
end

rec SendPrinterAgent[server : loc]
  declare
    var response : str
  begin
    out(MyPrinterAgent)@server;
    in(!response)@server;
    print "response is " | response
  end
```

```
mixin PrinterAgent
  expect print_doc(doc : str) : str;
  def start_agent() : str;
end

class LocalPrinter
  print_doc(doc : str) : str
  begin
    # real printing code omitted :-)
    return "printed " | doc
  end;
  init()
  begin
    nil # foo init
  end
end

rec ReceivePrinterAgent[ ]
  declare
    var rec_mixin : mixin PrinterAgent;
    var result : str
  begin
    in(!rec_mixin)@self;
    result :
      (new rec_mixin <> LocalPrinter).start_agent();
    out(result)@self
  end
```

**Listing 1.** The printer agent example

flexibility to such a system, while hiding these additional methods to the receiving site (since they are not specified in the receiving interface they are actually unknown statically to the compiler).

## 5   Conclusions and Related Work

We have presented the kernel language O'KLAIM, which extends the higher-order calculus KLAIM for mobile processes with mixin-based object-oriented code. The novel contributions of this paper, with respect to [8] (where we firstly presented design motivations for a mixin-based approach in a mobile context), can be summarized as follows:

1. we integrate the basic ideas of [8] into a mobile process calculus with an asynchronous and more sophisticated communication mechanism;
2. we refine the typing for the object-oriented component, we define a new typing system for KLAIM processes, and we study main typing concerns (in particular, a notion of substitution with renaming) in order to demonstrate the soundness of the proposed solution;
3. we present an implementation of O'KLAIM.

Keeping the O'KLAIM object-oriented calculus and the O'KLAIM processes separated may appear a limitation, but in fact this is not true. Our system consists of three components: the "surface" object-oriented component, a mixin/-

class subtyping relation, and a coordination calculus. If the object-oriented component is chosen to be an object-oriented concurrent/mobile language, the two components (object-oriented and concurrent/mobile) may interleave in a deeper way. A good example is the O'KLAIM implementation presented in Section 4: in there, X-KLAIM (extended with the proper object-oriented mixin-based primitives) is both the "surface" object-oriented calculus and the coordination language, so that method bodies can perform KLAIM actions. The matching mechanism that allows safe interactions during code exchange is based on the subtyping relation that acts as a general glue to glue together the two language components, of whichever nature they are (as long as the object-oriented one implements classes and mixins).

In the literature, there are several proposals of combining objects with processes and/or mobile agents. *Obliq* [16] is a lexically-scoped language providing distributed object-oriented computation. Mobile code maintains network references and provides transparent access to remote resources. In [15], a general model for integrating object-oriented features in calculi of mobile agents is presented where agents are extended with constructs for remote method invocations. Other works, such as, e.g., [20, 26, 25] do not deal explicitly with mobile distributed code. Our approach is more related to papers, as [29], where properties of distributed systems are enforced by a typing system equipped with subtyping. In our case the property we address is a flexible and type-safe coordination for exchanging code among processes, up- and down-loading classes and mixins from different sites.

Further extensions of O'KLAIM are topics for future developments: subtyping can be extended to *depth subtyping*, which offers a more flexible communication pattern (see [9] for a preliminary discussion) and the object-oriented component can be enriched with *incomplete objects*, i.e., objects instantiated from mixins [5].

# References

[1] D. Ancona, G. Lagorio, and E. Zucca. Jam - designing a java extension with mixins. *ACM Transaction on Programming Languages and Systems*, 2003. To appear. 20

[2] L. Bettini. A Java package for class and mixin mobility in a distributed setting. In *Proc. of FIDJI'03*, LNCS, 2003. To appear. 33

[3] L. Bettini. *Linguistic Constructs for Object-Oriented Mobile Code Programming & their Implementations*. PhD thesis, Dip. di Matematica, Università di Siena, 2003. Available at http://music.dsi.unifi.it. 29, 33

[4] L. Bettini, V. Bono, R. De Nicola, G. Ferrari, D. Gorla, M. Loreti, E. Moggi, R. Pugliese, E. Tuosto, and B. Venneri. The KLAIM Project: Theory and Practice. In *Global Computing – Trento*, LNCS. Springer, 2003. To appear. 21, 22

[5] L. Bettini, V. Bono, and S. Likavec. A core calculus of mixin-based incomplete objects. In *FOOL 11*, 2004. 36

[6] L. Bettini, V. Bono, and B. Venneri. MoMi - A Calculus for Mobile Mixins. Manuscript. 29

[7] L. Bettini, V. Bono, and B. Venneri. Towards Object-Oriented KLAIM. In *TOSCA 2001*, volume 62 of *ENTCS*. Elsevier, 2001. 21

[8] L. Bettini, V. Bono, and B. Venneri. Coordinating Mobile Object-Oriented Code. In *Proc. of Coordination Models and Languages*, volume 2315 of *LNCS*, pages 56–71. Springer, 2002. 21, 22, 23, 25, 35

[9] L. Bettini, V. Bono, and B. Venneri. Subtyping Mobile Classes and Mixins. In *Proc. of FOOL*, 2003. 36

[10] L. Bettini, R. De Nicola, G. Ferrari, and R. Pugliese. Interactive Mobile Agents in X-KLAIM. In *Proc. of WETICE*, pages 110–115. IEEE Computer Society Press, 1998. 33, 34

[11] L. Bettini, R. De Nicola, and R. Pugliese. X-KLAIM and KLAVA: Programming Mobile Code. In *TOSCA 2001*, volume 62 of *ENTCS*. Elsevier, 2001. 33, 34

[12] L. Bettini, R. De Nicola, and R. Pugliese. KLAVA: a Java package for distributed and mobile applications. *Software – Practice and Experience*, 32(14):1365–1394, 2002. 34

[13] V. Bono, A. Patel, and V. Shmatikov. A Core Calculus of Classes and Mixins. In *Proceedings ECOOP'99*, number 1628 in LCNS, pages 43–66. Springer, 1999. 31

[14] G. Bracha and W. Cook. Mixin-based inheritance. In *Proc. OOPSLA*, pages 303–311, 1990. 20

[15] M. Bugliesi and G. Castagna. Mobile Objects. In *Proc. of FOOL*, 2000. 36

[16] L. Cardelli. A Language with Distributed Scope. *Computing Systems*, 8(1):27–59, 1995. 36

[17] A. Carzaniga, G. P. Picco, and G. Vigna. Designing Distributed Applications with Mobile Code Paradigms. In *Proc. of ICSE*, pages 22–33. ACM Press, 1997. 21

[18] R. De Nicola, G. Ferrari, and R. Pugliese. KLAIM: a Kernel Language for Agents Interaction and Mobility. *IEEE Transactions on Software Engineering*, 24(5):315–330, 1998. 21, 22

[19] R. De Nicola, G. Ferrari, R. Pugliese, and B. Venneri. Types for Access Control. *Theoretical Computer Science*, 240(1):215–254, 2000. 28

[20] P. Di Blasio and K. Fisher. A Calculus for Concurrent Objects. In *Proc. of CONCUR*, volume 1119 of *LNCS*, pages 655–670, Pisa, Italy, 26–29 August 1996. Springer. 36

[21] K. Fisher and J. C. Mitchell. A Delegation-based Object Calculus with Subtyping. In *Proc. of FCT*, volume 965 of *LNCS*, pages 42–61. Springer, 1995. 32

[22] M. Flatt, S. Krishnamurthi, and M. Felleisen. Classes and mixins. In *Proc. POPL '98*, pages 171–183, 1998. 20, 33

[23] C. Fournet, G. Gonthier, J. J. Levy, L. Maranget, and D. Remy. A Calculus of Mobile Agents. In *Proc. of CONCUR*, volume 1119 of *LNCS*, pages 406–421. Springer, 1996. 22

[24] D. Gelernter. Generative Communication in Linda. *ACM Transactions on Programming Languages and Systems*, 7(1):80–112, 1985. 22

[25] A. Gordon and P. Hankin. A Concurrent Object Calculus: Reduction and Typing. In *Proc. of HLCL*, volume 16.3 of *ENTCS*. Elsevier, 1998. 36

[26] B. C. Pierce and D. N. Turner. Concurrent Objects in a Process Calculus. In *Proc. of TPPP*, volume 907 of *LNCS*, pages 187–215. Springer, 1995. 36

[27] J. G. Riecke and C. Stone. Privacy via Subsumption. *Information and Computation*, 172:2–28, 2002. 3rd special issue of Theory and Practice of Object-Oriented Systems (TAPOS). 32

[28] T. Thorn. Programming Languages for Mobile Code. *ACM Computing Surveys*, 29(3):213–239, 1997. Also Technical Report 1083, University of Rennes IRISA. 21

[29]  N. Yoshida and M. Hennessy. Subtyping and Locality in Distributed Higher Order Mobile Processes (extended abstract). In *Proc. of CONCUR'99*, volume 1664 of *LNCS*, pages 557–572. Springer-Verlag, 1999.  36

# On Calculi for Context-Aware Coordination

Pietro Braione and Gian Pietro Picco

Dipartimento di Elettronica e Informazione, Politecnico di Milano
P.za Leonardo da Vinci, 32, I-20133 Milano, Italy
{braione,picco}@elet.polimi.it

**Abstract.** Modern distributed computing demands unprecedented levels of dynamicity and reconfiguration. Mobile computing, peer-to-peer networks, computational grids, multi-agent systems, are examples of domains exhibiting a continuously changing system configuration. In these settings, the *context* where computation occurs is not only dynamically changing, but also affecting the components' behavior in a fundamental way, by enabling or inhibiting some of their actions.
This paper is a first step in laying the formal foundation for a process calculi specification style that: *i)* fosters a coordination approach by sharply separating the process behavior from the computational context defined by system changes; *ii)* enables the specifier to define her notion of context and the rules governing how it affects the application process behavior.

## 1 Introduction

Modern distributed computing demands unprecedented levels of dynamicity and reconfiguration. Mobile computing scenarios modify the physical topology of the system, and make communication transient and opportunistic. Mobile code changes the software fabric of a distributed computing system into a fluid one, by allowing program fragments to travel across hosts. Multi-agent systems, computational grids, and peer-to-peer networks are other examples of domains where the physical or logical structure of the system is continuously under reconfiguration.

The hallmark of these scenarios is that the *context* where computation occurs is no longer fixed as in traditional distributed computing. A mobile host often accesses only services that are provided by hosts in range. Mobile agents may use only the resources available on the host they reside on. Queries in a peer-to-peer system return results that depend on the current set of connected peers. Interestingly, context not only defines the allowed scope for interaction, but also affects the components' behavior in a fundamental way, by enabling or inhibiting some of their actions. A message can be reported by a soldier to the commander of a patrol only if the communication medium ensures an adequate level of secrecy. The result of a computation carried by a swarm of mobile agents can be computed only when they are all co-located on the same host. A particular music file can be downloaded from a peer only if no closer one offers an equivalent file.

R. de Nicola et al. (Eds.): COORDINATION 2004, LNCS 2949, pp. 38–54, 2004.

Dealing with a changing computational context is the fundamental challenge of mobility and, in general, modern distributed computing. As noted in [9], a coordination perspective is helpful in addressing this challenge, in that it allows to separate sharply the details of a component's internal behavior, concerned with application issues, from the details of the surrounding computational context, represented through coordination abstractions. Essentially, a coordination perspective allows context to emerge as a first-class element, and be treated accordingly. However, the complexity of the issues involved requires the use of formal thinking when tackling the design of systems in this environment.

*Process calculi* are a common way to formally describe concurrent, distributed systems, and have recently been used successfully for specifying the semantics of coordination models and languages. Unfortunately, these calculi only rarely address directly (i.e., with appropriate abstractions) the modeling of a changing computational context. Moreover, in these few cases the specifier is constrained by a (rather rigid) notion of context built-in the calculus. For instance, the Ambient calculus [3] assumes a space organized in hierarchical locations, and the context perceived by a process is determined by its position in the space tree. The resulting approach is undoubtedly elegant, in that the space structure is naturally mirrored by the very syntactic structure of terms. On the other hand, it forces *a priori* a space structure that may not be suitable for the specification task at hand. As an example, the inherently graph-based nature of mobile ad hoc networks and peer-to-peer systems can hardly be reduced to a hierarchy, and so are cases where physical or logical space areas (and hence contexts) overlap.

The specification of middleware and languages assuming alternative notions of space and context becomes then cumbersome—as we experienced directly. Our initial goal was in fact to formalize the LIME middleware [8] using process calculi. We soon discovered that describing the LIME semantics using a "raw" process calculus leads to a cumbersome specification, precisely because contextual information gets buried in technical details. Proper abstractions are required to simplify both the development and the understanding of the specification.

The contribution of this paper is a first step in laying the formal foundation for a process calculi specification style that: *i)* fosters a coordination approach by sharply separating the process behavior from computational context defined by system changes; *ii)* enables the specifier to define her notion of context and the rules governing how it affects the application process behavior. Hence, decoupling and flexibility in representing context are our driving motivations, with the goal of obtaining a formalism expressive enough to be used to model a real middleware. Process calculi is the formal tool we use to shape our ideas.

Our approach is based on *reactive systems* (RS), a kind of process calculi inspired by Berry and Boudol's Chemical Abstract Machine (CHAM) [1]. In a RS the elementary computational steps are described as transitions (the chemical reactions) that cause the rewriting of terms representing the current configuration of the system, expressed as a multiset of components (the chemical solution). Any such transition is interpreted as an interaction among a number of components which come in contact. The difficulty of representing a dynamic, subjective behavior in RSs stems from the fact that interactions are not disciplined: every computational context may host any interaction.

In this work, we generalize the notion of RS into a new class that we call *contextual reactive systems* (CRS). In these systems, it is possible to specify the computational context under which a class of interactions is allowed, and the contexts under which it is not. This allows to inhibit some behaviors according to the features of the context under which they should have been performed.

Our treatment of CRSs relies on categories. Capturing the fundamental properties at this high level of abstraction allows us to concentrate on the core concepts without being distracted by the technicalities of a specific calculus, and enables the definition of families of concrete calculi sharing the same abstract nature. To make the presentation more concrete, however, we show how the categorical framework can be instantiated in a process calculus, and demonstrate its effectiveness by formalizing a relevant subset of the LIME middleware [8]. More specifically, our approach is inspired by Leifer and Milner [6], where a categorical definition of RS is exploited to derive an equivalent labelled transition system (LTS). This approach allows to extend to RSs the notion of strong bisimulation found in LTSs, thus achieving both the ease of specification characteristic of RSs, and the availability of natural operational congruences based on strong bisimulation. While this paper presents only the formal definition of CRSs, our current work aims at obtaining similar equivalence results, and advantages, for CRSs.

This paper is organized as follows. Section 2 introduces a categorical formalization of RSs. A simple Linda-like calculus illustrates how a RS can implemented by a calculus, and serves as a reference example throughout the paper. Section 3 highlights the limitations of RSs when dealing with context. Section 4 contains the main contribution of this paper as a formalization of the notion of CRS. Section 5 shows how CRSs can be specified in practice, and discusses the advantages of our approach. Section 6 provides a concrete example by formalizing a subset of LIME. Section 7 elaborates on the findings of this paper, by suggesting relationships with other approaches and avenues for future research. Finally, Section 8 ends the paper with some brief concluding remarks.

## 2   Reactive Systems

The definition of RS assumed in this paper is slightly adapted from [6] and [10].

**Definition 1 (Reactive system).** *A* reactive system *(RS) is a* $(\mathcal{C}, I, \mathbf{R}, \mathcal{D})$ *quadruple, where* $\mathcal{C}$ *is a category,* $I \in Ob\mathcal{C}$, $\mathbf{R} \subseteq \bigcup_{x \in Ob\mathcal{C}} \mathcal{C}(I, x) \times \mathcal{C}(I, x)$, *and* $\mathcal{D} \leq \mathcal{C}$ *is composition-reflecting, i.e.,* $D_0 \, D_1 \in Mo\mathcal{D} \implies D_i \in Mo\mathcal{D}$, $i = 0, 1$.

We analyze each point of this definition[1]. The morphisms in $\mathcal{C}$ are called the *contexts* of the system. Among them, the *ground contexts* denote processes.

---

[1] In our notation, $\mathcal{C}(A, B)$ denotes the hom-set $\mathrm{Hom}_\mathcal{C}(A, B)$ of a category $\mathcal{C}$, and $\mathcal{D} \leq \mathcal{C}$ indicates that the category $\mathcal{D}$ is a sub-category of $\mathcal{C}$.

Ground contexts generalize the terms of a calculus, while all the other contexts generalize the "terms with a hole" obtained by replacing exactly one sub-term of a calculus' term with a special symbol $-$, the *hole*. Replacing the hole with a compatible sub-term is abstractly modeled, in the categorical framework, by morphism composition: $C\,C'$ corresponds to the term $C[C'/-]$. The objects of $\mathcal{C}$ serve the purpose of disciplinating composition, just like a sorting discipline rules substitution in a term algebra. Ground contexts are distinguished in the categorical framework by imposing that their source object is $I$, i.e., each of them belongs to some hom-sets $\mathcal{C}(I, x)$. $I$ is not necessarily initial.

**R** is the set of the *elementary rules*. An elementary rule is a pair $(l, r)$ of ground contexts, where $l$ is named the *redex* and $r$ the *contractum* of the rule. Elementary rules express the basic interactions for some simple, paradigmatic configurations. They are extended to form *composite rules*. The extension is performed as in the $\lambda$-calculus: When a redex appears as a sub-term of another term, *in some cases* it may be reduced to its contractum leaving the containing term (the context) unchanged. This idea is captured in the category-theoretic framework by defining the sub-category $\mathcal{D} \leq \mathcal{C}$ of *reactive contexts*, which specifies the contexts under which a rule may fire, and the following relationship:

**Definition 2 (Reaction relationship).** *The* reaction relationship, $\rightarrow$, *is defined as follows:*

$$a \rightarrow a' \quad \Longleftrightarrow \quad \exists\, (l, r) \in \mathbf{R},\, D \in Mo\,\mathcal{D}\, .\, a = Dl \wedge a' = Dr.$$

This relationship contains all the rules (both elementary and composite) of the RS, hence $\mathbf{R} \subseteq \rightarrow \subseteq \bigcup_{x \in \mathrm{Ob}\,\mathcal{C}} \mathcal{C}(I, x) \times \mathcal{C}(I, x)$. Restricting the context under which elementary rules can fire to a predefined class of "evaluation contexts" is a well-known technique, used for instance to impose evaluation disciplines over $\lambda$-calculi. In process calculi, reactive contexts are instead used to forbid the computation of "switched off" processes, e.g. guarded processes. Composition-reflectivity is necessary to ensure some basic properties to RSs.

*Example.* To make our formulation of RSs more concrete, we introduce a process calculus, slightly adapted from [2], describing a data-based coordination system inspired by Linda. Processes are sequential compositions of primitive actions. They execute concurrently and coordinate themselves by exchanging tuples through a global data space. The calculus' terms are generated by the abstract syntax in Table 1, where $v$ is a value in the set $\mathbf{V} = \{v_0, v_1, \ldots\}$, $c$ a coordination primitive (in or out), $P$ a process, $T$ a tuple, and $C$ a configuration. Infinite behaviors can be represented by processes in the form $\mathsf{rec}X.P$, where $X$ is a process variable and $P$ a process containing one guarded occurrence of $X$. We also require that all the occurrences of process variables in a term generated by $P$ are bound by some $\mathsf{rec}$. We define structural congruence $\equiv$ as the smallest congruence on terms such that:

$$
\begin{array}{ll}
C_1 \,|\, C_2 \equiv C_2 \,|\, C_1 & (C_1 \,|\, C_2) \,|\, C_3 \equiv C_1 \,|\, (C_2 \,|\, C_3) \\
C \,|\, 0 \equiv C & \mathsf{rec}X.P \equiv P[\mathsf{rec}X.P/X]
\end{array}
$$

**Table 1.** Syntax and semantics of the $\mathbf{L}_{RS}$ system

| Syntax: | Semantics: |
|---|---|
| $C ::= P \mid T \mid C \mid C$ | $in(v).P \mid \langle v \rangle \to P$  (2.1) |
| $P ::= 0 \mid X \mid c.P \mid recX.P$ | $out(v).P \to P \mid \langle v \rangle$  (2.2) |
| $T ::= \langle v \rangle$ | $\dfrac{C \to C'}{C \mid P \to C' \mid P}$  (2.3) |
| $c ::= in(v) \mid out(v)$ | $\dfrac{C \to C'}{C \mid T \to C' \mid T}$  (2.4) |
| | $\dfrac{D \equiv C \quad C \to C' \quad C' \equiv D'}{D \to D'}$  (2.5) |

Structural congruence equates terms which differ syntactically and nevertheless denote the same configuration. The operational semantics of the calculus are presented in Table 1: the rules are self-explanatory, and hence not commented.

Let us now see how the specification of $\mathbf{L}_{RS}$ maps onto our definition of RS. Elementary rules are represented by the semantic rules (2.1) and (2.2) in Table 1. Contexts are all the congruence classes of "terms with (at most) a hole". Reactive contexts are all the congruence classes of terms in the form $- \mid C$. Composite rules are expressed by the semantic rules (2.3) and (2.4) in Table 1, by recursion over the subclass of reactive contexts containing all the (congruence classes of) terms having the form $- \mid P$ and $- \mid T$.

The categorical definition of RS evidences some of its relevant features. First, while a context denotes a *locus*, i.e., an incomplete entity able to host another entity, a reactive context denotes a *computational locus*, i.e., a locus able to host an entity with a behavior and let it compute. Second, rules can be applied orthogonally under reactive contexts, i.e., *any* reactive context may host *any* reaction—with a correct composition typing. Hence, a reactive context can neither limit nor extend the internal behaviors of the entities it hosts. Third, by the very definition of composite rule, a reactive context is unaffected by the internal behaviors of the entities it hosts. We can summarize the last two observations by saying that computations in a RS are *pure* with respect to their context. As we describe in the rest of the paper, this orthogonality between reaction and context is the most relevant obstacle towards the decoupling and expressiveness we demand, and is lifted by our definition of contextual reactive systems.

# 3   Motivation

In the computing scenarios we target, computation is affected by the context[2] surrounding it (e.g., communication parties in range, set of services available, mobile agents co-located on the same host), and such context is dynamically and continuously changing. In these scenarios, the interactions between the components of an application often depend on the current configuration of the context.

Unfortunately, in some cases these situations are not easily modeled by means of a RS. We illustrate the issue with a simple example. A shared tuple space is used by printers to advertise their presence, and by processes to send them their jobs. A high-level print primitive is available to processes, whose effect is to automatically direct the job to the best printer among those currently advertised. Assuming, for the sake of simplicity, that only low-quality raw printers and high-quality PostScript printers are available, a possible configuration is:

$$\langle \text{pr:ps} \rangle \mid \langle \text{pr:raw} \rangle \mid \text{print(txt)}.0,$$

which contains two advertisements and a process which prints a job and then terminates. Our goal is to specify the semantics of print using a RS. In the first place, we must formalize how print generates jobs for both low-quality and high-quality printers. This can be done by rules in the form:

$$\text{print(txt)}.P \mid \langle \text{pr:raw} \rangle \rightarrow P \mid \langle \text{job,txt,raw} \rangle \mid \langle \text{pr:raw} \rangle$$
$$\text{print(txt)}.P \mid \langle \text{pr:ps} \rangle \rightarrow P \mid \langle \text{job,txt,ps} \rangle \mid \langle \text{pr:ps} \rangle$$

But how can we ensure that print generates jobs only for the PostScript printer, in the presence of both printers? We should forbid redexes as $\text{print(txt)}.P \mid \langle \text{pr:raw} \rangle$ to fire when they are placed in the same configuration with a tuple $\langle \text{pr:ps} \rangle$. Nevertheless, if we consider all the "contexts with a tuple" $- \mid \langle \ldots \rangle$ as reactive, this cannot be achieved since RSs allow *any* interaction to occur unrestrained under *any* reactive context. In the previous example with one printing processes and two advertisements, the system may perform one of two different transitions:

$$\langle \text{pr:ps} \rangle \mid \langle \text{pr:raw} \rangle \mid \text{print(txt)}.0 \rightarrow \langle \text{pr:ps} \rangle \mid \langle \text{pr:raw} \rangle \mid 0 \mid \langle \text{job,txt,raw} \rangle$$
$$\langle \text{pr:ps} \rangle \mid \langle \text{pr:raw} \rangle \mid \text{print(txt)}.0 \rightarrow \langle \text{pr:ps} \rangle \mid \langle \text{pr:raw} \rangle \mid 0 \mid \langle \text{job,txt,ps} \rangle$$

which are obtained by composing respectively the first and the second elementary rule with the reactive contexts $- \mid \langle \text{pr:ps} \rangle$ and $- \mid \langle \text{pr:raw} \rangle$.

This simple example evidences a characteristic of RSs that is central to the theme of this paper: It is not possible to forbid the reduction of a redex based on the properties of the context it is immersed in.

Besides being a limiting factor towards the ability to express computations that depend on the configuration of the physical context, this issue is frequently found in many aspects of coordination languages. For instance, similar problems

---

[2] It is worth noting how here we use the term *context* to refer to a concept that is different from the one defined for reactive systems.

arise when modeling the semantics of probe operations and reactive programming [2]. Moreover, they also arise in modeling the semantics of LIME, as pointed out in Section 6. We characterize the problem more precisely by considering an extension of $\mathbf{L}_{RS}$ with the bulk operation ing, which atomically removes all the tuples matching a specified value $v$. Removal of an unlimited number of matching tuples can be specified[3] through an infinite number of rules in the form $\text{ing}(v).P \mid \prod_n \langle v \rangle \to P$. Nevertheless, we cannot ensure that ing always removes *all* the matching tuples in a configuration. In fact:

*Claim.* There is no extension of $\mathbf{L}_{RS}$ capable of expressing the semantics of ing.

*Proof (Sketch).* Let us assume by contradiction that we can, i.e., that there is no rule $a \to a'$ where a $\text{ing}(v)$ prefix is consumed and at least one $\langle v \rangle$ tuple is not. Let us define two functions $\iota$ and $\tau$ yielding respectively the number of processes in $a$ with shape $\text{ing}(v).P$, and the number of tuples in $a$ with shape $\langle v \rangle$. (These functions can be defined by induction.) Then, if $\iota(a', v) = \iota(a, v) - 1$, it must be $\tau(a', v) = 0$. Let us consider any rule $a \to a'$ of the calculus, such as $\iota(a', v) = \iota(a, v) - 1$, and let us compose it with the reactive context $- \mid \langle v \rangle$. We obtain a composite rule $a'' \to a'''$ such as $\iota(a''', v) = \iota(a'', v) - 1$ and $\tau(a''', v) > 0$. This contradicts our assumption. $\square$

## 4   Contextual Reactive Systems

In the previous section we pointed out that the impossibility of inhibiting some reductions of a RS based on the properties of the context surrounding the redex hampers the style of modeling coordination constructs we are targeting. In this section we will define a new class of RSs overcoming this issue.

### 4.1   Fundamentals

To understand the spirit of our solution, let us focus on extending $\mathbf{L}_{RS}$ with ing, as discussed earlier. The problem we identified is that an elementary rule of ing is allowed to fire under any reactive context, including those containing additional matching tuples that hence ing cannot remove. In principle, one could solve it by simply removing from $\mathcal{D}$ all the reactive contexts containing one or more tuples. This solution, however, hinders the modularity of the specification since all the other elementary rules, which in principle are not affected by the presence of tuples, must be modified accordingly. In essence, the whole calculus must be revised to add a single primitive. We seek instead for a more flexible solution that limits the removal of the undesired contexts (i.e., those with matching tuples) only to the elementary rules for ing, and leaves the rest of the system unaffected.

The fundamental idea behind our approach is to lift the property of orthogonality between reactions and contexts characterizing RSs, and allow instead

---

[3] For the sake of simplicity we assume that, if no matching tuple is available, the process fails by becoming inert.

elementary rules to be extended only by *some* (i.e., not necessary by *any*) of the reactive contexts in $\mathcal{D}$. Composite rules are still obtained by recursively extending a core set of elementary rules with a set reactive contexts, representing the sub-configurations left unaffected by the transition. The important difference with RSs, however, is that each elementary rule is now associated to its own specific subset of reactive contexts–the only ones the rule can be composed with. These intuitions are formally captured by the following definitions, analogous to those enunciated for RSs.

**Definition 3 (Contextual reactive system).** *A contextual reactive system* (CRS) *is a* $(\mathcal{C}, I, \mathbf{R}, \mathcal{D}, \mathcal{D}[\![l,r]\!])$ *quintuple, such that* $(\mathcal{C}, I, \mathbf{R}, \mathcal{D})$ *is a* RS, *and* $\mathcal{D}[\![l,r]\!]$ *is a function mapping any elementary rule* $(l,r) \in \mathbf{R}$ *to a composition-reflecting sub-category of* $\mathcal{D}$.

**Definition 4 (Reaction relationship for contextual reactive systems).** *The* reaction relationship, $\rightarrow$, *is defined as follows:*

$$a \rightarrow a' \iff \exists\, (l,r) \in \mathbf{R},\, D \in Mo\,(\mathcal{D}[\![l,r]\!])\;.\; a = Dl \wedge a' = Dr$$

As with reactive systems, $\mathbf{R} \subseteq \rightarrow \subseteq \bigcup_{x \in \mathrm{Ob}\,\mathcal{C}} \mathcal{C}(I, x) \times \mathcal{C}(I, x)$.

Contextual reactive systems differ from RSs only for the presence of a function $\mathcal{D}[\![l,r]\!]$, which captures the association between elementary rules and their allowed reactive contexts, represented by a sub-category of $\mathcal{D}$. Accordingly, the definition of $\rightarrow$ now constrains $D$ to belong to $\mathcal{D}[\![l,r]\!]$, therefore forbidding all the other contexts from being composed with the elementary rule. In CRSs, different elementary rules may have different contextual constraints.

Interestingly, the class of CRSs strictly contains that of RSs. Indeed, the latter are obtained from the former by imposing that $\mathcal{D}[\![l,r]\!] = \mathcal{D}$ for all the $(l,r) \in \mathbf{R}$– i.e., as the CRSs where any elementary rule can be applied under any reactive context. Clearly, CRSs are more expressive, in that the computational locus is now able to influence which interactions can or cannot be performed by the components hosted in it. In a sense, reactive contexts are elevated to a first-class status, and this greatly simplifies the specification task, as discussed in the next section. On the other hand, in our formulation of CRSs an internal transitions performed by a group of components still does *not* affect the surrounding context.

## 4.2   Elementary Reactive Contexts

The reactive contexts of a RS can usually be expressed as the composition of a number of simpler, non-decomposable contexts. For instance, in the $\mathbf{L}_{\mathrm{RS}}$ system of Table 1, every reactive context is built by repeatedly composing in parallel either terms $T$, denoting tuples, or terms $P$, denoting processes. Hence, the set[4] $\mathbf{D}$ of the reactive contexts of $\mathbf{L}_{\mathrm{RS}}$ is generated by all the contexts in the form $-\,|\,P$ or $-\,|\,T$. This characteristic is fundamental for enabling a specification of

---

[4] To improve readability, we use the definitions $\mathbf{D} \stackrel{\mathrm{def}}{=} Mo\,\mathcal{D}$ and $\mathbf{D}[\![l,r]\!] \stackrel{\mathrm{def}}{=} Mo\,(\mathcal{D}[\![l,r]\!])$.

RSs using a rewrite system. Hence, in this section we define formally the notion of elementary context for a RS, and then see how this can be extended to CRSs.

Let us define, for any $\mathbf{X} \subseteq \mathbf{D}$, $\mathbf{X}^\star$ as the minimal set such that $\mathbf{X} \subseteq \mathbf{X}^\star$, and such that $D_0, D_1 \in \mathbf{X}^\star \implies D_0 D_1 \in \mathbf{X}^\star$, whenever $D_0 D_1$ is defined. The $\star$ operator is a closure on $\mathbf{D}$, which we call *composition closure*. The following definition is standard in universal algebra:

**Definition 5 (Elementary reactive context).** *An* (irredundant) basis *for* $\mathbf{D}$ *is a minimal generating set for* $\mathbf{D}$ *w.r.t. the closure operator* $\star$, *i.e., a subset* $\mathbf{B} \subseteq \mathbf{D}$ *such that* $\mathbf{B}^\star = \mathbf{D}$, *and such that* $\mathbf{B}' \subseteq \mathbf{B} \wedge \mathbf{B}'^\star = \mathbf{D} \implies \mathbf{B}' = \mathbf{B}$. *The elements of a basis* $\mathbf{B}$ *for* $\mathbf{D}$ *are called* elementary (reactive) contexts.

When $\mathbf{D}$ has a basis, any reactive context can be finitely decomposed on it, i.e., if $D \in \mathbf{D}$ then $D = B_{n-1} \ldots B_1 B_0$, for some $B_i \in \mathbf{B}$, $i = 0 \ldots n - 1$.

The existence of a basis is relevant as it enables us to express the composite rules of a RS by induction. Reactive systems are usually specified by means of a logic, whose axioms are the elementary rules, and whose inference rules describe how composite rules are constructed by composing a (not necessarily elementary) rule with an elementary context. As an example, in $\mathbf{L}_{\mathrm{RS}}$ these inference rules are rule (2.3) and (2.4) for parallel composition in Table 1. On the other hand, composite rules are formally defined as the composition of an elementary rule with a (not necessarily elementary) reactive context. For RSs the two approaches yield the same result, but for CRSs this symmetry is less obvious, because every elementary rule has its own allowed set of reactive contexts, determined by $\mathbf{D}[\![l, r]\!]$. Hence, it makes sense to ask whether every $\mathbf{D}[\![l, r]\!]$ has a basis. Not surprisingly, the answer is yes, assumed that $\mathbf{D}$ has one. Perhaps a little more surprising is the fact that every $\mathbf{D}[\![l, r]\!]$ has exactly the basis one would expect, namely, the projection of the basis of $\mathbf{D}$ on $\mathbf{D}[\![l, r]\!]$. This is stated formally by the following proposition, which we prove correct.

**Proposition 1.** *Let* $\mathbf{B}$ *be a basis for* $\mathbf{D}$, *and let us define* $\mathbf{B}[\![l, r]\!] \stackrel{def}{=} \mathbf{D}[\![l, r]\!] \cap \mathbf{B}$, *for each* $(l, r) \in \mathbf{R}$. *Then,* $\mathbf{B}[\![l, r]\!]$ *is a basis for* $\mathbf{D}[\![l, r]\!]$.

*Proof.* We begin by proving that $\mathbf{B}[\![l, r]\!]$ generates $\mathbf{D}[\![l, r]\!]$. $\mathbf{B}$ obviously generates $\mathbf{D}[\![l, r]\!]$, so every context in $\mathbf{D}[\![l, r]\!]$ can be decomposed on $\mathbf{B}$. But $\mathcal{D}[\![l, r]\!]$ is composition-reflecting, thus every component of this decomposition must also be in $\mathbf{D}[\![l, r]\!]$. This proves that every context in $\mathbf{D}[\![l, r]\!]$ can be decomposed on $\mathbf{D}[\![l, r]\!] \cap \mathbf{B} = \mathbf{B}[\![l, r]\!]$, i.e., that $\mathbf{D}[\![l, r]\!] \subseteq (\mathbf{B}[\![l, r]\!])^\star$. Being $\mathbf{B}[\![l, r]\!] \subseteq \mathbf{D}[\![l, r]\!]$, thus $(\mathbf{B}[\![l, r]\!])^\star \subseteq (\mathbf{D}[\![l, r]\!])^\star = \mathbf{D}[\![l, r]\!]$, we proved that $(\mathbf{B}[\![l, r]\!])^\star = \mathbf{D}[\![l, r]\!]$.

Now we prove by contradiction the irredundancy of $\mathbf{B}[\![l, r]\!]$. Let us assume the existence of $\mathbf{B}' \subset \mathbf{B}[\![l, r]\!]$, such as $\mathbf{B}'^\star = \mathbf{D}[\![l, r]\!]$. This means that for some $B \in \mathbf{D}[\![l, r]\!] \cap \mathbf{B}$ is $B \notin \mathbf{B}'$. But $\mathbf{B}'$ generates $\mathbf{D}[\![l, r]\!]$, of which $B$ is a member, thus $B = B_{n-1} \ldots B_1 B_0$, with $B_i \in \mathbf{B}'$. This implies that $\mathbf{B}'' = \mathbf{B} - \{B\} \subset \mathbf{B}$ generates $\mathbf{D}$, thus contradicting the assumption that $\mathbf{B}$ is a basis for $\mathbf{D}$.     □

Note that the intersection of a basis for an algebra with the carrier of one of its sub-algebras is *not*, in general, a basis for the latter: composition-reflectivity is the crucial additional hypothesis yielding this property. This result suggests that expressing composite rules by induction in a CRS is not harder than in a RS notwithstanding the proliferation of sets of contexts. This will the object of the next section.

## 5   Specifying Contextual Reactive Systems

In this section we move from the abstract, categoric-theoretic setting to a notation suitable for specification. We focus on configurations in the form of *flat* (non-structured) parallel composition of terms. Albeit we omit a formal definition of flat CRS, we remark that all the calculi in this paper are flat, and that flat systems always have a basis for $\mathbf{D}$.

### 5.1   Basics

A transition systems is usually specified by means of a logic whose sentences express the existence of a (possibly labelled) transition from one state to another. Sentences are built by means of recursive application of inference rules to a set of axioms. Incarnations of this basic principle have been formalized in literature, e.g., by transition systems specifications [5] and rewriting logic [7].

Since RSs differ from CRSs only due to the presence of the $\mathbf{D}[\![l, r]\!]$ function, the important issue to be dealt with in CRSs concerns how composite rules are defined. In a RS specification, appropriate inferences are introduced in the form

$$\frac{a \rightarrow a' \quad B \in \mathbf{B}}{B\,a \rightarrow B\,a'},$$

i.e., extending rules with elementary contexts. In a CRS, we must attain more strictly to the categorical definition of composite rule and write the inference as

$$\frac{(l, r) \in \mathbf{R} \quad D \in (\mathbf{B}[\![l, r]\!])^\star}{D\,l \rightarrow D\,r},$$

because we have no immediate way to recursively extend $\mathbf{D}[\![l, r]\!]$ to composite rules. For this reason, we define a different specification scheme, which evidences how the specification of an elementary rule is associated with the corresponding specification for its $\mathbf{D}[\![l, r]\!]$ set. This scheme has the form:

$$\{B \,.\, \mathcal{P}\}^\star \qquad L \rightarrow R \,.\, \mathcal{P}'$$

On the right hand side is the elementary rule scheme $L \rightarrow R \,.\, \mathcal{P}$, while on the left hand side is a set scheme $\{B \,.\, \mathcal{P}\}$. The two schemes are constrained by the predicates $\mathcal{P}$ and $\mathcal{P}'$ respectively. The schemes are instantiated by simultaneous substitution of all their free variables. This produces an elementary rule $l \rightarrow r$ on the right, and a set of elementary contexts on the left, which is closed with respect to context composition, yielding $(\mathbf{B}[\![l, r]\!])^\star = \mathbf{D}[\![l, r]\!]$. Juxtaposition of the set scheme and of the rule scheme stands for their composition, formally defined as $\mathbf{D}[\![l, r]\!] (l \rightarrow r) \overset{\text{def}}{=} \{D\,l \rightarrow D\,r \; . \; D \in \mathbf{D}[\![l, r]\!]\}$. This yields the set of all the composite rules generated by the elementary rule $l \rightarrow r$. When the elementary rules generated by a given scheme can be applied under any reactive context, we will omit to write the set scheme.

Specifications expressed with this notation are not very readable, since $\mathbf{B}[\![l, r]\!]$ does not bear an intuitive interpretation. Hence, we now present some notational improvements that simplify the specification task and, at the same time, shed a different light on the essence of CRSs.

## 5.2  Inhibitors and Enablers

Let us reconsider the printer example presented in Section 3. Now we can define a rule for printing on a raw printer, which does not fire if a PostScript printer is present:

$$\{- \mid \langle v \rangle \; . \; v \neq \mathrm{pr:ps}\}^\star \quad \mathsf{print}(\mathrm{txt}).P \mid \langle \mathrm{pr:raw} \rangle \rightarrow P \mid \langle \mathrm{job,txt,raw} \rangle \mid \langle \mathrm{pr:raw} \rangle$$

The set scheme can be rewritten more compactly in terms of its *complement*.

**Definition 6 (Inhibiting Elementary Context (Inhibitor)).** *Let us define, for any set* $\mathbf{X} \subseteq \mathbf{B}$*, the set* $\mathbf{X}^c \overset{\text{def}}{=} \mathbf{B} - \mathbf{X}$*. Then,* $\mathbf{I}[\![l, r]\!] \overset{\text{def}}{=} (\mathbf{B}[\![l, r]\!])^c$ *represents the set of* inhibiting elementary contexts (inhibitors), *or* anticatalysts, *of the elementary rule* $(l, r)$*.*

Using inhibitors, we can rewrite the previous rule as:

$$\{- \mid \langle \mathrm{pr:ps} \rangle\}^{c\star} \quad \mathsf{print}(\mathrm{txt}).P \mid \langle \mathrm{pr:raw} \rangle \rightarrow P \mid \langle \mathrm{job,txt,raw} \rangle \mid \langle \mathrm{pr:raw} \rangle.$$

This rule yields the same CRS as the previous one, since $(\mathbf{I}[\![l, r]\!])^{c\star} = (\mathbf{B}[\![l, r]\!])^\star$. Nevertheless, it allows us to describe what *must not* be present in the configuration at hand, rather than what *may* be present. We argue that the former is simpler and more intuitive in many cases, including those illustrated in Section 3. Primitives are affected only by a well defined and restricted class of entities, which are precisely those that must not be present, while those that may be present are, indeed, ininfluent.

In the elementary rule scheme for print we considered earlier, we can observe the presence of an invariant part, the tuple $\langle \mathrm{pr:raw} \rangle$. This tuple appears both in the redex and in the contractum of the rule: its presence is necessary for the rule to fire, but the state transition preserves it. In a sense, the tuple represents a portion of the rule context that is nonetheless necessary to its execution. This is a rather common situation, that we can capture formally as follows.

**Definition 7 (Maximal Invariant Context).** *We informally define the* maximal invariant context (MIC) *of a rule* $l \rightarrow r$ *as the reactive context* $D$ *such that* $l = D\,l'$ *and* $r = D\,r'$ *for some pair of ground contexts* $l', r'$*, and such that the new rule* $l' \rightarrow r'$ *is minimal, i.e. does not preserve in its contractum any of the entities appearing on its redex.*

Minimality can be formalized as the requirement that $l'$ and $r'$ are *relatively prime*, i.e., their decompositions on **B** have no elementary context in common besides the $-$. The MIC of the rule for print is $- \mid \langle \text{pr:ps} \rangle$. It is composed of a single elementary context, although in general the MIC of a rule may contain more than one. For uniformity, rather than exploiting directly the MIC in the specification we prefer to deal with its elementary contexts:

**Definition 8 (Enabling Elementary Context (Enabler)).** *The* enabling elementary contexts (enablers)*, or* catalysts*, of a rule are all the elementary contexts belonging to the rule's* MIC.

When enablers and inhibitors are both put in evidence, a specification becomes:

$$\{I \in \mathbf{B} \cdot \mathcal{P}\}^{c\star} \quad \{\!|E \in \mathbf{B} \cdot \mathcal{P}'|\!\}^; \quad L \to R \cdot \mathcal{P}''$$

with the constraint that the rules defined by the scheme $L \to R \cdot \mathcal{P}''$ must be minimal. The multiset scheme $\{\!|E \in \mathbf{B} \cdot \mathcal{P}'|\!\}$ specifies the enablers, and the semicolon operator (;) applied on a multiset of contexts, yields the composition of all the contexts in the multiset[5]. In this notation, the rule for print becomes:

$$\{- \mid \langle \text{pr:ps} \rangle\}^{c\star} \quad \{\!|- \mid \langle \text{pr:raw} \rangle|\!\}^; \quad \text{print(txt)}.P \to P \mid \langle \text{job,txt,raw} \rangle,$$

where the semicolon exponent is, in this case, pleonastic.

Enablers and inhibitors are similar: both determine how a behavior is affected by the surrounding environment. Nevertheless, they have different effects on the rule they are associated to. Inhibitors specify the entities that *must not* be present in a rule's context: their presence disables the firing of the rule. On the other hand, enablers define the entities that *must* be present in the context of a rule for it to fire. In the next section we show how these abstractions can be used to model a real middleware.

# 6 An Example: Formalizing LIME

In this section we set out to specify the $\text{Li}_{\text{CRS}}$ system, a subset of the LIME coordination middleware [8]. We first summarize informally its main features, and then show how it can be given a formal semantics effectively by using a CRS.

In $\text{Li}_{\text{CRS}}$ processes and tuples are organized in *agents*, the units of mobility. Agents may be members of *groups*. Group membership defines the set of tuples accessible to an agent. The tuples of an agent are transiently shared throughout the group the agent is member of: an in on the tuple space may return a local tuple as well as one belonging to another agent in the group. An agent joins a group through an *engagement* procedure, and leaves it through a *disengagement*. As the agent disengages, all its tuples become unavailable to the group. Insertion of a tuple in the tuple space is performed through a modified version

---

[5] This definition is unambiguous if $E_0 E_1 = E_1 E_0$ when both exist. For the systems we are considering this is precisely commutativity of parallel composition.

**Table 2.** Syntax and semantics of the Li$_{\text{CRS}}$ system

Syntax:

$$C ::= A \mid P \mid T \mid C \mid C \qquad\qquad A ::= \epsilon :: a \mid g :: a$$
$$P ::= a :: 0 \mid a :: X \mid a :: c.P \mid a :: \text{rec}X.P \qquad T ::= a :: \langle v \rangle @ a$$
$$c ::= \text{in}(v) \mid \text{out}[a](v) \mid \text{en}(g) \mid \text{den}$$

Rules:

$$a :: \text{in}(v).P \mid a :: \langle v \rangle @ a'' \rightarrow P \tag{6.1}$$

$$\mathbf{E}_1^i \quad a :: \text{in}(v).P \mid a' :: \langle v \rangle @ a'' \rightarrow P \tag{6.2}$$

$$\mathbf{E}_2^i \quad a :: \text{out}[a'](v).P \rightarrow a :: P \mid a :: \langle v \rangle @ a' \tag{6.3}$$

$$\mathbf{I}_1^{c\star} \ \mathbf{E}_3^i \quad a :: \text{out}[a'](v).P \rightarrow a :: P \mid a :: \langle v \rangle @ a' \tag{6.4}$$

$$\mathbf{E}_1^i \quad a :: \text{out}[a'](v).P \rightarrow a :: P \mid a' :: \langle v \rangle @ a' \tag{6.5}$$

$$a :: \text{den}.P \mid g :: a \rightarrow a :: P \mid \epsilon :: a \tag{6.6}$$

$$\mathbf{I}_2^{c\star} \ \mathbf{E}_4^i \quad a :: \text{en}(g).P \mid \epsilon :: a \mid \prod_{\mathbf{T}_a} a_i :: \langle v_i \rangle @ a \mid \prod_{\mathbf{T}_g} a :: \langle v_k \rangle @ a_k \rightarrow$$

$$a :: P \mid g :: a \mid \prod_{\mathbf{T}_a} a :: \langle v_i \rangle @ a \mid \prod_{\mathbf{T}_g} a_k :: \langle v_k \rangle @ a_k$$

$$. \, ((a' :: \langle v \rangle @ a \in \mathbf{T}_a \vee a :: \langle v \rangle @ a' \in \mathbf{T}_g) \implies g :: a' \in \mathbf{A}_g) \tag{6.7}$$

$$\frac{D \equiv C \quad C \rightarrow C' \quad C' \equiv D'}{D \rightarrow D'} \tag{6.8}$$

Contexts:

$$\mathbf{E}_1 = \{ - \mid g :: a \, , \, - \mid g :: a' \, . \, a \neq a' \} \qquad \mathbf{E}_2 = \{ - \mid \epsilon :: a \}$$
$$\mathbf{E}_3 = \{ - \mid g :: a \} \qquad\qquad\qquad\quad \mathbf{E}_4 = \{ - \mid g :: a' \, . \, g :: a' \in \mathbf{A}_g \}$$
$$\mathbf{I}_1 = \{ - \mid g :: a' \} \qquad\qquad\qquad\quad \mathbf{I}_2 = \{ - \mid g :: a' \, . \, g :: a' \notin \mathbf{A}_g \} \cup$$
$$\{ - \mid a' :: \langle v \rangle @ a \, . \, g :: a' \in \mathbf{A}_g \} \cup$$
$$\{ - \mid a :: \langle v \rangle @ a' \, . \, g :: a' \in \mathbf{A}_g \} \cup$$

of out, annotated with the name of a destination agent. If source and destination are engaged in the same group, the tuple is immediately delivered. Otherwise, it is retained at the source and tagged with the name of its destination; these tuples are said to be *misplaced*. Misplaced tuples are delivered as soon as the source and the destination agents become engaged in the same group.

The syntax of terms is shown at the top of Table 2. The $A$ term denotes the existence of an agent in a configuration, and has the form $g :: a$, where $a$ is the name of the agent and $g$ is the name of the group it belongs to. The symbol $\epsilon$ denotes the empty group, and is used to characterize disengaged agents, i.e., agents that are not members of any group. Tuples and processes are qualified with the agent they belong to. Tuples also report, after the @ symbol, the name of their destination agent. The out operation is annotated with the name of the destination agent. The engagement en and disengagement den operations, together with in, complete the calculus.

The semantics of the calculus is reported in the rest of Table 2. An evident difference with conventional calculi is that the specification is split in two parts: the behavioral rules and the (enabling and inhibiting) contexts constraining their execution. Structural congruence on terms is defined as for $\mathbf{L_{RS}}$, with the equation $C \,|\, 0 \equiv C$ replaced by $C \,|\, a \,::\, 0 \equiv C \; \Longleftarrow \; C \equiv C' \,|\, g :: a$.

The first two rules define the semantics of in. Rule $(6.1)$ defines input of local tuples, i.e., belonging to the same agent $a$ that issued the operation. Rule $(6.2)$ specifies an in withdrawing the tuple from the tuple space of a different agent $a'$, by virtue of transient sharing. In this case, $\mathbf{Li_{CRS}}$ prescribes that the two agents $a$ and $a'$ must be members of the same group. This requirement is captured by the enabling context $\mathbf{E}_1$. The out primitive is described by three rules. Rule $(6.3)$ defines the semantics of an out issued by a disengaged agent, while rule $(6.4)$ specifies an out issued by an engaged agent for a destination agent currently not engaged in the same group. In both cases, the emitted tuple is retained locally. Notably, the two rules are exactly the same: the different semantics is entirely captured by the associated contexts, i.e., the enabler $\mathbf{E}_2$ for $(6.3)$, and the combination of $\mathbf{E}_3$ and the inhibitor $\mathbf{I}_1$ for $(6.4)$. Finally, rule $(6.5)$ specifies the immediate delivery of the tuple when the source and destination agent are both engaged in $g$. Again, this rule is very similar to the other two, and leverages the enabler $\mathbf{E}_1$ previously used by rule $(6.2)$.

This first fragment of the semantics of $\mathbf{Li_{CRS}}$ evidences the significant advantages brought by our approach. The specification of behavior is sharply decoupled from the specification of the context where it may occur. This greatly simplifies the understanding of the specification, because it allows to grasp more directly the similarity between rules. In many cases it even elicits the fact that two rules with different semantics are in reality the same behavior applied in two different contexts (as with out), or two different behaviors taking place in the same context (as with $\mathbf{E}_1$). A specification with a traditional calculus is bound to bury these fundamental aspects in a direct representation of context, and hence obfuscates irremediably the true meaning of the semantic rules.

The specification of $\mathbf{Li_{CRS}}$ is completed by the engagement and disengagement of an agent $a$ to/from a group $g$. Disengagement is performed simply by changing the agent's group name in rule $(6.6)$. Engagement must also perform delivery of misplaced tuples. Rule $(6.7)$ relies on the definition of three sets: $\mathbf{A}_g$, containing the names of all the agents engaged in $g$, $\mathbf{T}_a$ and $\mathbf{T}_g$, containing respectively all the misplaced tuples in $g$ destined to $a$, and all the misplaced tuples in $a$ destined to some agent in $g$. The redex describes a situation where $a$ is currently disconnected and the system contains several misplaced tuples, both from agents in $g$ towards $a$ and vice versa. The contractum shows $a$ engaged in $g$ and all the misplaced tuples properly delivered. The predicate specifies that the misplaced tuples in $\mathbf{T}_a$ and $\mathbf{T}_g$ must, respectively belong and be destined to some agent in $\mathbf{A}_g$. The enabler $\mathbf{E}_4$ ensures that all the members of $\mathbf{A}_g$ are properly "expanded" around the rule. The inhibitor $\mathbf{I}_2$ forces three global constraints: $\mathbf{A}_g$ must contain *all* the agents in $g$; $\mathbf{T}_a$ must contain *all* the misplaced tuples in $g$ with $a$ as destination; $\mathbf{T}_g$ must contain *all* the misplaced tuples in $a$ with some agent in $g$ as destination. This prevents the rule from firing in contexts where some agents and/or tuples are "left behind" during engagement.

The specification of engagement is arguably more complex and less intuitive than the one for the other operations. However, some observations are noteworthy. First, engagement is the most complex portion of the original LIME model, both in terms of semantics and actual middleware implementation. Then, it is not surprising to see such complexity reflected in the specification. Second, dealing with misplaced tuples and their reconciliation essentially involves dealing explicitly with state- -something process calculi are notoriously not very good at. Third, without the level of abstraction provided by explicitly separating context, the specification would have been *much* more complicated and awkward. This is best understood by observing that the problem solved by the inhibitor $\mathbf{I}_2$ (i.e., ensuring that the rule fires in a context with *all* the agents and *all* their misplaced tuples) is very similar to the problem of implementing ing we discussed in Section 3. In our approach, the problem of ensuring that *all* of the necessary context is present and of preventing firing in all of the "partial" context configurations finds a natural and elegant solution in the use of inhibitors.

# 7   Discussion

In this paper we presented a new class of calculi which can be formally described by decoupling the specification of the computational units from that of the context where they execute. This decoupling, besides enabling natural modeling of physical or logical contexts, fosters separation of concerns, elicits similarities across the design, and hence improves expressiveness, understandability and reusability of the resulting specifications.

To our knowledge, none of the works in the lively field of calculi for distributed systems takes a perspective similar to ours. From a strictly technical point of view, the closest approach is described in [2], which gives a semantics for a Linda-like calculus with reactive programming constructs. However, all the rules are specified directly, with the allowed contexts explicitly mentioned in the rule schemes. This solution yields a RS somewhat similar to a CRS, although the authors do not strive towards a general framework, and hence the resulting model suffers from the drawbacks we discussed at the beginning of Section 4.1.

Since our study is at an early stage, the opportunities for further research are many, and we cite only some here. Firstly, the formal properties of CRSs are largely to be assessed. We are currently investigating if desirable operational congruences can be obtained by extending the techniques in [6], as discussed in the introduction. We conjecture that, when a RS has sufficient pushouts as in [6], bisimulation as congruence can be obtained for most, perhaps all, the CRSs that can be built from it by adding a $\mathcal{D}[\![l,r]\!]$ function. Another issue is assessing in which sense CRSs increase the expressive power of RSs. Since some affinities of CRSs with transition systems with negative premises [4] emerged during our research, we are investigating in that direction. Secondly, we are addressing the problem of describing models of space beyond flat (as in $\mathbf{Li}_{CRS}$) or hierarchical (as in the Ambient calculus) ones. Reflecting the space structure in the syntactic structure of the calculus terms, as done in the Ambient calculus, is no longer feasible in the general case. Finally, our long-term goal is to define an effective and usable specification framework. In this context, a CRS logic is a viable option to increase expressiveness and improve decoupling of the operational and the context-related parts of the specification. Formalization of other coordination models and middleware will be a necessary step to validate our approach.

## 8   Conclusions

In modern distributed computing the modeling of a dynamically changing context is becoming of paramount importance. Unfortunately, process calculi, a common formal tool for describing concurrent and distributed systems, do not provide specialized abstraction to deal effectively with context. In this paper, we set the grounds for *contextual reactive systems* (CRS), a generalization of the well-known reactive systems where the specification of the behavior of the system is sharply separated from the one of the contexts enabling or inhibiting its actions. We maintain that the features of our framework enable natural modeling of modern distributed systems, and in general improve separation of concerns, thus improving the understanding of the specification and simplifying its definition. Evidence for our hypothesis is provided in this paper by defining suitable process calculi abstractions based on our formulation of CRSs, and by presenting as an example the formalization of a subset of LIME, a coordination middleware for mobile computing.

## Acknowledgements

This work was partially supported by the projects: NAPI, funded by Microsoft Research, IS-MANET, funded by the National Research Council (CNR), SAHARA and VICOM, funded by the Ministry of Education, University, and Research (MIUR). The authors would like to thank Alessandra Cherubini for her comments on early drafts of this paper.

## References

[1] G. Berry and G. Boudol. The Chemical Abstract Machine. *Theoretical Computer Science*, 96:217–248, 1992.   39

[2] N. Busi, A. Rowstron, and G. Zavattaro. State- and event-based reactive programming in shared dataspaces. In F. Arbab and C. Talcott, editors, *Proc. of the 5<sup>th</sup> Int. Conf. on Coordination Models and Languages*, LNCS 2315. Springer, 2002.   41, 44, 52

[3] L. Cardelli and A. D. Gordon. Mobile ambients. In M. Nivat, editor, *Proc. of the 1^st Int. Conf. on Foundations of Software Science and Computation Structures (FoSSaCS'98)*, LNCS 1378, pages 140–155. Springer, 1998.  39

[4] J. F. Groote. Transition system specifications with negative premises. *Theoretical Computer Science*, 118(2):263–299, 1993.  53

[5] J. F. Groote and F. W. Vaandrager. Structured operational semantics and bisimulation as a congruence. *Information and Computation*, 100(2):202–260, 1992. 47

[6] J. J. Leifer and R. Milner. Deriving bisimulation congruences for reactive systems. In C. Palamidessi, editor, *Proc. of the Int. Conf. on Concurrency Theory (CONCUR 2000)*, LNCS 1187, pages 243–258. Springer, 2000.  40, 52

[7] José Meseguer. Conditional rewriting logic as a unified model of concurrency. *Theoretical Computer Science*, 96(1):73–155, 1992.  47

[8] A. L. Murphy, G. P. Picco, and G.-C. Roman. LIME: A Middleware for Physical and Logical Mobility. In F. Golshani et al., editors, *Proc. of the 21^st Int. Conf. on Distributed Computing Systems (ICDCS-21)*, pages 524–533, May 2001.  39, 40, 49

[9] G.-C. Roman, A. L. Murphy, and G. P. Picco. Coordination and Mobility. In A. Omicini et al., editors, *Coordination of Internet Agents: Models, Technologies, and Applications*, pages 254–273. Springer, 2000.  39

[10] V. Sassone and P. Sobociński. Deriving Bisimulation Congruences: A 2-Categorical Approach. In U. Nestmann and P. Panangaden, editors, *Proc. of the 9^th Int. Wksp. on Expressiveness in Concurrency (EXPRESS'02)*, volume 68 of *Electronic Notes in Theoretical Computer Science*. Springer, 2002.  40

# Probabilistic and Prioritized Data Retrieval in the Linda Coordination Model[*]

Mario Bravetti, Roberto Gorrieri, Roberto Lucchi, and Gianluigi Zavattaro

Dipartimento di Scienze dell'Informazione, Università degli Studi di Bologna,
Mura Anteo Zamboni 7, I-40127 Bologna, Italy.
{bravetti,gorrieri,lucchi,zavattar}@cs.unibo.it

**Abstract.** Linda tuple spaces are flat and unstructured, in the sense that they do not allow for expressing preferences of tuples; for example, we could be interested in indicating tuples that should be returned more frequently w.r.t. other ones, or even tuples with a low relevance that should be taken under consideration only if there is no tuple with a higher importance. In this paper we investigate, in a process algebraic setting, how probabilities and priorities can be introduced in the Linda coordination model in order to support a more sophisticated data retrieval mechanism. As far as probabilities are concerned, we show that the Linda pattern-matching data retrieval makes it necessary to deal with weights instead of just pure probabilities, as instead can be done in standard process algebras. Regarding priorities, we present two possible ways for adding them to Linda; in the first one the order of priorities is statically fixed, in the second one it is dynamically instantiated when a data-retrieval operation is executed.

## 1 Introduction

The native Linda coordination model is based on a shared tuple-space which is an unstructured and flat bag of tuples. All tuples have the same importance and relevance inside the shared repository, in the sense that when several tuples match the template of a data-retrieval operation, one of them is selected non deterministically. In some applications, we may be interested in expressing more sophisticated policy for selecting the tuple to be returned, for example, according to some priority based access (one tuple should be returned only if no other tuples of higher priority are currently available) or a probabilistic selection (one tuple should be returned with a higher probability w.r.t. another one).

Consider, for example, the problem of coordinating the collaboration among Web-Services; in particular, consider the problem of discovering a Web-Service willing to offer a particular service. A tuple-space could be exploited in this scenario as a registry where the available Web-Services register the kind of services they intend to offer, while the clients access the tuple-space in order to discover

---

[*] Work partially supported by MEFISTO Progetto "Metodi Formali per la Sicurezza e il Tempo".

R. de Nicola et al. (Eds.): COORDINATION 2004, LNCS 2949, pp. 55–70, 2004.
© Springer-Verlag Berlin Heidelberg 2004

the actual Web-Services availability. In the case more than one service is willing to offer the required service, according to the standard data-retrieval mechanism, one is chosen non deterministically. This is not satisfactory if we intend to distribute in a balanced way the workload, thus to avoid the overwhelming of requests towards one Web-Service while leaving other Services under-utilized.

As a second example, consider a master-worker application where the masters and the workers coordinate via a tuple-space: the masters produce job requests and store them inside the tuple-space, and the workers access the tuple-space to retrieve the description of the jobs to execute. We could assume that the jobs have different urgency levels, and that the workers must select a job for execution only if no jobs are currently registered with a higher priority. Another more sophisticated form of priority could be related to time constraints, e.g. assuming that a job must be executed before an expiration time, otherwise it can be left unexecuted. In this case, in order to limit the number of unexecuted jobs, each worker should select the job with the closest expiration time.

In the traditional Linda model these coordination patterns are rather difficult to be programmed. The reason is that the standard Linda data-retrieval coordination primitives (*in* and *rd*) access the tuple space on the basis of a *local* property, i.e., the conformance of the tuple w.r.t. the indicated template independently of the context in which the tuple is actually inserted. On the other hand, in the above examples *global* properties involving the entire group of matching tuples come into play. More precisely, in the examples the data-retrieval operation should select the tuple to be returned according to some function (either probabilistic or priority-based) that has all the matching tuples in its domain.

Extensions of Linda exist that support *global* operations. Consider, e.g., the *collect* primitive of [9] (that permits to withdraw all the tuples satisfying the template) or the non blocking *inp* operation supported in some Linda system [5] (that returns one tuple matching the template, if available, or terminates indicating the absence of matching tuples). These primitives permit to program the coordination patterns described above, but in a rather unsatisfactory way.

For example, if we want to force a specific probabilistic distribution of the returned tuple, we could decorate each tuple adding (as an extra field) a value that quantifies the level of relevance of the tuple. When a data-retrieval operation is executed from an agent, this agent could *collect* all the tuples satisfying the template, select the tuple according to the distribution of these values, and reintroduce the tuples in the space. Clearly, this pattern is not satisfactory because it requires to move from the tuple-space to the agent (and back) possibly huge quantities of tuples, and moreover this complex operation should be executed in a transactional manner, thus requiring consistent locks.

As far as the master-worker example is concerned, the priority-based coordination pattern that it requires could be programmed exploiting the *inp* operation. The level of priority could be associated to the tuples as an extra field. The workers that access the space could initially perform an *inp* taking into account the first level of priority, and passing to the subsequent levels only if no tuples are retrieved. This solution is satisfactory only if few levels of priority are considered, because it is necessary to explicitly access one level at a time. If the priorities are expressed in terms of an expiration time as described in the example above, this solution is clearly unfeasible because it requires a separate *inp* operation for each possible expiration time.

In light of these observations, we consider worth to investigate extensions of the Linda tuple-space coordination model with *probabilistic* as well as *prioritized* data retrieval. By probabilistic access we mean the possibility to specify the probabilistic distribution according to which the data to be returned are selected when a template is matched by more than one tuple. We observe that the most reasonable way for specifying this distribution is to associate weights to tuples indicating the absolute relevance of one tuple; when a data retrieval operation is performed, the weights of all the tuple matching the template are taken into account, and the tuple is probabilistically selected according to its relative weight w.r.t. the weights of the other tuples. Using this approach we can satisfactorily solve the problem of a balanced distribution of the workload of the Web-Services: each Web-Service indicates with a weight its current workload (the higher is the workload, the lower is the weight). When a client performs its discovery operation, a link to a Web-Service currently unloaded is more probably returned w.r.t. an overwhelmed one.

As far as the priority-based access is concerned, we investigate two possible scenarios; in the first one the order of the priorities is statically fixed; in the second one tuples are associated with a *symbolic* priority and the order relation among the symbolic priorities is defined from the processes at the time they execute the data-retrieval operations. Going back to the master-worker example, the first approach can easily solve the case in which there is a fixed hierarchy of urgency levels, simply by associating a different priority to each urgency level. On the other hand, in the case the job with the closest expiration time should be selected, we can proceed as follows: the expiration time of a job indicates its symbolic priority and, when a worker withdraws a job, it defines an order relation that privileges those with an expiration which is closer to the current time.

The paper is structured as follows. In Section 2 we present a formal description of the Linda coordination model that we use as the basis for our probabilistic and prioritized extensions. In Section 3 we discuss and formally introduce our probabilistic version of Linda, while in Section 4 we discuss and define the two extensions with a prioritized access to tuples. Finally, in Section 5 we draw some conclusive remark.

## 2    The Linda Coordination Model

The coordination primitives that we have in Linda are: $out(e)$, $in(t)$ and $rd(t)$. The output operation $out(e)$ inserts a tuple $e$ in the tuple space (TS for short). Primitive $in(t)$ is the blocking input operation: when an occurrence of a tuple $e$ matching with $t$ (denoting a template) is found in the TS, it is removed from the TS and the primitive returns the tuple. The read primitive $rd(t)$ is the blocking read operation that, differently from $in(t)$, returns the matching tuple $e$ without removing it from the TS.

Linda tuples are ordered and finite sequences of typed fields, while template are ordered and finite sequences of fields that can be either *actual* or *formal* (see [5]): a field is actual if it specifies a type and a value, whilst it is formal if the type only is given. For the sake of simplicity, in the formalization of Linda we are going to present fields are not typed.

Formally, let *Mess*, ranged over by $m$, $m'$, ..., be a denumerable set of messages and *Var*, ranged over by $x$, $y$, ..., be the set of data variables. In the following, we use $\boldsymbol{x}$, $\boldsymbol{y}$, ..., to denote finite sequences $x_1; x_2; \ldots; x_n$ of variables.

Tuples, denoted by $e$, $e'$, ..., are finite and ordered sequences of data fields, whilst templates, denoted by $t$, $t'$, ..., are finite and ordered sequences of fields that can be either data or wildcards (used to match with any message).

Formally, tuples are defined as follows:

$$e = <\boldsymbol{d}>$$

where $\boldsymbol{d}$ is a term of the following grammar:

$\boldsymbol{d} ::= d \mid d; \boldsymbol{d}$
$d ::= m \mid x.$

The definition of template follows:

$$t = <\boldsymbol{dt}>$$

where $\boldsymbol{dt}$ is a term of the following grammar:

$\boldsymbol{dt} ::= dt \mid dt; \boldsymbol{dt}$
$dt ::= d \mid null.$

A *data field* $d$ can be a message or a variable. The additional value *null* denotes the wildcard, whose meaning is the same of formal fields of Linda, i.e. it matches with any field value. In the following, the set *Tuple* (resp. *Template*) denotes the set of tuples (resp. templates) containing no variable.

The matching rule between tuples and templates we consider is the classical one of Linda, whose definition is as follows.

**Definition 1. *Matching rule* -** *Let $e = <d_1; d_2; \ldots; d_n> \in Tuple$ be a tuple, $t = <dt_1; dt_2; \ldots; dt_m> \in Template$ be a template; we say that $e$ matches $t$ (denoted by $e \triangleright t$) if the following conditions hold:*

1. $m = n$.
2. $dt_i = d_i$ or $dt_i = null$, $1 \leq i \leq n$.

Condition 1. checks if $e$ and $t$ have the same arity, whilst 2. tests if each non-wildcard field of $t$ is equal to the corresponding field of $e$.

Processes, denoted by $P$, $Q$, ..., are defined as follows:

| $P, Q, \ldots ::=$ | processes |
|---|---|
| **0** | null process |
| $\mid$ $out\ (e).P$ | output |
| $\mid$ $rd\ t(\boldsymbol{x}).P$ | read |
| $\mid$ $in\ t(\boldsymbol{x}).P$ | input |
| $\mid$ $P \mid P$ | parallel composition |
| $\mid$ $!P$ | replication |

A process can be a terminated program **0**, a prefix form $\mu.P$, the parallel composition of two programs, or the replication of a program. The prefix $\mu$ can be one of the following coordination primitives: i) $out\ (e)$, that writes the tuple $e$ in the TS; ii) $rd\ t(\boldsymbol{x})$, that given a template $t$ reads a matching tuple $e$ in the TS and stores the return value in $\boldsymbol{x}$; iii) $in\ t(\boldsymbol{x})$, that given a template $t$ consumes a matching tuple $e$ in the TS and stores the return value in $\boldsymbol{x}$. In both the $rd\ t(\boldsymbol{x})$ and $in\ t(\boldsymbol{x})$ operations $(\boldsymbol{x})$ is a binder for the variables in $\boldsymbol{x}$. The parallel composition $P \mid Q$ of two processes $P$ and $Q$ behaves as two processes running in parallel, whilst the replication operator $!P$ denotes the parallel composition of infinite copies of $P$.

In the following, $P[d/x]$ denotes the process that behaves as $P$ in which all occurrences of $x$ are replaced with $d$. We also use $P[\boldsymbol{d}/\boldsymbol{x}]$ to denote the process obtained by replacing in $P$ all occurrences of variables in $\boldsymbol{x}$ with the corresponding value in $\boldsymbol{d}$, i.e. $P[d_1; d_2; \ldots; d_n/x_1; x_2; \ldots; x_n] = P[d_1/x_1][d_2/x_2] \ldots [d_n/x_n]$.

We say that a process is *well formed* if each prefix operation of kind $rd/in\ < \boldsymbol{dt} > (\boldsymbol{x})$ is such that the variables $\boldsymbol{x}$ and the data $\boldsymbol{dt}$ have the same arity. Notice that in the $rd\ t(\boldsymbol{x})$ and $in\ t(\boldsymbol{x})$ operations we use a notation which is different from the standard Linda notation: we explicitly indicate in $(\boldsymbol{x})$ the variables that will be bound to the actual fields of the matching tuple, while in the standard Linda notation these variables are part of the template. Observe that the two notations are equivalent up to the fact that our notation introduces variables also in association to the formal fields of the template. We also say that a process is *closed* if it has no free variable. In the following, we consider only processes that are closed and well formed; *Process* denotes the set of such processes.

Let *DSpace*, ranged over by $DS$, $DS'$, ..., be the set of possible configurations of the TS, that is $DSpace = \mathcal{M}_{fin}(Tuple)$, where $\mathcal{M}_{fin}(S)$ denotes the set of all the possible finite multisets on $S$. In the following, we use $DS(e)$ to denote the number of occurrences of $e$ within $DS \in DSpace$. The set $System = \{[P, DS] \mid P \in Process, DS \in DSpace\}$, ranged over by $s$, $s'$, ..., denotes the possible configurations of systems.

The semantics we use to describe processes interacting via Linda primitives is defined in terms of a transition system $(System, \longrightarrow)$, where $\longrightarrow \subseteq System \times System$. More precisely, $\longrightarrow$ is the minimal relation satisfying the axioms and rules of Table 1 (symmetric rule of (4) is omitted). $(s, s') \in \longrightarrow$ (also denoted by $s \longrightarrow s'$) means that a system $s$ can evolve (performing a single action) in the system $s'$.

**Table 1.** Semantics of Linda

$$(1) \quad [out\ (e).P, DS] \longrightarrow [P, DS \oplus e]$$

$$(2) \quad \frac{\exists e \in DS : e \triangleright t}{[in\ t(\boldsymbol{x}).P, DS] \longrightarrow [P[e/\boldsymbol{x}], DS - e]}$$

$$(3) \quad \frac{\exists e \in DS : e \triangleright t}{[rd\ t(\boldsymbol{x}).P, DS] \longrightarrow [P[e/\boldsymbol{x}], DS]}$$

$$(4) \quad \frac{[P, DS] \longrightarrow [P', DS']}{[P \mid Q, DS] \longrightarrow [P' \mid Q, DS']}$$

$$(5) \quad \frac{[P, DS] \longrightarrow [P', DS']}{[!P, DS] \longrightarrow [P' \mid !P, DS']}$$

Axiom (1) describes the output operation that produces a new occurrence of the tuple $e$ in the shared space $DS$ ($DS \oplus e$ denotes the multiset obtained by $DS$ increasing by 1 the number of occurrences of $e$). Rules (2) and (3) describe the *in* and the *rd* operations, respectively: if a matching $e$ tuple is currently available in the space, it is returned at the process invoking the operation and, in the case of *in*, it is also removed from the space ($DS - e$ denotes the removal of an occurrence of $e$ from the multiset $DS$). Rule (4) represents a local computation of processes, whilst (5) the replication operator that produces a new instance of the process and copies itself.

# 3   Adding Probabilistic Data-Retrieval to Linda

In this section we extend the Linda language by introducing probabilities for retrieval of tuples stored in the TS. We start by discussing the probabilistic model that we will adopt (Section 3.1) and then we present the new extended Linda primitives: their syntax (Section 3.2) and their semantics (Section 3.3).

## 3.1   Probabilistic Model

In Linda expressing a probabilistic choice among entities reacting to a given communication request (e.g. tuples matching a "rd" or "in" request) requires a much more complex mechanism w.r.t. languages employing channel-based communication (like, e.g., those representable by standard process algebras). This is due to the greater complexity of Linda matching-based communication mechanism w.r.t. such a simpler form of communication. If we had channel-based communication then we could just consider probability distributions (i.e. functions assigning probabilities that sum up to 1 to elements of a given domain) over the messages $a(\boldsymbol{d})$ actually available on the channel type $a$; when a receive operation is performed on the channel of type $a$, the channel would "react" to the request by simply choosing a message $a(\boldsymbol{d})$ for some $d$ according to such a probability distribution (this is what would happen by adopting either the "reactive model" of probability [12] or the "simple model" of [10]). When we consider the Linda matching-based communication mechanism, we loose the separation above between the channel type (which decides the set of entities involved in the communication) and the datum $d$ that is read. Since the set of matching tuples $< d >$ is now established from a template $t$ on data that is chosen by the "rd" or "in" operation, it is unavoidable to deal with the situation in which the set of matching tuples is a proper subset of the domain of a probability distribution: in this case a re-normalization of "probability" values must be done in order to have them summing up to 1 (this is the same situation that arises for the restriction operator in generative models [12]). Note that the only way to avoid this would be to have an individual probability distribution for each datum $< \boldsymbol{d} >$ that is present in the shared space (over the several instances of such datum), i.e. by treating each different datum $< \boldsymbol{d} >$ in the same way as a channel type $a$ in channel-based communication. However, since in this case the channel type would coincide with the datum that is read from the tuple space, reading (or consuming) different tuples having the same channel type (i.e. different instances of the same datum $< \boldsymbol{d} >$) would have the same observable effect on the system, hence probability distributions would be useless.

As a consequence of this remark, since when the shared space is accessed the probabilities on matching tuples must be determined by using re-normalization (on the basis of the "selecting power" of the template in the "rd" or "in" operation), it is natural to express probability statically associated to tuples in the space by means of *weights* [11]. A weight is a positive real number which is associated to an entity that can be involved in a probabilistic choice: the actual probability that the entity assumes in the choice is determined from the associated weight depending on the context, i.e. from the weights of the other entities involved in the choice, by re-normalization.

*Example 1.* We indicate the weight $w$ of a tuple associating the notation $[w]$ to the tuple itself. Let us suppose that the tuple space contains three tuples $< m_1, m_2 > [w]$, $< m_1, m_2' > [w']$ and $< m_1', m_2'' > [w'']$, then the following happens. If the operation $rd \ < null, null > (x_1, x_2).P$ is performed, the variables $x_1, x_2$ are bound: to $m_1, m_2$ with probability $w/(w + w' + w'')$, to $m_1, m_2'$ with probability $w'/(w + w' + w'')$, and to $m_1', m_2''$ with probability $w''/(w + w' + w'')$. If the operation $rd \ < m_1, null > (x_1, x_2).P$ is performed, the variables $x_1, x_2$ are bound: to $m_1, m_2$ with probability $w/(w + w')$ and to $m_1, m_2'$ with probability $w'/(w + w')$. If the operation $rd \ < m_1, m_2 > (x_1, x_2).P$ is performed, the variables $x_1, x_2$ are bound: to $m_1, m_2$ with probability $w/w = 1$.

Moreover note that since the structure of the shared space is highly dynamic and tuples are introduced individually in the space, expressing weights associated to tuples seems to be preferable w.r.t. expressing a single probabilistic distribution over all tuples (generative approach of [12]) which is to be updated by re-normalization to value 1 every time a tuple is added or removed. Therefore, due to the inherent re-normalization behavior of Linda, and to the observations we have made, we adopt, like in [2, 1], the approach above based on weights.

## 3.2    Syntax

Formally, let $Weight$, ranged over by $w$, $w'$, ..., be the set of weights, i.e. positive (non-zero) real numbers. Tuples are now decorated with an attribute indicating the associated weight (representing their "appealing degree"), whilst templates have the classical structure as in Linda.

Tuples, denoted by $e$, $e'$, ..., are now defined as follows:

$$e = < \boldsymbol{d} > [w]$$

where $w \in Weight$ and $\boldsymbol{d}$ is a sequence of data fields (see Section 2) $d$ that are defined by the following grammar:

$$d ::= m \mid w \mid x.$$

A *data field* $d$ can be now a message, a weight, or a variable. We also define $\tilde{\cdot}$ as the function that, given a tuple $e$, returns its sequence of data fields (e.g. if $e = < \boldsymbol{d} > [w]$ then $\tilde{e} = \boldsymbol{d}$), and a function $W$ that, given a tuple, returns its weight (e.g., $W(< \boldsymbol{d} > [w]) = w$).

Similarly to Section 2, in the following we make use of $Tuple$ and $Template$ to denote sets of tuples and template. In general here and in the following sections we will assume them to take into account the current definition of tuples and templates. The same holds for the matching rule between tuples and templates, denoted by "▷", which is the classical one of Linda defined in Section 2 (the matching evaluation does not take into account the weight attributes associated to tuples).

The extended version of the Linda primitives has the following meaning:

- $out(e)$, where $e \in Tuple$ is the output operation; given a tuple $e$, where $e = < \boldsymbol{d} > [w]$, it writes it into the DS.
- $in(t)$, where $t \in Template$; if some tuple $e$ matching with template $t$ is available in the DS, the execution of $in$ causes the removal of one of such tuples $e$ from the space and returns $\tilde{e}$. The probability of removing a particular tuple $e = < \boldsymbol{d} > [w] \in DS$ with $e$ that matches $t$ is the ratio of $w$ to the sum of the weights $w'$ in the tuples $e' = < \boldsymbol{d'} > [w']$ in the DS such that $e'$ matches with $t$ (taking into account multiple occurrences of tuples).
- $rd(t)$, where $t \in Template$; if some tuple $e$ matching with template $t$ is available in the DS, one of such tuples is read and the returned value is $\tilde{e}$. The probability of reading a particular tuple $e$ with $e$ that matches $t$ is

evaluated as in the input case.

Note that this means that the probability of reading a particular matching sequence of data fields $< \boldsymbol{d} >$ contained in the DS is the ratio of the sum of weights $w$ associated with the several instances of $< \boldsymbol{d} >$ contained in the DS, to the sum of the weights of the tuples $e'$ in the DS matching with $t$.

It is worth noting that the probabilistic access to the tuples is at the level of the subspace that the agent can access using a specific template. More precisely, the probability distribution depends on the weights of all matching tuples stored in the DS.

## 3.3   Semantics

In this section we introduce the semantics of systems interacting via the probabilistic model of Linda. In particular, we describe how we replace -in the data retrieval operations- the standard non-deterministic choice of a tuple among the matching ones in the TS, with a probabilistic choice exploiting weights.

Let $Prob = \{\rho \mid \rho : System \longrightarrow [0,1] \wedge supp(\rho)$ is finite $\wedge \sum_{s \in System} \rho(s) = 1\}$, where $supp(\rho) = \{s \mid \rho(s) > 0\}$, be the set of probability distributions on configurations. The semantics we use to describe systems is defined in terms of probabilistic transition systems $(System, Prob, \longrightarrow)$, where $\longrightarrow \subseteq System \times Prob$. More precisely, $\longrightarrow$ is the minimal relation satisfying the axioms and rules of Table 2. $(s, \rho) \in \longrightarrow$ (also denoted by $s \longrightarrow \rho$) means that a system $s$ can reach a generic configuration $s'$ with a probability equal to $\rho(s')$. Note that, several probability distributions may be performable from the same state $s$, i.e. it may be that $s \longrightarrow \rho$ for several different $\rho$. This means that (like in the simple model of [10]) whenever the system is in state $s$, first a non-deterministic choice is performed which decides which of the several probability distributions $\rho$ must be considered, then the next configuration is probabilistically determined by the chosen distribution $\rho$. Note that the non-deterministic choice may, e.g., arise from several concurrent $rd$ operations which probabilistically retrieve data from the tuple-space. We use $s \longrightarrow s'$ to denote $s \longrightarrow \rho$, with $\rho$ the trivial distribution which gives probability 1 to $s'$ and probability 0 to all other configurations.

Table 3 defines: $(i)$ the probability distributions $\rho^p_{in\ t(\boldsymbol{x}).P,DS}$ and $\rho^p_{rd\ t(\boldsymbol{x}).P,DS}$ used for $in$ and $rd$ operations, respectively; $(ii)$ the operator $\rho|Q$ that, given $\rho$, computes a new probability distribution that accounts for composition with "$Q$". It is worth noting that $\rho^p_{in\ t(\boldsymbol{x}).P,DS}$ and $\rho^p_{rd\ t(\boldsymbol{x}).P,DS}$ are defined only for $t \in Template$ and $DS \in DSpace$ such that there exists $e \in DS : e \triangleright t$ (that is the condition reported in axioms (2) and (3)).

Axiom (1) describes the output of the tuple $e$, after the execution an occurrence of $e$ is added to the shared space $DS$ and the process continues with $P$. Axiom (2) describes the behaviour of $in$ operations; if a tuple $e$ matching with template $t$ is available in the $DS$, the $in$ execution produces the removal from the space of $e$ and then the process behaves as $P[\tilde{e}/\boldsymbol{x}]$. The probability of reaching a configuration where a matching tuple $e$ contained in the $DS$ is removed is the ratio of the total weight of the several instances of $e$ in the $DS$, to the sum of the

**Table 2.** Semantics of Linda with probabilistic access to tuples

$$(1) \quad [out\,(e).P, DS] \longrightarrow [P, DS \oplus e]$$

$$(2) \quad \frac{\exists e \in DS : e \triangleright t}{[in\,t(\boldsymbol{x}).P, DS] \longrightarrow \rho^{\mathrm{p}}_{\mathtt{in}\,\mathtt{t}\,(\boldsymbol{x})\,\mathtt{P}\,\mathtt{D}\mathtt{S}}}$$

$$(3) \quad \frac{\exists e \in DS : e \triangleright t}{[rd\,t(\boldsymbol{x}).P, DS] \longrightarrow \rho^{\mathrm{p}}_{\mathtt{rd}\,\mathtt{t}\,(\boldsymbol{x})\,\mathtt{P}\,\mathtt{D}\mathtt{S}}}$$

$$(4) \quad \frac{[P, DS] \longrightarrow \rho}{[P \mid Q, DS] \longrightarrow \rho|Q}$$

$$(5) \quad \frac{[P, DS] \longrightarrow \rho}{[!P, DS] \longrightarrow \rho|!P}$$

**Table 3.** Probability distributions

$$\rho^{\mathrm{p}}_{\mathtt{in}\,\mathtt{t}\,(\boldsymbol{x})\,\mathtt{P}\,\mathtt{D}\mathtt{S}}\,(s) =$$
$$\begin{cases} \dfrac{W(e) \cdot DS(e)}{\sum_{e' \in DS\,:e'\,\mathtt{t}} W(e') \cdot DS(e')} & \begin{array}{l} if\ s = [P[\tilde{e}/\boldsymbol{x}], DS - e] \\ with\ e \in DS \wedge e \triangleright t \end{array} \\ \\ 0 & o.w. \end{cases}$$

$$\rho^{\mathrm{p}}_{\mathtt{rd}\,\mathtt{t}\,(\boldsymbol{x})\,\mathtt{P}\,\mathtt{D}\mathtt{S}}\,(s) =$$
$$\begin{cases} \dfrac{\sum_{e' \in DS\,:e'\,\mathtt{t} \wedge \mathtt{P}\,[\tilde{e}'/\boldsymbol{x}] = \mathtt{P}\,[\tilde{e}/\boldsymbol{x}]} W(e') \cdot DS(e')}{\sum_{e' \in DS\,:e'\,\mathtt{t}} W(e') \cdot DS(e')} & \begin{array}{l} if\ s = [P[\tilde{e}/\boldsymbol{x}], DS] \\ with\ e \in DS \wedge e \triangleright t \end{array} \\ \\ 0 & o.w. \end{cases}$$

$$\rho|Q(s) = \begin{cases} \rho([P', DS]) \ if\ s = [P' \mid Q, DS], \\ \qquad\qquad P' \in Process \wedge\ DS \in DSpace. \\ \\ 0 \qquad o.w. \end{cases}$$

total weights of the several instances of the matching tuples currently available in the $DS$. In this way, the probability to reach a system configuration takes into account the multiple ways of removing $e$ due to the several occurrences of $e$ in the $DS$. The axiom (3) describes $rd$ operations; if a tuple $e$ matching with template $t$ is available in the $DS$, then the process behaves as $P[\tilde{e}/\boldsymbol{x}]$. Differently from the previous axiom, $rd$ operations do not modify the tuple space, i.e. reached states do not change the configuration of $DS$, therefore they are simply differentiated by the continuation $P[\tilde{e}/\boldsymbol{x}]$ of the reading process. For example, let us consider two different tuples $e'$ and $e''$ that contain the same value in some of their fields. If the reading process considers only the common fields, we have that $P[\tilde{e'}/\boldsymbol{x}] = P[\tilde{e''}/\boldsymbol{x}]$, thus it is not possible to discriminate the selection of the two different tuples. Therefore, the probability of reaching a configuration $s$ that is obtained by reading a tuple $e$ matching with $t$ in the DS (yielding value $e$) is the ratio of the sum of the total weights associated to the several instances of tuples $e'$ matching with $t$ in the DS such that the continuation of the reading process obtained by reading tuple $e'$ is the same as the one obtained by reading $e$, to the sum of the total weights of the several instances of the matching tuples currently available in the $DS$. Rule (4) describes the behaviour of the parallel composition of processes (the symmetric rule is omitted): if configurations reachable from $[P, DS]$ are described by the probability distribution $\rho$, and $P$ performs an action in the system $[P \mid Q, DS]$ (the process that proceeds between $P$ and $Q$ is non-deterministically selected), then the reachable configurations are of the form $[P' \mid Q, DS']$, for some $P' \in Process$ and $DS' \in DSpace$. The probability values of such configurations do not depend on $Q$ (that is "inactive") and are equal to $\rho([P', DS'])$. Finally, rule (5) describes the behaviour of process replication operator: $!P$ behaves as an unbounded parallel composition of the process $P$.

# 4    Adding Prioritized Data-Retrieval to Linda

Priorities on tuples represent an absolute preference of the currently available tuples in the shared space. More precisely, if a process performing a $rd/in$ operation receives as the return value a tuple $e$, there is no currently available matching tuple $e'$ in TS such that its priority level is greater than the one of $e$. In Section 4.1 we present a model with *static priorities*: priorities on tuples are set by the output operations and the data-retrieval operations return a matching tuple with the highest priority among the available ones. In Section 4.2 we propose another solution which supports *dynamic priorities*: tuples are partitioned by associating a partition name with each tuple (set by the output operations) and processes performing $rd/in$ operations can express a priority level to be dynamically assigned to partitions for the data-retrieval.

## 4.1    Static Priorities

Following the approach used to introduce weights, tuples are now further extended by adding, similarly as in [2, 1], an additional attribute indicating their priority. Templates keep the classical structure as well as the classical Linda matching rule given in Definition 1.

Formally, let $Priority$, ranged over by $l, l', \ldots$, be the set of possible priorities, i.e. positive (non-zero) natural numbers.

Tuples are now defined as follows:

$$e = <\boldsymbol{d}> [w, l]$$

where $w \in Weight$, $l \in Priority$ and $\boldsymbol{d}$ is a sequence of data fields $d$ that are defined by the following grammar:

$$d ::= m \mid w \mid l \mid x.$$

A data field $d$ now can be a message, a weight, a priority level, or a variable.

In the following, we denote with $PL$ the function that, given a tuple, returns its priority level (e.g., if $e = <\boldsymbol{d}> [w, l]$ then $PL(e) = l$), and with $DS_l$ the partition of $DS$ determined by selecting all the tuples $e$ with priority level $l$, i.e. the multiset contained in $DS$ such that for any $e \in Tuple$ if $e \in DS$ and $PL(e) = l$ then $DS_l(e) = DS(e)$, otherwise $DS_l(e) = 0$. We also define $L(DS, t)$ as the function that, given a space $DS$ and a template $t$, returns the highest priority level of tuples matching with $t$,i.e. $L(DS, t) = \max\{l \mid \exists e \in DS_l : e \triangleright t\}$. Note that the function $L(DS, t)$ is defined only in the case $DS$ contains at least one matching tuple within $DS$ and, since we consider only $DS$ that are finite multisets of $Tuple$, it can be computed for any $DS \in DSpace$.

The semantics of the Linda model with priority and weights on tuples is obtained from Table 2, by replacing $\rho^p_{rd\ t(\boldsymbol{x}).P,DS}$ and $\rho^p_{in\ t(\boldsymbol{x}).P,DS}$ with $\rho^{p,l}_{rd\ t(\boldsymbol{x}).P,DS}$ and $\rho^{p,l}_{in\ t(\boldsymbol{x}).P,DS}$, respectively, which are defined in Table 4. The definition of the new probability distributions in Table 4 makes use of the probability distributions previously defined in Table 3 for the pure probabilistic case. Informally, the idea is that the search space is restricted to the partition of $DS$ which has the greatest priority level and contains a matching tuple. On this subspace, the probabilistic data-retrieval is governed by weights of the matching tuples it contains. More precisely, $\rho^{p,l}_{in\ t(\boldsymbol{x}).P,DS}([P', DS'])$ is defined by using the corresponding probabilistic version applied on the restricted space, i.e. $\rho^p_{in\ t(\boldsymbol{x}).P,DS_{L(DS,t)}}([P', DS'_{L(DS,t)}])$. This "reduction" is applied only if $DS - DS_{L(DS,t)} = DS' - DS'_{L(DS,t)}$ (where "−" is the usual multiset difference operator), that is if the partitions of the space not involved in the restrictions of $DS$ and $DS'$ used by $\rho^p$ do not change. The same kind of "reduction" and condition have been used to define the probability distribution for $rd$ operations.

## 4.2   Dynamic Name-Based Priorities

Priority attributes on tuples introduced in the previous section logically partition the tuple space: each partition is identified by a priority level and contains all tuples with that specific priority level, i.e. $DS = \sum_{l \in Priority} DS_l$, for any $DS \in DSpace$.

**Table 4.** Probability distributions with priority

$$\rho^{\mathrm{p,l}}_{\mathrm{in}\, t\,(x)\,P\,DS} \left([P', DS']\right) =$$

$$\begin{cases} \rho^{\mathrm{p}}_{\mathrm{in}\, t\,(x)\,P\,DS\,\,L(DS,t)} \left([P', DS'_{\mathrm{L}(DS,t)}]\right) & if\ DS - DS_{\mathrm{L}(DS,t)} = \\ & \qquad DS' - DS'_{\mathrm{L}(DS,t)} \\[2ex] 0 & o.w. \end{cases}$$

$$\rho^{\mathrm{p,l}}_{\mathrm{rd}\, t\,(x)\,P\,DS} \left([P', DS']\right) =$$

$$\begin{cases} \rho^{\mathrm{p}}_{\mathrm{rd}\, t\,(x)\,P\,DS\,\,L(DS,t)} \left([P', DS'_{\mathrm{L}(DS,t)}]\right) & if\ DS - DS_{\mathrm{L}(DS,t)} = \\ & \qquad DS' - DS'_{\mathrm{L}(DS,t)} \\[2ex] 0 & o.w. \end{cases}$$

In this section we discuss how to manage dynamically priorities by providing, at the process that is willing to perform a $rd/in$ operation, a manner to express in which partition of the tuple space to search the matching tuple (by associating an absolute preference to partitions), thus providing a way to restrict the search space to a subset of the tuple space.

Tuples have now an attribute weight and another one that is a "key": the name used to identify the partition. In order to express in which partitions to search matching tuples and with which priority, templates are decorated by adding a partial function that maps keys on priority levels. In this way, producers of tuples do not assign an absolute preference on the tuples, that is dynamically described by the processes performing a $in/rd$ operation.

Formally, let $Key$, ranged over by $k$, $k'$, ..., be the set of keys, and $KL = \{f \mid f : Key \hookrightarrow Priority\}$, ranged over by $f$, $f'$, ..., be the set of partial functions mapping keys to priority levels; we denote with $Dom(f)$ the domain of the function $f$.

The definition of tuple is as follows:

$$e =< \boldsymbol{d} > [w, k]$$

where $w \in Weight$, $k \in Key$ and $\boldsymbol{d}$ is a sequence of data fields $d$ that can be set to a message, a key, a weight, or a variable. In the following, we use $PK(e)$ to denote the key associated to the tuple $e$, i.e. $PK(< \boldsymbol{d} > [w, k]) = k$.

The structure of templates is the following:

$$t =< \boldsymbol{dt} > [f]$$

where $f \in KL$ and $\boldsymbol{dt}$ is a sequence of data fields that, in addition to those ones used by tuples, can also be set to wildcard value.

**Table 5.** $rd$ and $in$ semantics with dynamic priority

$$(2') \quad \frac{\exists e \in DS : e \triangleright t \quad PK(e) \in Dom(f)}{[in\ <dt>[f](x).P, DS] \longrightarrow \rho_{in\ <\ dt>[f](x)\ P\ DS}^{p\ dl}}$$

$$(3') \quad \frac{\exists e \in DS : e \triangleright t \quad PK(e) \in Dom(f)}{[rd\ <dt>[f](x).P, DS] \longrightarrow \rho_{rd\ <\ dt>[f](x)\ P\ DS}^{p\ dl}}$$

We also define $DS_{\{k_1, k_2, \ldots, k_n\}}$ as the function that given a $DS \in DSpace$ and a set of keys $\{k_1, k_2, \ldots, k_n \mid k_i \in Key, 1 \le i \le n\}$ returns the multiset containing all the tuples in $DS$ associated with one of the keys in the given set, i.e. for any $e \in Tuple$ if $e \in DS$ and $PK(e) = k_i$ for some $1 \le i \le n$ then $DS_{\{k_1, k_2, \ldots, k_n\}}(e) = DS(e)$, otherwise $DS_{\{k_1, k_2, \ldots, k_n\}}(e) = 0$.

Finally, we define the functions $L(DS, t, f)$ and $K(DS, t, f)$ that, given a configuration of the tuple space $DS \in DSpace$, a template $t \in Template$ and a function $f \in KL$, return the highest priority level and the set of keys with the highest priority level of the available matching tuples in $DS$, respectively. They are defined as it follows:

$$L(DS, t, f) = \max\{f(k) \mid k \in Dom(f) \wedge \exists e \in DS_{\{k\}} : e \triangleright t\}$$

$$K(DS, t, f) = \{k \mid k \in Dom(f) \wedge f(k) = L(DS, t, f)\}$$

Note that the functions $L$ and $K$ are defined only for $DS$, $t$ and $f$ such that there exists at least one matching tuple $e \in DS$ having an associated key $k$ contained in the domain of $f$.

The semantics of the model with dynamic priority and weights on tuples is obtained by using rules (1), (4) and (5) of Table 2, rules (2') and (3') of Table 5 and the probability distributions reported in Table 6.

Differently from $rd$ and $in$ operations with priority proposed in the previous section, the corresponding ones with dynamic priority can be performed only if a tuple with one of the specified priority levels is found in the space. Therefore, (2') and (3') differ from (2) and (3) of Table 2 because we need to test not only the presence in $DS$ of a matching tuple, but also that it has an associated symbol $k$ that is in the domain of $f$ (indicated by the template). The definition of the probability distributions of Table 6 follows the same idea used in those ones for static priority: we exploit the definition of probability distributions $\rho^p$ by restricting the space $DS$ to that one containing only tuples having a key corresponding to the highest priority level containing matching tuples.

**Table 6.** Probability distributions for dynamic priorities

$$\rho^{\text{p,dl}}_{\text{in}<\ dt>\ [\text{f}](x)\,\text{P}\,\text{DS}} ([P', DS']) =$$

$$\begin{cases} \rho^{\text{p}}_{\text{in}<\ dt>\ [\text{f}](x)\,\text{P}\,\text{DS}\ K(DS,t,f)} ([P', DS'_{\text{K (DS},t,\text{f })}]) & if\ DS - DS_{\text{K (DS},t,\text{f })} = \\ & \qquad\qquad DS' - DS'_{\text{K (DS},t,\text{f })} \\[2ex] 0 & o.w. \end{cases}$$

$$\rho^{\text{p,dl}}_{\text{rd}<\ dt>\ [\text{f}](x)\,\text{P}\,\text{DS}} ([P', DS']) =$$

$$\begin{cases} \rho^{\text{p}}_{\text{rd}<\ dt>\ [\text{f}](x)\,\text{P}\,\text{DS}\ K(DS,t,f)} ([P', DS'_{\text{K(DS},t,\text{f })}]) & if\ DS - DS_{\text{K (DS},t,\text{f })} = \\ & \qquad\qquad DS' - DS'_{\text{K (DS},t,\text{f })} \\[2ex] 0 & o.w. \end{cases}$$

## 5   Conclusion

In this paper we have introduced, in a process algebraic setting, probabilities and priorities on the the data-retrieval mechanisms of Linda. We have technically motivated the use of weights on tuples -instead of classic probability distribution- to express probabilities, and discussed two possible forms of priority mechanisms on tuples, one using static priorities and another one using dynamic priorities defined by the process when they execute data-retrieval operations. To the best of our knowledge, the unique paper that addresses probabilities in the context of Linda-like languages is Probabilistic Klaim [8]. Klaim [7] is a distributed mobile version of Linda where processes may migrate among nodes in a net; in Probabilistic Klaim probabilities are used to describe probabilistic forms of mobility.

In [3] we describe an implementation of a Linda-like repository that exploits the probabilistic data-retrieval described in this paper. This repository is intended to be used to distribute the workload among collaborating Web Services, as briefly described in the Introduction section. More precisely, we describe how to implement a registry service that supports registration, deregistration, discovery and update of Web Services descriptions. In particular, the update operation allows for run-time modification of the weight associated to a tuple.

As future work, a natural extension of the model with dynamic priorities is to provide a manner for limiting the scope of the symbolic priorities; in other words, we want to ensure that the data associated to a specific symbolic priority can be accessed only from a restricted group of processes. In terms of security properties, this corresponds to a form of secure group communication. Linda is not expressive enough to provide security solutions and, more precisely, access control mechanisms on the tuple space. Therefore, we need to model probabilities and priorities on a more sophisticated Linda-like language supporting these features (e.g., [4, 13, 7, 6]). In particular, we intend to investigate on a possible solution that exploits the access control mechanism provided by SecSpaces [4] because it is mainly based on partitions which shares common features with the notion of symbolic priorities.

# References

[1] M. Bravetti. *Specification and Analysis of Stochastic Real-Time Systems*. PhD thesis, Dottorato di Ricerca in Informatica. Università di Bologna, Padova, Venezia, February 2002. Available at http://www.cs.unibo.it/~bravetti/. 62, 65

[2] M. Bravetti and M. Bernardo. Compositional asymmetric cooperations for process algebras with probabilities, priorities, and time. In *Proc. of the 1st Int. Workshop on Models for Time-Critical Systems, MTCS 2000,* State College (PA), volume 39(3) of *Electronic Notes in Theoretical Computer Science.* Elsevier, 2000. 62, 65

[3] Mario Bravetti, Roberto Gorrieri, Roberto Lucchi, and Gianluigi Zavattaro. Web Services for E-commerce: guaranteeing security access and quality of service. In *Proc. of ACM Symposium on Applied Computing (SAC'04).* ACM Press, 2004. 69

[4] Nadia Busi, Roberto Gorrieri, Roberto Lucchi, and Gianluigi Zavattaro. Secspaces: a data-driven coordination model for environments open to untrusted agents. In *1st International Workshop on Foundations of Coordination Languages and Software Architectures*, volume 68.3 of *ENTCS*, 2002. 70

[5] Scientific Computing Associates. *Linda: User's guide and reference manual.* Scientific Computing Associates, 1995. 56, 58

[6] N. Minsky, Y. Minsky, and V. Ungureanu. Safe Tuplespace-Based Coordination in Multi Agent Systems. *Journal of Applied Artificial Intelligence*, 15(1), 2001. 70

[7] R. De Nicola, G. Ferrari, and R. Pugliese. KLAIM: A Kernel Language for Agents Interaction and Mobility. *IEEE Transactions on Software Engineering*, 24(5):315–330, May 1998. Special Issue: Mobility and Network Aware Computing. 69, 70

[8] A. Di Pierro, C. Hankin, and H. Wiklicky. Probabilistic Klaim. In *Proc. of 7th International Conference on Coordination Models and Languages (Coordination 04)*, LNCS. Springer Verlag, 2004. 69

[9] A. Rowstron and A. Wood. Solving the Linda multiple rd problem using the copy-collect primitive. *Science of Computer Programming*, 31(2-3):335–358, 1998. 56

[10] R. Segala. *Modeling and Verification of Randomized Distributed Real-Time Systems*. PhD thesis, Department of Electrical Engineering and Computer Science, Massachusetts Institute of Technology, 1995. 61, 63

[11] C. M. N. Tofts. Processes with probabilities, priority and time. *Formal Aspects of Computing*, 6:534–564, 1994. 61

[12] R. J. van Glabbeek, S. A. Smolka, and B. Steffen. Reactive, Generative and Stratified Models of Probabilistic Processes. *Information and Computation*, 121:59–80, 1995. 61, 62

[13] Jan Vitek, Ciarán Bryce, and Manuel Oriol. Coordinating Processes with Secure Spaces. *Science of Computer Programming*, 46:163–193, 2003. 70

# Measuring Component Adaptation

Antonio Brogi[1], Carlos Canal[2], and Ernesto Pimentel[2]

[1] Department of Computer Science, University of Pisa, Italy
[2] Department of Computer Science, University of Málaga, Spain

**Abstract.** Adapting heterogeneous software components that present mismatching interaction behaviour is one of the crucial problems in Component-Based Software Engineering. The process of component adaptation can be synthesized by a transformation from an initial specification (of the requested adaptation) to a revised specification (expressing the actual adaptation that will be featured by the deployed adaptor component). An important capability in this context is hence to be able to evaluate to which extent an adaptor proposal satisfies the initially requested adaptation. The aim of this paper is precisely to develop different metrics that can be employed to this end. Such metrics can be fruitfully employed both to assess the acceptability of an adaptation proposal, and to compare different adaptation solutions proposed by different servers.

## 1  Introduction

One of the general objectives of coordination models is to support the successful interoperation of heterogeneous software elements that may present mismatching interaction behaviour [12]. In the area of Component-Based Software Engineering, the problem of component adaptation is widely recognised to be one of the crucial issues for the development of a true component marketplace and for component deployment in general [5, 6]. Available component-oriented platforms address software interoperability at the signature level by means of Interface Description Languages (IDLs), a sort of *lingua franca* for specifying the functionality offered by heterogeneous components possibly developed in different languages. While IDL interfaces allow to overcome signature mismatches, there is no guarantee that the components will suitably interoperate, as mismatches may also occur at the protocol level, due to differences in the interaction behaviour of the components involved [18].

The need for component adaptation is also motivated by the ever-increasing attention devoted to developing extensively interacting distributed systems, consisting of large numbers of heterogeneous components. Most importantly, the ability of dynamically constructing software adaptors will be a must for the next generation of nomadic applications consisting of wireless mobile computing devices that will need to require services from different hosts at different times.

In our previous work [2, 3, 4], we have developed a formal methodology for component adaptation that supports the successful interoperation of heterogeneous components presenting mismatching interaction behaviour. The main ingredients of the methodology can be summarised as follows:

R. de Nicola et al. (Eds.): COORDINATION 2004, LNCS 2949, pp. 71–86, 2004.

- *Component interfaces.* IDL interfaces are extended with a formal description of the behaviour of components, which explicitly declares the interaction protocol followed by a component.
- *Adaptor specification.* Adaptor specifications are simply expressed by a set of correspondences between actions of two components. The distinguishing aspect of the notation used is that it yields a high-level, partial specification of the adaptor.
- *Adaptor derivation.* A concrete adaptor is fully automatically generated, given its partial specification and the interfaces of two components, by exhaustively trying to build a component which satisfies the given specification.

The methodology has proven to succeed in a number of diverse situations [2], where a suitable adaptor is generated to support the successful interoperation of heterogeneous components presenting mismatching interaction behaviours. The separation of adaptor specification and adaptor derivation permits the automation of the error-prone, time-consuming task of constructing a detailed implementation of a correct adaptor, thus notably simplifying the task of the (human) software developer. One of the distinguishing features of the methodology is the simplicity of the notation employed to express adaptor specifications. Indeed the desired adaptation is simply expressed by defining a set of (possibly nondeterministic) correspondences between the actions of the two components.

Consider for instance a typical scenario where a client component wishes to use some of the services offered by a server. (For instance, a client wishing to access a remote system via the network, or a mobile client getting into the vicinity of a stationary server.) The client will ask for the server interface, and then submit its service request in the form of an adaptor specification (together with its own interface). The server will run the adaptor derivation procedure to determine whether a suitable adaptor can be generated to satisfy the client request. If the client request can be satisfied, the server will notify the client by presenting a (possibly modified) adaptor specification which states the type of adaptation that will be effectively featured. The client will then decide whether to accept the adaptation proposal or not. (In the latter case the client may decide to continue the trading process by submitting a revised adaptor specification, or to address another server.)

Expressing adaptation trading by means of adaptor specification features two main advantages:

- *Efficiency.* Clients and servers exchange light-weighted adaptor specifications rather than component code. Besides contributing to the efficiency of communications, this notably simplifies the trading process, when the client has to analyse the adaptation proposed by the server.
- *Non-disclosure.* The server does not have to present the actual adaptor component in its full details, thus communicating only the "what" of the offered adaptation rather than the "how".

Summing up, the process of component adaptation can be synthesized by an adaptor specification $S$, representing the client request, and by a (possibly modified) adaptor specification $C$, representing the actual adaptation offered by the server. The specification $C$ is then interpreted as a contract guaranteeing that:

1. The client will be able to interoperate successfully with the adaptor (viz., the client will not get stuck), and
2. all the client actions occurring in $C$ will be effectively executable by the client.

An important issue in this context is hence how to evaluate to which extent a contract proposal satisfies the initial specification defining the requested adaptation. The aim of this paper is precisely to develop different metrics for component adaptation. Such metrics can be fruitfully employed both to assess the acceptability of an adaptation proposal and to compare different adaptations proposed by different servers.

The rest of the paper is organised as follows. Section 2 recalls the key aspects of the methodology for component adaptation developed in [2, 3, 4]. Section 3 is devoted to present several metrics to assess the acceptability of an adaptation proposal. Such metrics are then extended in Section 4 to deal with additional quantitative information. Finally, some concluding remarks are drawn in Section 5.

## 2   Component Adaptation

Throughout this paper we will use an example concerning a Video-on-Demand system (VoD), simplified to some extent. The VoD is a Web service providing access to remote clients to a repository of movies in video format.

When interacting with a client, the VoD executes client's instructions, represented by the different input messages the VoD is able to react to (message names are in italics in the description that follows). For instance, clients may *search* the VoD catalog for a movie, or ask the service which is the *première* of the day. Once a certain movie is selected, the client may decide to *preview* it for a few minutes, or to *view* it all. In either case, the client must indicate whether it wants to *play* the movie (which will be shown by a viewer), or to *record* it on its disk. During video transmission, chunks of data are sent by the server by means of repeated *stream* output messages, while the end of the transmission is marked with an *eof* output message.

Following [2], component interfaces are extended with a description of the interactive behaviour of components using a process algebra (here, we use the $\pi$-calculus [16]). Suppose that the behaviour of the VoD server during the video data transmission phase is described by a term of the form:

$$Server \;=\; stream!(y).\; Server \;+\; \tau.\; eof!().\, 0$$

where $\tau$ is an internal silent action.

Consider now a simple *Client* that (repeatedly) receives data by performing an input action *data*, and which may decide autonomously to abort the data transmission by performing an output action *abort*:

$$Client \; = \; data?(x). \; Client \; + \; \tau. \; abort!(). \; 0$$

It is worth observing that the mismatch between the two components above is not limited to signature differences (viz., the different names of actions employed, such as *stream* in the server and *data* in the client), but it also involves behavioral differences, in particular the way in which either component may close the communication unexpectedly.

## 2.1   Hard Adaptation

The objective of software adaptation is to deploy a software component, called *adaptor*, capable of acting as a component-in-the-middle between two components and of supporting their successful interoperation. Following our approach, a concrete adaptor will be automatically generated starting from the interfaces of the components and from a specification of the adaptor itself. Such a specification simply consists of rules establishing correspondences between actions of the two components. More precisely, an adaptor specification is a set of rules of the form:

$$a_1, \ldots, a_m \; \Diamond \; b_1, \ldots, b_n \; ;$$

where $a_i$ and $b_j$ are the input or output actions performed by the components to be adapted. By convention, given a specification $S$, actions on the left-hand side of rules refer to one of the components to be adapted (in the examples here, the client), and we will refer to them by $[S]_{cl}$, while actions on the right-hand side of rules refer to the other component (the server), and will be denoted by $[S]_{sr}$. To simplify notation, and without loss of generality, we assume that the sets of client and server actions are disjoint.

The formal semantics of adaptor specifications is defined in [4], here we shall recall this semantics informally by means of examples. For instance, the adaptation required for the video transmission between the server and the client can be naturally expressed by the specification:

$$S_1 = \left\{ \begin{array}{l} data?(u) \; \Diamond \; stream!(u) \; ; \\ abort!() \; \Diamond \; stream!(u) \; ; \\ abort!() \; \Diamond \qquad\qquad ; \\ \qquad\quad \Diamond \; eof!() \qquad ; \end{array} \right\}$$

The first rule in $S_1$ states that the input action *data?* in the client matches or corresponds to the output action *stream!* in the server. This same *stream!* action is also matched to client's *abort!* in the second rule, stating that the client may abort the transmission even when the server is trying to send video data. Thus, combining both rules we have that the action *stream!* may correspond non-deterministically to either *data?* or *abort!*, depending on the evolution of the client. In the third and fourth rules, actions *abort!* and *eof!* are represented without a corresponding action in the other side. For instance, the fourth rule of $S_1$ indicates that the execution of an *eof!* server action does not necessarily call for a corresponding client action. Notice that rules in an adaptor specification may establish one-to-one, one-to-many, and many-to-many correspondences among actions of the two components. They can also be employed to express asymmetries naturally, typically when the execution of an action in one of the component may not require a corresponding action to be executed by the other component.

Given an adaptor specification and the interfaces of two components, a fully automated procedure [2] returns non-deterministically one of the possible adaptors components (if any) that satisfy the specification, and that let the two components interoperate successfully. For instance, for the specification $S_1$ above the generation procedure may return the adaptor:

$$A = \quad stream?(u).\ (data!(u).\ A + abort?().\ eof?().\ 0)$$
$$+$$
$$eof?().\ abort?().\ 0$$

In this example a full adaptation is achieved, and hence the server will return the submitted specification $S_1$ as the contract proposal. However, in general, the server may be able to offer the client only a partial adaptation, namely a contract $C$ which is a proper subset of the submitted specification $S$.

To illustrate the idea, let us develop further our example of the VoD system. Suppose now that the client uses different action names for accessing the service than those considered by the server (again action names are in italics in the description that follows). For instance, the client wishes to perform its *info* action either for requesting information on a particular movie (by indicating its title), or for asking the service to suggest a movie (by using in this case the empty string as parameter), and its *watch* and *store* actions to play and record a movie, respectively. Hence the client submits the adaptor specification $S_2$ below, establishing correspondences with the previously described server actions[1]:

$$S_2 = \left\{ \begin{array}{l} info!(t) \lozenge search?(t)\ ; \\ info!("\ ") \lozenge premiere?()\ ; \\ watch!(m) \lozenge view?(m), play?()\ ; \\ store!(m) \lozenge view?(m), record?()\ ; \end{array} \right\}$$

Let us suppose that as a reply to the specification $S_2$, the client receives from the server the following contract $C_A$:

$$C_A = \{\ info!(t) \lozenge search?(t)\ ;\ \}$$

The straightforward reading of the contract proposal $C_A$ is that while the server commits to let the client search the movies database, for some reason it will not

---

[1] For the sake of simplicity, we omit here the correspondences concerning the data transfer actions (*data, abort, stream, eof*) already described in specification $S_1$.

feature the adaptation required to let the client watch or store such movies. (For instance, the server might decide to feature a partial adaptation even if a full adaptation would be feasible, in order to balance its current workload or for other internal service policies.)

Hence, given an adaptor specification $S$, the type of component adaptation that we have described so far:

- either it yields a (possibly partial) adaptation proposal $C$ (where $C$ is a subset of $S$),
- or it fails when no adaptation is possible.

The sole possibility of removing some rules from the initial specification obviously limits the success possibilities of yielding a (partial) adaptation. Indeed there are many situations in which more flexible ways of weakening the initial specification may lead to deploying a suitable partial adaptor, as we shall discuss in the next section.

## 2.2   Soft Adaptation

The methodology for *hard* adaptation described in [2] has been extended in [3] to feature forms of *soft* adaptation. One of the key notions introduced in [3] is the notion of *subservice*. Intuitively speaking, a subservice is a kind of surrogate of a service, which features only a limited part of such service. Formally, subservices are specified by defining a partial order $\sqsubset$ over the actions of a component:

$$b_j \quad \sqsubset \quad b_i$$

indicating that the service $b_j$ is a subservice of $b_i$.

It is important to observe that adding subservice declarations to component interfaces paves the way for more flexible forms of adaptation. Indeed, subservice declarations support a flexible configuration of components in view of their (dynamic) behaviour, without having to modify or to make more complex the protocol specification of component interfaces.

As one may expect, the introduction of subservices increases notably the possibilities of successful adaptations, as an initial specification can be suitably weakened by providing (when needed) subservices in place of the required services. A direct consequence of enabling soft adaptation is that a client that submits an adaptor specification may now receive a rather different contract proposal, in which the server may declare its intention both to feature only some of the services requested and to subservice some of them. Hence, the process of soft adaptor generation in presence of subservice declarations can be described as follows.

1. The initial adaptor specification $S$ is actually interpreted as the specification $S^*$ obtained by expanding every rule $r$ in $S$ with a new set $subs(r)$ of correspondence rules that are obtained by replacing one or more (server) actions in $r$ with a corresponding subservice. That is, $S^* = S \cup subs(S)$, where $subs(S) = \cup_{r \in S} subs(r)$.

2. The process of adaptor construction generates (if possible) a partial adaptor that satisfies a subset $C$ of the extended specification $S^*$.

(Notice that while both $C$ and $S$ are subsets of $S^*$, in general $C$ is not a subset of $S$ since possibly some service requests have been subserviced.)

For instance, in the Video-on-Demand service, offering a clip preview of a movie can be considered a typical subservice of offering the whole movie, while starting to view a movie could be considered as a subservice of downloading it into the hard disk of the client. These subservice definition are expressed as follows:

$$
\begin{array}{lll}
preview?(m) & \sqsubseteq & view?(m) \ ; \\
play?() & \sqsubseteq & record?() \ ;
\end{array}
$$

The previous adaptor specification $S_2$ is hence actually interpreted by the server as the following expanded specification $S_2^*$:

$$
S_2 = \left\{
\begin{array}{l}
info \lozenge search \ ; \\
info \lozenge premiere \ ; \\
watch \lozenge view, play \ ; \\
store \lozenge view, record \ ;
\end{array}
\right\}
\quad
S_2^* = \left\{
\begin{array}{l}
info \lozenge search \ ; \\
info \lozenge premiere \ ; \\
watch \lozenge view, play \ ; \\
watch \lozenge preview, play \ ; \\
store \lozenge view, record \ ; \\
store \lozenge view, play \ ; \\
store \lozenge preview, record \ ; \\
store \lozenge preview, play \ ;
\end{array}
\right\}
$$

where for simplicity we have omitted signs and parameters in the actions of both components.

Depending both on the actual protocols of the components, and on the server's policy, the server may return different contract proposals, for instance:

$$
C_B = \left\{
\begin{array}{l}
info \lozenge search \ ; \\
watch \lozenge view, play \ ; \\
watch \lozenge preview, play \ ; \\
store \lozenge preview, record \ ;
\end{array}
\right\}
$$

where the contract proposal $C_B$ indicates that some *watch* requests will be adapted into previews, while all *store* requests will be adapted into previews.

As in the case of the partial adaptation described in the previous section, it is worth noting that a server may decide to subservice some of the client requests even if this is not strictly necessary in order to achieve a successful interoperation of the two components. Hence, the contract proposal returned may present relevant differences with respect to the original client requests, and some additional information would be of help for deciding whether or not to accept a proposed adaptation. Thus, together with the contract proposal, the server should provide the client with some explanation of why some requests have not been satisfied, such as for instance "temporarily unavailable service", "insufficient access rights", or "unsolved protocol mismatch", as discussed in [3].

However, this kind of "qualitative" information is usually insufficient and most of the times the client needs a "quantitative" estimation on how close to the original request is a certain contract proposal with respect to an alternative one (either provided by the same server or by a different one). The main aim of this work is exploring different possibilities for achieving a quantitative measure of adaptation.

## 3   Measuring Adaptation

In this section we develop two initial metrics to compare an initial specification $S$ with a contract proposal $C$.

### 3.1   Rule Satisfaction

A first way to measure the distance between an initial specification $S$ and a contract proposal $C$ is to inspect how many rules of $S$ are "satisfied" by $C$.

For the case of hard adaptation, where $C$ is a subset of $S$, one may simply count the number of correspondence rules of $S$ that are contained in $C$, that is consider the ratio:

$$\frac{\sharp\, C}{\sharp\, S}$$

where $\sharp\, X$ denotes the number of rules in a specification $X$.

However, the above ratio does not make much sense in the context of soft adaptation, where in general the rules of $C$ are not a subset of the rules of $S$. Indeed, as we have already mentioned, both $S$ and $C$ are subsets of $S^*$, but $C$ may even contain more rules than $S$.

In the general context of soft adaptation, one should measure how many rules of $S$ are "satisfied" by $C$, either because they are included *verbatim* in $C$ or because a subserviced version of them is included in $C$. More precisely, we can single out three possible cases for each rule $r$ in $S$:

1. *r is fully satisfied by $C$.* Namely, $r$ belongs to $C$, but no subserviced version of $r$ belongs to $C$. Formally:

$$r \in C \ \wedge \ subs(r) \cap C = \emptyset$$

2. *r is partly satisfied by $C$ with some subservicing.* Namely, some subserviced version of $r$ belongs to $C$. Formally:

$$subs(r) \cap C \neq \emptyset$$

3. *r is not satisfied by $C$.* Namely, neither $r$ nor any subserviced version of $r$ belongs to $C$. Formally:

$$r \notin C \ \wedge \ subs(r) \cap C = \emptyset$$

Based on the above observation, we define the metric $m_1(S, C)$ which, given a specification $S$ and a contract $C$, returns two values. The first value indicates the percentage of rules of $S$ that are fully satisfied by the contract proposal $C$. The second value indicates the percentage of rules of $S$ that are partly satisfied, that is subserviced, by the contract proposal $C$. Formally:

$$m_1(S, C) \left\langle \frac{\sharp \{r \in S \cap C \mid subs(r) \cap C = \emptyset\}}{\sharp\, S} \, , \, \frac{\sharp \{r \in S \mid subs(r) \cap C \neq \emptyset\}}{\sharp\, S} \right\rangle$$

For instance, consider again the specification $S_2$ and the contract $C_B$ already presented, together with the new contract proposal $C_C$:

$$C_C = \left\{ \begin{array}{l} info \, \Diamond \, search \; ; \\ watch \, \Diamond \, view, play \; ; \\ store \, \Diamond \, view, play \; ; \end{array} \right\}$$

We have that $m_1(S_2, C_B) = \langle \frac{1}{4}, \frac{2}{4} \rangle$, while $m_1(S_2, C_C) = \langle \frac{2}{4}, \frac{1}{4} \rangle$, from which we could deduce that the contract proposal $C_B$ is worse than $C_C$ with respect to the specification $S_2$, since $C_B$ presents less rules fully satisfied and more subserviced rules than $C_C$.

## 3.2   Action Enabling

The simple inspection of the percentage of rules satisfied by a contract proposal does not however deal adequately with specifications that contain nondeterministic correspondence rules. For instance, consider once more the specification $S_2$ and the contract $C_B$ already presented, together with the new contract proposal $C_D$:

$$C_D = \left\{ \begin{array}{l} info \, \Diamond \, search \; ; \\ info \, \Diamond \, premiere \; ; \\ watch \, \Diamond \, preview, play \; ; \end{array} \right\}$$

We observe that, according to metric $m_1$, $m_1(S_2, C_B) = \langle \frac{1}{4}, \frac{2}{4} \rangle$, while on the other hand $m_1(S_2, C_D) = \langle \frac{2}{4}, \frac{1}{4} \rangle$, from which we should conclude that the contract proposal $C_D$ is closer to the specification $S_2$ than $C_B$, since in $C_D$ the number or rules of $S_2$ fully satisfied are greater than in $C_B$. However, the adaptor corresponding to the new contract $C_D$ will allow the client to perform a smaller number of actions than $C_B$ (viz., action $store$ is not present in $C_D$). Hence, a finer metric should consider the percentage of client actions (instead of rules) whose execution will be actually enabled by the adaptor proposal. Again, for the case of hard adaptation, one may simply consider the ratio between the number of client actions occurring in $C$ and in $S$, formally:

$$\frac{\sharp\, [C]_{cl}}{\sharp\, [S]_{cl}}$$

However, the above ratio is a bit coarse in the general context of soft adaptation, since it does not consider the subservicing possibly operated by the adaptor. More precisely, we can single out three possible cases for a client action $a$ occurring in $S$ (viz., for each $a \in [S]_{cl}$):

1. *a is fully enabled by C.* Namely the execution of $a$ is enabled by $C$ without introducing subservicing, that is, $a$ only occurs in rules of $C$ that were in $S$ too. Formally:

$$a \in [C]_{cl} \land a \notin [C \cap subs(S)]_{cl}$$

2. *a is partly enabled by C with some subservicing.* Namely the execution of $a$ is enabled by $C$ via some subservicing, that is, $a$ occurs in some subserviced version of rules of $S$. Formally:

$$a \in [C \cap subs(S)]_{cl}$$

3. *a is not enabled by C.* Namely $a$ does not occur in (any rule of) $C$. Formally:

$$a \notin [C]_{cl}$$

Based on the above observation, we define a new metric $m_2(S, C)$ which, given a specification $S$ and a contract $C$, returns two values. The first value indicates the percentage of client actions in $S$ that are fully enabled by $C$. The second value indicates the percentage of client actions in $S$ that are partly enabled by $C$. Formally:

$$m_2(S, C) = \left\langle \frac{\sharp \left([C]_{cl} \backslash [C \cap subs(S)]_{cl}\right)}{\sharp [S]_{cl}} \, , \, \frac{\sharp [C \cap subs(S)]_{cl}}{\sharp [S]_{cl}} \right\rangle$$

For instance, considering again the specification $S_2$ along with the contracts $C_B$ and $C_D$, we observe that $m_2(S_2, C_B) = \langle \frac{1}{3}, \frac{2}{3} \rangle$ while $m_2(S_2, C_D) = \langle \frac{1}{3}, \frac{1}{3} \rangle$, from which we should now conclude that $C_B$ –in which all client actions are being adapted– represents a better adaptation than $C_D$ –in which no adaptation for action *store* is featured. In other words, if we only take into account the number of (partially) satisfied rules (as given by metric $m_1$), the contract proposal $C_D$ presents a greater level of satisfaction for the specification $S_2$. Nevertheless, from an intuitive point of view, $C_B$ seems closer to $S_2$ than $C_D$, which is correctly reflected by metric $m_2$.

## 4   Adding Quantitative Information

So far we have assumed that contract specifications are plain sets of correspondence rules, some of which may have been introduced because of subservicing. We now consider the case in which contract specifications are enriched so as to contain additional quantitative information denoting usage percentage of the individual rules during the construction of the adaptor. For instance, consider again the specification $S_2$ already presented, together with the following annotated version of the contract proposal $C_B$:

$$C_{B'} = \left\{ \begin{array}{ll} info \, \Diamond \, search & : 1; \\ watch \, \Diamond \, view, play & : .8; \\ watch \, \Diamond \, preview, play & : .2; \\ store \, \Diamond \, preview, record & : 1; \end{array} \right\}$$

The intended meaning of the numbers annotated on the right of the correspondence rules is to provide an estimation of the degree of subservicing employed in the adaptation. For instance, the first rule of $C_{B'}$ indicates that the first rule of $S_2$ is kept as is in $C_B$, i.e., without subservicing it (while the second rule of $S_2$ has not been used at all during the construction of the adaptor). On the other hand, the second and third rules of $C_{B'}$ state that the third rule of $S_2$ has been used 80% of the times during the adaptor construction to match client action *watch*, while its subserviced version has been employed the remaining 20% of the times. Finally, the fourth rule of $C_{B'}$ states that the fourth rule of $S_2$ has been always subserviced.

Hence, we can refine metric $m_1$ so as to measure the *percentage* with which the rules of $S$ are satisfied without or with subservicing by $C$:

$$m_3(S,C) \left\langle \frac{\sum_{r \in S} \{p \mid \langle r : p \rangle \in C\}}{\sharp S} , \frac{\sum_{r \in subs(S)} \{p \mid \langle r : p \rangle \in C\}}{\sharp S} \right\rangle$$

For instance, for the contract $C_{B'}$ above we have that $m_3(S_2, C_{B'}) = \left\langle \frac{1.8}{3}, \frac{1.2}{3} \right\rangle$, which offers a more precise information on the adaptation proposal than that provided by $m_1(S_2, C_B) = \langle \frac{1}{4}, \frac{2}{4} \rangle$ for the non-annotated version $C_B$ of the same contract proposal.

The metric $m_3(S, C)$ above allows to exploit the information provided by annotated contracts in order to measure the percentage of *overall* subservicing of the original specifications. However, subservices may not be all the same for clients. Typically, a client may consider a subservice $b_j$ to be an acceptable surrogate of $b_i$, while a different subservice $b_k$ of $b_i$ may not be of interest or valuable for the client. Therefore, a finer metric should try to combine the information provided by an annotated contract together with an assessment of subservices performed by the client.

We hence consider that a client may wish to set its own criteria to assess the quality of a soft adaptor obtained in response to its request for adaptation. As soft adaptors employ subservicing, clients may wish to assess how much the employed subservicing will affect the quality of the adaptation proposed. For instance, in our VoD system, the client may wish to weight the subservice relation presented by the server on the basis of its own assessment. For instance, the client may annotate the above subservice relation as follows:

$$\begin{aligned} preview \quad &\sqsubseteq_{.5} \quad view \, ; \\ play \quad &\sqsubseteq_1 \quad record \, ; \end{aligned}$$

where the first annotation ($\sqsubseteq_{.5}$) indicates that the client will be half satisfied if the *preview* subservice will be provided in place of the *view* service. The second annotation ($\sqsubseteq_1$) instead indicates that the subservicing of *record* with *play* is not relevant for the client. Annotations must maintain some kind of consistency. In fact, they must satisfy the following property:

$$a \sqsubseteq_u b \ \land \ b \sqsubseteq_v c \quad implies \quad a \sqsubseteq_{u \times v} c$$

which ensures that $\sqsubseteq$. is also a partial order.

The annotated subservice relation can be lifted to rules as follows:

$$r' \sqsubseteq_v r \quad \textit{iff} \quad v = \begin{cases} \min_{a' \in [r']_{sr}, a \in [r]_{sr}} \{x \mid a' \sqsubseteq_x a \} & \textit{if} \ \ r' \in subs(r) \\ 1 & \textit{if} \ \ r' = r \end{cases}$$

We can hence refine metric $m_3$ to take into account the subservicing assessment made by the client:

$$m_4(S, C) \ = \ \frac{\sum_{r \in S} \{p \times v \mid \langle r' : p \rangle \in C \ \wedge \ r' \sqsubseteq_v r \}}{\sharp S}$$

For instance, for the above specification $S_2$ and the annotated contract $C_{B'}$, we have that $m_4(S_2, C_{B'}) = (1 \times 1 + .8 \times 1 + .2 \times .5 + 1 \times .5) \div 3 = .8$, which can be considered as a measure of the optimality of the contract for the client, i.e., of the degree of satisfaction achieved during adaptor construction.

The introduction of quantitative annotations (both in contracts and in subservice relations) paves the way for a more precise assessment of the actions or services whose execution will be enabled by an adaptor proposal. However, such an assessment should consider the actual interaction protocols followed by the components and the adaptor. Consider for instance the following specification $S_3$, and the contract proposal $C_E$:

$$S_3 = \{\, watch \, \Diamond \, view, play \, ; \} \qquad C_E = \begin{cases} watch \, \Diamond \, view, play & : .5; \\ watch \, \Diamond \, preview, play : .5; \end{cases}$$

where as before $preview \sqsubseteq_{.5} view$. The quantitative annotations in $C_E$ denote the usage percentage of the rules *during the construction* of the adaptor, resulting in a satisfaction measurement $m_4(S_3, C_E) = (1 \times .5 + .5 \times .5) \div 2 = .375$.

However, let us suppose now that the contract $C_E$ corresponds for instance to the actual adaptor:

$$A \ = \ watch. \, (\, preview. \, A \ + \ view. \, A \,)$$

It is easy to observe that the real percentage of subservicing employed by the server to enable the execution of client actions depends on the actual protocols of the components involved (in the example, the frequency with which the server drives the adaptor to perform action *preview* instead of *view*). Furthermore, a simple inspection of the protocols of the two components may not suffice. Suppose for instance that the protocol of the server is:

$$Server = \ preview. \, Server \ + \ view. \, Server$$

From that, we cannot conclude that the adaptor will perform the actions *preview* and *view* with the same frequency, since the choice between the two branches of the alternative may depend on internal policies of the *Server* not represented at the protocol level. Hence, the amount of times that action *watch* will be subserviced when using the adaptor $A$ above will not depend merely on the protocol describing the adaptor, but mainly on the actual behaviour of the *Server* and the *Client* which determines the frequency with which these components present the actions complementary to those offered by the adaptor.

Hence, a quantitative assessment of the actual, possibly subserviced, execution of client actions should take into account also probabilistic information associated with protocols (e.g., see [9, 14]). For instance a probabilistic definition of the previous process *Server*, as:

$$Server = preview.\, Server\ _{.9}+_{.1}\ view.\, Server$$

indicates that the left branch of the alternative will be executed with probability .9. Hence, most of the times the subservice *preview* will be offered to the client instead of the service *view* originally requested. This information should be taken into account in order to refine metrics like $m_3$ and $m_4$ in order to yield a more precise information on the adaptation proposal.

## 5    Concluding Remarks

When heterogeneous software components have to be combined in order to construct complex systems, one of the crucial problems to be solved is the mismatching of interaction behaviours they may present. To the best of our knowledge, in spite of the relevance of this topic, not many efforts have been devoted to develop well-founded component adaptation theories.

A number of practice-oriented studies have analysed different issues encountered in (manually) adapting a third-party component for using it in a (possibly radically) different context (e.g., see [10, 11, 19]). The problem of software adaptation from a more formal point of view was specifically addressed by the work of Yellin and Strom [21], which constitutes the starting point for our work. They used finite state grammars to specify interaction protocols between components, to define a relation of compatibility, and to address the task of (semi)automatic adaptor generation. The main advantage of finite state machines is that their simplicity supports an efficient verification of protocol compatibility. However, such a simplicity is a severe expressiveness bound for modelling complex open distributed systems. On the contrary, process algebras feature more expressive descriptions of protocols and enable more sophisticated analysis of concurrent systems. For this reason, several authors propose their use for the specification of component interfaces and for the analysis of component compatibility [1, 7]. A technique for automatically synthetising connectors is discussed in [13] by focussing on avoiding deadlocks caused by mismatching coordination policies among COM/DCOM components that present compatible interfaces. A different approach is that of [20], where software composition is addressed in the context of category theory. The connection between components is obtained by *superposition*, defining a morphism between actions in both components. Morphisms are similar to our specifications, though the kind of adaptation provided is more restrictive, limiting adaptation to a kind of name translation similar to that provided by IDL signature descriptions. Finally, in [17], type systems and finite state automata are used for describing component interfaces, and a game-theoretic framework is defined for the automatic generation of adaptors avoiding component deadlock. Their proposal is quite appealing, although it shares most of the limitations of those based on finite automata.

Following the above comparison with significant related works in the literature, we argue that our approach [2, 3, 4] facilitates the adaptation of components by combining expressiveness and effectiveness in a formally grounded methodology. Our proposal is based on the idea of deriving a concrete adaptor, given its specification and the behaviour description of the two components to be adapted. As full adaptation is not always possible (e.g., because behavioral protocols cannot be matched, or because the requested services are not –fully– available), soft adaptation features a flexible way of adapting components, and calls for mechanisms to assess the appropriateness of proposed adaptors.

Component adaptation is also a relevant issue in the context of mobile computation, where nomadic applications (client components) will need to require services from different hosts (server components). Again, the behaviours mismatching can be solved by adapting both client and server protocols, considering an initial adaptation (given by a set of rules) requested by the client. If the server cannot fully satisfy these initial requests, it could offer an alternative (partial) adaptation (given by a set of –possibly– revised rules) , whose appropriateness should be evaluated by using the previously mentioned mechanisms.

If the references to formal adaptation of software components are scarce in the literature, those trying to address a measurement of the results obtained are probably non-existing. There are quite a few proposals for measuring the quality of component-based systems, usually dealing with measuring the adequacy of the components in a repository w.r.t. the particular needs of a software developer (see for instance [8] for catching a glimpse on the state-of-the-art in this field). Although there are works, as [15], dealing with measuring the semantic distance between functional specifications on a formally based setting, most of the proposals in the component-based field deal with component specification and metrics using long lists of mostly qualitative attributes. Some of these metrics are proposed as an estimation of the effort required for adapting (manually) software components.

At the best of our knowledge, this work is the first proposal addressing the measurement of the (automatic) process of software adaptation and of its result (the adaptor). In this paper, we have defined a set of behaviour-oriented metrics which feature different ways of measuring the distance between an adaptor request and the adaptor which will be effectively deployed. Thus, $m_1$ gives a measure based on the satisfied adaptation rules, whereas $m_2$ defines a metric where enabled services are taken into account. On the other hand metrics $m_3$ and $m_4$ take into account additional quantitative information provided by the server and client components, respectively.

It is worth noting that the metrics $m_1$, $m_2$, and $m_3$ can be computed directly by server components (they only need the client protocol specification and the initial adaptor request). Thus, servers may ultimately send back to the client only metric values rather than adaptor proposal specifications, hence increasing further the non-disclosure of information.

Our plans for future work include integrating the adaptation methodology in existing CBSE development environments, so as to allow experimenting and assessing the methodology on large numbers of available components. Another interesting direction for future work is to extend the adaptation methodology to deal with probabilistic descriptions of behaviour, as suggested at the end of Section 4.

# References

[1] R. Allen and D. Garlan. A formal basis for architectural connection. *ACM Transactions on Software Engineering and Methodology*, 6(3):213–49, 1997. 83

[2] A. Bracciali, A. Brogi, and C. Canal. A formal approach to component adaptation. *Journal of Systems and Software, Special Issue on Automated Component-Based Software Engineering*, (in press). A preliminary version of this paper was published in *COORDINATION 2002: Fifth International Conference on Coordination Models and Languages*, LNCS 2315, pages 88–95. Springer, 2002. 71, 72, 73, 75, 76, 84

[3] A. Brogi, C. Canal, and E. Pimentel. Soft component adaptation. *Electronic Notes in Theoretical Computer Science (ENTCS)*, 85(3), 2003. 71, 73, 76, 77, 84

[4] A. Brogi, C. Canal, and E. Pimentel. On the specification of software adaptation. In *FOCLASA'03, Electronic Notes in Theoretical Computer Science (ENTCS)*, 90 (in press), 2003. 71, 73, 74, 84

[5] A. W. Brown and K. C. Wallnau. The current state of CBSE. *IEEE Software*, 15(5):37–47, 1998. 71

[6] G. H. Campbell. Adaptable components. In *ICSE 1999*, pages 685–686. IEEE Press, 1999. 71

[7] C. Canal, E. Pimentel, and J. M. Troya. Compatibility and inheritance in software architectures. *Science of Computer Programming*, 41:105–138, 2001. 83

[8] A. Cechich, M. Piattini, and A. Vallecillo (Eds). Component-Based Software Quality. LNCS 2693. Springer, 2003. 84

[9] A. Di Pierro, C. Hankin, H. Wiklicky. Approximate Non-Interference. In *CSFW'02*, IEEE Press, pages 3–17, 2002. 83

[10] S. Ducasse and T. Richner. Executable connectors: Towards reusable design elements. In *ESEC/FSE'97*, LNCS 1301. Springer, 1997. 83

[11] D. Garlan, R. Allen, and J. Ockerbloom. Architectural mismatch: Why reuse is so hard. *IEEE Software*, 12(6):17–26, 1995. 83

[12] D. Gelernter and N. Carriero. Coordination languages and their significance. *Communications of the ACM*. 35(2):97–107. 1992. 71

[13] P. Inverardi and M. Tivoli. Automatic synthesis of deadlock free connectors for COM/DCOM applications. In *ESEC/FSE'2001*. ACM Press, 2001. 83

[14] B. Jonsson, K. G. Larsen, and W. Yi. Probabilistic extensions of process algebras. *Handbook of Process Algebra*. Elsevier, 2001. 83

[15] R. Mili et al. Semantic distance between specifications. *Theoretical Computer Science*, 247:257–276, Elsevier 2000. 84

[16] R. Milner, J. Parrow, D. Walker. A calculus of mobile processes. *Journal of Information and Computation*, 100:1–77. 1992. 73

[17] R. Passerone et al. Convertibility Verification and Converter Synthesis: two faces of the same coin. In *Proc. of the Int. Conference on Computer-Aided Design*. ACM Press, 2002.  83

[18] A. Vallecillo, J. Hernández, and J. M. Troya. New issues in object interoperability. In *Object-Oriented Technology*, LNCS 1964, pages 256–269. Springer, 2000.  71

[19] K. Wallnau, S. Hissam, and R. Seacord. *Building Systems from Commercial Components*. SEI Series in Soft. Engineering, 2001.  83

[20] M. Wermelinger and J. L. Fiadeiro. Connectors for mobile programs. *IEEE Transactions on Software Engineering*, 24(5):331–341, 1998.  83

[21] D. M. Yellin and R. E. Strom. Protocol specifications and components adaptors. *ACM Transactions on Programming Languages and Systems*, 19(2):292–333, 1997.  83

# An Operational Semantics for StAC, a Language for Modelling Long-Running Business Transactions

Michael Butler[1] and Carla Ferreira[2]

[1] School of Electronics and Computer Science, University of Southampton
Highfield, Southampton SO17 1BJ, United Kingdom
mjb@ecs.soton.ac.uk
[2] Department of Computer Science, Technical University of Lisbon
Av. Rovisco Pais, 1049-001 Lisbon, Portugal
carla.ferreira@dei.ist.utl.pt

**Abstract.** This paper presents the StAC language and its operational semantics. StAC (Structured Activity Compensation) is a business process modelling language and a distinctive feature of the language is its support for compensation. A compensation is an action taken to recover from error or cope with a change of plan, especially when rollback of a process is not possible. StAC is similar to a process algebraic language such as Hoare's CSP or Milner's CCS but has additional operators dealing with compensation and with exception handling. In this paper we present an operational semantics for the language.

## 1 Introduction

The StAC language (**St**ructured **A**ctivity **C**ompensation) was introduced in [3] as a business process modelling language and includes constructs for modelling compensation in business processes. In the context of business transactions, Gray [11] defines a compensation as the action taken to recover from error or cope with a change of plan. Compensation is a useful feature when modelling long running business transactions where rollback is not always possible because parts of a transaction will have been committed or because parts of a transaction (e.g., communications with external agents) are inherently impossible to undo. Consider the following example: a client buys some books in an on-line bookstore and the bookstore debits the client's account as the payment for the book order. The bookstore later realises that one of the books in the client's order is out of print. To compensate the client for this problem, the bookstore can credit the account with the amount wrongfully debited and send a letter apologising for their mistake. This example shows that compensation is more general than traditional rollback in database transactions. Compensation is important when a system cannot control everything, such as when interaction with humans is involved.

StAC gives a precise interpretation to the mechanics of compensation, including the combination of compensation with parallel execution, hierarchy and

R. de Nicola et al. (Eds.): COORDINATION 2004, LNCS 2949, pp. 87–104, 2004.

**Table 1.** StAC Syntax

| Process ::= | $A$ | (activity label) | | $P \sqcap Q$ | (internal choice) |
|---|---|---|---|---|---|
| | $skip$ | (skip) | | $P\{Q\}R$ | (attempt block) |
| | $b \ \& \ P$ | (condition) | | $\odot$ | (early termination of attempt) |
| | $call(N)$ | (call named process) | | $P \div Q$ | (compensation pair) |
| | $P \setminus S$ | (hiding) | | $\boxtimes$ | (reverse) |
| | $P; Q$ | (sequence) | | $\boxdot$ | (accept) |
| | $P \parallel_X Q$ | (parallel) | | $[P]$ | (compensation scoping) |
| | $P \ [\!]\ Q$ | (external choice) | | | |

exceptions. StAC was inspired by the BPBeans framework [6] that allows an application to be built by a nested hierarchy of business processes. Like BPBeans, StAC provides ways to coordinate basic acivities by supporting sequential and concurrent processes, as well as compensation and exceptions. Similar coordination mechanisms are found in the BizTalk [15] and BPEL4WS [7] business coordination languages.

## 2   The StAC Language

StAC has taken inspiration from other process algebras, especially Milner's Calculus for Communicating Systems (CCS) [16] and Hoare's Communicating Sequential Processes (CSP) [12]. Both CCS and CSP model processes in terms of the atomic events in which they can engage. The languages provide operators for defining structured processes such as sequencing, choice, parallel composition, communication and hiding. StAC provides a similar process term language along with operators for compensation and exceptions. A StAC process has global data state associated with it and this state is changed by atomic events (or activities). Typically the data states of a StAC process are represented using state variables and the effect of atomic activities is represented using assignment to variables.

Formally a system is described by a set of equations of the form $N_i = P_i$, where each $N_i$ is a process name and $P_i$ is a StAC process expression. The syntax of StAC processes is presented in Table 1. Note that recursion is allowed since a process $P_i$ may contain a call to a process named $N_j$.

The specification of a system is not complete with the StAC equations alone, as we might also want to specify the effect of the basic activities on the information structures. Instead of extending StAC to include variables and expressions we use existing state-based formal notations to define the state variables and activities. Possible notations are Z [19], VDM [13], B [1] and the guarded command language [8]. Any formal notation where it is possible to define a state, and where operations are partial relations on that state may be used to complement StAC. Examples of the use of the B notation to specify the data states of a StAC process and the effect of activities on the variables may be found in [3, 9, 10].

The StAC language allows sequential and parallel composition of processes, and the usual process combinators. Besides these, it has specific combinators to deal with compensation. An overview of the language is given in this section. Each activity label $A$ (in StAC) has an associated activity $\overset{A}{\rightarrow}$ representing an atomic change in the state: if $\Sigma$ is the set of all possible states, then $\overset{A}{\rightarrow}$ is a relation on $\Sigma$. The process *skip* does nothing and immediately terminates successfully. This process has a similar interpretation to the CSP *skip* that describes successful termination. The process call *call(N)* calls the process named $N$ returning if and when $N$ terminates successfully. Hiding is identical to the CSP hiding operator. With hiding one can make the execution of activities invisible to the environment.

**Sequential and Parallel Operators.** The sequential construct combines two processes, $P; Q$. In process $P; Q$, $P$ is executed first, and only when P terminates successfully can $Q$ be executed.

In parallel process $P \underset{X}{\parallel} Q$, the execution of the activities of $P$ and $Q$ is synchronised over the activities in X, while the execution of the remaining activities of $P$ and $Q$ is interleaved. Synchronisation can introduce deadlock, *e.g.*, process $P$ may be waiting to synchronise with $Q$ over an activity $A$ and that activity will never occur in $Q$. If set $X$ is empty (no synchronisation) we will represent the parallel process as $P \parallel Q$.

**Condition.** In the conditional operator, process $P$ is guarded by a boolean function $b$. This boolean function can consult the state, *i.e.*, $b : \Sigma \rightarrow \textbf{BOOL}$. Process $b \& P$ behaves as $P$ if $b$ evaluates to true in the current state. Conversely, if $b$ is false, the conditional process will block.

**Choice.** The external choice $P \,[]\, Q$ selects whichever of $P$ or $Q$ is enabled (i.e., not blocked). If both $P$ and $Q$ are enabled, the choice is made by the environment and it is resolved at the first activity. The environment could be a user selecting one of the options in a menu, for example. Notice that the $[]$ operator causes nondeterminism in some cases. Consider the following example:

$$(A; B) \,[]\, (A; C).$$

When activity $A$ occurs it is not possible to determine which one of the two behaviours $A; B$ or $A; C$ will be chosen. In this case, the choice is made internally by the system rather than by the environment. Internal nondeterminism may be specified directly using the internal choice operator ($\sqcap$).

The parallel and choice operators may be extended to generalised versions over (possibly infinite) sets of indexed processes. For example, a process that allows a user to choose a book could be described in StAC as:

$$[] \, b \in BOOK \bullet ChooseBook.b$$

Details of the generalised versions of the operators may be found in [9]

**Attempt Block and Early Termination.** An important feature in business processing is the possibility of terminating processes before they have concluded their main tasks. Early termination might arise if an exception occurs or a customer decides to abandon a transaction. It might also arise in the case of speculative parallelism, where several tasks, representing alternative ways of achieving a goal, are commenced in parallel and when one completes, the remaining tasks may be abandoned. We have included in StAC what we term an *attempt* block. An attempt block $P\{Q\}R$ first executes $Q$, and if $Q$ terminates successfully it then continues with $P$. If an early termination operation ($\odot$) is executed within $Q$, the block continues with $R$. For example, the process

$$C\{A; \odot; B\}D$$

will first execute $A$, then the early termination will cause $B$ to be skipped over and $D$ to be executed. Any behaviour sequentially following the execution of early termination within an attempt block will be skipped. So an attempt block $P\{Q\}R$ can be viewed as an exception construct, with early termination representing the raising of an exception and $R$ representing the exception handler.

The effect of the early termination is limited to the attempt block so in the following process, the early termination in the attempt block has no effect on the process $S$ running in parallel with the block:

$$\{(P; \odot; Q)\} \parallel S$$

(We write $\{Q\}$ as short for $skip\{Q\}skip$.)

In the case of parallel processes within an attempt block, a termination instruction within one of the parallel process also affects the other processes. For example, in the process

$$\{ (P; \odot; Q) \parallel R \}$$

the early termination after $P$ allows $R$ to terminate early. Our use of the term 'allows' is deliberate here. $R$ is not required to terminate immediately. It may continue for several more steps before terminating early, it may continue to completion or it may execute forever if it is a non-terminating process. In any case, if and when the main body of an attempt block terminates and at least one of its constituent process has executed an early termination, then the whole of the main body is deemed to have terminated early.

**Compensation Operators.** The next few StAC operators are related to compensation. In the *compensation pair* $P \div Q$, $P$ is the primary process and $Q$ is the compensation process. When a compensation pair runs, it runs the primary task, and once the primary process has successfully completed, the compensation process is remembered (installed) for possible later invocation.

The *reverse* operation ($\boxtimes$) causes the currently installed compensation handlers to be invoked. For example $(A \div A'); \boxtimes$ will execute $A$, install $A'$ and then the reverse operation will cause $A'$ to be executed. The overall behaviour is $A; A'$.

In the case of activities composed using sequential composition, the compensation process is constructed in the reverse order to the primary process execution. Consider the process $(A \div A'); (B \div B')$. This process behaves as $A; B$

and has the compensation task $B'; A'$. A sequential compensation task can be viewed as a stack where compensation processes are pushed on to the top of the stack. The process $(A \div A'); (B \div B'); \boxtimes$ behaves as $A; B$, and then the $\boxtimes$ operator causes the compensation task to be executed, so the overall behaviour is $(A; B); (B'; A')$ (which we write as $A; B; B'; A'$).

In the case of parallel processes, execution of compensations is also performed in parallel. The parallel process $(A \div A') \parallel (B \div B')$ executes $A$ and $B$ concurrently and the resulting compensation process is $A' \parallel B'$.

The *accept* operation ($\boxdot$) indicates that currently installed compensations should be cleared, meaning that after an accept the compensation task is set to *skip*. The process $(A \div A'); (B \div B'); \boxdot; \boxtimes$ executes $A$ and $B$, when the $\boxtimes$ operation is called the compensation task $B'; A'$ has already been cleared by the $\boxdot$ operator so $B'; A'$ will not be executed.

Next we will consider the combination of compensation with choice. The process $(A \div A') \,[\!]\, (B \div B')$ behaves as either $A$ or $B$, the choice between $A$ and $B$ is made by the environment. The compensation task in the case that $A$ is chosen is $A'$ and in the other case is $B'$.

If the primary process terminates early, the compensation process will not be installed. For example, in the process: $(A; \odot; B) \div C$ compensation C would not be installed because of the early termination in the primary process.

In the case that a compensation pair is running in parallel with a process that executes an early termination, this early termination cannot affect the compensation pair while the compensation pair is executing. So the compensation pair will either not get executed at all or will be expected to execute to completion, including installation of the compensation handler. For example, the process $\{\, (A \div B) \parallel \odot \,\}$ will either behave as *skip* or as $(A \div B)$.

**Scoping of Compensation.** The compensation scoping brackets $[\cdots]$ provide nested compensation scoping are used to delimit the scope of the acceptance and reversal operators. All StAC processes have an implicit outer compensation scope. The start of scope creates a new compensation task, and invoking a reversal instruction within that scope will only execute those compensation activities that have been remembered since the start of the scope. In the process

$$(A \div A'); [\, (B \div B'); \boxtimes \,],$$

the overall process would behave as $A; B; B'$. Compensation $A'$ is not invoked because its outside the scope of the reversal instruction. An acceptance instruction, within a scope, will only clear the compensation activities that have been recorded since the start of the scope. For example, the process:

$$(A \div A'); [\, (B \div B'); \boxdot \,]; (C \div C')$$

after $A$, $B$ and $C$ have been executed, has $C'; A'$ as compensation. Since the acceptance instruction is within the compensation scope, it just clears the compensation process $B'$ that is within the brackets. Another feature of compensation scoping is that compensation is remembered beyond a scope if a reversal instruction is not performed, as in the example:

$$(A \div A'); [(B \div B')]; (C \div C').$$

Here, after executing $A; B; C$ the compensation process is $C'; B'; A'$, which includes the compensation process $B'$ of the inner scope. $B'$ is retained because there is no acceptance instruction within the brackets.

### Example: Order Fulfillment

To illustrate the use of StAC we present the order fulfillment example described in [4] and [5]. ACME Ltd distributes goods which have a relatively high value to its customers. When the company receives an order from a customer, the first step is to verify whether the stock is available. If not available the customer is informed that his/her order can not be accepted. Otherwise, the warehouse starts preparing the order for shipment, and a courier is booked to deliver the goods to the customer. Simultaneously with the warehouse preparing the order, the company does a credit check on the customer to verify that the customer can pay for the order. The credit check is performed in parallel because it normally succeeds, and in this normal case the company does not wish to delay the order unnecessarily. If the credit check fails the preparation of the order is stopped. Here we present a very simple representation of the order acceptance and focus on the order fulfillment part in more detail.

Before presenting the ACME process, we introduce the following syntactic sugar:

$$TRY\ P\ THEN\ Q\ ELSE\ R\ =\ Q\{P\}R$$
$$IF\ G\ THEN\ P\ ELSE\ Q\ =\ G\&P\ [\!]\ \neg G\&Q$$

At the top level the application is defined as a sequence as follows:

$$ACME = \mathbf{AcceptOrder} \div \mathbf{RestockOrder};$$
$$TRY\ FulfillOrder\ THEN\ \boxtimes\ ELSE\ \boxtimes$$

The first step in the $ACME$ process is a compensation pair. The primary action of this pair is to accept the order and deduct the order quantity from the inventory database. The compensation action is simply to add the order quantity back to the total in the inventory database. Following the compensation pair, the $FulfillOrder$ process is invoked. If the order has been fulfilled correctly ($FulfillOrder$ terminates sucessfully), the order is accepted, otherwise ($FulfillOrder$ terminates early) the order is reversed.

Notice that some processes are written with a bold font, e.g., **AcceptOrder**, this means that those processes are activity labels, so they are not further decomposed.

The order is fulfilled by packaging the order at the warehouse while concurrently doing a credit check on the customer. If the credit check fails, the

*FulfillOrder* process is terminated early:

$$FulfillOrder = WarehousePackaging$$
$$\| \ (\textbf{CreditCheck}; \textit{IF} \ \neg \textbf{okCreditCheck} \ \textit{THEN} \ \odot \ \textit{ELSE skip})$$

Because *WarehousePackaging* is within the scope of the early termination, a failed credit check allows *WarehousePackaging* to terminate early, possible before all the items in the order have been packed.

The *WarehousePackaging* process consists of a compensation pair in parallel with the *PackOrder* process:

$$WarehousePackaging = (\textbf{BookCourier} \div \textbf{CancelCourier}) \ \| \ PackOrder$$

The compensation pair books the courier, with the compensation action being to cancel the courier booking. **CancelCourier** might result in a second message being sent to the courier rather than reversing the send of the message which booked the courier. The *PackOrder* process packs each of the items in the order in parallel. Each **PackItem** activity is reversed by a corresponding **UnpackItem**:

$$PackOrder \ = \ \| i \in \textbf{order} \ \bullet \ (\textbf{PackItem}(i) \div \textbf{UnpackItem}(i))$$

In the case that a credit check fails, the *FulfillOrder* process terminates early with the courier possibly having been booked and possibly some of the items having being packed. The reversal instruction will then be invoked and will result in the appropriate compensation activity being invoked for those activities that did take place.

## 3   Semantics

In this section we will present the operational semantics for StAC. To do this we introduce a variant of the language called StAC$_i$ to which we give an operational semantics. We refer to StAC$_i$ as the semantic language. In StAC$_i$, a process can have several simultaneous compensation tasks associated with it. A process decides which task to attach the compensation activities to, and each individual compensation task can be reversed or accepted. This contrasts with the language presented in Section 2, where scoping of compensation is hierarchical and each scope has a single implicit compensation task. To distinguish different compensation tasks, the operators that deal with compensation, *i.e.*, compensation pair, acceptance and reversal, are indexed by the compensation task index to which they apply. The syntax of StAC$_i$ is presented in Table 2. Later we define a translation from StAC to StAC$_i$.

### 3.1   Semantic Language

Several of the StAC$_i$ operators are retained from StAC without any alterations. The changes concern operators that deal with compensation and early termination (indicated with bold font in Table 2).

**Table 2.** $StAC_i$ Syntax ($[P]$ and $P \div Q$ are derived operators)

| Process ::= $A$ | (*activity label*) | $\mid \odot$ | (*early termination*) |
|---|---|---|---|
| $\mid skip$ | (*skip*) | $\mid P\{Q\}_v R$ | (**attempt block**) |
| $\mid b \;\&\; P$ | (*conditional*) | $\mid early$ | (**premature termination**) |
| $\mid call(N)$ | (*named process call*) | $\mid \lvert P \rvert_v$ | (**protection block**) |
| $\mid P \setminus S$ | (*hiding*) | $\mid new(i).P_i$ | (**new compensation task**) |
| $\mid P; Q$ | (*sequence*) | $\mid \boxtimes_i$ | (**indexed reverse**) |
| $\mid P \parallel_X Q$ | (*parallel*) | $\mid \boxdot_i$ | (**indexed accept**) |
| $\mid P \sqcap Q$ | (*internal choice*) | $\mid \uparrow_i P$ | (**push**) |
| $\mid P \mathbin{[\!]} Q$ | (*external choice*) | $\mid J \triangleright i$ | (**merge**) |

After an early termination, the process within an attempt block may continue to execute for several steps before terminating. To deal with this we have added a boolean flag $v$ to the attempt block representing the following two possibilities:

$P\{Q\}_{false} R$ – Process $Q$ can continue its execution since no early termination instruction has been invoked within $Q$.

$P\{Q\}_{true} R$ – An early termination instruction has previously been invoked within the attempt block and process $Q$ may terminate prematurely.

The term *early* represents a process that has terminated early. It is used to distinguish a process that has terminated early from a process that has terminated successfully (*skip*).

In some case we require that a process that has already commenced execution, e.g., a compensation pair, be protected from early termination caused by another process within an attempt block. This is achieved using the protection block $\lvert P \rvert_v$. The boolean flag $v$ will initially be *false*, and once the protected process executes its first visible activity the flag will be changed to *true* and $P$ will then be protected from an early termination originating from outside the protection block. A protection block may still be terminated by an early termination invocation within the protection block.

In our semantics, the compensation information of a process is maintained by a compensation function that maps each compensation task index to a compensation process. The accept and reverse operators are subscripted with the index of the compensation process to which they should be applied. In the $StAC_i$ language we introduce the *push* operator that stores a compensation process in a compensation task, i.e., $\uparrow_i Q$ will store $Q$ on top of compensation task $i$, where $i$ is an index. A compensation pair $P \div_i Q$ can be defined in terms of the push operator as follows:

$$\lvert\, P; \uparrow_i Q \,\rvert_{false}.$$

Here, $P$ will be executed first and after it has concluded its execution the process *push* will store $Q$ in task $i$. The protection block ensures that, once the process $P; \uparrow_i Q$ has commenced, it is not affected by early termination emanating from outside the protection block.

An important operator in $StAC_i$ is the merge operator. The expression $J \rhd i$, where $J$ is a set of indices, merges all compensation tasks belonging to $J$ into the compensation task $i$. All compensation tasks in $J$ are put in parallel, the result is added to the compensation task $i$ and all compensation tasks $J$ are cleared. For example, in the process

$$(A \div_i A'); (B \div_j B'); \{i, j\} \rhd k$$

the merge operator will compose in parallel the compensation task $i$ ($A'$) with compensation task $j$ ($B'$), and add parallel process $A' \parallel B'$ to compensation task $k$. Compensation tasks $i$ and $j$ will be removed.

Consider the following process that uses three individual compensation tasks:

$$(A \div_i A'); (B \div_j B'); (C \div_k C'); \{i, j\} \rhd k.$$

Initially it executes $A$, $B$ and $C$ and then merges compensation tasks $i$ and $j$ into compensation task $k$. Joining compensation tasks $i$ and $j$ results in the parallel process $A' \parallel B'$, that will be put in front of the compensation task $k$, giving $(A' \parallel B'); C'$ as the resulting compensation for task $k$.

The $new(i).P_i$ construct in $StAC_i$ creates a new compensation task identified by bound variable $i$. This can be used to model the compensation scope of StAC. For example, the StAC process

$$(A \div A'); [(B \div B'); \boxtimes; (C \div C')]$$

can be represented in $StAC_i$ as

$$(A \div_i A'); new(j).((B \div_j B'); \boxtimes_j; (C \div_j C'); \{j\} \rhd i)$$

When the reversal instruction is invoked on compensation task $j$ it will only execute $B'$. Compensation process $A'$ that in StAC was outside the scope, in $StAC_i$ is in a different compensation task, and does not get invoked. The merge is used to preserve any compensations not reversed within the scoping brackets.

## 3.2    Operational Semantics for Compensation

This section presents the operational semantics for the $StAC_i$ operators excluding termination operators. The semantics of termination is described in Section 3.3. Plotkin [18] describes how to use transition systems to define an operational semantics; here a system is defined in terms of transition rules between configurations. For the operational semantics of $StAC_i$, a configuration is a tuple:

$$(P, C, \sigma) \in Process \times (I \to Process) \times \Sigma$$

In the above tuple, $C$ is a function that returns the compensation process $C(i)$, for each compensation index $i$. If $C(i) = \perp$, then the compensation is not in use. $\Sigma$ represents the data state and $\Sigma$ is included in our model of StAC processes since we want to model the ability of a basic activity to change the data state. The labelled transition

$$(P,\ C,\ \sigma) \xrightarrow{A} (P',\ C,\ \sigma') \qquad\qquad (1)$$

denotes that the execution of a basic activity $A$ may cause a configuration transition from $(P,\ C,\ \sigma)$ to $(P',\ C,\ \sigma')$. Notice that the execution of a basic activity does not alter the compensation function. Instead, only the compensation operators may alter the compensation function.

In the configuration transition (1) we used an activity as the transition label, but two other labels may be used, they are $\tau$ and $\odot$. The set $\mathcal{B}$ of all possible transition labels is defined as:

$$\mathcal{B} = \mathcal{A} \cup \{\tau,\ \odot\}$$

where $\mathcal{A}$ represents the set of all activity labels. The label $\tau$ is a special label that represents an operation not visible to the external environment. In the transition rules we consider that label $B \in \mathcal{B}$, while $A \in \mathcal{A}$.

*Activity.* We assume that an activity is a relation from states to states, and write $\sigma \xrightarrow{A} \sigma'$ when $\sigma$ is related to $\sigma'$ by $\xrightarrow{A}$. The execution of an activity imposes a change in the state, leaving the compensation function unchanged:

$$\frac{\sigma \xrightarrow{A} \sigma'}{(A,\ C,\ \sigma) \xrightarrow{A} (skip,\ C,\ \sigma')}$$

*Conditional.* In the conditional process $b \ \& \ P$ the execution of $P$ is guarded by a boolean function $b$. If the boolean function $b$ is true in the current state $\sigma$, then $P$ may be executed:

$$\frac{(P,\ C,\ \sigma) \xrightarrow{B} (P',\ C',\ \sigma') \ \wedge \ b(\sigma) = true}{(b \ \& \ P,\ C,\ \sigma) \xrightarrow{B} (P',\ C',\ \sigma')}$$

Notice that when $B$ is an activity, the guard is evaluated in the state to which the activity $B$ is applied, ensuring that $b$ holds when the activity is executed. Since there is no transition rule dealing with a false guard, a false guard causes the process to block.

*Name Process Call.* The call of a process $N$ (where $N = P$ is an equation) will substitute $call(N)$ by the process on the left-side of the equation:

$$\frac{N = P}{(call(N),\ C,\ \sigma) \xrightarrow{\tau} (P,\ C,\ \sigma)}$$

*Hiding.* The rule on the left below says that the hiding operator makes the occurrence of an activity labelled from set $S$ invisible to the environment. The rule on the right states that the occurrence of an activity not labelled from $S$ is visible:

$$\frac{(P,\ C,\ \sigma) \xrightarrow{A} (P',\ C',\ \sigma') \wedge A \in S}{(P \setminus S,\ C,\ \sigma) \xrightarrow{\tau} (P' \setminus S,\ C',\ \sigma')} \qquad \frac{(P,\ C,\ \sigma) \xrightarrow{B} (P',\ C',\ \sigma') \wedge B \notin S}{(P \setminus S,\ C,\ \sigma) \xrightarrow{B} (P' \setminus S,\ C',\ \sigma')}$$

Hiding events in *skip* is the same as *skip*:

$$\frac{}{(skip \setminus S, C, \sigma) \xrightarrow{\tau} (skip, C, \sigma)}$$

*Sequence.* The next rule shows the execution of activities within the first process of a sequential composition:

$$\frac{(P, C, \sigma) \xrightarrow{B} (P', C', \sigma')}{(P; Q, C, \sigma) \xrightarrow{B} (P'; Q, C', \sigma')}$$

If the first process in the sequence has terminated successfully, then the second process can be executed immediately:

$$\frac{}{(skip; Q, C, \sigma) \xrightarrow{\tau} (Q, C, \sigma)}$$

*Parallel.* The rule below shows that the occurrence of activity $A \in X$ requires processes $P$ and $Q$ to synchronise in $P \parallel_X Q$:

$$\frac{A \in X \;\wedge\; (P, C, \sigma) \xrightarrow{A} (P', C, \sigma') \;\wedge\; (Q, C, \sigma) \xrightarrow{A} (Q', C, \sigma')}{(P \parallel_X Q, C, \sigma) \xrightarrow{A} (P' \parallel_X Q', C, \sigma')}$$

Notice that both processes refer to the same basic activity which updates the state from $\sigma$ to $\sigma'$. This is because the state is intended to be global and the parallel processes do not have their own local state.

The following two rules specify that parallel processes can evolve independently for $B \notin X$:

$$\frac{B \notin X \wedge (P, C, \sigma) \xrightarrow{B} (P', C', \sigma')}{(P \parallel_X Q, C, \sigma) \xrightarrow{B} (P' \parallel_X Q, C', \sigma')} \qquad \frac{B \notin X \wedge (P, C, \sigma) \xrightarrow{B} (P', C', \sigma')}{(Q \parallel_X P, C, \sigma) \xrightarrow{B} (Q \parallel_X P', C', \sigma')}$$

The rule below states that the parallel process $P \parallel_X Q$ terminates (i.e., reduces to *skip*) when both $P$ and $Q$ terminate:

$$\frac{}{(skip \parallel_X skip, C, \sigma) \xrightarrow{\tau} (skip, C, \sigma)}$$

*Internal Choice.* Internal choice decides nondeterministically which process $P$ or $Q$ will occur:

$$\frac{}{(P \sqcap Q, C, \sigma) \xrightarrow{\tau} (P, C, \sigma)} \qquad \frac{}{(P \sqcap Q, C, \sigma) \xrightarrow{\tau} (Q, C, \sigma)}$$

*External Choice.* The next two rules state that in $P \, [\!] \, Q$ only one of the processes $P$ or $Q$ is executed:

$$\frac{(P, C, \sigma) \xrightarrow{B} (P', C', \sigma') \wedge B \neq \tau}{(P \, [\!] \, Q, C, \sigma) \xrightarrow{B} (P', C', \sigma')} \qquad \frac{(P, C, \sigma) \xrightarrow{B} (P', C', \sigma') \wedge B \neq \tau}{(Q \, [\!] \, P, C, \sigma) \xrightarrow{B} (P', C', \sigma')}$$

The following rules state that the occurrence of internal actions will not resolve the choice between $P$ and $Q$:

$$\frac{(P,\, C,\, \sigma) \xrightarrow{\tau} (P',\, C',\, \sigma')}{(P \,[\!]\, Q,\, C,\, \sigma) \xrightarrow{\tau} (P' \,[\!]\, Q,\, C',\, \sigma')} \qquad \frac{(Q,\, C,\, \sigma) \xrightarrow{\tau} (Q',\, C',\, \sigma')}{(P \,[\!]\, Q,\, C,\, \sigma) \xrightarrow{\tau} (P \,[\!]\, Q',\, C',\, \sigma')}$$

*Create Compensation Task.* The rule for the *new* construct selects an index for a compensation task that is not in use and sets that task to *skip*:

$$\frac{C(k) = \perp}{(new(i).P_i,\, C,\, \sigma) \xrightarrow{\tau} (P_k,\, C[k := skip],\, \sigma)}$$

$C[k := skip]$ denotes that compensation task $k$ is set to *skip*.

*Push.* The rule for the *push* operator adds the compensation process $Q$ to the compensation function $C$:

$$\frac{}{(\uparrow_i Q,\, C,\, \sigma) \xrightarrow{\tau} (skip,\, C[i := (Q; C(i))],\, \sigma)}$$

$C[i := Q; C(i)]$ denotes that compensation task $i$ is set to $Q$ in sequence with the previous compensation for task $i$. In this manner, the compensation process is built in the reverse order of the execution of the primary processes.

*Reverse.* In the next rule, the operator $\boxtimes_i$ causes the compensation task $i$ to be executed, and also resets that compensation task to *skip*:

$$\frac{}{(\boxtimes_i,\, C,\, \sigma) \xrightarrow{\tau} (C(i),\, C[i := skip],\, \sigma)}$$

Note that compensation tasks do not store any state with them: if the state changes between the compensation being stored and executed, the current state is used.

*Accept.* The operator $\boxdot_i$ clears the compensation task $i$ to *skip* without executing it:

$$\frac{}{(\boxdot_i,\, C,\, \sigma) \xrightarrow{\tau} (skip,\, C[i := skip],\, \sigma)}$$

*Merge.* The operator $J \rhd i$ merges all compensation tasks of set $J$ in parallel on to the front of compensation task $i$:

$$\frac{}{(J \rhd i,\, C,\, \sigma) \xrightarrow{\tau} (skip,\, C[\, i := (\|_{j \in J} . C(j)); C(i),\quad J := \perp\, ],\, \sigma)}$$

In the above rule the expression $J := \perp$ denotes attributing to all tasks of set $J$ the value $\perp$ meaning these tasks are no longer in use. Set $J$ must be disjoint from $i$.

## 3.3    Operational Semantics for Termination

This section concludes the presentation of $StAC_i$ semantics by defining the operational rules related to early termination.

*Protected Block.* This rule states that the occurrence of a basic activity within a protected process $P$ will place the label *true* on the protection block. It is not necessary to distinguish whether the value $v$ is initially *true* or *false*, in both cases the final label will be *true*:

$$\frac{(P,\, C,\, \sigma) \xrightarrow{B} (P',\, C',\, \sigma') \ \wedge\ B \neq \tau \ \wedge\ v \in BOOL}{(\, |P|_v\,,\, C,\, \sigma\,) \xrightarrow{B} (\, |P'|_{true}\,,\, C',\, \sigma'\,)}$$

Note that occurrence of a $\tau$ is not regarded as commencing a protection block so the above rule does not apply to $\tau$. The following rule deals with $\tau$:

$$\frac{(P,\, C,\, \sigma) \xrightarrow{\tau} (P',\, C',\, \sigma') \ \wedge\ v \in BOOL}{(\, |P|_v\,,\, C,\, \sigma\,) \xrightarrow{\tau} (\, |P'|_v\,,\, C',\, \sigma'\,)}$$

A terminated protection block becomes *skip*:

$$\frac{}{(\, |skip|_v\,,\, C,\, \sigma\,) \xrightarrow{\tau} (\, skip,\, C,\, \sigma\,)}$$

*Early Termination.* Invocation of the early termination operation causes a process to execute a visible $\odot$-event and then become the *early* process:

$$\frac{}{(\odot,\, C,\, \sigma) \xrightarrow{\odot} early,\, C,\, \sigma)}$$

Later, when the rules for the attempt block are presented, it will be seen that this early termination event will cause the enclosing attempt block to commence early termination and that the event will be contained within the enclosing attempt block and will not be visible outside it.

In a sequential process if the first process has terminated early, the overall sequential process is interrupted and terminates early:

$$\frac{}{(early;\, P,\, C,\, \sigma) \xrightarrow{\tau} (terminate(P);\, early,\, C,\, \sigma)}$$

The *terminate* function terminates all constituents of $P$ except for compensation merge operations and protected blocks that have commenced execution. The *early* process is added to ensure that the indication of early termination is maintained. Allowing the merge to be executed is important because merging of compensations will typically be required before exiting an attempt block. The *terminate* function is defined later in this section.

A consequence of the previous rule is that if in a compensation pair the primary process terminates early, the overall process terminates early and the compensation process $Q$ will not be installed.

Hiding or protection of an early terminated process gives an early terminated process:

$$\frac{}{(early \setminus S, C, \sigma) \xrightarrow{\tau} (early, C, \sigma)} \quad \frac{}{(|early|_v, C, \sigma) \xrightarrow{\tau} (early, C, \sigma)}$$

In a parallel process if both have terminated early, or one has terminated early and the other has terminated early, the overall process will terminate early:

$$\frac{}{(early \underset{X}{\|} early, C, \sigma) \xrightarrow{\tau} (early, C, \sigma)}$$

$$\frac{}{(early \underset{X}{\|} skip, C, \sigma) \xrightarrow{\tau} (early, C, \sigma)} \quad \frac{}{(skip \underset{X}{\|} early, C, \sigma) \xrightarrow{\tau} (early, C, \sigma)}$$

*Attempt Block.* If the main body of an attempt block can engage in an early termination event, then its termination flag is set to *true* and the early termination event is made invisible:

$$\frac{(Q, C, \sigma) \xrightarrow{\odot} (Q', C, \sigma)}{(P\{Q\}_v R, C, \sigma) \xrightarrow{\tau} (P\{Q'\}_{true} R, C, \sigma)}$$

When the main body of an attempt block terminates successfully, the left hand continuation process will be executed:

$$\frac{}{(P\{skip\}_v R, C, \sigma) \xrightarrow{\tau} (P, C, \sigma)}$$

(The flag $v$ will always be *false* whenever an attempt block body evolves to *skip*.)

When the main body of an attempt block terminates prematurely, the right hand continuation process will be executed:

$$\frac{}{(P\{early\}_v R, C, \sigma) \xrightarrow{\tau} (R, C, \sigma)}$$

An attempt block may also evolve by executing events of the main body other than $\odot$, regardless of the value of the flag $v$:

$$\frac{(Q, C, \sigma) \xrightarrow{B} (Q', C', \sigma') \ \wedge \ B \neq \odot}{(P\{Q\}_v R, C, \sigma) \xrightarrow{B} (P\{Q'\}_v R, C', \sigma')}$$

When the termination flag has been set to *true*, the main body of an attempt block may terminate early. However, all protected blocks that have started their execution are made to complete their execution. This is provided for in as follows:

$$\frac{}{(P\{Q\}_{true} R, C, \sigma) \xrightarrow{\tau} (P\{terminate(Q)\}_{false} R, C, \sigma)}$$

Note that setting the termination flag back to *false* in this rule prevents *terminate* being applied infinitely which would otherwise cause an infinite cycle of $\tau$ events.

*Function terminate.* The *terminate* function clears all processes that no longer should continue and keeps the protected blocks that have already started. The first three definitions below show processes that may continue running, as they may contain protected blocks. The fourth rule says that a merge of compensation tasks is allowed to execute. The fifth rule shows that early termination is propagated by *terminate*:

$$
\begin{aligned}
terminate(P; Q) &= terminate(P); terminate(Q) \\
terminate(P \parallel_X Q) &= terminate(P) \parallel_X terminate(Q) \\
terminate(P\{Q\}_vR) &= \{terminate(Q)\}_v \\
terminate(J \rhd i) &= J \rhd i \\
terminate(early) &= early
\end{aligned}
$$

The next rule shows that a protected block that has not started its execution (its flag is *false*) is terminated immediately. The rule following that states that a protected block that has started its execution (its flag is *true*) can continue until it has finished:

$$
\begin{aligned}
terminate(|P|_{false}) &= skip \\
terminate(|P|_{true}) &= |P|_{true}
\end{aligned}
$$

The final rule applies to any process not matching the previous rules for *terminate*. Such processes are made to finish immediately:

$$
terminate(P) = skip
$$

It is easy to show that *terminate* is idempotent.

## 3.4    Translation from StAC to StAC$_i$

We define a semantics for the StAC language by defining a translation of StAC processes into StAC$_i$ processes. This way the interpretation of a StAC process is given in terms of a StAC$_i$ process.

For each process definition of the form $N = P$, we construct an indexed process definition:

$$
N_i = \mathbb{T}(P, i)
$$

where $\mathbb{T}$ translates a process written in the syntax of StAC to a process in the syntax of StAC$_i$ in the context of compensation index $i$. The translation function $\mathbb{T}$ is shown in Table 3. For the translation to work correctly, the root StAC process definition should be of the form $N = [P]$, ensuring that the outermost compensation task is properly created.

The first three rules of the translation function $\mathbb{T}$ show that basic activities, *skip* and $\odot$ have the same representation in StAC and StAC$_i$. The next rule shows that a call to process named $N$ in the context of index $i$ becomes a call to process $N_i$.

**Table 3.** Translation Rules

$$
\begin{aligned}
\mathbb{T}(A, i) &= A & \mathbb{T}(P \div Q, i) &= |\mathbb{T}(P, i) \div_i \mathbb{T}(Q, i)|_{false} \\
\mathbb{T}(skip, i) &= skip & \mathbb{T}(b \,\&\, P, i) &= b \,\&\, \mathbb{T}(P, i) \\
\mathbb{T}(\odot, i) &= \odot & \mathbb{T}(P \setminus S, i) &= \mathbb{T}(P, i) \setminus S \\
\mathbb{T}(call(N), i) &= call(N_i) & \mathbb{T}(P; Q, i) &= \mathbb{T}(P, i)\,;\,\mathbb{T}(Q, i) \\
\mathbb{T}(\boxtimes, i) &= \boxtimes_i & \mathbb{T}(P \,[\!]\, Q, i) &= \mathbb{T}(P, i) \,[\!]\, \mathbb{T}(Q, i) \\
\mathbb{T}(\boxdot, i) &= \boxdot_i & \mathbb{T}(P \sqcap Q, i) &= \mathbb{T}(P, i) \sqcap \mathbb{T}(Q, i)
\end{aligned}
$$

$$
\begin{aligned}
\mathbb{T}(P\{Q\}R, i) &= \mathbb{T}(P, i)\{\mathbb{T}(Q, i)\}\mathbb{T}(R, i) \\
\mathbb{T}([P], i) &= new(j).(\ \mathbb{T}(P, j); \{j\} \rhd i\ ) \\
\mathbb{T}(P \parallel_X Q, i) &= new(j, k).(\ (\mathbb{T}(P, j) \parallel_X \mathbb{T}(Q, k)); \{j, k\} \rhd i\ )
\end{aligned}
$$

The $\text{StAC}_i$ representation for the compensation operators accept, reverse, and compensation pair, is obtained by adding a compensation task index to each of them.

The remaining rules (except the last two), show how to translate composite constructs. The translation rules are defined on the constituents of the constructor.

Because the order of execution of $P \parallel_X Q$ is not known, their compensation should not have a predefined order of execution. So each parallel process will have a new compensation task. This way their compensation processes will also be a parallel process: the parallel composition of the new compensation tasks. In the translation rule for $P \parallel Q$, two new compensations tasks $j$ and $k$ are created and processes $P$ and $Q$ are translated using $j$ and $k$. The resulting processes will be composed in parallel. Lastly, the new compensation tasks $j$ and $k$ are merged into the initial task $i$, which means that the compensations of the parallel processes are retained (unless they have been explicitly committed). Notice that compensation tasks are merged in parallel, so the outcome of the merge is process $C(j) \parallel C(k)$, that will be pushed on top of $C(i)$.

The compensation scoping brackets $[P]$ are translated to a new compensation task $j$ and process $P$ is translated using index $j$. Then the compensation task $j$ is merged into the initial index $i$, so all the compensation information that was not reversed or accepted can be preserved by adding it to compensation task $i$.

## 4    Conclusions

The semantic definition of StAC is somewhat complicated, in particular the use of indexed compensation tasks. An alternative approach would be to embed the installed compensations within the process terms, for example, by representing a scope in the form $[P, Q]$ where $P$ is the remaining process to be executed within the scope and $Q$ represents the compensation installed so far for this scope. However the interaction between early termination and compensation means that installed compensations must be preserved whenever a scope terminates early. Because scopes can be nested, this requires that the installed compensations for the nested scopes need to be accumulated before a process terminates. We found it easier to describe this by separating the installed compensations from the process terms which in turn required the use of indexed compensation.

In [5] we have used indexed compensation to explore generalisations of the modelling language in which processes may have multiple compensation 'threads'. It is not clear how useful this is in its full generality, but two idioms do appear to be useful: selective compensation, where some activities are compensated and others are not (yet) compensated, and alternative compensation, where activities can have several alternative compensations and the compensation to be selected may depend on the nature of the exception.

The use of indexed compensation should also make it possible to model the style of compensation used in BPEL4WS [7]. BPEL4WS supports similar operators to StAC, such as compensation, concurrency, and sequencing. In BPEL4WS, reversal is invoked through exception handlers, while acceptance is implicit in scoping. Reversal (called *compensate* in BPEL4WS) can identify particular subprocesses which should be compensated and this can be modelled using indexed compensation. BPEL4WS is layered on top of XML (its processes and data are specified in the BPEL dialect of XML), and at the moment BPEL4WS does not have a formal semantics. We plan to investigate further the use of StAC to give a semantics to BPEL4WS.

In [14], a compensation is formalised in terms of the properties it has to guarantee. However, [14] does not provide a modelling language as StAC does, rather it provides a characterisation of properties of compensation. Bocchi et al [2] define a language $\pi t$-calculus for modelling long-running transactions based on Milner's $\pi$-calculus [17]. The $\pi t$-calculus includes a transaction construct that contains a compensation handler and a fault manager. ConTracts [20] attempt to provide a structured approach to compensation. In ConTracts the invocation of a particular compensation has to be made explicitly within a conditional instruction (if the outcome of a step is false, then a specific task is executed to compensate for this). ConTracts do not have the notion of installing a compensation handler nor acceptance nor reversal found in StAC.

# References

[1] J. R. Abrial. *The B-Book: Assigning Programs to Meanings*. Cambridge University Press, 1996. 88

[2] L. Bocchi, C. Laneve, and G. Zavattaro. A calulus for long-running transactions. In *FMOODS'03*, volume LNCS, to appear. Springer-Verlag, 2003. 103

[3] M. Butler and C. Ferreira. A process compensation language. In *Integrated Formal Methods(IFM'2000)*, volume 1945 of *LNCS*, pages 61 – 76. Springer-Verlag, 2000. 87, 88

[4] M. Chessell, D. Vines, and C. Griffin. An introduction to compensation with business process beans. Technical report, Transaction Processing Design and New Technology Development Group, IBM UK Laboratories, August 2001. 92

[5] M. Chessell, D. Vines, C. Griffin, M. Butler, C. Ferreira, and P. Henderson. Extending the concept of transaction compensation. *IBM Systems Journal*, 41(4):743–758, 2002. 92, 103

[6]  M. Chessell, D. Vines, C. Griffin, V. Green, and K. Warr. Business process beans: System design and architecture document. Technical report, Transaction Processing Design and New Technology Development Group, IBM UK Laboratories, January 2001. 88

[7]  F. Curbera, Y. Goland, J. Klein, F. Leymann, D. Roller, S. Thatte, and S. Weerawarana. Business process execution language for web services, version 1.1. http://www-106.ibm.com/developerworks/library/ws-bpel/, 2003. 88, 103

[8]  E. Dijkstra. *A Discipline of Programming.* Prentice-Hall, 1976. 88

[9]  C. Ferreira. *Precise Modelling of Business Processes with Compensation.* PhD thesis, University of Southampton, 2002. 88, 89

[10]  C. Ferreira and M. Butler. Using B Refinement to Analyse Compensating Business Processes. In *Third International ZB Conference (ZB'2003)*, volume 2651 of *LNCS*. Springer-Verlag, 2003. 88

[11]  J. Gray and A. Reuter. *Transaction Processing: Concepts and Techniques.* Morgan Kaufmann Publishers, 1993. 87

[12]  C. A.R Hoare. *Communicating Sequential Processes.* Prentice-Hall, 1985. 88

[13]  C. Jones. *Systematic Software Development Using VDM.* Prentice-Hall, 1986. 88

[14]  H. Korth, E. Levy, and A. Silberschatz. A formal approach to recovery by compensating transactions. In *16th VLDB Conference*, Brisbane, Australia, 1990. 103

[15]  B. Metha, M. Levy, G. Meredith, T. Andrews, B. Beckman, J. Klein, and A. Mital. BizTalk Server 2000 Business Process Orchestration. *IEEE Data Engineering Bulletin*, 24(1):35–39, 2001. 88

[16]  R. Milner. *Communication and Concurrency.* Prentice-Hall, 1989. 88

[17]  R. Milner, J. Parrow, and D. Walker. A calculus of mobile processes, I and II. *Inform. and Comput.*, 100(1):1–40,41–77, 1992. 103

[18]  G. Plotkin. A structural approach to operational semantics. Technical Report DAIMI FN-19, Aarhus University, Computer Science Department, September 1981. 95

[19]  J. Spivey. *The Z Notation.* Prentice Hall, New York, 1989. 88

[20]  H. Wachter and A. Reuter. The ConTract model. In A. Elmagarmid, editor, *Database Transaction Models for Advanced Applications*. Morgan Kaufmann Publishers, 1992. 103

# From Endogenous to Exogenous Coordination Using Aspect-Oriented Programming

Sirio Capizzi, Riccardo Solmi, and Gianluigi Zavattaro

Dipartimento di Scienze dell'Informazione,Università di Bologna,
Mura A.Zamboni 7, I-40127 Bologna, Italy
{capizzi,solmi,zavattar}@cs.unibo.it

**Abstract.** One of the main goals of coordination models and languages is to support a clear and distinct separation between computation and coordination in applications based on cooperating components. Nevertheless, this separation is not always reflected at the level of the source code. This is the case for the so-called *endogenous* coordination models and languages (see e.g. Linda) that provide coordination primitives that must be incorporated within a computational language. In this way, there is no piece of source code identifiable as the coordination module, thus losing the advantages of a distinct design and development.

In this paper, we investigate aspect-oriented programming as a technology for supporting the modularization of the coordination part even if an endogenous coordination model is considered. More precisely, we propose to encapsulate the coordination actions inside *aspects* while describing the single points of the computational part in which coordination comes into play as *join points*. Following this approach, we show that we can rewrite a distributed application, moving from an underlying endogenous data-driven to an endogenous event-driven coordination model, simply by replacing the coordination aspects and leaving the computational code unchanged.

## 1 Introduction

Coordination languages are a class of programming notations which offer a solution to the problem of specifying and managing the interactions among computing entities. In fact, they generally offer language mechanisms for composing, configuring, and controlling systems made of independent, even distributed, active components.

Gelernter and Carriero introduced a programming-specific meaning of the term *Coordination* presenting the following equation [7]:

$$\text{Programming} = \text{Computation} + \text{Coordination}$$

They formulated this equation arguing that there should be a clear separation between the specification of the components of the computation and the specification of their interactions or dependencies. On the one hand, this separation facilitates the reuse of components; on the other hand, the same patterns

R. de Nicola et al. (Eds.): COORDINATION 2004, LNCS 2949, pp. 105–118, 2004.
© Springer-Verlag Berlin Heidelberg 2004

of interaction usually occur in many different problems – so it might be possible to reuse the coordination specification as well.

Nevertheless, this separation is not always supported at the level of the source code as pointed out by the Arbab's classification of coordination models and languages as either *endogenous* or *exogenous* [1]:

> Endogenous models and languages provide primitives that must be incorporated *within* a computation for its coordination. In applications that use such models, primitives that affect the coordination of each module are inside the module itself. In contrast, exogenous models and languages provide primitives that support the coordination of entities from *without*. In applications that use exogenous models, primitives that affect the coordination of each module are outside the module itself.

Endogenous models lead to intermixing of coordination primitives with computation code. This entangles the semantics of computation with coordination, thus making the coordination part inside the application implicit and sometimes nebulous. However, endogenous coordination models are quite natural for a huge variety of applications. Consider, for example, the success and popularity of the Linda tuple-space coordination model [6]. The naturality and flexibility of this coordination model is demonstrated by the fact that, even if it has been designed more than twenty years ago for programming parallel computers, it is still considered a referring model in the rather different context of distributed programming (see e.g. the Sun Microsystem's JavaSpaces [13] or the IBM's T-Spaces [12]).

In this paper we investigate the problem of combining the advantages deriving from both the modularization of exogenous models, and the naturality and understandability of endogenous languages. To meet our goal, we start from the observation that coordination can be seen as a *cross-cutting* concern when an endogenous language is considered. By cross-cutting concern we mean behaviour that span multiple, often unrelated, implementation modules that cannot be neatly separated from each other. In general, cross-cutting concerns are poorly localized in the code thus making the code harder to reuse and limiting the evolution of the application. Several techniques such as design patterns [5] and mixin classes [4] have been recently developed for dealing with the problem of modularization of cross-cutting concerns. One of the most advanced and sophisticated techniques is Aspect-Oriented Programming (AOP) [8], a programming paradigm that intends to do for cross-cutting concerns what Object-Oriented Programming has done for object encapsulation and inheritance.

The main concepts at the basis of Aspect-Oriented Programming are:

**Join points:** the points inside the code in which the cross-cutting concerns come into play,
**Advice:** the behaviour to be associated to the join points,
**Weaver:** the responsible for hooking, in the corresponding join points, the advice in the code.

By *aspect* we mean a group of join points equipped with the corresponding advice. For a more detailed description of AOP, and the technologies available for supporting this paradigm, see Section 2.

Following the AOP paradigm we can solve the problem of modularizing the coordination part of applications based on an endogenous coordination model. This can be simply achieved by encapsulating the coordination code inside advices, and indicating as the corresponding join points the part of the computational code where the coordination aspects should come into play.

More radically, our thesis is that the application developer can separate since the design phase the computational from the coordination concerns. For example, let us consider a *chat* system based on agents willing to perform two possible operations: the first one used to produce a new message and the second one used to download the new messages produced by the other agents. The computational behaviour of an agent can be written abstracting away from the actual implementation of the two operations. Subsequently, an aspect can be defined that captures as join points those points inside the computational code where the two operations are executed. After, the implementation of the two operations can be written (exploiting any possibly available coordination infrastructure) and encapsulated inside two advices. For example, in the case a tuple space is used, the first operation could simply produce a tuple, while the second operation retrieves the tuples containing the required messages. On the other hand, if an event based system is taken into account, the first operation could raise an event (that is caught and stored locally by each agent), while the second operation returns the locally stored messages. Once the single agents and the aspects have been programmed, the whole application is obtained simply weaving the aspects together with the computational code.

To support our thesis, we consider a less trivial case study: the implementation of a (distributed) spreadsheet. A spreadsheet is composed of cells, each of which has a unique identifier; each cell contains a numeric value or a numeric expression, and the expression may contain references to other cells; when the content of a cell is modified, all the other cells containing an expression depending on that cell should be updated.

In Section 3 we discuss the design and development of the spreadsheet according to our proposed approach. More precisely, we describe the structure of the computational code and of three different aspects used to describe the way a cell retrieves the content of the other cells on which it depends, and how a cell modification is notified to the dependent cells. The three aspects consider three different scenarios: a local implementation (all the cells executes on the same machine and they can directly invoke one each other), a distributed implementation based on a shared tuple space (namely, IBM T-Spaces [12]), and a distributed implementation based on an event based infrastructure (namely, Java Message Service(JMS) [14]).

## 2   Aspect-Oriented Programming

Aspect Oriented Programming (AOP for short) is a meta programming notation that permits to manipulate programs; as any other meta programming technique, it needs abstractions to manipulate a program at a meta level. AOP is neither a complete programming model, nor a full meta programming system; it is a language extension pluggable on top of every existing *host* language. The most important abstractions considered in AOP are the *join points* and the *advices*. As briefly described in the Introduction, the join points are the points of the program which are affected by the manipulation, while the advices are the actions to be taken when the join points are reached during the program execution; in AOP terminology, we say that an aspect is *woven* at a join point.

More precisely, *join points* are well-defined points in the program flow; they are instances of program locations that have a meaning in the domain of the programming language. The *pointcut* is the language construct introduced in AOP to pick out certain join points. An *aspect* is a collection of pointcuts, advices and introductions. The *advices* are language constructs used to implement crosscutting behavior. An advice is code executed when a pointcut is reached. Beyond advices, also *introductions* are usually supported by the AOP systems: introductions are similar to mixin classes [4] and give the possibility to add interfaces and implementations to existing classes.

The AOP systems, see e.g. AspectJ [8], Prose [10], and JAC [9], mainly differ in the join point model and in the weaving time.

The joint point model is tied to the features of the host programming language; for an object oriented host language it may support advising of static and member fields, static and member methods, method calls. It may also support advising of exceptions, caller side pointcuts, and constraining the weaving to a given control flow.

In general, we distinguish between *static* and *dynamic* pointcuts. Static pointcuts capture the static structure of a program such as class members and relationship between classes. Dynamic poincuts, on the other hand, capture operations taken at run-time such as method invocation depending on the actual control flow. A poincut can also expose its context at the matched join points and the woven aspects can use that context to implement the crosscutting behaviour.

Aspect Oriented features can be added or by extending the syntax of a core language, or by introducing both a library (API) and a runtime code weaver; in the first case we have *static* (compile time) weaving, in the second we have *dynamic* (runtime) weaving. Both choices have their strengths and weaknesses, neither one alone can satisfy all needs.

For our case study, we have chosen the AspectJ aspect-oriented extension to the Java language; but before presenting it, let us give you a few examples written in AspectJ.

Let us consider the two following pointcuts:

```
pointcut updatingOperation(Container c):
  call(void Container.setValue(Object)) && target(c);
```

```
pointcut internalUpdatingOperations(Container c):
  updatingOperation(c) && within(mypackage.*);
```

The former picks out all calls (i.e. each join point that is a call) to the method of the class `Container` that has the signature `void setValue(object)` and exposes the object target of the call with the identifier `c`. The latter pointcut example extends the former capturing only the calls within the `mypackage` Java package modules.

In the example below, we capture all calls to the method `remove` (with the given signature) executed inside the control flow of a call to the method `retainAll` of a `Collection` class.

```
pointcut removedElements():
  call(boolean Collection.remove(Object o))
  && cflow(call(boolean Collection.retainAll(Collection c)));
```

Pointcuts capture a set of join points and permit to identify them introducing a name that reflects the intent of the programmer to denote the place in the program flow where a crosscutting behaviour occurs. Pointcuts alone do not do anything, but they introduce a vocabulary of pointcut names in the domain of the program allowing the programmer to write a separate code. The *advice* is the language construct used in AOP to implement crosscutting behavior. For example, the advice:

```
after (Container c) : updatingOperation(c) {
  // ... advice code body written in Java
}
```

executes the `advice body` method whenever a value has changed (after each join point captured by the pointcut `updatingOperation`). Note that the `advice body` code may operate on the object that has changed.

Often, in addition to affecting dynamic behavior using advice, it is necessary for aspects to affect the static structure in a crosscutting manner. AspectJ provides a mechanism called *introduction* to introduce such members into the specified classes and interfaces. For example, the introductions:

```
private List Container.listeners;
```

```
public Iterator Container.listenersIterator() {
  return listeners.iterator();
}
```

introduce in the class `Container` both a data member `listeners` and a method `listenersIterator`.

The language construct *aspect* in AspectJ is a simple container that wrap up pointcuts, advices, and introductions in a modular unit of crosscutting implementation. For example, the aspect:

```
public abstract aspect DataBaseAccessLogger {
  abstract pointcut dbAccessPoint();

before(): dbAccessPoint { /* log begin of a~DB operation */ }
after(): dbAccessPoint { /* log end of a~DB operation */ }
}
```

defines an aspect containing a pointcut declaration and two advices; the pointcut is abstract and should be defined in a concrete aspect that inherits from `DataBaseAccessLogger`.

## 3    A Case Study: A (Distributed) Spreadsheet

As a case study showing the benefits of the AOP paradigm applied to the development of an application based on a coordination infrastructure, we consider a spreadsheet, i.e. a set of cells containing either values or expressions that could contain references to the content of other cells. We will show that all the code regarding the coordination concerns is encapsulated in a *coordination aspect*; in this way a better separation of concerns is achieved. The main advantage is that the coordination part of the application become clear and visible and the application itself is more reusable and it is not bound to a specific underlying coordination infrastructure. Developers are able to adapt it to a new environment simply reimplementing the aspect and thus avoiding the tedious work that is normally done, especially when the changes are spread across the code.

In order to show that AOP effectively supports the possibility to move from one coordination infrastructure to another one, we present three different versions of the coordination aspect: the first one assumes that the cells can directly invoke one each other and simply implements a form of coordination based on the *Observer* pattern [5], the second one implements the interaction among the cells exploiting a data-driven coordination infrastructure (namely, T-Spaces [12]), on the contrary the third one is based on an event-based coordination system (namely, Java Message Service (JMS) [14]). The last two aspects supports a distributed version of the spreadsheet, in the sense that the cells may be located at different sites.

Three different versions of the applications are achieved automatically simply weaving one of the coordination aspects with the computational code, which is exactly the same one for all the versions of the applications. This distinct separation between the computational and the coordination concerns, and the possibility to combine them automatically, represents the main novelty of the AOP approach; indeed, in this way several changes on the code can be done in a limited time and with effectiveness.

The structure of our application is shown in Figure 1. It is composed of two structurally separated parts:

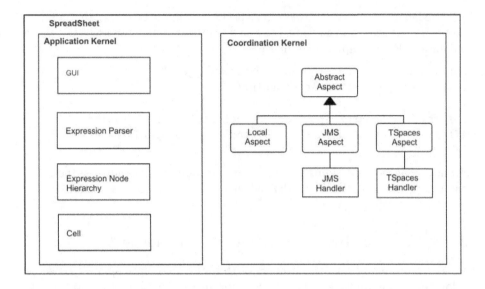

**Fig. 1.** The structure of the spreadsheet application

- The *application* kernel which contains the GUI, the expression parser and some other classes needed by the cells.
- The *coordination* kernel, which is encapsulated in the aspect, and some other classes that provide the support for operating on the underlying coordination infrastructure.

The application kernel is a Java application that introduces the class `Cell` describing the behaviour of the cells. It essentially provides methods that permits to display the value associated to a cell or to handle the content of the cell represented in terms of an expression tree. We have developed the application kernel without assuming any specific mechanism for managing the interaction among the cells; we simply introduce in the `Cell` class the methods `setValue` and `evaluate` that respectively change the contents of the cell and evaluate the expression tree associated with the cell.

The coordination kernel is instead composed of a hierarchy of aspects written using AspectJ [15]. The hierarchy is itself an example of separation of concerns and abstraction. In fact, the join points at which the coordination part should come into play are constant and fixed unless the application kernel changes, therefore we have decided to create an abstract aspect that captures exactly those join points. The abstract aspect, moreover, associates abstract operations to the indicated join points. These abstract operations are then implemented by concrete aspects that provide the specific behaviour needed by the actually exploited coordination infrastructure.

The coordination part of the application is responsible for managing the dependencies among the cells; we say that a cell depends on another one if the expression inside the first cell contains a reference to the second one. Besides providing a common interface to the join points and the corresponding abstract behaviour, the abstract aspect introduces inside the `Cell` class two data structures: the listeners and the dependency lists. The listeners of a cell `c` are the cells that depend on `c`, while the dependency list of `c` is composed of the cells on which `c` depends. We have encapsulated the declaration of these two data structures inside the coordination part of the application because we do not consider them part of the computational logic. Indeed, alternative mechanisms could be exploited in order to manage the interdependencies among the cells such as, e.g., storing locally the current content of all the cells instead of maintaining track of the cell dependencies only.

The two data structures can be managed following a well-known design pattern [5], namely the *Observer* pattern. This pattern assumes the existence of one `subject` object and a group of `observer` objects. The `subject` provides three methods: the first one is invoked from an object in order to register itself as an `observer`, the second one is invoked by a registered `observer` for deregistration, while the third one is responsible for notifying a state change to the whole set of registered `observers`. More precisely, when the `subject` object changes its content, all the registered `observers` will be notified via the invocation of a specific method provided by the `observer` themselves.

The points where the register, deregister, and notify operations of the Observer pattern should be invoked are captured from join points. The notification must be executed after every change of the value inside a cell; this can be achieved from the lines of code reported below:[1]

```
pointcut changingValue(Cell c):
  call(void Cell.setValue(Object)) && target(c);

after (Cell c) : changingValue(c) {
  notifyListener(c);
}
```

The registration operations are executed during the evaluation of the expression tree, each time a node is encountered which contains a reference to a cell. The definition of this point cut is clearly more complex with respect to the previous one: in fact, it is necessary to take under consideration all the eval operations performed on each of the nodes of the expression tree. In this case, the lines of code are as follows:

```
pointcut retrievingValue(Cell dest, CellIDNode source):
  call(Object ExpNode.eval()) && target(source)
  && cflow( call(Object Cell.evaluate(ExpNode)) && target(dest));

Object around (CellIDNode n, Cell c) : retrievingValue(c,n) {
  return retrieveValue(n.id,c);
}
```

---

[1] The code is taken from the abstract aspect that we have entirely reported in the Appendix A.

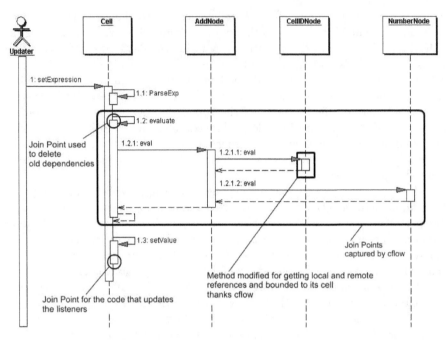

**Fig. 2.** An example of expression update with the join points captured by the aspects

The pointcut `retrievingValue` captures all calls to the method `eval` (used to evaluate an intermediary node of an expression tree) executed inside the control flow (i.e. in the execution stack) of a call to the method `evaluate` of the `Cell` class. The registration operation is intended to be part of the `retrieveValue` method. Finally, the deregistration occurs at the beginning of the parse of a new expression tree with the result that all previous registrations (related to the previous expression tree) are cancelled:

```
pointcut expressionParse(Cell c):
   call(ExpNode ExpParser.parse(String)) && this(c);

before (Cell c) : expressionParse(c)  {
   removeDependences(c);
}
```

In the figure 2 we report a graphical representations of the join point described above.

Besides the join points related to the Observer pattern, other points must be taken into account (see Appendix A) in order to capture, e.g., the activation of the application because we need to initialise the data structures for the coordination kernel.

We have implemented the abstract aspects in three different ways based on three different coordination infrastructures. The main difference among the three aspects is related to the way the value inside a cell is retrieved, and the way the notification required from the Observer pattern is realized. In the first concrete aspect we assume that the cells are all local and can directly invoke one each other: thus these operation are simply mapped on direct method invocations. In the other two concrete aspects a cell may be either local or remote. In the case the cell is remote, a specialized handler is needed.

In the implementation based on T-Spaces the content of the cell is retrieved by the handler accessing the shared tuple space, where the contents of the cells are stored. The notification mechanism, on the other hand, is realized exploiting the event system of T-Spaces. This system allows an object to register for some event in the tuple space like writing or deleting of a tuple. In this way, the handler behaves like a tuple space observer, and receives notification about updates.

In the implementation that uses Java Message Service the notification mechanism is realized exploiting the publish/subscribe system supported by JMS: each update is forwarded as a message to a predefined `Topic`, created by the J2EE server, and at which the handlers are subscribed. Through the filters specified by each handler at subscribing time, the message is delivered only to the interested ones. Another server object, in this case a `Queue`, is used as a peer-to-peer communication the first time a reference value is needed.

## 4   Conclusion

In this paper we have discussed the exploitation of the Aspect Oriented Programming paradigm as a technology for supporting a clear separation between the computational and the coordination concerns. This separation has been always considered the main goal of coordination models and languages, while at the level of code this separation is not always supported. In order to prove the effectiveness of AOP in the context of coordination models and languages, we have considered as a case study the implementation of a (distributed) spreadsheet.

The development process of our application has been quite different from a traditional one. In fact, the expressive power of the AOP paradigm has allowed us to develop the application kernel and the coordination kernel in two different and independent phases.

In the first phase we have implemented the application kernel; in the second phase we have developed the coordination kernel (which is a separate module) in terms of aspects containing the pointcut (the description of the points inside the application kernel where the coordination operation should be hooked) and the corresponding advices (the code to be attached in the join points).

A first advantage of an independent and separate development of the two kernels is concerned with the the application debug. After a good debug of the application kernel, the developer can focus his attention only on the bugs inserted by the coordination aspects that are well localized in the code.

The application that we have developed shows that the use of a new emerging technology such as the AOP would be very useful in the coordination field. In fact the use of aspects has enriched our spreadsheet with the following major characteristics:

- The coordination code is well encapsulated and not mixed with the other code.
- Thanks to the aspects the application is independent from both the coordination technology used and the model on which it is based.
- The AOP permits fast code refactoring and offers a quite simple way to expand the application with features that were not expected at design-time.
- The application and the coordination kernels are more reusable. In fact the second can survive to several application changes thanks to some powerful AOP constructs like wildcards for capturing classes or subclasses not yet present in the source code.

Manifold [2] is considered the most prominent representative of the family of exogenous coordination languages, i.e., languages supporting separation between the computation and the coordination code. Another example of exogenous approach is given by Mobile UNITY [11] that permits to program the cooperation among mobile components in terms of abstract variables, whose content is transiently shared when the components are physically connected. It is worth noting that AOP supports an even more radical separation. In fact, in Manifold the computation code explicitly contains coordination operations (that are managed by the Manifold coordinators) such as the raising of events and the sending/receiving of messages through/from ports. In Mobile UNITY, on the other hand, the coordination operations corresponds to the read/write operations on the shared variables. On the contrary, our approach also removes this explicit coordination operations from the computation code because the actual points in which the coordination operations should be performed are defined by the pointcuts incorporated inside the coordination aspects.

As future work, we intend to investigate the possibility to associate to the computing components the coordination aspects at run time. Emerging AOP systems such as Prose [10] supports this possibility. This could be particularly useful for introducing mobility and context awareness in our application: consider, e.g., an agent based system where the coordination rules of the agents depends on the current site, and these rules are associated to the agents when they enter the site. A similar support for mobility and application of the coordination behaviour at run-time is realized by MoMi (Mobile Mixins) [3]. The main difference between MoMi and our proposal is that MoMi exploits mixin classes [4] instead of AOP. Mixins are class definitions parameterized over the superclass, and they have the ability to affect their actual superclass by adding and/or overriding methods. Beyond this possibility, supported by the *introductions* of AOP (see Section 2), Aspect Oriented Programming permits also to attach behaviours in other points thanks to the pointcut language.

# References

[1] F. Arbab. What Do You Mean, Coordination? In the March '98 Issue of the Bulletin of the Dutch Association for Theoretical Computer Science (NVTI). Available at http://homepages.cwi.nl/≈ farhad/. 106

[2] F. Arbab, I. Herman and P. Spilling. An Overview of Manifold and its Implementation. In *Concurrency - Practice and Experience*, 5(1): 23–70, 1993. 115

[3] L. Bettini, V. Bono and B. Venneri. Coordinating Mobile Object-Oriented Code. In proc. of *Coordination Models and Languages*, volume 2315 of *Lecture Notes in Computer Science*, pages 56–71. Springer-Verlag, Berlin, 2002. 115

[4] G. Bracha and W. Cook. Mix-in Based Inheritance In Proc. of of the Conference on Object-Oriented Programming: Systems, Languages, and Applications (OOPSLA'90), pages 303-311. ACM Press, 1990. 106, 108, 115

[5] E. Gamma, R. Helm, R. Johnson, and J. Vlissides. Design Patterns: Elements of Reusable Object-Oriented Software. Addison Wesley Professional Computing Series, 1994 106, 110, 112

[6] D. Gelernter. Generative Communication in Linda. *ACM Transactions on Programming Languages and Systems*, 7(1):80–112, 1985. 106

[7] D. Gelernter and N. Carriero. Coordination Languages and Their Significance. *Communications of the ACM*, 35(2):97–107, February 1992. 105

[8] G. Kiczales, J. Lamping, A. Mendhekar, C. Maeda, C. Lopes, J.-M. Loingtier, and J. Irwin. Aspect-Oriented Programming, In Proc. of European Conference on Object-Oriented Programming (ECOOP'97), volume 1241 of *Lecture Notes in Computer Science*, pages 220–242. Springer-Verlag, Berlin, 1997. 106, 108

[9] Renaud Pawlak, Lionel Seinturier, Laurence Duchien, Gerard Florin. JAC: A Flexible Framework for AOP in Java. *Reflection'01*, Kyoto, Japan, 2001. 108

[10] A. Popovici, T. Gross, G. Alonso. Dynaminc Weaving for Aspect Oriented Programming. In Proc. of *em1st International Conference on Aspect-Oriented Software Development* (AOSD02), Enschede, The Netherlands, April 2002. 108, 115

[11] G.-C. Roman, P. J. McCann, and J. Y. Plun. Mobile UNITY: reasoning and specification in mobile computing. *ACM Transactions on Software Engineering and Methodology*, 6(3):250–282, 1997. 115

[12] P. Wyckoff, S. McLaughry, T. Lehman, and D. Ford. T spaces. *IBM Systems Journal*, 37(3):454–474, 1998. 106, 107, 110

[13] J. Waldo et al. Javaspace specification - 1.0. Technical report, Sun Microsystems, March 1998. 106

[14] M. Hapner et al. Java Message Service specification - 1.1. Technical report, Sun Microsystems, April 2002. 107, 110

[15] Xerox Corporation. The AspectJ Programming Guide. 1998-2000, http://www.aspectj.org 111

# A    The Abstract Aspect of the Coordination Kernel

```
package TSDistCell;

import java.util.Vector;
import java.util.HashMap;
import TSDistCell.spreadSheet.*;

/* The base aspect of introduces the basic pointcut to handle
 * and implements the Observer patterns upon the cells */

privileged abstract aspect CoordinationAspect {

  Vector Cell.dependences=new Vector();
  Vector Cell.listeners=new Vector();

  CoordinationAgent agent;

  /* Initialize the aspect at program startup */
  public abstract void initAspect(String[] args);

  /* Removes old dependences */
  public abstract void removeDependences(Cell c);

  /* Notify the listener of this cell after an update */
  public abstract void notifyListener(Cell c);

  /* Retrieves the value form an ID in the expression and manage
   * this new dependence */
  public abstract Object retrieveValue(String sourceID, Cell dest);

  public void Cell.addChangeEventListener(Cell l) {
    listeners.add(l);
  }

  public void Cell.removeChangeEventListener(Cell l) {
    listeners.remove(l);
  }

  /* Informs the cell that a~dependence's value has changed */
  public void Cell.stateChanged() {
    setValue(evaluate(expTree));
  }

  pointcut applicationStart(String[] arguments):
    call(SpreadSheet.new()) && cflow(call(void SpreadSheet.main(String[]))
    && args(arguments));

  pointcut retrievingValue(Cell dest, CellIDNode source):
    call(Object ExpNode.eval()) && target(source)
```

```
    && cflow( call(Object Cell.evaluate(ExpNode)) && target(dest));

  pointcut expressionParse(Cell c):
    call(ExpNode ExpParser.parse(String)) && this(c);

  pointcut changingValue(Cell c):
    call(void Cell.setValue(Object)) && target(c);

  /* Initialize the coordination infrastructure at application start */
  before (String[] a): applicationStart(a) {
    initAspect(a);
  }

  /* Removes all dependences */
  before (Cell c) : expressionParse(c)  {
    removeDependences(c);
  }

  /* Updates listeners */
  after (Cell c) : changingValue(c) {
    notifyListener(c);
  }

  /* Fetches cell values and updates dependences if needed */
  Object around (CellIDNode n, Cell c) : retrievingValue(c,n) {
    return retrieveValue(n.id,c);
  }

}
```

# Probabilistic KLAIM

Alessandra Di Pierro[1], Chris Hankin[2], and Herbert Wiklicky[2]

[1] Dipartimento di Informatica, Università di Pisa, Italy
[2] Department of Computing, Imperial College London, UK

**Abstract.** We introduce a probabilistic extension of KLAIM, where the behaviour of networks and individual nodes is determined by a probabilistic scheduler for processes and probabilistic allocation environments which describe the logical neighbourhood of each node. The resulting language has two variants which are modelled respectively as discrete and continuous time Markov processes. We suggest that Poisson processes are a natural probabilistic model for the coordination of discrete processes asynchronously communicating in continuous time and we use them to define the operational semantics of the continuous time variant. This framework allows for the implementation of networks with independent clocks on each site.

## 1 Introduction

The design of languages supporting network programming is a necessary step towards the formalisation of distributed and mobile computing. The existence of an abstract semantic framework constitutes the basis for a formal analysis of such systems. The KLAIM paradigm [1] provides such a semantic framework by introducing basic concepts and primitives addressing the key aspects of the coordination of interacting located processes. We extend this basic paradigm with probabilistic constructs with the aim of introducing a semantic basis for a quantitative analysis of networks. A quantitative analysis allows in general for the consideration of more "realistic" situations. For example, a probabilistic analysis allows for establishing the security of a system up to a given tolerance factor expressing how much the system is actually vulnerable. This is in contrast to a qualitative analysis which typically might be used to validate the absolute security of a given system. In a distributed environment quantitative analysis is also of a great practical use in the consideration of timing issues which involve the asynchronous communications among processes running with different clocks.

Specifically in our probabilistic version of KLAIM, which we call pKLAIM, we introduce probabilities in a number of ways. At the local level, we introduce probabilistic parallel and choice operators. In addition we use probabilistic allocation environments which associate distributions on physical sites with logical localities. We propose two variants of pKLAIM which differ in the way in which probabilities are introduced at the network level. In the *discrete time* variant each node also has a probability associated with it; this indicates the chance that the process at that node will be selected for execution. The *continuous*

R. de Nicola et al. (Eds.): COORDINATION 2004, LNCS 2949, pp. 119–134, 2004.
© Springer-Verlag Berlin Heidelberg 2004

**Table 1.** Syntactic Categories

| | | | |
|---|---|---|---|
| $s \in S$ | (physical) sites | $v \in Val$ | (basic) values |
| $l \in Loc$ | (logical) locality | $e \in Exp$ | (basic) expressions |
| $\ell \in Loc \cup S$ | (general) locality | $A \in Proc$ | (predefined) processes |
| $x \in Var$ | (value) variable | | |
| $u \in LVar$ | (locality) variable | $\varrho \in View$ | allocation environment |
| $X \in PVar$ | (process) variable | | |

*time* variant instead associates a "rate" with each node; this determines how often a node is active.

In the next section we introduce the language in its two variants. Sections 3 through to 5 present the operational semantics of pKLAIM; we present the local semantics, which is common to both variants, in Section 3, the discrete time model in Section 4 and the continuous time model in Section 5. Section 5 ends with an example which highlights the differences between the two variants. Our main motivation is to provide a basis for quantitative analysis; one example of this kind of analysis might be to look at the rate at which a virus can spread through a network. We sketch the way in which such a scenario can be modelled in the final main section.

## 2  Syntax of pKLAIM

The syntax of pKLAIM is based essentially on the one given for KLAIM originally in [1]. It is based on the syntactic categories in Table 1.

The process terms in pKLAIM are formed according to rules which are very similar to the ones in the original KLAIM language [1]. The main difference is the probabilistic weighting of choice and local parallelism in Table 2.

The syntax of pKLAIM networks can be defined according to two different models: in the *discrete time* model the transition from one network configuration to another is done with a certain probability in one single step which determines the clock for all nodes in the network; in the *continuous time* execution model the notion of a "single step transition probability" is replaced by the notion of "transition rate" which describes how probability is distributed in the time between state changes. Thus, transition probabilities are now functions of the time; in particular they are governed by an exponential distribution of parameter given by the specified rate. The syntax of the discrete time variant of pKLAIM is given on the left hand side of Table 3 while the continuous time variant is defined on the right hand side of Table 3. The difference between the network syntax of standard KLAIM is the *scheduling probability* $q$, which is a real number in the interval $[0, 1]$ used in the discrete time version of pKLAIM, and the *execution rate* $\lambda$, which is a positive real number determining the behaviour of the network for the continuous time execution model of pKLAIM.

**Table 2.** Process Syntax

| $P ::=$ **nil** | null process | $a ::=$ **out**$(t)@\ell$ | sending tuples |
|---|---|---|---|
| $\mid$ $a.P$ | action prefix | **in**$(t)@\ell$ | receiving tuples |
| $\mid$ $\mid_{i=1}^{n} p_i : P_i$ | probabilistic parallelism | **read**$(t)@\ell$ | inspecting tuples |
| $\mid$ $+_{i=1}^{n} p_i : P_i$ | probabilistic choice | **eval**$(P)@\ell$ | remote evaluation |
| $\mid$ $X$ | process variable | **newloc**$(u)$ | new location |
| $\mid$ $A(P, \ell, e)$ | process call | | |

| $t ::= t_1, t_2$ tuple | | | |
|---|---|---|---|
| $e$ | expression tuple | !$x$ | expression template |
| $P$ | process tuple | !$u$ | locality template |
| $\ell$ | locality tuple | !$X$ | process template |

**Table 3.** Network Syntax (Discrete and Continuous Time Variants)

| $N ::= s ::_\varrho^q P$ | node |
|---|---|
| $\mid$ $N_1 \parallel N_2$ | composition |

| $N ::= s ::_\varrho^\lambda P$ | node |
|---|---|
| $\mid$ $N_1 \parallel N_2$ | composition |

In both the discrete and the continuous time execution model of pKLAIM we make use of *probabilistic allocation environments* $\varrho$. These allow us to associate logical localities with a probability distribution on the set of physical sites. A probabilistic allocation environment is formally defined as a partial map:

$$\varrho : Loc \rightarrow Dist(S),$$

where $Dist(S)$ is the set of all distributions on physical sites. We extend this definition to the set $S$ of physical sites, by defining $\varrho(s)$ as the distribution which assigns probability 1 to $s$ and 0 to all the other $s' \in S$. We denote by $\phi$ the probabilistic allocation environment which is undefined on all $l \in Loc$.

The stratification procedure, which allows to extend an inner allocation environment $\sigma$ with an outer one $\varrho$ (as in standard KLAIM), is defined for probabilistic allocation environments by:

$$(\sigma \bullet \varrho) = \begin{cases} \sigma \text{ iff } \sigma \neq \phi \\ \varrho \text{ otherwise} \end{cases}$$

As long as there is an inner allocation $\sigma$ for $\ell$ we randomly identify $\ell$ with one of the possible sites according to the distribution $\sigma(\ell)$; only if $\sigma = \phi$ do we allocate $\ell$ according to $\varrho(\ell)$.

**Table 4.** The Local Structural Semantics

$$\mathbf{out}(t)@\ell.P \xrightarrow[\phi]{o(t)@\ell} {}_1 P \quad \mathbf{in}(t)@\ell.P \xrightarrow[\phi]{i(t)@\ell} {}_1 P \quad \mathbf{read}(t)@\ell.P \xrightarrow[\phi]{r(t)@\ell} {}_1 P$$

$$\mathbf{eval}(Q)@\ell.P \xrightarrow[\phi]{e(Q)@\ell} {}_1 P \quad \mathbf{newloc}(u)@\ell.P \xrightarrow[\phi]{n(u)@\ell} {}_1 P$$

$$\frac{P_j \xrightarrow[\varrho]{\mu} {}_p P_j'}{+_{i=1}^{n} p_i : P_i \xrightarrow[\varrho]{\mu} {}_{p \cdot p_j} P_j'} \quad \frac{P_j \xrightarrow[\varrho]{\mu} {}_p P_j'}{|_{i=1}^{n} p_i : P_i \xrightarrow[\varrho]{\mu} {}_{p \cdot p_j} \;|_{j \neq i=1}^{n} P_i \mid P_j'} \quad \frac{P \xrightarrow[\varrho]{\mu} {}_p P'}{P\{\sigma\} \xrightarrow[\varrho \bullet \sigma]{\mu} {}_p P'\{\sigma\}}$$

$$\frac{P[Q/X, \ell/u, e/x] \xrightarrow[\varrho]{\mu} {}_p P'}{A(Q, \ell, e) \xrightarrow[\varrho]{\mu} {}_p P'} \quad \text{with } P \equiv A(X, u, x)$$

# 3   Operational Semantics of pKLAIM: Local Semantics

The operational semantics for pKLAIM is defined via probabilistic versions of the two levels of the operational semantics of KLAIM. The local transition relation

$$P_1 \xrightarrow[\varrho]{action} {}_p P_2$$

is the same for the discrete and continuous time versions of pKLAIM and is defined in Table 4. As in the original semantics for KLAIM, we use the label *action* to describe the activities performed in the evolution; thus, for example $o(t)@\ell$ refers to the action of sending the tuple $t$ in the tuple space specified by $\ell$, and $r(t)@\ell$ is the action of consuming the tuple $t$ in the tuple space specified by $\ell$. Following the conventions in [1] we use additional "book-keeping terms" — which are not part of the pKLAIM syntax — in the description of the operational semantics; for example we use "$P\{\rho\}$" in order to indicate the encapsulation of mobile processes.

Tuple evaluation is slightly different from standard KLAIM, as we have to take into account that allocation environments are probabilistic identifications of localities with sites. Each time we evaluate a locality $\ell$ we might obtain another physical site $s$. If $\langle s, p \rangle \in \varrho(\ell)$, we denote the probability $p$ by $\varrho(\ell)(s)$.

The evaluation function for tuples is defined in Table 5, where $\mathcal{E}[\![e]\!]$ represents an evaluation mechanism for closed expressions. The matching of tuples (with templates) in Table 5 is defined exactly as in standard KLAIM. We will also write $X \simeq Y$ for $match(X, Y)$.

# 4   Operational Semantics of pKLAIM: Discrete Time

For the discrete time execution model the update principle simulates a global scheduler: At every time step one node is selected according to the scheduling

**Table 5.** Probabilistic Tuple Evaluation and Tuple Matching

$$\mathcal{T}[\![e]\!]_\varrho = \mathcal{E}[\![e]\!]$$
$$\mathcal{T}[\![P]\!]_\varrho = P\{\varrho\}$$
$$\mathcal{T}[\![\ell]\!]_\varrho = s \text{ with } p = \varrho(\ell)(s)$$
$$\mathcal{T}[\![!x]\!]_\varrho = !x$$
$$\mathcal{T}[\![!X]\!]_\varrho = !X$$
$$\mathcal{T}[\![!u]\!]_\varrho = !u$$
$$\mathcal{T}[\![t_1, t_2]\!]_\varrho = \mathcal{T}[\![t_1]\!]_\varrho, \mathcal{T}[\![t_2]\!]_\varrho$$

$$match(v, v) \quad match(P, P) \quad match(s, s)$$
$$match(!x, v) \quad match(!X, P) \quad match(!u, s)$$

$$\frac{match(et_1, et_2) \quad match(et_3, et_4)}{match((et_1, et_3), (et_2, et_4))}$$

$$\frac{match(et_1, et_2)}{match(et_2, et_1)}$$

probabilities and executed. The result is a discrete time Markov chain (DTMC), cf. e.g. [2, 3].

In order to update a network (configuration) the global scheduler has to perform at each time step the following tasks:

1. select a node which could initiate a global update, according to the scheduling probabilities $q_i$,
2. check if the selected node can indeed cause a global transition (e.g. it can make an **out** transition or it has an **in** pending with a matching **out** somewhere),
3. execute one of the possible updates, as defined by the local semantics of the node in question.

If the first node selected is unable to perform a local transition an alternative one has to be selected. This means that the scheduler is effectively choosing only among the "active" nodes.

We will implement this scheduling principle by normalising the scheduling probabilities $q_i$; this is also needed to accommodate for dynamically created nodes (which inherit their scheduling probabilities from their ancestor). We will also normalise the probabilities $p$ of active processes at a single node and the selection probabilities $p_s$ we have encoded in the probabilistic allocation environments for **in** and **read** actions. These normalisation procedures, which we define below, guarantee that the probabilities of all global updates add up to one.

Based on the local semantics, we define the global semantics for discrete time pKLAIM in Table 6. We assume the usual structural equivalences as in KLAIM [1], so for example we have the identification:

$$s ::_\varrho^q P' \mid p : \mathbf{out}(et) \equiv s ::_\varrho^q P' \mid p : \mathbf{out}(et).\mathbf{nil}.$$

Moreover, we omit the probability associated to a process when it is 1.

In order to keep the presentation of the semantical rules as simple as possible, we will define the involved normalisation procedures — i.e. the "side computations" of $\tilde{p}$, etc. — outside the table. Furthermore, in the rules in Table 6 we omit the context of the entire network and only describe the transitions of at most two nodes involved in a global transition. This means that, for example, the first rule in Table 6 (for an $n$ node network) should actually be read as:

$$\frac{P_n \xrightarrow[\sigma]{o(t)@\ell}_p P'_n \quad \langle s_n, p_{s_n} \rangle \in (\sigma \bullet \varrho)(\ell) \quad et = \mathcal{T}[\![t]\!]_{\sigma \bullet \varrho}}{N_{n-1} \parallel s_n ::_{\varrho_n}^{q_n} P_n \xRightarrow{\tilde{q}_n \cdot p_{s_n} \cdot \tilde{p}} N_{n-1} \parallel s_n ::_{\varrho_n}^{q_n} P'_n \mid \mathbf{out}(et)}$$

with $N_{n-1} \equiv s_1 ::_{\varrho_1}^{q_1} P_1 \parallel s_2 ::_{\varrho_2}^{q_2} P_2 \parallel \ldots \parallel s_{n-1} ::_{\varrho_{n-1}}^{q_{n-1}} P_{n-1}$, and that the normalisation of $q_n$ involves all probabilities in $N_{n-1}$.

The probabilities attached to each global transitions in Table 6 denote the probability that this particular transition will be executed at a certain time step. Each of these involves typically a normalised scheduling probability $\tilde{q}$ — reflecting the fact that a particular node was selected by the scheduler — a normalised local probability $\tilde{p}$ — indicating the chances that a certain process at the selected node gets executed — and a selection probability $p_s$ which stands for the probability that a logical locality is associated to a certain physical site.

For the global transitions initiated by **in** and **read** actions we need to normalise the selection probabilities $\tilde{p}_s$ as only those nodes can be selected which have indeed a data item, i.e. an **out**$(t)$, available. This is not necessary for proper **out** and **eval** action as they will always succeed. For **in** and **read** actions we also need to determine the probabilities that — in case there are several possible data items available — a particular one is consumed or inspected by the **in** and **read** action respectively.

The normalisation of the local probabilities involves only either all the "competing" **outs** at a certain node or all the "competing" **ins** and **reads**. It is defined as $\tilde{p} = \frac{p}{P}$, where $P$ is either the sum of all the probabilities associated to $o(t)@\mathbf{self}$ transitions or the sum of the probabilities attached to transitions on $i(t)@\ell$ or $r(t)@\ell$ actions at a particular node.

In the following we will use the abbreviation **out**$(t)$ for the action **out**$(t)@\ell$, and the analogous abbreviations for **in**, **read** and **eval**. We denote by $p_a$ the probability attached to a local transition where the action label corresponds to the prefix $a$ (e.g. $p_{\mathbf{out}(t)} = p$ if there is a transition $\mathbf{out}(t)@\ell.P \xrightarrow[\phi]{o(t)@\ell}_p P$).

Moreover, we say that an action $a_1$ *matches* an action $a_2$ if $a_1 = \mathbf{out}(t_1)$ and $a_2 = \mathbf{in}(t_2)$ or $a_2 = \mathbf{read}(t_2)$ and $match(et_1, et_2)$, or vice versa. In order to formalise these normalisation procedures we define **Top** to extract top-level actions:

$$\begin{aligned}
\mathbf{Top}(\mathbf{nil}) &= \emptyset \\
\mathbf{Top}(a.P) &= \{a\} \\
\mathbf{Top}(\,|_{i=1}^{n}\, p_i : P_i) &= \bigcup_{i=1}^{n} \mathbf{Top}(P_i) \\
\mathbf{Top}(+_{i=1}^{n}\, p_i : P_i) &= \bigcup_{i=1}^{n} \mathbf{Top}(P_i)
\end{aligned}$$

We next define the *active* **in**/**reads** and **outs**:

$$\mathbf{Act}_{out}(s_1 :: P_1) = \{\mathbf{out}(t) \mid \mathbf{out}(t) \in \mathbf{Top}(P_1)\}$$

**Table 6.** The Global Structural Discrete Time Semantics

$$\frac{P \xrightarrow[\sigma]{o(t)@\ell}_p P' \quad \langle s, p_s \rangle \in (\sigma \bullet \varrho)(\ell) \quad et = \mathcal{T}[\![t]\!]_{\sigma \bullet \varrho}}{s ::_\varrho^q P \xLongrightarrow{\tilde{q} \cdot p_s \cdot \tilde{p}} s ::_\varrho^q P' \mid \mathbf{out}(et)}$$

$$\frac{P_1 \xrightarrow[\sigma_1]{o(t)@\ell}_p P_1' \quad \langle s_2, p_{s_2} \rangle \in (\sigma_1 \bullet \varrho_1)(\ell) \quad et = \mathcal{T}[\![t]\!]_{\sigma_1 \bullet \varrho_1}}{s_1 ::_{\varrho_1}^{q_1} P_1 \parallel s_2 ::_{\varrho_2}^{q_2} P_2 \xLongrightarrow{\tilde{q}_1 \cdot p_{s_2} \cdot \tilde{p}} s_1 ::_{\varrho_1}^{q_1} P_1' \parallel s_2 ::_{\varrho_2}^{q_2} P_2 \mid \mathbf{out}(et)}$$

$$\frac{P_1 \xrightarrow[\sigma]{i(t)@\ell}_{p_1} P_1' \quad \langle s, p_s \rangle \in (\sigma \bullet \varrho)(\ell) \quad P_2 \xrightarrow[\phi]{o(et)@\mathbf{self}}_{p_2} P_2' \quad et \simeq \mathcal{T}[\![t]\!]_{\sigma \bullet \varrho}}{s ::_\varrho^q P_1 \mid P_2 \xLongrightarrow{\tilde{q} \cdot \tilde{p}_1 \cdot \tilde{p}_s \cdot \tilde{p}_2} s ::_\varrho^q P_1'[et/\mathcal{T}[\![t]\!]_{\sigma \bullet \varrho}] \mid P_2'}$$

$$\frac{P_1 \xrightarrow[\sigma_1]{i(t)@\ell}_{p_1} P_1' \quad \langle s_2, p_{s_2} \rangle \in (\sigma_1 \bullet \varrho_1)(\ell) \quad P_2 \xrightarrow[\phi]{o(et)@\mathbf{self}}_{p_2} P_2' \quad et \simeq \mathcal{T}[\![t]\!]_{\sigma_1 \bullet \varrho_1}}{s_1 ::_{\varrho_1}^{q_1} P_1 \parallel s_2 ::_{\varrho_2}^{q_2} P_2 \xLongrightarrow{\tilde{q}_1 \cdot \tilde{p}_1 \cdot \tilde{p}_{s_2} \cdot \tilde{p}_2} s_1 ::_{\varrho_1}^{q_1} P_1'[et/\mathcal{T}[\![t]\!]_{\sigma \bullet \varrho}] \parallel s_2 ::_{\varrho_2}^{q_2} P_2'}$$

$$\frac{P_1 \xrightarrow[\sigma]{r(t)@\ell}_{p_1} P_1' \quad \langle s, p_s \rangle \in (\sigma \bullet \varrho)(\ell) \quad P_2 \xrightarrow[\phi]{o(et)@\mathbf{self}}_{p_2} P_2' \quad et \simeq \mathcal{T}[\![t]\!]_{\sigma \bullet \varrho}}{s ::_\varrho^q P_1 \mid P_2 \xLongrightarrow{\tilde{q} \cdot \tilde{p}_1 \cdot \tilde{p}_s \cdot \tilde{p}_2} s ::_\varrho^q P_1'[et/\mathcal{T}[\![t]\!]_{\sigma \bullet \varrho}] \mid P_2}$$

$$\frac{P_1 \xrightarrow[\sigma_1]{r(t)@\ell}_{p_1} P_1' \quad \langle s_2, p_{s_2} \rangle \in (\sigma_1 \bullet \varrho_1)(\ell) \quad P_2 \xrightarrow[\phi]{o(et)@\mathbf{self}}_{p_2} P_2' \quad et \simeq \mathcal{T}[\![t]\!]_{\sigma_1 \bullet \varrho_1}}{s_1 ::_{\varrho_1}^{q_1} P_1 \parallel s_2 ::_{\varrho_2}^{q_2} P_2 \xLongrightarrow{\tilde{q}_1 \cdot \tilde{p}_1 \cdot \tilde{p}_{s_2} \cdot \tilde{p}_2} s_1 ::_{\varrho_1}^{q_1} P_1'[et/\mathcal{T}[\![t]\!]_{\sigma \bullet \varrho}] \parallel s_2 ::_{\varrho_2}^{q_2} P_2}$$

$$\frac{P \xrightarrow[\sigma]{e(Q)@\ell}_p P' \quad \langle s, p_s \rangle \in (\sigma \bullet \varrho)(\ell)}{s ::_\varrho^q P \xLongrightarrow{\tilde{q} \cdot p_s \cdot \tilde{p}} s ::_\varrho^q P' \mid Q}$$

$$\frac{P_1 \xrightarrow[\sigma_1]{e(Q)@\ell}_p P_1' \quad \langle s_2, p_{s_2} \rangle \in (\sigma_1 \bullet \varrho_1)(\ell)}{s_1 ::_{\varrho_1}^{q_1} P_1 \parallel s_2 ::_{\varrho_2}^{q_2} P_2 \xLongrightarrow{\tilde{q}_1 \cdot p_{s_2} \cdot \tilde{p}} s_1 ::_{\varrho_1}^{q_1} P_1' \parallel s_2 ::_{\varrho_2}^{q_2} P_2 \mid Q}$$

$$\frac{P \xrightarrow[\sigma_1]{n(u)@\mathbf{self}}_p P' \quad s' \in S \quad s \neq s'}{s ::_\varrho^q P \xLongrightarrow{\tilde{q} \cdot \tilde{p}} s ::_\varrho^q P'[s'/u] \parallel s' ::_{[s'/\mathbf{self}] \bullet \varrho}^q \mathbf{nil}}$$

$$\frac{s ::_\varrho^q P_1 \xRightarrow{p} s ::_\varrho P_1'}{s ::_\varrho^q P_1 \mid P_2 \xLongrightarrow{\tilde{q} \cdot \tilde{p}} s ::_\varrho^q P_1' \mid P_2}$$

$$\mathbf{Act}_{in}(s_1 :: P_1, s_2 :: P_2) = \{\mathbf{in}(t) \mid \mathbf{in}(t) \in \mathbf{Top}(P_1) \text{ and there exists}$$
$$\mathbf{out}(t') \in \mathbf{Top}(P_2) \text{ s.t. } \mathbf{out}(t') \text{ matches } \mathbf{in}(t)\}$$
$$\cup \{\mathbf{read}(t) \mid \mathbf{read}(t) \in \mathbf{Top}(P_1) \text{ and there exists}$$
$$\mathbf{out}(t') \in \mathbf{Top}(P_2) \text{ s.t. } \mathbf{out}(t') \text{ matches } \mathbf{read}(t)\},$$

and then compute

$$P_o = \sum_{a \in \mathbf{Act}_{out}(s_1 :: P_1)} p_a,$$

so that for the active **outs** we get the normalised probabilities as

$$\tilde{p}_i = \frac{p_i}{P_o},$$

and

$$P_i = \sum_{a \in \mathbf{Act}_{in}(s_1 :: P_1, s_2 :: P_2)} p_a,$$

so that for the active **ins** we get the normalised probabilities as

$$\tilde{p}_j = \frac{p_j}{P_i}.$$

A normalisation is needed also for the probability of the selected site. Given a site $s_1 ::_{\varrho_1} P_1$, suppose that $\mathbf{in}(t)@\ell \in \mathbf{Top}(P_1)$. Then a site $s_2$ is *active* (willing to communicate) if there is a matching **out** action possible at $s_2$. We define

$$P_s = \sum (\sigma_1 \bullet \varrho_1)(l)(s_2)$$

where the sum is over all selection probabilities of nodes which are willing to communicate, and $\sigma_1$ is the environment of the local transition of $P$, and then we normalise:

$$\tilde{p}_{s_2} = \frac{p_{s_2}}{P_s}.$$

*Example 1.* Consider the two node network:

$$N \equiv l_1 ::_\phi^{\frac{1}{4}} P_1 \parallel l_2 ::_\phi^{\frac{3}{4}} P_2$$

with

$$P_1 \equiv \mathbf{out}(t)@l_1.P_1$$
$$P_2 \equiv \frac{1}{3} : \mathbf{out}(t_1)@l_2.P_2 + \frac{2}{3} : \mathbf{out}(t_2)@l_2.P_2.$$

If we look at the possible global transitions $N \overset{p}{\Longrightarrow} N'$ in one time unit/step we see that there are two cases: The network update can be initiated by node $n_1 \equiv l_1 ::_\phi^{\frac{1}{4}} P_1$ or by node $n_2 \equiv l_2 ::_\phi^{\frac{3}{4}} P_2$. The chances that each of these updates is happening is $\frac{1}{4}$ and $\frac{3}{4}$, respectively.

In the case the update is initiated the by $n_1$ there is only one possible global transition, namely:

$$l_1 ::_\phi^{\frac{1}{4}} P_1 \parallel l_2 ::_\phi^{\frac{3}{4}} P_2 \overset{\frac{1}{4}}{\Longrightarrow} l_1 ::_\phi^{\frac{1}{4}} P_1 \mid \mathbf{out}(t) \parallel l_2 ::_\phi^{\frac{3}{4}} P_2$$

For a global transition initiated by $n_2$ we get two possibilities, each of which have probabilities $\frac{3}{4}\frac{1}{3} = \frac{1}{4}$ and $\frac{3}{4}\frac{2}{3} = \frac{1}{2}$, respectively:

$$l_1 ::_\phi^{\frac{1}{4}} P_1 \parallel l_2 ::_\phi^{\frac{3}{4}} P_2 \overset{\frac{1}{4}}{\Longrightarrow} l_1 ::_\phi^{\frac{1}{4}} P_1 \parallel l_2 ::_\phi^{\frac{3}{4}} P_2 \mid \mathbf{out}(t_1)$$

$$l_1 ::_\phi^{\frac{1}{4}} P_1 \parallel l_2 ::_\phi^{\frac{3}{4}} P_2 \overset{\frac{1}{2}}{\Longrightarrow} l_1 ::_\phi^{\frac{1}{4}} P_1 \parallel l_2 ::_\phi^{\frac{3}{4}} P_2 \mid \mathbf{out}(t_2)$$

In other words the one step global transitions $N \overset{p}{\Longrightarrow} N'$ lead to a network in which either $n_1$ or $n_2$ is changed.

# 5  Operational Semantics of pKLAIM: Continuous Time

The continuous time semantics of pKLAIM relies on the idea that state changes (transitions) do not occur at regularly spaced intervals like in the previously defined discrete time semantics; instead the time between state transitions is exponentially distributed. The resulting model is therefore a continuous time Markov chain (CTMC), cf. e.g. [4, 2, 3].

In the discrete case, the global scheduler determines which node (according to the global scheduling priorities) can initiate the change. In the continuous case each node can initiate a network update independently at any moment in time with a certain probability.

In this paper we will consider a very basic mechanism describing the chance of a certain node initiating an update. We assume that each node "fires", i.e. initiates an update, via a so called Poisson process, where the chances are governed by an exponential distribution. Such processes can be specified by a single real parameter, the *rate*, which essentially describes a probability over the time between two updates (see e.g. [2, Sect 2.4]). This parameter is specified by the superscript $\lambda$ in the syntax of a node.

The global semantics for the continuous time pKLAIM is defined in Table 7. The transition relation is now labelled by a probability $p(t)$ which is a continuous function of the time $t$.

The following examples illustrate how the local probabilities, in a choice or a local parallel construct and the global update probabilities interact with each other.

*Example 2.* Consider the following network which is the same as the one in Example 1 but for the scheduling probabilities which are replaced by rates:

$$N \equiv l_1 ::_\phi^1 P_1 \parallel l_2 ::_\phi^2 P_2$$

**Table 7.** The Global Continuous Time Structural Semantics

$$\frac{P \xrightarrow[\sigma]{o(t)@\ell}_p P' \quad \langle s,p_s\rangle \in (\sigma \bullet \varrho)(\ell) \quad et = \mathcal{T}[\![t]\!]_{\sigma\bullet\varrho}}{s ::_\varrho^\lambda P \xLongrightarrow{p_s\cdot\tilde{p}\cdot e^{-\lambda t}} s ::_\varrho^\lambda P' \mid \mathbf{out}(et)}$$

$$\frac{P_1 \xrightarrow[\sigma_1]{o(t)@\ell}_p P_1' \quad \langle s_2,p_{s_2}\rangle \in (\sigma_1 \bullet \varrho_1)(\ell) \quad et = \mathcal{T}[\![t]\!]_{\sigma_1\bullet\varrho_1}}{s_1 ::_{\varrho_1}^{\lambda_1} P_1 \parallel s_2 ::_{\varrho_2}^{\lambda_2} P_2 \xLongrightarrow{p_{s_2}\cdot\tilde{p}\cdot e^{-\lambda_1 t}} s_1 ::_{\varrho_1}^{\lambda_1} P_1' \parallel s_2 ::_{\varrho_2}^{\lambda_2} P_2 \mid \mathbf{out}(et)}$$

$$\frac{P_1 \xrightarrow[\sigma]{i(t)@\ell}_{p_1} P_1' \quad \langle s,p_s\rangle \in (\sigma \bullet \varrho)(\ell) \quad P_2 \xrightarrow[\phi]{o(et)@\mathbf{self}}_{p_2} P_2' \quad et \simeq \mathcal{T}[\![t]\!]_{\sigma\bullet\varrho}}{s ::_\varrho^\lambda P_1 \mid P_2 \xLongrightarrow{\tilde{p}_1\cdot\tilde{p}_s\cdot\tilde{p}_2\cdot e^{-\lambda t}} s ::_\varrho^\lambda P_1'[et/\mathcal{T}[\![t]\!]_{\sigma\bullet\varrho}] \mid P_2'}$$

$$\frac{P_1 \xrightarrow[\sigma_1]{i(t)@\ell}_{p_1} P_1' \quad \langle s_2,p_{s_2}\rangle \in (\sigma_1 \bullet \varrho_1)(\ell) \quad P_2 \xrightarrow[\phi]{o(et)@\mathbf{self}}_{p_2} P_2' \quad et \simeq \mathcal{T}[\![t]\!]_{\sigma_1\bullet\varrho_1}}{s_1 ::_{\varrho_1}^{\lambda_1} P_1 \parallel s_2 ::_{\varrho_2}^{\lambda_2} P_2 \xLongrightarrow{\tilde{p}_1\cdot\tilde{p}_{s_2}\cdot\tilde{p}_2\cdot e^{-\lambda_1 t}} s_1 ::_{\varrho_1}^{\lambda_1} P_1'[et/\mathcal{T}[\![t]\!]_{\sigma\bullet\varrho}] \parallel s_2 ::_{\varrho_2}^{\lambda_2} P_2'}$$

$$\frac{P_1 \xrightarrow[\sigma]{r(t)@\ell}_{p_1} P_1' \quad \langle s,p_s\rangle \in (\sigma \bullet \varrho)(\ell) \quad P_2 \xrightarrow[\phi]{o(et)@\mathbf{self}}_{p_2} P_2' \quad et \simeq \mathcal{T}[\![t]\!]_{\sigma\bullet\varrho}}{s ::_\varrho^\lambda P_1 \mid P_2 \xLongrightarrow{\tilde{p}_1\cdot\tilde{p}_s\cdot\tilde{p}_2\cdot e^{-\lambda t}} s ::_\varrho^\lambda P_1'[et/\mathcal{T}[\![t]\!]_{\sigma\bullet\varrho}] \mid P_2}$$

$$\frac{P_1 \xrightarrow[\sigma_1]{r(t)@\ell}_{p_1} P_1' \quad \langle s_2,p_{s_2}\rangle \in (\sigma_1 \bullet \varrho_1)(\ell) \quad P_2 \xrightarrow[\phi]{o(et)@\mathbf{self}}_{p_2} P_2' \quad et \simeq \mathcal{T}[\![t]\!]_{\sigma_1\bullet\varrho_1}}{s_1 ::_{\varrho_1}^{\lambda_1} P_1 \parallel s_2 ::_{\varrho_2}^{\lambda_2} P_2 \xLongrightarrow{\tilde{p}_1\cdot\tilde{p}_{s_2}\cdot\tilde{p}_2\cdot e^{-\lambda_1 t}} s_1 ::_{\varrho_1}^{\lambda_1} P_1'[et/\mathcal{T}[\![t]\!]_{\sigma\bullet\varrho}] \parallel s_2 ::_{\varrho_2}^{\lambda_2} P_2}$$

$$\frac{P \xrightarrow[\sigma]{e(Q)@\ell}_p P' \quad \langle s,p_s\rangle \in (\sigma \bullet \varrho)(\ell)}{s ::_\varrho^\lambda P \xLongrightarrow{p_s\cdot\tilde{p}\cdot e^{-\lambda t}} s ::_\varrho^\lambda P' \mid Q}$$

$$\frac{P_1 \xrightarrow[\sigma_1]{e(Q)@\ell}_p P_1' \quad \langle s_2,p_{s_2}\rangle \in (\sigma_1 \bullet \varrho_1)(\ell)}{s_1 ::_{\varrho_1}^{\lambda_1} P_1 \parallel s_2 ::_{\varrho_2}^{\lambda_2} P_2 \xLongrightarrow{p_{s_2}\cdot\tilde{p}\cdot e^{-\lambda_1 t}} s_1 ::_{\varrho_1}^{\lambda_1} P_1' \parallel s_2 ::_{\varrho_2}^{\lambda_2} P_2 \mid Q}$$

$$\frac{P \xrightarrow[\sigma_1]{n(u)@\mathbf{self}}_p P' \quad s' \in S \quad s \neq s'}{s ::_\varrho^\lambda P \xLongrightarrow{\tilde{p}\cdot e^{-\lambda t}} s ::_\varrho^\lambda P'[s'/u] \parallel s' ::_{[s'/\mathbf{self}]\bullet\varrho}^\lambda \mathbf{nil}}$$

$$\frac{s ::_\varrho^\lambda P_1 \xRightarrow{p} s ::_\varrho^\lambda P_1'}{s ::_\varrho^\lambda P_1 \mid P_2 \xLongrightarrow{\tilde{p}\cdot e^{-\lambda t}} s ::_\varrho^\lambda P_1' \mid P_2}$$

with

$$P_1 \equiv \mathbf{out}(t)@l_1.P_1$$

$$P_2 \equiv \frac{1}{3} : \mathbf{out}(t_1)@l_2.P_2 + \frac{2}{3} : \mathbf{out}(t_2)@l_2.P_2$$

In a similar way as in Example 1 we can look at the possible transitions of $N$ in a single time unit, i.e. the probabilities for $N \xrightarrow{p(1)} N'$.

Again the global transitions of $N$ can be initiated by two events: both $n_1 \equiv l_1 ::_\phi^1 P_1$ and $n_2 \equiv l_2 ::_\phi^2 P_2$ can initiate a global update. The difference with Example 1 is the fact that the statement that either of the two happens in one transition step does no longer make sense in the continuous time setting. Instead we observe that each of them, both together or none of them might happen in one time unit. In order to express this situation we introduce the notation $P^n = P \mid P \mid \ldots \mid P$ to stand for the $n$-fold parallel composition of copies of $P$, and define

$$P_{1k} \equiv P_1 \mid \mathbf{out}(t)^k$$

$$P_{2nm} \equiv P_2 \mid \mathbf{out}(t_1)^n \mid \mathbf{out}(t_2)^m.$$

Among the possible transitions we have the following:

$$l_1 ::_\phi^1 P_1 \parallel l_2 ::_\phi^2 P_2 \xrightarrow{\exp(-1)} l_1 ::_\phi^1 P_{1,1} \parallel l_2 ::_\phi^2 P_{2,0,0}$$

$$l_1 ::_\phi^1 P_1 \parallel l_2 ::_\phi^2 P_2 \xrightarrow{\exp(-1)\frac{1}{3}} l_1 ::_\phi^1 P_{1,0} \parallel l_2 ::_\phi^2 P_{2,1,0}$$

$$l_1 ::_\phi^1 P_1 \parallel l_2 ::_\phi^2 P_2 \xrightarrow{\exp(-2)\frac{2}{3}} l_1 ::_\phi^1 P_{1,0} \parallel l_2 ::_\phi^2 P_{2,0,1}$$

Note that the cases on the right hand side of these transitions are not mutually exclusive and that thus the probabilities do not sum up to one. Moreover, contrary to the discrete case, a number of other transitions are also possible since each of the two processes can be executed any number $i$ of times in an interval of length $t$. From the theory of Poisson processes the following formula expresses the probability $p_i(t)$ that exactly $i$ events occur in an interval of length $t$:

$$p_i(t) = \frac{(\lambda t)^i e^{-\lambda t}}{i!},$$

where $\lambda$ is is the parameter of the Poisson distribution, e.g. [4, Thm 1.2.1].

We can then calculate the probability $p$ of transition

$$l_1 ::_\phi^1 P_1 \parallel l_2 ::_\phi^2 P_2 \xrightarrow{p(1)} l_1 ::_\phi^1 P_{1,n} \parallel l_2 ::_\phi^2 P_{2,0,0}$$

by simply instantiating the above formula with $\lambda = 1$, $i = n$ and $t = 1$: $p(1) = \frac{e^{-1}}{n!}$. Analogously, we get the transition:

$$l_1 ::_\phi^1 P_1 \parallel l_2 ::_\phi^2 P_2 \xrightarrow{p(1)} l_1 ::_\phi^1 P_{1,0} \parallel l_2 ::_\phi^2 P_{2,n,m}$$

with probability $p(1) = \frac{2^k e^{-2}}{k!}$, where $k = n + m$, and the transition:

$$l_1 ::_\phi^1 P_1 \parallel l_2 ::_\phi^2 P_2 \overset{p(1)}{\Longrightarrow} l_1 ::_\phi^1 P_{1,s} \parallel l_2 ::_\phi^2 P_{2,n,m}$$

with probability $p(1) = \frac{e^{-1}}{s!} \cdot \frac{2^k e^{-2}}{k!}$, where $k = n + m$.

Comparing Example 1 and Example 2 we see that in the latter case we obtain a much richer set of possible transitions in one time unit. In the continuous case a single transition might happen in a time unit, none at all or more than one, while in the discrete case exactly one transition happens (provided that no deadlock occurs).

Furthermore, the continuous time model realises true concurrency as several transitions *seem* to happen in "parallel". In fact, two transitions are actually never happening at exactly the same moment, as the probability for this is zero. However, after a single time unit we can observe that two or more transitions have happened.

This allows us to avoid considering "clashes" like for example two **in**($t$) actions trying to access the same token: the probability of this happening vanishes. We can however ask for the probability that either of the two **in**'s is executed first and in this way determine the chances that the token in question has been consumed by the first or the second **in** after a given time (or, as also could be the case, that neither of them has already consumed the token).

# 6    Example: Computer Viruses

We now present a more sophisticated example, motivated by the security literature. Computer viruses and worms have been very much in the news recently with the SoBig.F virus and the Blaster worm both making the headlines over the summer (of 2003). We have recently been looking at how probabilistic program analysis techniques can be used to predict the rate of spread of such viruses [5]. The techniques used in *op. cit.* were applied to a much smaller language than that treated here and they are beyond the scope of this paper. However, we will give a flavour of how such phenomena may be modelled in pKLAIM.

## 6.1    pKLAIM Program

Consider the following program implementing a "computer virus":

$$V \equiv \mathbf{out}(V)@\ell.V.\mathbf{nil}$$

which transmits itself to another location $\ell$ and executes some "malicious code".

At each node in the network we assume that there is an "operating system" running which either accepts any process it receives and executes it:

$$O \equiv \mathbf{in}(!P)@\mathbf{self}.Seq(P, O).\mathbf{nil}$$

i.e. an open system, or ignores processes it receives:

$$C \equiv \mathbf{in}(!P)@\mathbf{self}.C$$

i.e. a closed system. Note that $O$ and $C$ actually do nothing else but recursively receiving processes. The *Seq* process is defined as follows:

$$Seq(A, B) \equiv \mathbf{eval}(A)@\mathbf{self}.\mathbf{eval}(B)@\mathbf{self}.\mathbf{nil}$$

## 6.2   Discrete Time

Consider the following set of ('top', 'middle' and 'bottom') sites:

$$S = \{t_1, \ldots, t_9, m_1, m_2, m_3, b_1, \ldots, b_9\}$$

and define the following (probabilistic) allocation environments:

$$\tau = \left\{ \begin{array}{l} \langle [\ell/t_1], 1/12 \rangle, \ldots, \langle [\ell/t_9], 1/12 \rangle, \\ \langle [\ell/m_1], 1/12 \rangle, \langle [\ell/m_2], 1/12 \rangle, \langle [\ell/m_3], 1/12 \rangle \end{array} \right\}$$

$$\mu = \left\{ \begin{array}{l} \langle [\ell/m_1], 1/12 \rangle, \langle [\ell/m_2], 1/12 \rangle, \langle [\ell/m_3], 1/12 \rangle, \\ \langle [\ell/b_1], 1/12 \rangle, \ldots, \langle [\ell/b_9], 1/12 \rangle \end{array} \right\}$$

$$\lambda = \{ \langle [\ell/b_1], 1/9 \rangle, \ldots, \langle [\ell/b_9], 1/9 \rangle \}$$

Then a network which can informally be described by the following diagram:

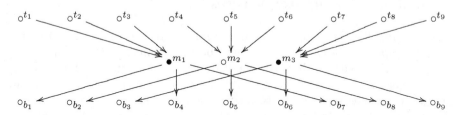

is formally specified by the following pKLAIM specification:

$$t_1 ::_\tau^{\frac{1}{7}} O \parallel \ldots \parallel t_9 ::_\tau^{\frac{1}{7}} O$$
$$\parallel m_1 ::_\mu^{\frac{1}{21}} C \parallel m_2 ::_\mu^{\frac{1}{21}} O \parallel m_3 ::_\mu^{\frac{1}{21}} C \parallel$$
$$b_1 ::_\lambda^{\frac{1}{21}} O \parallel \ldots \parallel b_9 ::_\lambda^{\frac{1}{21}} O$$

We have assumed a uniform distribution — each node has probability $\frac{1}{21}$ associated with it. In the following we will omitted these probabilities on nodes.

Note that in the formal specification the nodes in each layer are fully connected and that each node on the top level is connected with all nodes in the middle layer (not all of these connections had been depicted in the above diagram). The idea is that at site $m_1$ and $m_3$ virus resistant processes are situated while all other nodes are vulnerable to "infections". Now assume that one top node (e.g. $t_1$) gets infected by the virus, i.e. consider the execution of:

$$t_1 ::_\tau V \parallel \ldots \parallel t_9 ::_\tau O$$
$$\parallel m_1 ::_\mu C \parallel m_2 ::_\mu O \parallel m_3 ::_\mu C \parallel$$
$$b_1 ::_\lambda O \parallel \ldots \parallel b_9 ::_\lambda O$$

Then there are two prototypical changes possible: Either $V$ spreads to an open node, like $m_2$, or to a closed one, like $m_1$. The probability for each of the neighbours that this might happen is $\frac{1}{12}$. Whilst in the former case the virus gets activated, in the later case the virus stays untouched and encapsulated.

$$t_1 ::_\tau V \parallel \ldots \parallel t_9 ::_\tau O$$
$$\parallel m_1 ::_\mu C \parallel m_2 ::_\mu O \parallel m_3 ::_\mu C \parallel$$
$$b_1 ::_\lambda O \parallel \ldots \parallel b_9 ::_\lambda O$$
$$\overset{1/12}{\Longrightarrow}$$
$$t_1 ::_\tau V \parallel \ldots \parallel t_9 ::_\tau O$$
$$\parallel m_1 ::_\mu C \parallel m_2 ::_\mu O \mid \mathbf{out}(V) \parallel m_3 ::_\mu C \parallel$$
$$b_1 ::_\lambda O \parallel \ldots \parallel b_9 ::_\lambda O$$
$$\overset{1}{\Longrightarrow}$$
$$t_1 ::_\tau V \parallel \ldots \parallel t_9 ::_\tau O$$
$$\parallel m_1 ::_\mu C \parallel m_2 ::_\mu V.O \parallel m_3 ::_\mu C \parallel$$
$$b_1 ::_\lambda O \parallel \ldots \parallel b_9 ::_\lambda O$$

and

$$t_1 ::_\tau V \parallel \ldots \parallel t_9 ::_\tau O$$
$$\parallel m_1 ::_\mu C \parallel m_2 ::_\mu O \parallel m_3 ::_\mu C \parallel$$
$$b_1 ::_\lambda O \parallel \ldots \parallel b_9 ::_\lambda O$$
$$\overset{1/12}{\Longrightarrow}$$
$$t_1 ::_\tau V \parallel \ldots \parallel t_9 ::_\tau O$$
$$\parallel m_1 ::_\mu C \mid \mathbf{out}(V) \parallel m_2 ::_\mu O \parallel m_3 ::_\mu C \parallel$$
$$b_1 ::_\lambda O \parallel \ldots \parallel b_9 ::_\lambda O$$

Analysing all possible network transitions together with their probabilities allows us to answer questions like: What is the chance that a certain node is infected after $n$ steps? In other words, we can *formally* study and analyse the patterns of how a virus might spread through a network with a certain topology; in our simple example above we can determine, for example, how the number of closed nodes in the middle layer slows down the spread of a virus from the top to the bottom layer.

## 6.3   Continuous Time and Analysis

The continuous time version of the network is based upon the same process definitions. The only difference in the formal description is that probabilities associated with nodes are replaced by rates. We can then answer questions about the probability that a node becomes infected at a certain point given some initial configuration. As we have observed above, the continuous time model captures some aspects of true concurrency and, therefore in some senses, gives a more accurate model of virus/worm propagation in a network.

The preceding subsections constitute a work programme rather than a catalogue of results. Ideally we would like to produce automatic tools that could assist systems administrators in assessing the vulnerability of their networks to such infections. The approach we advocate in [5] is to model the network by a Markov process and then to use linear algebraic techniques to "abstract" the network by an *infection matrix* which enables us to study the propagation of viruses. The work we have done to date has been focused on discrete time models for a first-order restriction of pKLAIM. The analysis of full pKLAIM and the ultimate production of automated tools remains for future work.

# 7    Conclusions

We have presented an approach to introducing probabilities into coordination languages. Our proposals has been presented in the context of the KLAIM language where we introduced probabilities both at the local (or process) level and at the network level. The natural role of probabilities at the process level is in scheduling parallel threads and deciding choice operators. We have proposed two alternative ways of introducing probabilities at the network level: discrete time and continuous time. In the former case, we have used probabilities to schedule network parallelism. In the latter case we use rates to determine how often a node is active. We have illustrated the difference between these two approaches with a simple example and also sketched a more complex example of virus propagation. We have shown that the continuous time model captures some aspects of true concurrency.

The probabilistic version(s) of KLAIM we have introduced in this paper are closely related to various *probabilistic programming languages* and *probabilistic process calculi* proposed in the recent literature. Among these one can find discrete time approaches — e.g. PCCS [6, 7], PCCP [8], etc. — as well as continuous time approaches — e.g. PEPA [9], Stochastic $\pi$ calculus [10], to name just a few. Work in performance analysis is often based on probabilistic process calculi, for example, on Hillston's PEPA [11], or EMPA by Bernardo and Gorrieri [12]. One of the long term aims of the work presented in this paper is the development of semantics based approaches towards *performance analysis* along similar lines as in classical program analysis. We also aim to investigate more closely the relation of our work to recent work on probabilistic verification and model checking, such as PRISM [13] and de Alfaro [14]. The virus example discussed in Section 6 is part of a more general probabilistic approach towards *security analysis* which attempts to investigate more "realistic" measures for confidentiality, security, etc., see e.g. [15, 16].

In our continuous time model we only consider the simplest time processes, the so called Poisson processes. More complicated continuous time behaviour could be considered, but this might require more parameters than just rate to describe the time distributions. The language could also be extended to allow for dynamic change of probabilities and rates, i.e. for rate and probability variables. This would require some care in the choice of range of e.g. $p$; taking all the reals might lead to paradoxes regarding computability. These last two extensions require further work as does a detailed analysis of the virus example presented in Section 6.

# References

[1] De Nicola, R., Ferrari, G., Pugliese, R.: KLAIM: A kernel language for agents interaction and mobility. IEEE Transactions on Software Engineering **24** (1998) 315–330   119, 120, 122, 123

[2] Norris, J.: Markov Chains. Cambridge Series in Statistical and Probabilistic Mathematics. Cambridge University Press, Cambridge (1997)   123, 127

[3] Bause, F., Kritzinger, P. S.: Stochastic Petri Nets – An Introduction to the Theory. second edn. Vieweg Verlag (2002)   123, 127

[4] Tijms, H. C.: Stochastic Models – An Algorithmic Approach. John Wiley & Sons, Chichester (1994)   127, 129

[5] Di Pierro, A., Hankin, C., Wiklicky, H.: Analysing the propagation of computer viruses. Journal of Functional Programming (2003) (submitted).   130, 133

[6] Giacalone, A., Jou, C. C., Smolka, S.: Algebraic reasoning for probabilistic concurrent systems. In: Proceedings of the IFIP WG 2.2/2.3 Working Conference on Programming Concepts and Methods, North-Holland (1990) 443–458   133

[7] Jonsson, B., Yi, W., Larsen, K.: 11. In: Probabilistic Extentions of Process Algebras. Elsevier Science, Amsterdam (2001) 685–710 see [17].   133

[8] Di Pierro, A., Wiklicky, H.: Quantitative observables and averages in Probabilistic Concurrent Constraint Programming. In: New Trends in Constraints. Number 1865 in Lecture Notes in Computer Science, Springer Verlag (2000)   133

[9] Hillston, J.: PEPA: Performance enhanced process algebra. Technical Report CSR-24-93, University of Edinburgh, Edinburgh, Scotland (1993)   133

[10] Priami, C.: Stochastic $\pi$-calculus. Computer Journal **38** (1995) 578–589   133

[11] Hillston, J.: A Compositional Approach to Performance Modelling. Cambridge University Press (1996)   133

[12] Bernardo, M., Gorrieri, R.: A tutorial on EMPA: A theory of concurrent processes with nondeterminism, priorities, probabilities and time. Technical Report UBLCS-96-17, Department of Computer Science, University of Bologna (1997)   133

[13] Kwiatkowska, M., Norman, G., Parker, D.: Probabilistic symbolic model checking with PRISM: A hybrid approach. In Katoen, J. P., Stevens, P., eds.: Proceedings of TACAS'02. Volume 2280 of Lecture Notes in Computer Science., Springer Verlag (2002) 52–66   133

[14] de Alfaro, L.: Formal Verification of Probabilistic Systems. PhD thesis, Stanford University, Department of Computer Science (1998)   133

[15] Di Pierro, A., Hankin, C., Wiklicky, H.: Approximate Non-Interference. Journal of Computer Security **12** (2004) 37–81   133

[16] Aldini, A., Bravetti, M., Gorrieri, R.: A process algebraic approach for the analysis of probabilistic non-interference. Journal of Computer Security (2004)   133

[17] Bergstra, J., Ponse, A., Smolka, S., eds.: Handbook of Process Algebra. Elsevier Science, Amsterdam (2001)   134

# A Lightweight Coordination Middleware for Mobile Computing

Chien-Liang Fok, Gruia-Catalin Roman, and Gregory Hackmann

Department of Computer Science and Engineering
Washington University in Saint Louis
Saint Louis, Missouri 63130-4899, USA
{liang, roman, gwh2}@cse.wustl.edu
http://www.cse.wustl.edu/mobilab

**Abstract.** This paper presents Limone, a new coordination model that
facilitates rapid application development over ad hoc networks consisting
of logically mobile agents and physically mobile hosts. Limone assumes
an agent-centric perspective on coordination by allowing each agent to
define its own acquaintance policy and by limiting all agent-initiated
interactions to agents that satisfy the policy. Agents that satisfy this
acquaintance policy are stored in an acquaintance list, which is automatically maintained by the system. This asymmetric style of coordination allows each agent to focus on relevant peers. Coordination activities
are restricted to tuple spaces owned by agents in the acquaintance list.
Limone tailors Linda-like primitives for mobile environments by elimi-
nating remote blocking and complex group operations. It also provides
timeouts for all distributed operations and reactions that enable asynchronous communication with agents in the acquaintance list. Finally,
Limone minimizes the granularity of atomic operations and the set of
assumptions about the environment. In this paper we introduce Limone,
explain its key features, and explore its capabilities as a coordination
model. A universal remote control implementation using Limone provides a concrete illustration of the model and the applications it can
support.

## 1 Introduction

Mobile devices with wireless capabilities have experienced rapid growth in recent
years due to advances in technology and social pressures from a highly dynamic
society. Many of these devices are capable of forming ad hoc networks. By elim-
inating the reliance on the wired infrastructure, ad hoc networks can be rapidly
deployed in disaster situations where the infrastructure has been destroyed, or
in military applications where the infrastructure belongs to the enemy. Ad hoc
networks are also convenient in day-to-day scenarios where the duration of the
activity is too brisk and localized to warrant the establishment of a permanent
network infrastructure. Applications for ad hoc networks are expected to quickly
grow in importance because they address challenges set forth by several important application domains.

R. de Nicola et al. (Eds.): COORDINATION 2004, LNCS 2949, pp. 135–151, 2004.
© Springer-Verlag Berlin Heidelberg 2004

The salient properties of ad hoc networks create many challenges for the application developer. The inherent unreliability of wireless signals and the mobility of nodes result in frequent unannounced disconnections and message loss. In addition, mobile devices have limited battery and computing power. The limited functionality of mobile devices and the peer-to-peer nature of the network lead to strong mutual dependencies among devices, which have to cooperate to achieve a variety of common goals. This results in an increased need for coordination support. For example, in a planetary exploration setting, miniature rovers, each equipped with a single sensor, may need to perform experiments that demand data from any arbitrary combination of sensors.

Designing a coordination middleware for ad hoc networks is difficult. It must be lightweight in terms of the amount of power, memory, and bandwidth consumed. Depending on the application, it may have to operate over a wide range of devices with different capabilities: some devices, such as a laptop, may have plenty of memory and processing ability, while others, such as a sensor network Mote, may have extremely limited resources. A coordination middleware for ad hoc networks must be flexible in order to adapt to a dynamic environment; for example, in a universal remote control application, a remote held by the user must interact with a set of devices within its vicinity, a set that changes as the user moves. Furthermore, wireless signals are prone to interference from the environment. Thus, the middleware must be designed to handle unpredictable message loss.

Coordination middleware facilitates application development by providing high-level constructs such as tuple spaces [5], blackboards [4], and channels [8], in place of lower-level constructs such as sockets. Tuple spaces and blackboards are both shared-memory architectures. Tuple spaces differ from blackboards in that they use pattern-matching for retrieving data; in a blackboard, the data is generally accessed by type alone. Channels are similar to sockets in that data is inserted at one end and is retrieved from the other. They differ in that the end points of a channel may be dynamically rebound.

This paper introduces Limone (Lightly-coordinated Mobile Networks), a lightweight coordination model and middleware for mobile environments supporting logical mobility of agents and physical mobility of hosts. Limone agents are software processes that represent units of modularity, execution, and mobility. In a significant departure from existing coordination research, Limone emphasizes the individuality of each agent by focusing on asymmetric interactions among agents. Each agent contains an *acquaintance list* that defines a personalized view of remote agents within communication range. For each agent, Limone discovers remote agents and updates its acquaintance list according to customizable policies.

As in most coordination models, traditional Linda-like primitives over tuple spaces facilitate the coordination of agent activities. However, Limone allows each agent to maintain strict control over its local data, provides advanced pattern matching capabilities, permits agents to restrict the scope of their operations, and offers a powerful repertoire of reactive programming constructs.

The autonomy of each agent is maintained by the exclusion of distributed transactions and remote blocking operations. Furthermore, Limone ensures that all
distributed operations contain built-in mechanisms to prevent deadlock due to
packet loss or disconnection. For these reasons, Limone is resilient to message
loss and unexpected disconnection. This allows Limone to function in realistic
ad hoc environments in which most other models cannot.

The paper starts with a review of existing coordination models in Section 2. It
then presents an overview of Limone in Section 3. Section 4 discusses the design
of Limone followed by an evaluation of its performance in Section 5. A sample
universal remote control application is presented in Section 6. The paper ends
with conclusions in Section 7.

## 2   Related Work

The unique characteristics of wireless ad hoc networks, such as a dynamic topology and limited node capabilities, increase the need for coordination support. To
address this need, numerous coordination models have been proposed. These include JEDI [3], MARS [2], and LIME [9]. Of these, LIME is the only coordination
middleware designed explicitly for ad hoc networks as it is the only model that
provides a discovery protocol, which is necessary for a node to determine who it
can coordinate with. We consider the other two models because they could be
adopted to function in an ad hoc network by adding a discovery protocol. In this
section, we present each model and analyze their effectiveness for supporting the
universal remote control application. This application consists of a universal remote held by the user that discovers controllable devices within its environment
and enables the user to control them over a wireless ad hoc network.

JEDI offers a publish-subscription paradigm where nodes interact by exchanging events through a logically centralized event dispatcher. An event is
modelled as an ordered set of strings where the first is the name of the event,
and the rest are application-specified parameters. Nodes subscribe to events using regular expressions on the event name. When a node publishes an event, the
event dispatcher passes it to all nodes subscribed to it. Since all communication is done through the event dispatcher, the publisher is decoupled from the
subscriber(s).

The universal remote control application can be implemented in JEDI as
follows. Devices publish *description events* that describe how they are controlled,
and the remote control subscribes to these events. Similarly, the universal remote
publishes *control events* with instructions for a particular device, and each device
subscribes to control events that are destined for it. The main problem, however,
is the lack of event persistency. When a device publishes a description event,
the event dispatcher passes it to all universal remotes subscribed to it. But in
a mobile environment, the universal remote may not be present at the time
when the event was published. Thus, the device must periodically re-publish
its description event to ensure all remote controls receive it, which increases
bandwidth and battery power consumption.

MARS consists of logically mobile agents that migrate from one node to another. Each node maintains a local tuple space that is accessed by agents residing on it. The tuple space is enhanced with reactive programming, which allows an agent to respond to actions performed on it. An agent can only co-ordinate with other agents that reside on the same node. Agent migration is required for inter-node communication. MARS adapts to mobile environments by allowing agents to "catch" connection events that indicate the presence of a remote node to which they may migrate.

The universal remote control application can be implemented in MARS as follows. Whenever a device's agent detects the presence of a universal remote, it spawns a new agent that migrates to the universal remote, and inserts a *device description tuple*. The universal remote control's agent reacts to the insertion, and thus learns about the device. A similar mechanism can be used whenever the universal remote wishes to control the device. This design is inefficient since it requires an agent migration for each operation that is more costly than message passing.

LIME is a coordination model that utilizes logically mobile agents running on physically mobile hosts. It offers a group membership paradigm where neighboring hosts form a group that share one or more logically centralized tuple spaces enhanced with reactive programming. Agents coordinate by exchanging tuples through the tuple space. Reactive programming allows the system to notify an agent when a particular tuple is in the tuple space. LIME provides strong atomicity and functional guarantees by utilizing distributed transactions. For example, when two groups merge, the logical merging of the two tuple spaces is done atomically. While powerful, this atomicity comes at a cost because it requires a symmetric relationship between nodes and assumes connectivity throughout the transaction, which may be difficult to guarantee in an ad hoc environment.

The universal remote control can be implemented in LIME as follows. The remote discovers controllable devices by reacting to *device description tuples* inserted by the devices. To control the devices, the remote inserts *control tuples* that the targeted device reacts to. The main problem, however, is the underlying symmetric engagement enforced by group membership. Since LIME forms groups of hosts, all devices must be in the same group as the universal remote limiting scalability.

The universal remote can be implemented in existing coordination models, but result in implementations that limit efficiency and flexibility. In the next section, we introduce a new coordination model called Limone that addresses the issues identified in this section.

## 3   Model Overview

Limone emerged out of an effort to build a lightweight version of LIME suitable for use on small devices and in unstable environments. The ultimate result was a novel model having a distinct character. Ultimately, Limone has been shaped by a set of highly pragmatic software engineering concerns, particularly,

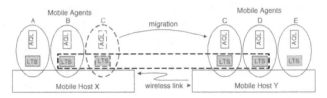

**Fig. 1.** An overview of Limone where agents are ovals. Each agent owns a local tuple space (LTS) and an acquaintance list (AQL). Agent C is shown migrating to host Y. The dotted rectangle surrounding the tuples spaces of agents B, C, and D highlight those that are accessible from C

by the desire to facilitate rapid mobile application development under realistic environmental assumptions. While other models are willing to rely on strong assumptions such as precise knowledge about the status of communication links, we readily acknowledge the unpredictable and dynamic nature of wireless ad hoc networks. As such, we do not presume to know when communication links go up or down or the range of the wireless signals. The model starts with the premise that a single round trip message exchange is possible and, under this minimalist assumption, it offers a precise and reasonable set of functional guarantees.

The willingness to accommodate a high degree of uncertainty about the physical state of the system raised important research questions regarding the choice of coordination style and associated constructs. A minimalist philosophy, combined with the goal of achieving high levels of performance, led to the emergence of a novel model whose elements appear to support fundamental coordination concerns. Central to the model is the organization of all coordination activities around an *acquaintance list* that reflects the current local view of the global operating context, and whose composition is subject to customizable admission policies. From the application's perspective, all interactions with other components take place by referring to individual members of the acquaintance list. All operations are content-based, but can be active or reactive. This perspective on coordination, unique to Limone, offers an expressive model that enjoys an effective implementation likely to transfer to small devices.

Limone assumes a computational model consisting of mobile devices (hosts) capable of forming ad hoc networks; mobile agents that reside on hosts but can migrate from one host to another; and data owned by agents that is stored in local tuple spaces. The relationship between hosts, agents, and tuple spaces is shown in Figure 1. The features of Limone can be broadly divided into four general categories: context management, explicit data access, reactive programming, and code mobility.

Central to the notion of context management is an agent's ability to discover neighbors and to selectively decide on their relevance. Limone provides a beacon-based discovery protocol that informs each agent of the arrival and departure of other agents. Limone notifies each agent of its relevant neighbors by storing them in individualized acquaintance lists, where relevance is determined by a customizable *engagement policy*. Since each agent has different neighbors and engagement policies, the context of each agent may differ from that of its peers.

Many existing coordination models for mobility in ad hoc environments presume a symmetric and transitive coordination relation among agents that is not scalable. In such systems, every node must coordinate with every other node in the group. As the number of nodes increase, the likelihood that some nodes move out of range also increases. This results in frequent group reconfigurations, which consumes valuable resources. By allowing an agent to restrict coordination to agents it is interested in, Limone scales better to dense ad hoc networks and to devices with limited memory resources. For example, if an agent is surrounded by hundreds of other agents but is interested only in two of them, it can concentrate on these two and ignore the rest, thus minimizing memory usage and processor cycles. This asymmetry increases the level of decoupling among agents and results in a more robust coordination model that requires fewer assumptions about the underlying network [6].

Limone accomplishes explicit data access in a manner similar to that employed by most other coordination models. Each agent owns a single tuple space that provides operations for inserting and retrieving tuples. Explicit data access spans at most two agents. The agent initiating the data access (called the reference agent) must have the target agent in its acquaintance list. Our initial approach was to allow the reference agent to perform operations on the target agent's tuple space. But upon further review, we decided for security and simplicity reasons that the reference agent can only *request* a target agent to perform the operation for it. By doing this, each agent maintains full control over its local data and can implement policies for rejecting and accepting requests from remote agents. This is accomplished using an *operation manager*.

The operation manager controls which requests are performed and is customizable. It greatly enhances the expressiveness of Limone since it can be customized to perform relatively complex tasks. For example, suppose each agent creates a public/private key pair and publishes its public key in a "read-only" tuple. The read-only nature of this tuple can be enforced by the operation manager by preventing all requests that would remove it from executing. Using this read-only tuple, secrecy and authentication can be achieved. Suppose a reference agent wishes to place a tuple onto a remote agent's tuple space. To do this, it can encrypt the data first by its private key, then by the remote agent's public key. The remote agent knows that the tuple is secret if it is able to decrypt it using its private key. It also knows that the tuple was sent by the reference agent if it can decrypt it using the reference agent's public key. This example illustrates how the operation manager can be configured to perform one complex task, e.g., authentication. The possibilities are endless.

Reactive programming constructs enable an agent to automatically respond to particular tuples in the tuple spaces belonging to agents in its acquaintance list. Two state variables within each agent, the *reaction registry* and *reaction list*, support this behavior. A reference agent registers a reaction by placing it in its reaction registry. Once registered, Limone automatically propagates the reaction to all agents in the acquaintance list that satisfy certain properties specified by the reaction (e.g., the agent's name or location). At the receiving end, the operation manager determines whether to accept the reaction. If accepted, the reaction is placed into the reaction list, which holds the reactions that apply to the local tuple space.

When the tuple space contains a tuple satisfying the trigger for a reaction in the reaction list, the agent that registered the reaction is sent a notification containing a copy of the tuple and a value identifying which reaction was fired. When this agent receives the notification, it executes the code associated with the reaction atomically. This mechanism, originally introduced in Mobile UNITY [7], and later deployed in LIME, is distinct from that employed in traditional publish/subscribe systems in that it reacts to state properties rather than to data operations. For instance, when a new agent is added to the acquaintance list, its tuples may trigger reactions regardless of whether the new agent performed any operations.

Code mobility is supported in Limone by allowing agents to migrate from one host to another. When an agent migrates, Limone automatically updates its context and reactions. There are many benefits to agent to migration. For example, if a particular host has a large amount of data, an agent that needs access to it over an extended period of time can relocate to the host holding the data and thus have reliable and efficient access to it despite frequent disconnection among hosts. Another example is software update deployment. Suppose an agent is performing a certain task and a developer creates a new agent that can perform the task more efficiently. The old agent can be designed to shutdown when the new agent arrives. Thus, simply having the new agent migrate to the same host as the old agent updates the application. To date, such updates are common practice on the Internet. However, agent migration promises to be even more beneficial in the mobile setting.

## 4   Design

Limone provides a runtime environment for agents via the Limone server, a software layer between the agent and the underlying operating system. By using different ports, multiple Limone servers may operate on a single host. However, for the sake of simplicity, we will treat each host as having one Limone server.

An application uses Limone by interacting with an agent. Each agent contains a tuple space, acquaintance list, reaction registry, reaction list, and operation manager. The overall structure of Limone is shown in Figure 2. An agent allows the application to customize its profile, engagement policy, and operation manager. An agent's profile describe its properties. Its engagement policy specifies which agents are relevant based on their profiles. The operation manager specifies which remote operation requests are accepted. This section describes how Limone fulfills its responsibilities and is organized around the key elements of the run-time environment, i.e., agent discovery, management, reactions, and agent mobility.

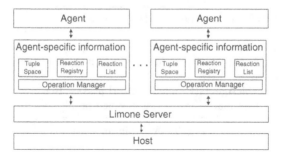

**Fig. 2.** The overall structure of Limone

**Discovery Mechanism.** Since connectivity between hosts in an ad hoc network is dynamic, Limone provides a *discovery protocol* based on beacons that allows an agent to discover the arrival and departure of other agents. Each Limone server periodically broadcasts a beacon containing a *profile* for each agent running on top of it. A profile is a collection of triples each consisting of a property name, type, and value. The two system-defined entries include the host on which the agent resides and a unique agent identifier. Additional entries can be added by the application. When the Limone server receives a beacon, it forwards it to each of its agents. When an agent receives a beacon, it extracts the profiles and passes them to its *acquaintance handler,* which uses the agent's *engagement policy* to differentiate the relevant profiles, and places them in the acquaintance list. If a particular agent's profile is already in the list, the acquaintance handler ensures that it is up to date and that it still satisfies the engagement policy. Once a profile is added to the acquaintance list, the acquaintance handler continuously monitors the beacons for the profile. If it is not received for an application-customizable period of time, the acquaintance handler removes the profile from the acquaintance list.

The acquaintance list, shown in Figure 3, contains a set of profiles representing the agents within range that have satisfied the engagement policy. The addition of a profile into the acquaintance list signifies an *engagement* between the reference agent and the agent represented by the profile. Once the reference agent has engaged with another agent, it gradually propagates its relevant reactive patterns (the trigger portion of the reaction) to the remote agent. While the addition of the profile to the acquaintance list is atomic, the propagation of reactive patterns is gradual, avoiding the need for a distributed transaction.

The removal of a remote agent's profile from the acquaintance list signifies *disengagement* between the reference and remote agent. When this occurs, the reference agent removes all of the remote agent's reactive patterns from its reaction list. The removal of the profile from the acquaintance list and the reactive patterns from the reaction list is performed atomically, which is possible because it is done locally.

---

**ABSTRACT STATE:** A set of profiles, $\{p_1, p_2, \ldots\}$

**INTERFACE SPECIFICATION:**
**boolean contains(AgentID aID)** — Returns *true* if the list contains a profile that has the specified AgentID.
**Profile[] getApplicableAgents(ProfileSelector[] pss)** — Returns all of the profiles within the list that match any of the specified profile selectors.

---

**Fig. 3.** Acquaintance list

**Tuple Space Management.** All application data is stored in individually owned tuple spaces, each containing a set of tuples. Limone tuples contain data fields distinguished by name and store user-defined objects and their types. The ordered list of fields characterizing tuples in Linda is replaced by unordered collections of named fields in Limone. This results in a more expressive pattern matching mechanism similar to the $\Psi$-terms in [1] that can handle situations where a tuple's arity is not known in advance. For example, in the universal remote application, the following tuple may be created by the remote control destined for a device:

$$tuple\{\langle\text{``type''}, \ String, \ \text{``command''}\rangle,$$
$$\langle\text{``device ID''}, \ String, \ \text{``CD Player''}\rangle,$$
$$\langle\text{``instruction''}, \ String, \ \text{``play''}\rangle\}$$

Agents use templates to access tuples in the tuple space. A template is a collection of named constraints, each defining a name and a predicate called the *constraint function* that operates over the field type and value. A template matches a tuple if each constraint within the template has a matching field in the tuple. A constraint matches a field if the field's name, type, and value satisfy the constraint function. For example, the following template matches the message tuple given above:

$$template\{\langle\text{``type''}, \ String, \ \text{valEql}(\text{``command''})\rangle\}$$
$$\langle\text{``device ID''}, \ String, \ \text{valEql}(\text{``CD Player''})\rangle\}^1$$

Notice that the tuple may contain more fields than the template has constraints. As long as each constraint in the template is satisfied by a field in the tuple, the tuple matches the template. This powerful style of pattern matching provides a higher degree of decoupling since it does not require prior knowledge of the ordering of fields within a tuple, or its arity, to create a template for it.

**Local Tuple Space Operations.** The operations an agent can perform on its tuple space are shown in Figure 4. The **out** operation places a tuple into the tuple space. The operations **in** and **rd** block until a tuple matching the template is found in the tuple space. When this occurs, **in** removes and returns the tuple, while **rd** returns a copy without removing it. The operations **inp** and **rdp** are

---

[1] `valEql(p)` is a constraint function that returns *true* if the value within the field is equal to $p$.

**INTERFACE SPECIFICATION:**

**void out(Tuple t)** — Places a tuple into the tuple space.

**Tuple rd(Template template)** — A blocking operation that returns a copy of a tuple matching the template.

**Tuple rdp(Template template)** — A non-blocking operation that returns a copy of a tuple matching the template, or $\varepsilon$ if none exists.

**Tuple[] rdg(Template template)** — Same as **rd** except it returns a copy of all matching tuples.

**Tuple[] rdgp(Template template)** — Same as **rdp** except it returns all matching tuples that exist.

**Tuple in(Template template)** — Same as **rd** except it removes the tuple.

**Tuple inp(Template template)** — Same as **rdp** except it removes the tuple.

**Tuple[] ing(Template template)** — Same as **rdg** except it removes the tuples.

**Tuple[] ingp(Template template)** — Same as **ingp** except it removes the tuples.

**Fig. 4.** Local tuple space operations

the same as **in** and **rd** except they do not block. If no matching tuple exists within the tuple space, $\varepsilon$ is returned. The operations **ing** and **rdg** are similar to **in** and **rd** except they find and return *all* matching tuples within the tuple space. Similarly, **ingp** and **rdgp** are identical to **ing** and **rdg** except they do not block. If they do not find a matching tuple, $\varepsilon$ is returned. All of these operations are performed atomically, which is possible because they are performed locally.

**Remote Tuple Space Operations.** To allow for inter-agent coordination, an agent can request a remote agent to perform an operation on their tuple space. To do this, Limone provides remote operations **out**, **inp**, **rdp**, **ingp**, and **rdgp**, as shown in Figure 5. These differ from the local operations in that they require an `AgentLocation` parameter that specifies the target agent. When a remote operation is executed, the reference agent sends a request to the remote agent specified by the `AgentLocation`, sets a timer, and remains blocked till a response is received or the timer times out. When the remote agent receives the request, it passes it to its operation manager, which may reject or approve it. If rejected, an exception is returned to allow the reference agent to distinguish between a rejection and a communication failure. If accepted, the operation is performed atomically on the remote agent, and the results are sent back. The timer is necessary to prevent deadlock due to message loss. If the request or response is lost, the operation will time-out and return $\varepsilon$. To resolve the case when an operation times out while the response is still in transit, each request is enumerated and the remote agent includes this value in its response.

**Reaction Mechanism.** Reactions enable an agent to inform other agents within its acquaintance list of its interest in tuples matching a particular template. A reaction contains an application-defined call-back function that is executed by the agent that created it when a matching tuple is found in a tuple

---

**INTERFACE SPECIFICATION:**

**void out(AgentLocation loc, Tuple t)** — Asks the agent at **loc** to place a
 tuple in its tuple space.

**Tuple rdp(AgentLocation loc, Template template)** — Asks the agent at **loc** to
 perform a **rdp** operation. Returns the results, or $\varepsilon$ if the operation times out.

**Tuple[] rdgp(AgentLocation loc, Template template)** — Asks the agent at **loc** to
 perform a **rdgp** operation. Returns the results, or $\varepsilon$ if the operation times out.

**Tuple inp(AgentLocation loc, Template template)** — Asks the agent at **loc** to
 perform a **inp** operation. Returns the results, or $\varepsilon$ if the operation times out.

**Tuple[] ingp(AgentLocation loc, Template template)** — Asks the agent at **loc** to
 perform a **ingp** operation. Returns the results, or $\varepsilon$ if the operation times out.

---

**Fig. 5.** Operations on a remote tuple space

space that the reaction is registered on. Reactions fit particularly well with ad
hoc networks because they provide an asynchronous form of communication between agents by transferring the responsibility of searching for a tuple from one
agent to another, which eliminates the need to poll continuously for data.

A reaction consists of a *reactive pattern* and a *call-back function*. The reactive
pattern contains a template that indicates which tuples trigger it and a list
of profile selectors that determine which agents the reaction should propagate
to. The call-back function executes when the reaction *fires* in response to the
presence of a tuple that matches its template in the tuple space it is registered
on. The firing of a reaction consists of sending a copy of the matching tuple to
the agent that registered the reaction. When the matching tuple is received, the
reference agent executes the reaction's call-back function atomically. To prevent
deadlock, the call-back function cannot perform blocking operations. Notice that
the message containing the tuple may be lost, meaning there is no guarantee that
a reaction's callback function will be executed even if a matching tuple is found.

The list of profile selectors within the reactive pattern determines which
agents it should be propagated to. Implementation-wise, a profile selector is
a template and a profile is a tuple. They are subject to the same pattern matching
mechanism but are functionally different because profiles are not placed in tuple
spaces. A reaction's reactive pattern propagates to a remote agent if the remote
agent's profile matches *any* of the reactive pattern's profile selectors. Multiple
profile selectors are used to lend the developer greater flexibility in specifying
a reaction's domain. For example, returning to our universal remote example,
a device would have the following profile:

$$profile\{\langle\text{``type''}, \ String, \ \text{``Device''}\rangle\}$$

and a reaction created by the universal remote control would contain the following profile selector to restrict its propagation to device agents:

$$profile \ selector\{\langle\text{``type''}, \ String, \ \texttt{valEql}(\text{``Device''})\rangle\}$$

This ensures that the reactive pattern only propagates to agents whose profile
contains a property called "*type*," with a *String* value equal to "*Device.*"

---

**ABSTRACT STATE:** — A set of reactions, $\{r, \ldots\}$

**INTERFACE SPECIFICATION:**
**ReactionID addReaction(Reaction rxn)**— Adds a reaction to the reaction registry
and returns the reaction's ReactionID.
**Reaction removeReaction(ReactionID rID)** — Removes and returns the reaction
with the specified ReactionID.
**Reaction get(ReactionID rID)** — Retrieves the reaction with the specified
ReactionID.
**Reaction get(Profile profile)** — Retrieves all reactions containing profile selectors
that match the given profile.

---

**Fig. 6.** Reaction Registry

As in LIME, reactions may be of two types: ONCE or ONCE_PER_TUPLE.
The type of the reaction determines how long it remains active once registered
on a tuple space. A ONCE reaction fires once and automatically deregisters itself
after firing. When a ONCE reaction fires and the reference agent receives the
resulting tuple(s), it deregisters the reaction from all other agents, preventing the
reaction from firing later. If a ONCE reaction fires several times simultaneously
on different tuple spaces, the reference agent chooses one of the results non-
deterministically and discards the rest. This does not result in data loss because
no tuples were removed. ONCE_PER_TUPLE reactions remain registered after
firing, thus firing once for each matching tuple. These reactions are deregistered
at the agent's request or when network connectivity to the agent is lost. To
keep Limone as lightweight as possible, no history is maintained regarding where
reactions were registered. Thus, if network connectivity breaks and later reforms,
the formerly registered reactions will be re-registered and will fire again.

Two additional state components, the *reaction registry* and *reaction list,* are
required for the reaction mechanism. The reaction registry, shown in Figure 6,
holds all reactions created and registered by the reference agent. An agent uses
its reaction registry to determine which reactions should be propagated following
an engagement and to obtain a reaction's call-back function when a reaction fires.

The reaction list, shown in Figure 7, contains the reactive patterns registered on the reference agent's tuple space. The reactive patterns within this list
may come from *any* agent within communication range, including agents *not*
in the acquaintance list. Thus, to maintain the validity of the reaction list, the
acquaintance handler notifies its agent when *any* agent moves out of communication range, not just the agents within its acquaintance list. The reaction list
determines which reactions should fire when a tuple is placed into the local tuple
space or when a reactive pattern is added to it.

**Agent Mobility.** Coordination within Limone is based on the logical mobility of agents and physical mobility of hosts. Agents are logically mobile
since they can migrate from one host to another. Agent mobility is accomplished using $\mu$Code [10]. $\mu$Code provides primitives that support light-weight

---

**ABSTRACT STATE:** — A set of reactive patterns, $\{rp_1, rp_2, \ldots\}$

**INTERFACE SPECIFICATION:**
**boolean addReactivePattern(ReactivePattern rp)** — Adds a reactive pattern to
  the reaction list, returns true if it was successfully added.
**void clear()** — Clears the reaction list by removing all reactive patterns within it.
**ReactivePattern[] getApplicablePatterns(Tuple tuple)** — Retrieves all of the
  reactive patterns within the list that should fire on the specified tuple.
**void removeReactivePattern(ReactivePattern rp)** — Removes the specified
  reactive pattern from the list if it is in the list.
**void removeReactivePatterns(AgentID aID)** — Removes all reactive patterns
  from the list that were registered by the agent with the specified AgentID.

---

**Fig. 7.** Reaction List

mobility preserving code and state. Of particular interest is the $\mu$CodeServer
and $\mu$Agent. A $\mu$Agent maintains a reference to a $\mu$CodeServer and provides
a go(String *destination*) method that moves the agent's code and data state
to the destination. The agent's thread state is not preserved because doing so
would require modifying the Java virtual machine, limiting Limone to propri-
etary interpreters. Thus, after an agent migrates to a new host, it will start fresh
with its variables initialized to the values they were prior to migration.

Limone cooperates with $\mu$Code by running a $\mu$CodeServer alongside each
Limone server and having the Limone agent extend $\mu$Agent. By extending
$\mu$Agent, the Limone agent inherits the go(String *destination*) method. However, Limone abstracts this into a migrate(HostID $hID$) method that moves
the agent to the destination host by translating the HostID to the string accepted by $\mu$Code. Prior to migration, the agent first deregisters all of its reactive
patterns from remote agents, and removes its profile from the beacons. Once on
the new host, the agent resumes the broadcasting of its beacons. This allows
remote agents to re-engage with the agent at its new location.

## 5   Evaluation

A prototype of Limone has been implemented in Java that strictly adheres to
the model given in Section 3, where each construct is a distinct object that
implements the interface and behavior described in Section 4. A LimoneServer
object serves as a foundation that listens for incoming messages and beacons.
It periodically broadcasts beacons containing the profiles of all agents residing
on it. An application can load its agents onto the LimoneServer by calling
loadAgent(), or by using a special Launcher object that communicates with
the server through its single-cast port. This allows new agents to be dynamically
loaded, possibly from a remote device.

As a testament to how lightweight Limone is, its jar file is only 111.7KB. To
analyze its performance, we calculated the round trip time for a tuple containing
eight bytes of data to be pulled onto a remote agent and back using reactions as

triggers. The test was performed using two 750MHz laptops running Java 1.4.1 in 802.11b ad hoc mode with a one second beaconing period. The laptops were located in a "clean room" environment where they are stationary and placed next to each other. To compare Limone's performance, we also performed the same operation using LIME and raw TCP sockets. Averaged over 100 rounds, the results of our tests are shown in Figure 1. They show that Limone adds some overhead over raw sockets, but not as much as LIME. Interestingly, in this simple test, Limone requires more code than LIME. This is due to Limone's more expressive pattern matching mechanism and engagement policy.

## 6  Sample Application

This section presents the universal remote control application we developed using Limone. Limone is ideal for this task because it automatically discovers all controllable devices within range of the remote control, allows the device's state to be shared and controlled amongst multiple remotes, and is lightweight enough to run on embedded devices such as electrical appliances.

When the Universal Remote is started, it briefly displays the notice shown in Figure 8(a) while it finds devices in range. As soon as it finds devices in range, it displays them in a tabbed list, as shown in Figure 8(b). Devices that go in or out of range are added to or removed from the list of tabs, ensuring that users cannot control devices that are no longer available. In addition to the controls for each device, a fixed row of controls is available along the bottom of the window to scroll the display, show or hide the grid, edit button placement, or show context-sensitive help (as shown in Figure 8(c)).

Each device runs a `LimoneServer` and has an associated agent. These agents insert information about the device into their local tuple space: namely, the advertised list of controls (buttons, sliders, etc.), the "help text" associated with each of these controls, and the current state of each control.

In order to further simplify the creation of device agents, we implemented a `GenericDeviceAgent` class as well as a `DeviceDefinition` interface. The `GenericDeviceAgent` is a Limone agent that accepts any `DeviceDefinition` interface as a plug-in; this interface exposes information about the device (such as its advertised controls) to the `GenericDeviceAgent` as well as exposing specific operations (i.e., pressed buttons or moved sliders) to the device. This allows the device-specific code to be implemented with little to no knowledge of Limone.

**Table 1.** Application code size and round-trip message passing time using reactions as a trigger, averaged over 100 rounds

| Model | Lines of Code | Time (ms) |
|---|---|---|
| Limone | 250 | 50.3 |
| LIME | 170 | 73.6 |
| Raw Sockets | 695 | 44.6 |

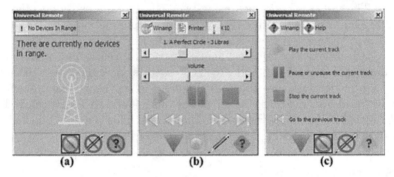

**Fig. 8.** The Universal Remote (a) at start-up before finding any devices,(b) after finding several available devices, and (c) displaying help for the selected device

As an example, we simulated a remotely-controllable stereo by writing a `WinampDeviceDef` to control Winamp [11]. This required implementing the eleven methods in the `DeviceDefinition` interface, which took about 250 lines of code and about an hour to write. The agent is started by loading a `GenericDeviceAgent` onto the device running Winamp, and instructing it to interface with the `WinampDeviceDef` class.

The `GenericDeviceAgent` instantiates a `WinampDeviceDef` and obtains basic information about the device such as its name, icon, functions, state, and help text. Based on this information, the `GenericDeviceAgent` inserts advertisement, state, and help text tuples into its tuple space using the local **out** operation, which the `UniversalRemoteAgent` reacts to and uses to create its display.

When the `UniversalRemoteAgent` alters the state of a device (such as by toggling a button), it creates an `ActionTuple` that describes the change and inserts it into the device's local tuple space using the remote **out** operation. The `GenericDeviceAgent` reacts to this tuple and notifies the `WinampDeviceDef`, which handles the change (such as by pausing the song if the pause button was toggled) and passes any change to the device's state (such as that the pause button is now lit) back to the `GenericDeviceAgent`. The `GenericDeviceAgent` then encapsulates the information in a `StateTuple` and inserts it into its local tuple space using the local **out** operation. The `UniversalRemoteAgent` reacts to this `StateTuple` and updates its display accordingly.

Aside from the SWT graphics library, no third-party libraries were needed in the implementation of the `UniversalRemoteAgent`, and no third-party libraries were needed for the implementation of the device agents aside from libraries specific to each device (e.g., an X10 communication library for the X10 agent). Further, since Limone uses a small subset of the Java API, both the client and server could be run on a device with limited Java support, like a PocketPC.

## 7   Conclusions

Limone is a lightweight but highly expressive coordination model and middleware tailored to meet the needs of developers concerned with mobile applications over ad hoc networks. Central to Limone is the management of context-awareness in a highly dynamic setting. The context is managed transparently and is subject to policies imposed by each agent in response to its own needs at a particular point in time. Explicit manipulation of the context is provided by operations that access data owned by agents in the acquaintance list. Each agent retains full control of its local tuple space since all remote operations are simply requests to perform a particular operation for a remote agent and are subject to policies specified by the operation manager. This security provision encourages a collaborative type of interaction among agents. An innovative adaptation of the reaction construct facilitates rapid response to environmental changes. As supported by evidence to date, the result of this unique combination of context management features is a coordination model and middleware that promise to reduce development time for mobile applications.

subcaption*Acknowledgements This research was supported in part by the National Science Foundation under grant No. CCR-9970939 and by the Office of Naval Research under MURI Research Contract N00014-02-1-0715. Any opinions, findings, and conclusions or recommendations expressed in this paper are those of the authors and do not necessarily reflect the views of the research sponsors.

# References

[1] Antonio Brogi, Jean-Marie Jacquet, and Isabelle Linden. On modeling coordination via asynchronous communication and enhanced matching. In Antonio Brogi and Jean-Marie Jacquet, editors, *Electronic Notes in Theoretical Computer Science*, volume 68. Elsevier, 2003. 143

[2] G. Cabri, L. Leonardi, and F. Zambonelli. MARS: A programmable coordination architecture for mobile agents. *Internet Computing*, 4(4):26–35, 2000. 137

[3] G. Cugola, E. Di Nitto, and A. Fuggetta. The JEDI event-based infrastructure and its application to the development of the OPSS WFMS. *IEEE Transactions on Software Engineering*, 27(9):827–850, September 2001. 137

[4] R. Englemore and T. Morgan. *Blackboard systems*. Addison-Wesley Publishing Company, 1988. 136

[5] D. Gelernter. Generative communication in Linda. *ACM Trans. on Prog. Languages and Systems*, 7(1):80–112, 1985. 136

[6] C. Julien and G.-C. Roman. Egocentric context-aware programming in ad hoc mobile environments. In *Proc. of the $10^{th}$ Int'l. Symp. on Foundations of Software Engineering*, 2002. 140

[7] Peter J. McCann and Gruia-Catalin Roman. Compositional programming abstractions for mobile computing. *IEEE Transactions on Software Engineering*, 24(2):97–110, 1998. 141

[8] Robin Milner, Joachim Parrow, and David Walker. A calculus of mobile processes, parts I and II. Technical Report 89-86, 1989. 136

[9] A. L. Murphy, G. P. Picco, and G.-C. Roman. LIME: A middleware for physical and logical mobility. In *Proc. of the $21^{st}$ Int'l. Conf. on Distributed Computing Systems*, pages 524–533, April 2001. 137

[10] Gian Pietro Picco. code: A lightweight and flexible mobile code toolkit. In Kurt Rothermel and Fritz Hohl, editors, *Proceedings of the 2nd International Workshop on Mobile Agents*, Lecture Notes in Computer Science, pages 160–171, Berlin, Germany, 1998. Springer-Verlag. 146

[11] Winamp. http://www.winamp.com/. 149

# Enforcement of Communal Policies for P2P Systems *

Mihail Ionescu, Naftaly Minsky, and Thu D. Nguyen

Department of Computer Science, Rutgers University
110 Frelinghuysen Rd, Piscataway, NJ, 08854
{ionescu, minsky, tdnguyen}@cs.rutgers.edu

**Abstract.** We consider the question of how to establish and enforce *communal* policies for peer-to-peer (P2P) communities. Generally, members of each P2P community must conform to an application specific communal policy if the community is to operate smoothly and securely. An open question, however, is how can such communal policies be established reliably and in a scalable manner? While some communities can rely on voluntary compliance with their stated policies, voluntary compliance will not be sufficient for many future P2P applications. We illustrate the nature of policies that must be *enforced* to be reliable by means of an example of a community that operates like Gnutella, but which is established to exchange more sensitive and critical information than music files. Then, we propose to employ the intrinsically distributed control mechanism called *Law-Governed Interaction* (LGI) for the scalable enforcement of communal P2P policies. To demonstrate the efficacy of the proposed approach, we show how our example policy can be formulated and enforced under LGI. Finally, we modify an existing open-source Gnutella client to work with LGI and show that the use of LGI incurs little overhead.

## 1 Introduction

Peer-to-peer (P2P) computing, where members of a community of agents interact *directly* with each other rather than through intermediary servers, is a potentially powerful paradigm for collaboration over the Internet [24]. But, a P2P community can collaborate harmoniously and securely only if all its members conform to a certain *communal policy*, or protocol. A Gnutella community, for example, relies on a flooding protocol to be carried out correctly by its members, in their collaborative effort to execute searches; and it depends on members not to issue too many queries, which might overburden the community, resulting in a kind of *tragedy of the commons*. Generally speaking, the purpose of such a policy is (a) to provide for effective coordination between members of the community, and (b) to ensure the security of community members, and of the information they share with each other. To achieve these purposes, the policy might impose

---

* This work was supported in part by Panasonic Information and Networking Technologies Laboratory and by NSF grant No. CCR-98-03698.

R. de Nicola et al. (Eds.): COORDINATION 2004, LNCS 2949, pp. 152–169, 2004.

constraints on both the membership of the community and on the behavior of its members when they are interacting with each other—all these in a highly application dependent manner.

**The Question We Address in this Paper** is how can such a communal policy be established reliably and scalably? That is, how can one ensure—in a manner consistent with the decentralized nature of P2P communication—that all members of a given P2P community comply with its communal policy?

There are essentially two ways for establishing communal policies: by *voluntary compliance*, and by *enforcement*. A policy $P$ can be established by *voluntary compliance* as follows: once $P$ is declared as a standard for the community in question, each member is simply expected to abide by it, or to be carefully constructed according to it, or to use a widely available tool (or "middleware"), which is built to satisfy this policy. For example, to join a Gnutella community, one employs a Gnutella *servent*—several implementation of which are available—which is supposed to carry out the Gnutella flooding protocols for finding neighbors and information. This is entirely voluntary, and there is no way for a member to ensure, or verify, that its interlocutors use correct Gnutella servents.

However, for voluntary compliance to be reliable, the following two conditions need to be satisfied: (a) it must be in the vested interest of everybody to comply with the given policy $P$; and (b) a failure to comply with $P$, by some member, somewhere, should not cause any serious harm to anybody else. If condition (a) is not satisfied then there is little chance for $P$ to be generally observed. If condition (b) is not satisfied than one has to worry about someone not observing $P$, maliciously or inadvertently, and thus causing harm to others.

The boundary between communal policies that can, and cannot, be established by voluntary compliance is not sharp. There are, in particular, communities whose policies have been designed carefully to be resilient to some amount of violations; this is the case, for example, for the *Free Haven* [10] and *Freenet* [7] communities, which attempt to provide anonymity, and to prevent censorship. There are also communities whose activity is not important enough to worry about violations, even if conditions (a) and (b) above are not satisfied. A case in point is a Gnutella community when it is used to exchange music files: the exchange of music is not a critical activity for most people and so the risk of members violating the implicit communal policy is not considered prohibitive.

But many of the policies required for P2P collaboration do not satisfy conditions (a) and (b) above, and do not lend themselves to implementation by voluntary compliance alone. Such policies, we maintain, *need to be enforced to be reliable*. We illustrate the nature of such policies, and their enforcement difficulty, by means of the following example of a community that operates like Gnutella, but which is established to exchange more critical information than music files.

**A Motivating Example:** Consider a collection of medical doctors, specializing in a certain area of medicine, who would like to share some of their experiences with each other—despite the fact that they may be dispersed throughout the world, and that they may not know each other personally. Suppose that they decided to form a Gnutella-like P2P community, to help in the location and dissemination of files that each of them would earmark for sharing with other community members.

The main difference between this case and music sharing is that the reliability of the information to be exchanged could be critical, and cannot always be judged simply by reading it. Moreover, some people, like representative of drug companies, may have vested interest to provide false treatment advice to promote their drug. One way to enhance the trustworthiness of the information exchanged is to limit the membership in the community to *trustworthy* people, however this may be defined. Policy *MDS* (for "Medical Data Sharing") below, attempts to do that, in a manner which is consistent with the decentralized nature of P2P communication. This policy also attempts to prevent the overloading of the community with too many messages, by budgeting the rate in which members can pose their queries; and it helps the receiver of information to evaluate its quality by providing him with the *reputation* of the source of each file he receives. Policy *MDS* is stated below, in somewhat abstract form.

1. Membership: An agent $x$ is allowed to join this community if it satisfies one of the following two conditions:
   (a) If $x$ is one of the *founders* of this community, as certified by a specific certification authority (CA) called here $ca1$. (Note: we assume that there are at least three such founders.)
   (b) (i) if $x$ is a medical doctor, as certified by the CA called $ca2$, representing the medical board; and
   (ii) if $x$ garners the support of at least three current members of this community.

   And, a regular member (not a founder) is *removed* from this community if three different members vote for his removal.
2. Regulating the Rate of Queries: Every query has a cost, which must be paid for from the budget of the agent presenting it. (We will elaborate later on the cost of different queries, and on the way in which agents get their budgets.)
3. Reputation: Each member must maintain a *reputation value* that summarizes other members' feedback on the quality of his responses to posted queries. Further, this reputation must be presented along with every response to a query. (Again, we will elaborate on the exact mechanism for maintaining this reputation later.)

It should be clear that this policy cannot be entrusted to voluntary compliance. The question is: how can one enforce a single policy of this kind over a large and distributed community? A recent answer given to this question [11], in the context of distributed enterprise systems, is to adopt the traditional concept of *reference monitor* [3], which mediates all the interactions between the members of the community. Of course, a single reference monitor is inherently unscalable, since it constitutes a dangerous single point of failure, and could become a bottleneck if the system is large enough. This difficulty can be alleviated when dealing with static (stateless) policies, simply by replicating the reference monitor–as has been done recently in [14].

But replication is very problematic for dynamic policies, such as our *MDS*, which are sensitive to the history, or *state*, of the interactions being regulated. This is because every state change sensed by one replica needs to be propagated, synchronously, to all other replicas of the reference monitor. In the case of our *MDS* policy, in particular, all replicas would have to be informed synchronously about every request made by each member, lest this member circumvents his budget by routing different requests through different replicas. Such synchronous update of all replica could be very expensive, and is quite unscalable.

We propose in this paper to employ the intrinsically distributed control mechanism called *Law-Governed Interaction* (LGI) [20, 22] for the governance of P2P communities. LGI is outlined in Section 2. To demonstrate the efficacy of this approach for P2P computing, we show, in Section 3, how our example policy *MDS* can be formulated and enforced under LGI. This is carried out in a strictly decentralized and scalable manner, using the Gnutella file-sharing mechanism. Finally, to show that LGI imposes only a modest amount of overhead, we have modified an existing Gnutella servent to inter-operate with LGI. Section 4 presents the measured overhead, both in terms of increased latency for each message-exchange and overheads of running the LGI law enforcement middleware.

## 2   Law-Governed Interaction: An Overview

Broadly speaking, LGI is a message-exchange mechanism that allows an *open group* of distributed agents to engage in a mode of interaction *governed* by an explicitly specified policy, called the *law* of the group. The messages thus exchanged under a given law $\mathcal{L}$ are called $\mathcal{L}$-messages, and the group of agents interacting via $\mathcal{L}$-messages is called a *community* $\mathcal{C}$, or, more specifically, an $\mathcal{L}$-community $\mathcal{C}_\mathcal{L}$. The concept of LGI has been originally introduced (under a different name) in [20], and has been implemented via a middleware called Moses [22].

By the phrase "open group" we mean (a) that the membership of this group (or, community) can change dynamically, and can be very large; and (b) that the members of a given community can be heterogeneous. In fact, we make here no assumptions about the structure and behavior of the agents[1] that are members of a given community $\mathcal{C}_\mathcal{L}$, which might be software processes, written in an arbitrary languages, or human beings. All such members are treated as black boxes by LGI, which deals only with the interaction between them via $\mathcal{L}$-messages, making sure it conforms to the law of the community. (Note that members of a community are neither prohibited from non-LGI communication nor from participation in other LGI-communities.)

---

[1] Given the popular usages of the term "agent," it is important to point out that we do not imply by it either "intelligence" nor mobility, although neither of these is being ruled out by this model.

For each agent x in a given community $\mathcal{C}_{\mathcal{L}}$, LGI maintains what is called the *control-state* $\mathcal{CS}_x$ of this agent. These control-states, which can change dynamically, subject to law $\mathcal{L}$, enable the law to make distinctions between agents, and to be sensitive to dynamic changes in their state. The semantics of control-states for a given community is defined by its law and can represent such things as the role of an agent in this community, and privileges and tokens it carries. For example, under law $\mathcal{MDS}$ to be introduced in Section 3, as a formalization of our example *MDS* policy, the term member in the control-state of an agent denotes that this agent has been certified as a doctor and admitted into the community.

We now elaborate on several aspects of LGI, focusing on (a) its concept of law, (b) its mechanism for law enforcement and their deployment, and (c) its treatment of digital certificates. Due to lack of space, we do not discuss here several important aspects of LGI, including the *interoperability* between communities and the treatment of *exceptions*. For these issues, and for a more complete presentation of the rest of LGI, and of its implemetation, the reader is referred to [22, 31, 4].

## 2.1    The Concept of Law

Generally speaking, the law of a community $\mathcal{C}$ is defined over a certain types of events occuring at members of $\mathcal{C}$, mandating the effect that any such event should have–this mandate is called the *ruling* of the law for a given event. The events subject to laws, called *regulated events*, include (among others): the *sending* and the *arrival* of an $\mathcal{L}$-message; the *coming due of an obligation* previously imposed on a given object; and the *submission of a digital certificate*. The operations that can be included in the ruling of the law for a given regulated event are called *primitive operations*. They include, operations on the control-state of the agent where the event occured (called, the "home agent"); operations on messages, such as forward and deliver; and the imposition of an obligation on the home agent.

Thus, a law $\mathcal{L}$ can regulate the exchange of messages between members of an $\mathcal{L}$-community, based on the control-state of the participants; and it can mandate various side effects of the message-exchange, such as modification of the control states of the sender and/or receiver of a message, and the emission of extra messages, for monitoring purposes, say.

**On The Local Nature of Laws:** Although the law $\mathcal{L}$ of a community $\mathcal{C}$ is *global* in that it governs the interaction between all members of $\mathcal{C}$, it is enforceable *locally* at each member of $\mathcal{C}$. This is due to the following properties of LGI laws:

- $\mathcal{L}$ only regulates local events at individual agents.
- The ruling of $\mathcal{L}$ for an event e at agent x depends only on e and the local control-state $\mathcal{CS}_x$ of x.
- The ruling of $\mathcal{L}$ at x can mandate only local operations to be carried out at x, such as an update of $\mathcal{CS}_x$, the forwarding of a message from x to some other agent, and the imposition of an obligation on x.

The fact that the same law is enforced at all agents of a community gives LGI its necessary global scope, establishing a *common* set of ground rules for all members of $\mathcal{C}$ and providing them with the ability to trust each other, in spite of the heterogeneity of the community. And the locality of law enforcement enables LGI to scale with community size.

Finally, we note here that, as has been shown in [22], the use of strictly local laws does not involve any loss in expressive power. That is, any policy that can be implemented with a centralized reference monitor, which has the interaction state of the entire community available to it, can be implemented also under LGI–although the efficieny of the two types of implementation can vary.

**On the Structure and Formulation of Laws:** Abstractly speaking, the law of a community is a function that returns a *ruling* for any possible regulated event that might occur at any one of its members. The ruling returned by the law is a possibly empty sequence of primitive operations, which is to be carried out locally at the *home* of the event.

In the current implementation of LGI, a law can be written either in Prolog or Java. Under the Prolog implementation, which will be assumed in this paper, a law $\mathcal{L}$ is defined by means of a Prolog-like program L which, when presented with a goal e, representing a regulated event at a given agent x, is evaluated in the context of the control-state of this agent, producing the list of primitive-operations representing the ruling of the law for this event.

In addition to the standard types of Prolog goals, the body of a rule may contain two distinguished types of goals that have special roles to play in the interpretation of the law. These are the *sensor-goals*, which allow the law to "sense" the control-state of the home agent, and the *do-goals* that contribute to the ruling of the law. A *sensor-goal* has the form t@CS, where t is any Prolog term. It attempts to unify t with each term in the control-state of the home agent. A *do-goal* has the form do(p), where p is one of the above mentioned primitive-operations. It appends the term p to the ruling of the law.

**The Concept of Enforced Obligation:** Obligations, along with permissions and prohibitions, are widely considered essential for the specification of policies for financial enterprises [16]. The concept of obligation being employed for this purpose is usually based on conventional *deontic logic* [18], designed for the specification of normative systems, or on some elaborations of this logic, such as taking into account interacting agents [5]. These types of obligations allows one to reason about what an agent must do, but they provide no means for ensuring that what needs to be done will actually be done [17]. LGI, on the other hand, features a concept of obligation that can be enforced.

Informally speaking, an obligation under LGI is a kind of *motive force*. Once an obligation is imposed on an agent–which can be done as part of the ruling of the law for some event at it–it ensures that a certain action (called *sanction*) is carried out at this agent, at a specified time in the future, when the obligation is said to *come due*–provided that certain conditions on the control state of the agent are satisfied at that time. The circumstances under which an agent may incur an obligation, the treatment of pending obligations, and the nature of the

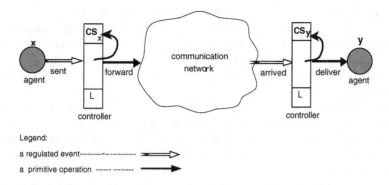

**Fig. 1.** Law enforcement in LGI. Specifically, this figure shows the sequence of events and operations resulting from the sending of an $\mathcal{L}$-message from $x$ to $y$. When x initiates the send, a **sent** event is triggered at $\mathcal{T}_x$, which in turns causes a ruling at $\mathcal{T}_x$ that updates $\mathcal{CS}_x$ and forwards the message to $\mathcal{T}_y$. When the message arrives at $\mathcal{T}_y$, an **arrived** event is triggered, which in turns causes a ruling at $\mathcal{T}_y$ that updates $\mathcal{CS}_y$ and delivers the message to $y$

sanctions, are all governed by the law of the community. For a detailed discussion of obligations the reader is referred to [22].

## 2.2   The Law-Enforcement Mechanism

We start with an observations about the term "enforcement," as used here. We do not propose to coerce any agent to exchange $\mathcal{L}$-messages under any given law $\mathcal{L}$. The role of enforcement here is merely to ensure that *any exchange of $\mathcal{L}$-messages, once undertaken, conforms to law $\mathcal{L}$.* More specifically, our enforcement mechanism is designed to ensure the following properties: (a) the sending and receiving of $\mathcal{L}$-messages conforms to law $\mathcal{L}$; and (b) a message received under law $\mathcal{L}$ has been sent under the same law (i.e., it is not possible to forge $\mathcal{L}$-messages).

Since we do not compel anybody to operate under any particular law, or to use LGI, for that matter, how can we be sure that all members of a community will adopt a given law? The answer is that an agent may be *effectively compelled* to exchange $\mathcal{L}$-messages, if he needs to use services provided only under this law, or to interact with agents operating under it. For instance, if the members of the medical information-sharing community posed as an example in Section 1 only accept $\mathcal{MDS}$-messages, then anybody wishing to participate in the community would be compelled to send $\mathcal{MDS}$-messages to them.

**Distributed Law-Enforcement:** Broadly speaking, the law $\mathcal{L}$ of community $\mathcal{C}$ is enforced by a set of trusted agents called *controllers*, that mediate the exchange of $\mathcal{L}$-messages between members of $\mathcal{C}$. Every member x of $\mathcal{C}$ has a controller $\mathcal{T}_x$ assigned to it ($\mathcal{T}$ here stands for "trusted agent") which maintains the control-state $\mathcal{CS}_x$ of its client x. And all these controllers, which are logically placed between the members of $C$ and the communications medium (as illustrated in Figure 1) carry the *same law* $\mathcal{L}$. Every exchange between a pair of agents x and y is thus mediated by *their* controllers $\mathcal{T}_x$ and $\mathcal{T}_y$, so that this enforcement is inherently decentralized. Although several agents can share a single controller, if such sharing is desired. (The efficiency of this mechanism, and its scalability, are discussed in [22].)

Controllers are *generic*, and can interpret and enforce any well formed law. A controller operates as an independent process, and it may be placed on any trusted machine, anywhere in the network. We have implemented a prototype *controller-service*, which maintains a set of active controllers. To be effective in a P2P setting, such a service would likely need to be well dispersed geographically so that it would be possible to find controllers that are reasonably close to their prospective clients.

**On the Basis for Trust Between Members of a Community:** For a members of an $\mathcal{L}$-community to trust its interlocutors to observe the same law, one needs the following assurances: (a) that the exchange of $\mathcal{L}$-messages is mediated by controllers interpreting the *same law* $\mathcal{L}$; (b) that all these controllers are *correctly implemented*; and (c) all controllers run on trusted executing environments that will not maliciously cause them to misbehave even when they are correctly implemented. If these conditions are satisfied, then it follows that if y receives an $\mathcal{L}$-message from some x, this message must have been sent as an $\mathcal{L}$-message; in other words, that $\mathcal{L}$-messages cannot be forged.

To ensure that a message forwarded by a controller $\mathcal{T}_x$ under law $\mathcal{L}$ would be handled by another controller $\mathcal{T}_y$ operating under the *same* law, $\mathcal{T}_x$ appends a one-way hash [27] H of law $\mathcal{L}$ to the message it forwards to $\mathcal{T}_y$. $\mathcal{T}_y$ would accept this as a valid $\mathcal{L}$-message under $\mathcal{L}$ if and only if H is identical to the hash of its own law.

With respect to the correctness of the controllers and their execution environments, controllers must authenticate themselves to each other via certificates signed by a certification authority acceptable to the law $\mathcal{L}$. Note that different laws may, thus, require different certification levels for the controllers (and their execution environments) used for its enforcement. Messages sent across the network must be digitally signed by the sending controller, and the signature must be verified by the receiving controller. Such secure inter-controller interaction has been implemented in Moses ([21]).

**On the Deployment of LGI:** To deploy LGI, one needs a set of trustworthy controllers and a way for a prospective client to locate an available controller. While this requirement is reminiscent of the centralized reference monitor solution, there is a critical difference: *controllers can be distributed to limit the computing load placed on any one node, allow easy scaling, and avoid a single point of failure.* Further, due to the local enforceability of laws, each controller only has to mediate interactions that involve agents connected to itself.

One possible deployment strategy for P2P computing is to run controllers on a subset of the peers that are trusted by the community. A new member can query its peers for the addresses of these controllers. As the community grows, this subset of trusted peers can grow to accommodate the additional computing load. A second possible solution would be to use a controller service. An example of an analogous non-commercial service is the set of Mixmaster anonymous remailers [23].

# 3   Regulating Gnutella-Based Information Sharing: A Case Study

We now show how the policy *MDS* introduced in Section 1 can be explicitly specified and enforced using LGI. To provide a concrete context for our study, we assume that the community of doctors in question are sharing their medical data using Gnutella. We start this section with an outline of the critical aspects of the Gnutella protocol. We then introduce the law in three parts, the first part regulates membership, the second regulates the searches carried out by members, and the third part deals with the reputation of members. For each part, we first motivate the appropriate portion of policy *MDS*, then expand on the policy itself as necessary, and, finally, discuss the details of the law itself–although we do not present the last part of the law, which deals with reputation, because of space constraints; we instead refer the interested reader to [13].

Finally, before proceeding, we note that we did not choose Gnutella because it is necessarily the best P2P system. Rather, we choose Gnutella because: (a) it is a *real* protocol being used by a thriving community of users, (b) there are many different implementations of the Gnutella servent so that the community cannot rely on built-in safe-guards to enforce acceptable behavior, and (c) its protocol is relatively simple, ensuring that our study is not bogged down with many irrelevant details.

## 3.1   Gnutella: A Brief Overview

The Gnutella protocol is comprised of three main parts:

**Joining** An agent joins a Gnutella community by simply connecting (using TCP) to one or more active members.

**Peer discovery** After successfully contacting at least one active member, the joining agent uses a flooding *ping/pong* protocol to discover more active members (peers). This protocol is very similar to the search protocol that we will describe next.

**Search** An agent searches for shared content by flooding a query through the community. In particular, the querying agent sends its query along with a time-to-live (TTL) to a subset of its known peers. When a peer receives a query, (a) it decrements the TTL and forwards the query to a subset of its known peers if the TTL is greater than 0; and (b) it searches its local store for files matching the query. If relevant files are found, it sends a *query-hit* message containing the names of the matching files directly to the querying agent. As the querying agent receives query-hit messages, it decides which file to download (if any) and does so by directly contacting the source of the appropriate query-hit message using HTTP.

## 3.2   Regulating Membership

We start our case study by considering the problem of controlling membership. While the set of criteria for admission and removal can be arbitrarily complex, fundamentally, there seems to be three concerns for our supposed community: (a) members should be doctors since sensitive medical data should not be shared with non-doctors, (b) members should have some level of trust in each other– again, because of the sensitive nature of the information being shared, and (c) if a member misbehaves, it must be possible to revoke his membership. These requirements led us to the membership part of policy *MDS* presented in Section 1.

Figure 2 gives the first part of law $\mathcal{L}_{MDS}$, which implements the membership portion of policy *MDS*. This, like other LGI laws, is composed of two parts: a *preamble* and a set of *rules*. Each rule is followed by a comment (in italic), which, together with the explanation below, should be understandable even for a reader not well versed in the LGI language of laws (which is based on Prolog).

The preamble of law $\mathcal{L}_{MDS}$ has several clauses. The first two specify that this community is willing to accept certificates from two certifying authorities, ca1 and ca2, identified by the given public keys. Then, there is an initialCS clause that defines the initial control-state of all agents in this community, which in this case is empty. We now examine the rules of this law in detail, showing how they establish the provisions of the policy at hand.

Rule $\mathcal{R}1$ allows the bootstrapping of a community by admitting three founding members certified by ca1. Rule $\mathcal{R}2$ allows an agent wishing to join the community to present a certificate from ca2 to prove that its user is a doctor. Once certified as a founder, the term member will be inserted into the agent's control state.

Rule $\mathcal{R}3$ specifies that an agent wishing to sponsor the entry of a new member must already be a member of the community. Furthermore, this rule specifies that a member can only sponsor each distinct agent at most once. If this agent has previously sent permission to Y to join, return a message saying already accepted Y in the past. Rule $\mathcal{R}4$ specifies that if three members have approved the admittance of an agent, then that agent is admitted to the community as a new member. Each message granting permission is also delivered to the destination agent. Note the distributed enforcement of the approval process: for example, the controller of the approver ensures that it is a member while the controller of the agent being sponsored ensures that it is a certified doctor. This distributed regulation is important for scalability because the requesting agent's controller does not have to gather information about the granting agent; it simply knows that, according to the law, if it gets a reply granting permission, the proper conditions must have been checked and met at the granting agent's controller.

Finally, rules $\mathcal{R}5$ and $\mathcal{R}6$ regulate the removal of members from the community in a similar manner to how admittance is regulated.

$\mathcal{P}$*reamble:*
   authority(ca1, CA1PublicKey). authority(ca2, CA2PublicKey). initialCS([]).
$\mathcal{R}$1.
```
   certified(X,cert(issuer(ca1),subj(X),attr([found(X)])))
       :- do(+member).
```
*The agent is accepted into the community without requiring approval from already admitted members if it can present a certificate from ca1 stating that it is a founder.*
$\mathcal{R}$2.
```
   certified(X,cert(issuer(ca2),subj(X),attr([md(X)])))
       :- do(+certified).
```
*The agent must establish that it is representing a doctor by presenting a certificate from ca2 with the attribute MD.*
$\mathcal{R}$3.
```
   sent(X,allow,Y)  :- member@CS,
           if (friend(Y)@CS) then do(deliver(X,alreadyAccept,X))
           else do(+friend(Y)), do(forward(X,allow,Y)).
```
*If the agent attempts to send a message approving admittance of another agent, forward the message if (a) the agent has membership, and (b) have not previously given Y permission to join.*
$\mathcal{R}$4.
```
   arrived(X,allow,Y)  :- certified@CS,
           do(deliver),
           if (nrfriends(M)@CS) then
           if (M>=3) then do(+member), do(-nrfriends(M)), else
           do(incr(nrfriends(M),1)), else do(+nrfriends(1)).
```
*When 3 approval messages have been received, the agent will be allowed to join the community (by having the member term added to its control state).*
$\mathcal{R}$5.
```
   sent(X,revoke,Y)  :- member@CS,
           if (enemy(Y)@CS) then do(deliver(X,alreadyRevoke,X))
           else do(+enemy(Y)), do(forward).
```
*The agent (X) can request that another agent (Y) to be removed from the community by sending a revoke message to Y.*
$\mathcal{R}$6.
```
   arrived(X,revoke,Y)  :- member@CS, if (nrenemies(M)@CS) then
           if (M>=4) then do(-member), do(-nrenemies(M)), else
           do(incr(nrenemies(M),1)), else do(+nrenemies(1)).
```
*If 4 current members have requested removal of this agent, then the agent is removed from the community.*

**Fig. 2.** $\mathcal{L}_{MDS}$, part 1: regulating membership

## 3.3   Avoiding the Tragedy of the Commons

We now turn our attention to preventing members from abusing the community. In particular, we regulate the rate with which each member can make queries, to ensure that careless and/or selfish members cannot overwhelm the community.

Before presenting the law, we expand on the synopsis of this part of policy *MDS* given in Section 1.

**Policy *MDS*, part (2): Limiting Query Rates**

2(a)  Each agent has a query budget that starts at 500, and is incremented by 500 every minute up to a maximum of 50,000.

2(b)  Each query has a cost as follows: $Cost = n \times 2^{TTL}$, where $n$ is the number of peers that the querying agent sends the query to and TTL is the query's TTL.

2(c)  An agent is only allowed to pose a query if its budget is greater than the cost of the query. When the query is posed, the cost is deducted from the agent's query budget.

Note that even in the above expanded policy, we have chosen to ignore the issue of ensuring that agents faithfully follow the Gnutella flooding protocol. By ignoring this issue, we are ignoring a number of possible threats: for example, an agent might increase the TTL of a peer's query instead of decreasing it, using searches from other members as a method for denial-of-service attack on the community, or an agent might selectively refuse to forward queries from a subset of community members (perhaps because the owner of the agent doesn't like this subset of members). We have chosen not to address this issue, however, for two reasons: (1) for simplicity of presentation and to meet the space constraint; and (2) in our view, carelessness and/or selfish self-interest, as represented by someone trying to index the communal set of information [8], is a much more likely threat than a malicious insider attempting to perpetrate a denial-of-service attack.

Figure 3 shows the second part of our law, which implements the second part of policy *MDS* described above. In Figure 3, the `preamble` is first modified to have a budget term that starts with 500 credits and an obligation imposed to be fired in 60 seconds. The firing of the obligation is handled by Rule $\mathcal{R}9$, which increases the agent's budget by 500 credits and then reimpose the obligation to be fired in another 60 seconds. Thus, effectively, the agent's budget is increased by 500 credits every minute until a cap of 50,000 is reached.

Rule $\mathcal{R}7$ deducts from the budget whenever the agent sends a query; if the agent does not have enough budget accumulated, the message is dropped and the agent notified with a message saying it has exceeded its budget. The specific values chosen were aimed at allowing a normal Gnutella search of ($TTL = 7, fan\text{-}out = 3$) every minute and a maximal search of ($TTL = 14, fan\text{-}out = 3$), which can be posted once every 100 minutes. Clearly, these parameters can be changed easily to accommodate the specific needs of the community. Also, note that we do not account for large fan outs once the query reaches an intermediary peer. We could handle this by complicating the law but do not do so here because there's no incentives for intermediary nodes to use huge fan outs (unless that

---

$\mathcal{P}$*reamble:*
    initialCS([budget(500)]).
    obligation(budgetincr,60).

$\mathcal{R}7$.
    sent(X,query(S,T,TTL),Y) :- member@CS, if (X=S) then
        budget(B)@CS, pow(2,TTL,C),
        if (B >= C) then do(decr(budget(B),C)),
        do(forward(X,query(T,TTL),Y))
        else do(deliver(X,nobudget,X)),
        else do(forward(X,query(T,TTL),Y)).
    *Only an accepted agent can send query messages to the community. The content*
    *of the query is contained in T. If the agent is the source of the query, then a charge*
    *of $2^{TTL}$ will be assessed against its budget.*
$\mathcal{R}8$.
    arrived(X,query(S, T,TTL),Y) :- member@CS,
        do(deliver(X,query(T,TTL),Y)).
    *On the arrival of a query message, deliver it to the destination agent if it has*
    *been certified and accepted into the community. We assume that the agent itself*
    *is responsable for the forwarding of query messages.*
$\mathcal{R}9$.
    obligationDue(budgetincr) :- budget(M)@CS,
        if (M < 50,000) then do(incr(budget(M),500)),
        do(imposeObligation(budgetincr,60)).
    *Impose an obligation to be fired every 60 seconds to increase the agent's messag-*
    *ing budget by 500.*

---

**Fig. 3.** $\mathcal{L}_{MDS}$, part 2: controlling querying behaviors

node was malicious and wanted to perform a denial of service attack, a threat that we are explicitly not addressing).

Finally, note that we currently only keep a budget for query messages. Ping messages are costly as well. A community may or may not choose to regulate ping messages. The governance of these messages would be basically the same as that for the query messages so we do not consider them further here.

## 3.4   Maintaining Reputations

The last part of our case study involves a simple yet general reputation system to aid members in assessing the reliability of information provided by each others. We do not include the law itself because of space constraints. Rather, we expand on the third part of policy *MDS* to give the general idea of the reputation system and then refer the interested reader to [13] for the details of the law.

A number of interesting reputation systems have already been designed [30, 2]. Most of these systems, however, have relied on a centralized server for computing and maintaining the reputations. Here, we show how a reputation system could be built using LGI's distributed enforcement mechanism. This reputation system is interesting because it maintains the reputation local to each peer (or, more precisely, local to the controller of that peer) so that the reputation can easily be embedded in every peer-to-peer query exchange without involving a third party. This allows scalable, per-transaction, on-line updates of reputations.

**Policy *MDS*, part 3: Reputation**

3(a)  Each member of a community has a numeric reputation in the range of $-1000$ to $1000$, which is attached to every query-hit message so that the querier can decide whether to trust the answer or not. Larger numeric reputation values imply greater trust.

3(b)  Each member starts with a reputation of 0 when it first joins the community. Whenever a member receives a query-hit message from a peer, it is allowed to rate the quality of the answer given by that peer. This rating can range from $-10$ to $10$ and is simply added to the peer's reputation. A member is allowed to make only one rating per answering peer per query.

### 3.5   Maintaining Persistent State

To close the section, we observe that peers in P2P networks often represent people; for example, in our example community, each member represents a doctor. Thus, persistent state such as membership and reputation should be associated with the person, not with the particular agent that he happens to be using at the moment. This is because as the real person moves around (between work and home, say), he may wish to employ different agents–the one installed on his work computer when at work and the one installed on his home computer when at home–at different locations. We use a feature of LGI called *virtual agents* [19] to provide the needed persistency. Again, we refer the interested reader to [13] for the details of this implementation.

## 4   Performance

We have modified the Furi Gnutella agent [29] to work with LGI to show that it is practical to make software "LGI-aware" as well as to measure the imposed overheads. This LGI-aware (Furi-LGI) version preserves the full functionality of the original agent–it searches for files, keeps a list of active neighbors, etc.–but passes most messages (per law $\mathcal{L}_M DS$) through an LGI controller instead of sending directly to peers on the Gnutella network.

To give an idea of the cost of using LGI, we measured two aspects of Furi-LGI: (1) the added latency of passing through LGI's controllers for a pair of message exchange, and (2) the overhead of running a controller. Measurements were taken on two 440 MHz Sparc Ultra10 machines connected by an Ethernet hub. Results are as follows. A query/query-hit message exchange between two normal Furi agents took 4ms compared to 15ms for two Furi-LGI agents. The added overhead for Furi-LGI is due to 4 LGI evaluations and 4 additional inter-process but intra-machine messages. A controller supporting 35 constantly interacting clients used on average 20% of the CPU and 30MB of main memory. While we did not measure the system extensively, these results provide evidence that LGI does not impose undue overheads and so provides a practical vehicle for establishing communal policies for P2P systems.

## 5   Related Work

While current P2P systems such as Gnutella [12], and KaZaA [15] have been very successful for music and video sharing communities, little attention has been paid to community governance. The very fact that these communities are not regulating themselves has led to the illegal sharing of material and so much of the legal trouble between these communities and the entertainment industries.

Much recent work has studied the problem of how to better scale P2P systems to support an enormous number of users [33, 26, 28, 25]. These efforts have typically not concern themselves with security, however, which is the focus of our work.

Two recent works have considered how to implement reputation systems for P2P communities: Cornelli et. al have considered implementing a reputation-aware Gnutella servent [9] while Aberer and Despotovic have considered implementing a binary trust system in the P-Grid infrastructure [1]. These efforts take a fundamentally different approach than ours in that they do not rely on a TCB as we do (i.e., the LGI controllers). Instead, they propose a system that uses historical information about past pair-wise interactions among the members of a community to compute a trust metric for each member. The underlying premise is that if only a few individuals are misbehaving, then it should be possible to identify these individuals by statistical analysis of the maintained historical information. Thus, these efforts differ from our work in two critical dimensions. First, these efforts limit their focus to reputation whereas our work uses reputation as a case study, aiming at the broader context of governing P2P communities. Second, these efforts rely on members of the community to participate in a reliable P2P storage and retrieval infrastructure while we rely on the network of controllers to provide a TCB.

A related effort that attempts to provide a more general framework than Cornelli et al. and Aberer and Despotovic is Chen and Yeager's Pablano web-of-trust [6]. While considerably more complex than the above two reputation systems, fundamentally, this work differs from our in similar ways.

Finally, it may be possible that some principles/invariants can be achieved even in the absence of universal conformance. One example of such a principle is anonymity: a number of P2P systems preserve the anonymity of their users by implementing anonymous storage and retrieval protocols that are resilient to a small number of misbehaving members [7, 32]. Our work differs from these efforts in that the LGI middleware allows a wide variety of policies to be specified and explicitly enforced without significant effort in protocol design, analysis, and implementation.

## 6  Conclusion

In this paper we propose LGI as the mechanism for specifying and enforcing the policies required for the members of a P2P community to collaborate harmoniously and securely with each other. LGI is well-suited to the P2P computing model because while it enforces *global* policies, it uses a *decentralized* enforcement mechanism that only depend on *local* information. This allows the use of LGI to easily scale with community sizes, avoids a single point of failure, and avoid needed centralized resources to start a community.

We provide supporting evidence for our proposal by presenting a case study of a Gnutella-based information sharing community. We show how a law regulating important aspects of such communities, including membership, resource usage, and reputation control can be written in a straightforward manner in LGI. Further, modifying a Gnutella agent to be compatible with LGI was a matter of a small number of weeks of work by one programmer. Finally, we observe that while our proposed solution requires the deployment of a trusted computing infrastructure, i.e., the set of law enforcement controllers, we believe that such an infrastructure is critical to the enforcement of policies that cannot rely on voluntary compliance. Further, this trusted computing infrastructure scales with the value of the collaboration being protected by the communal policy. Thus, a voted set of trusted nodes may be entirely adequate for the enforcement of many policies over many communities. Beyond this simple method, security may be escalated through a variety of approaches, such as the use of secure co-processors or a commercial controller service.

## References

[1]  Karl Aberer and Zoran Despotovic. Managing Trust in a Peer-2-Peer Information System. In *Proceedings of the 10th International Conference on Information and Knowledge Management (ACM CIKM)*, 2001. 166
[2]  Advogado. Website: http://www.advogato.org/. 164
[3]  J. P. Anderson. Computer security technology planning study. Technical Report TR-73-51, Air Force Electronic System Division., 1972. 154
[4]  X. Ao, N. Minsky, T. Nguyen, and V. Ungureanu. Law-governed communities over the internet. In *Proc. of Fourth International Conference on Coordination Models and Languages; Limassol, Cyprus; LNCS 1906*, pages 133–147, September 2000. 156
[5]  M. Brown. Agents with changing and conflicting commitments: a preliminary study. In *Proc. of Fourth International Conference on Deontic Logic in Computer Science (DEON'98)*, January 1998. 157
[6]  Rita Chen and William Yeager. Poblano: A Distributed Trust Model for Peer-to-Peer Networks. http://www.jxta.org/docs/trust.pdf. 166

[7] Ian Clarke, Oskar Sandberg, Brandon Wiley, and Theodore W. Hong. Freenet: A Distributed Anonymous Information Storage and Retrieval System. In *Proceedings of the ICSI Workshop on Design Issues in Anonymity and Unobservability*, number 2009 in LNCS, pages 46–66, 2000. 153, 166

[8] Clip2 DSS. Gnutella: To the Bandwidth Barrier and Beyond. http://www.clip2.com/gnutella.html, November 2000. 163

[9] Fabrizio Cornelli, Ernesto Damiani, Sabrina De Capitani di Vimercati, Stefano Paraboschi, and Pierangela Samarati. Implementing a Reputation-Aware Gnutella Servent. In *Proceedings of International Workshop on Peer to Peer Computing*, 2002. 166

[10] Roger Dingledine, Michael J. Freedman, and David Molnar. The Free Haven Project: Distributed Anonymous Storage Service. In *Proceedings of the ICSI Workshop on Design Issues in Anonymity and Unobservability*, number 2009 in LNCS, pages 67–95, 2000. 153

[11] D. Ferraiolo, J. Barkley, and R. Kuhn. A role based access control model and refernce implementation within a corporate intranets. *ACM Transactions on Information and System Security*, 2(1), February 1999. 154

[12] Gnutella. http://gnutella.wego.com. 166

[13] Mihail Ionescu, Naftaly Minsky, and Thu Nguyen. Enforcement of communal policies for p2p systems. Technical Report DCS-TR-537, Department of Computer Science, Rutgers University, Dec. 2003. 160, 164, 165

[14] G. Karjoth. The authorization service of tivoli policy director. In *Proc. of the 17th Annual Computer Security Applications Conference (ACSAC 2001)*, December 2001. (to appear). 155

[15] KaZaA. http://www.kazaa.com/. 166

[16] P. F. Linington. Options for expressing ODP enterprise communities and their policies by using UML. In *Proceedings of the Third Internantional Enterprise Distributed Object Computing (EDOC99) Conference*. IEEE, September 1999. 157

[17] P. F. Linington, Z. Milosevic, and K. Raymond. Policies in communities: Extending the odb enterprise viewpoint. In *Proceedings of the Second Internantional Enterprise Distributed Object Computing (EDOC98) Conference*. IEEE, November 1998. 157

[18] J. J. Ch. Meyer, R. J. Wieringa, and Dignum F. P. M. The role of deontic logic in the specification of information systems. In J. Chomicki and G. Saake, editors, *Logic for Databases and Information Systems*. Kluwer, 1998. 157

[19] Naftaly Minsky and Victoria Ungureanu. Scalable Regulation of Inter-Enterprise Electronic Commerce. In *Proceedings of the Second International Workshop on Electronic Commerce*, 2001. 165

[20] N. H. Minsky. The imposition of protocols over open distributed systems. *IEEE Transactions on Software Engineering*, February 1991. 155

[21] N. H. Minsky and V. Ungureanu. A mechanism for establishing policies for electronic commerce. In *The 18th International Conference on Distributed Computing Systems (ICDCS)*, pages 322–331, May 1998. 159

[22] N. H. Minsky and V. Ungureanu. Law-governed interaction: a coordination and control mechanism for heterogeneous distributed systems. *TOSEM, ACM Transactions on Software Engineering and Methodology*, 9(3):273–305, July 2000. 155, 156, 157, 158, 159

[23] Mixmaster. http://mixmaster.sourceforge.net. 160

[24] Andy Oram, editor. *PEER-TO-PEER: Harnessing the Benefits of a Disruptive Technology*. O'Reilly & Associates, Inc., 2001. 152

[25] Sylvia Ratnasamy, Paul Francis, Mark Handley, Richard Karp, and Scott Shenker. A scalable content addressable network. In *Proceedings of the ACM SIGCOMM '01 Conference*, 2001. 166

[26] A. Rowstron and P. Druschel. Pastry: Scalable, distributed object location and routing for large-scale peer-to-peer systems. In *Proceedings of the IFIP/ACM International Conference on Distributed Systems Platforms (Middleware)*, 2001. 166

[27] B. Schneier. *Applied Cryptography*. John Wiley and Sons, 1996. 159

[28] Ion Stoica, Robert Morris, David Karger, M. Frans Kaashoek, and Hari Balakrishnan. Chord: A Scalable Peer-to-peer Lookup Service for Internet Applications. In *Proceedings of the ACM SIGCOMM '01 Conference*, August 2001. 166

[29] The Furi Project. Website: http://www.furi.org. 165

[30] The SlashDot Home Page. Website: http://www.slashdot.org/. 164

[31] V. Ungureanu and N. H. Minsky. Establishing business rules for inter-enterprise electronic commerce. In *Proc. of the 14th International Symposium on DIStributed Computing (DISC 2000); Toledo, Spain; LNCS 1914*, pages 179–193, October 2000. 156

[32] Marc Waldman, Aviel D. Rubin, and Lorrie Faith Cranor. Publius: A Robust, Tamper-Evident, Censorship-Resistant, Web Publishing System. In *Proceedings of the 9th USENIX Security Symposium*, August 2000. 166

[33] Y. Zhao, J. Kubiatowicz, and A. Joseph. Tapestry: An infrastructure for fault-tolerant wide-area location and routing. Technical Report UCB/CSD-01-1141, University of California, Berkeley, 2000. 166

# An Infrastructure to Build Secure Shared Grid Spaces

Javier Jaén[1] and Elena Navarro[2]

[1] Departamento de Sistemas Informáticos y Computación
Universidad Politécnica de Valencia
fjaen@dsic.upv.es
[2] Departamento de Informática
Universidad de Castilla-La Mancha
enavarro@info-ab.uclm.es

**Abstract.** Grid applications need for coordination infrastructures that are secure and scalable with both the vast number of potential users and the enormous volume of information that may be exchanged. However, building middleware for these purposes that scales to accommodate the Grid requirements remains a complex problem. In this paper we present a middleware infrastructure that supports the creation of secure shared spaces scaling virtually to any number of users by defining security policies with regular expressions over distinguished names. We propose an XML representation for tuples in the shared space, an infrastructure of XSQL pages for accessing them, and a security model that supports authentication, privacy, integrity and authorization. Our approach leverages on existing standard technologies like XML, XSL, and HTTP favouring coordination between existing applications and future Web Services.

## 1 Introduction

In the last decades, applications have shifted towards distributed environments due to the increasing number of either the complex mathematical operations to be carried out (High Performance Computing) or the items to be processed per unit of time (High Throughput Computing). In these applications, distributed processing is completed over heterogeneous environments that have to work cooperatively but loosely coupled. An example of such environments are Grids [6] which support a new model of computing that has emerged from conventional distributed computing but focusing on large-scale resource sharing and innovative scientific applications. In this context, sharing is concerned about a highly controlled access to software, data, computers, etc, according to sharing rules defined by resources providers. Rules that have to define, clearly and carefully, *what* is shared, *who* is allowed to share, and *how* this sharing happens.

This new type of computing environments raise new challenges with respect to coordination, namely the heterogeneity of the coordinated processes, the volume and volatility of the shared information and the potentially vast number of processes that require an homogeneous way of communication, abstracting the machine-dependent details[7].

The coordination paradigm has ranged over a wide set of alternatives to address the issues related to the development of complex and distributed applications. Most of the proposed coordination models have evolved from the notion of shared spaces, which

R. de Nicola, et al. (Eds.): COORDINATION 2004, LNCS 2949, pp. 170-182, 2004.
© Springer-Verlag Berlin Heidelberg 2004

are common structures for the insertion and withdrawal of information, allowing inter-process communication and providing a decoupling in time and space. However, Linda [2], its most prominent representative, together with other approaches as BONITA[21] JavaSpaces [23], IBM T SPACE[14], lack security mechanisms.

In order to overcome this issue, several improvements have been proposed as SECOS[22] or LIME [19]. Both propose model extensions to overcome this deficiency when traditional shared spaces are applied to domains with strong security requirements like integrity for mobile agents, for the former, or control access and encrypted communications for ad-hoc networking, for the latter. Nevertheless, security for shared spaces in grid applications still have some peculiarities that underline major differences with respect to other applications like mobile agents: scalability of the authorization policies, heterogeneity and volatility of the number controlled of users/processes, and flexibility for the dynamic and rapid deployment of secure spaces.

In this paper we present a middleware infrastructure that supports the creation of secure shared spaces in this context. We propose an XML representation for tuples in the shared space, an infrastructure of XSQL pages for accessing them, and a security model that supports authentication, privacy, integrity and authorization at both coarse and fine grain levels. Our approach leverages on existing standard technologies like XML, XSL, and HTTP favouring interoperability among applications. The reminder of the paper is organized as follows: Section 2 describes XSQL[17] as a valid technology to develop shared dataspaces by providing a set of LINDA-like primitives. Section 3 details the security limitations of this technology and describes our security infrastructure to cope with the requirements listed above. Conclusions and future works round up the paper in Section 4.

## 2    Building Shared Spaces

The term shared dataspace [20] refers to the general class of models and languages in which the principal means of communication is a common, content-addressable data structure (called *Tuple Space*). All involved process can communicate via this medium, by means of the insertion and withdrawal of elements. In terms of Grid Applications, this structure allows that the involved virtual organizations cooperate by the insertion and withdrawal of their resources, both data and processes, as tuples.

As was stated above, LINDA is one of the most prominent languages to manage this communication model. Linda is defined as a set of four some simple coordination primitives:

- *out(t)* puts a passive tuple *t* in the tuple space,
- *in(t)* retrieves a passive tuple *t* from the tuple space,
- *rd(t)* retrieves a copy of *t* from the tuple space (i.e., t is still there)
- *eval(p)* puts an active tuple *p* (i.e., a process that turns into ordinary passive tuples after the completion of their execution) the tuple space.

To show that our approach is feasible we show a prototype shared space that support Linda-like operations. To increase the readability, only *rd* and *in* operations are brought into play.

## 2.1  XSQL for a Tuple Space

XSQL is a framework that allows any person familiar with SQL to create templates (XSQL pages) to produce XML documents from parametric SQL queries. Architecturally, this framework is implemented as a Java Servlet[11] running on a Web server which is compliant with the Java Servlets specification[12]. One important aspect of this technology is that it is not bound to any specific vendor server-side infrastructure, e.g. the framework has successfully been tested with several platforms as *Oracle9i Internet Application Server, Allaire JRun 2.3.3 and 3.0.0 Apache Tomcat 3.1 o 3.2 Web Server + Servlet Engine, Weblogic 5.1 Web Server, NewAtlanta ServletExec 2.2 and 3.0 for IIS/PWS 4.0, etc.*

A basic usage scenario of XSQL in a web server would be as follows (figure 1): a Web server receives a request of an XSQL page (.xsql extension). The server recognizes that an XSQL servlet is up and running and forwards the request. The servlet contains a processor of XSQL pages which is activated. The processor analyses the contents of the requested page, executes the SQL queries within it, transform the obtained results into a standard XML format and finally, if required, applies some XSLT transformations. Finally, the resulting document is returned to the requesting entity using HTPP as the underlying protocol.

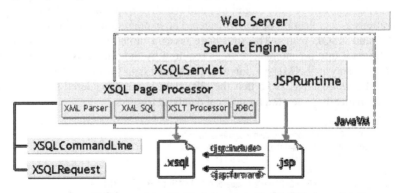

**Fig. 1.** Architectural view of the XSQL framework (Oracle9i Release 2.9.2)

This mechanism may be used in the context of our problem to implement shared spaces as relational databases that are accessed via standard HTTP requests to retrieve or insert tuples that are represented as XML documents. In doing so,  several advantages are obtained: first, tuples in the shared space may be manipulated and transformed in a very flexible and powerful way by using the many existing XML toolkits and APIs; second, setting up and managing new shared spaces is easy and cost-effective because only standard Web servers and a collection of XSQL pages are required to be in place, third, XSQL is platform independent and every JDBC compliant commercial RDBMS could be used to obtain scalable and performing spaces; finally, integration of shared spaces with future Web Services is straightforward because XML is the ground representation language.

In our approach tuples are represented as XML documents containing a sequence of fields and each field is, in general, an XML fragment. Having fields represented as XML fragments is an important issue because powerful matching XPath [25] expressions can be defined as will be shown later. An example of trivial tuple consisting of three fields is:

```
<?xml version="1.0"?>
<TUPLE>
    <FIELD id="1">
        <VALUE>
            <METADATA>
                <DESCRIPTION> http://data_repository /derived_data.dat</DESCRIPTION>
                <AUTHOR> Javier Jaen</AUTHOR>
                <TITLE> Callibration derived data </TITLE>
                <DATE>08/May/1970</DATE>
            </METADATA>
        </VALUE>
    </FIELD>
    <FIELD id="2"> <VALUE>23</VALUE></FIELD>
    <FIELD id="3"> <VALUE>This is just a string</VALUE></FIELD>
</TUPLE>
```

Internally, every tuple is assigned a URI[16] to uniquely identify it. Fields are stored in a simple relational table named *TUPLES* that, for the moment[1], has three columns *(URI,FIELDNUM,XMLFIELD)*, where *(URI, FIELDNUM)* is the primary key and *XMLFIELD* is the XML representation of the stored field of a tuple.

Having this simple data model in mind we have implemented the Linda *in* and *rd* operations as a collection of XSQL pages. The *in* operation is defined with two simple XSLT and XSQL pages. The first page takes a tuple as the one shown above and transforms it into a canonical form as required by the *<xsql:insert-request>* tag [17] then, this canonical XML document is the source data for the XSQL page that inserts it into the *tuples* table. Note that the URI field is not considered here because URIs are automatically generated by internal database triggers.

```
<?xml version = '1.0'?>
/* XSL Transformation to obtain a canonical form */
<ROWSET xmlns:xsl="http://www.w3.org/1999/XSL/Transform">
    <xsl:for-each select="/TUPLE/FIELD ">
        <ROW>
            <FIELDNUM><xsl:value-of select="/[@id]"/></ FIELDNUM>
            <XMLFIELD><xsl:value-of select="/VALUE"/></XMLFIELD>
        </ROW>
    </xsl:for-each>
</ROWSET>

<?xml version="1.0?>
/*XSQL page for inserting a tuple in the shared space*/
<xsql:insert-request xmlns:xsql="urn:oracle-xsql"
    connection="demo-shared-space"
    table="tuples"
transform="tuple-into-cannonical.xsl"/>
```

Implementing the *rd* operation in terms of XSQL pages is a bit more complex because we allow, for matching purposes, XPath expressions to be defined over the fields of a tuple. As an example, the following XML document included as part of an

---

[1]  Both the data model and its XML representation will be extended when considering security issues

*rd* request would match our previous tuple (note that non existing fields are interpreted as wildcards):

```
<?xml version="1.0"?>
<TUPLE>
    <FIELD id="1" xpath="/VALUE/METADATA[AUTHOR='Javier Jaen']"/>
    <FIELD id="3" xpath="/[VALUE= 'This is just a string ']"/>
</TUPLE>
```

In order to obtain the matching tuples, this document is passed as an HTTP request parameter (*rd-expr*) and processed during the execution of the following XSQL page:

```
<?xml version="1.0?>
/*XSQL page for reading from the shared space*/
<xsql:rd connection="demo-shared-space" expression=@rd-expr />
```

We have taken advantage of the extensibility properties of XSQL where new tags and associated Java handlers can be implemented. We have defined a new XSQL tag *<xsql:rd>* whose associated handler takes the XPath expressions, defined in the selection expression, evaluates them against the data stored in our database and finally assembles the fields of the matching tuples returning them as an XML document. The details about how to do it are out of the scope of this paper but, summarizing, a process of iterative matching of XPath expressions against the stored data is performed. The resulting tuples are returned in XML format as a response to the HTTP request.

# 3  A Security Infrastructure for Grid Shared Spaces

Security in XSQL pages is implemented by explicitly defining connection identifiers which are internally mapped into database connections (in our previous examples "demo-shared-space"). However, this mechanism is not well suited for our problem because of the following issues: first, processes requesting an XSQL page to execute a Linda operation are not authenticated (**authentication**); second, the transferred information is not encrypted and sensitive data is visible (**privacy**); third, processes other than the communicating ones may interfere in the transmission (**integrity**); fourth, policies to grant access to tuples or even fields within a tuple only to specific authorized parties may not be defined (**authorization**); finally, all this must be done taking into account that in a grid environment possibly thousands of processes (users) must be granted access in a secure way (**scalability**). Therefore, we need a security infrastructure that supports all these requirements in the context of our problem.

### Authentication, Privacy and Integrity

Since HTTP is the protocol used in our design to reach XSQL pages using standard URLs, it is easy to see that a straightforward access control mechanism can be implemented. One could use a secure extension of HTTP to restrict access to XSQL pages to authorized users only. Such a secure extension is already available and is widely known as HTTP over Secure Sockets Layer (SSL)[13]. The Secure Sockets Layer protocol is a protocol layer which may be placed between a reliable connection-oriented network layer protocol (e.g. TCP/IP) and the application protocol layer (in our case HTTP). SSL provides for secure communication between client and server by allowing mutual authentication, the use of digital signatures for integrity, and encryption for privacy. The protocol is designed to support a range of choices for specific algorithms used for cryptography, digests, and signatures.

**Authorization**

The access control mechanism described above is definitely valid for implementing basic level security, however there are some unresolved issues. First, when using SSL, access control is enforced by inspecting the certificate that the client side presents during the handshake process. In this case access control policies are defined in terms of existing fields in the certificate (the validity period, the signing certificate authority, the distinguished name, etc). These fields can be even extended with X509 v3 extensions and most implementations of SSL provide mechanisms to access such extensions and implement complex policies. Though this is feasible, this access control mechanism is not bound to XSQL. This means that complex policies defined at the X509 certificate level cannot be implemented at higher levels like the shared spaces that we are proposing. Besides, even if this information could be propagated, data providers would need to write code in order to implement group level access policies; this is unfeasible for non experts in security issues.

In our context we need a mechanism that allows users to be mapped dynamically to the appropriate shared spaces (different database connections) based on identity (as expressed in X509 certificates) and roles so that a same individual or process may access different shared spaces depending on the role she is playing. This authorization mechanisms has already been implemented for XSQL pages and is detailed in [9]. In short, a new XSQL tag for authorization purposes was defined <xsql:auth> so that database connections are dynamically generated by inspecting the X509 certificate and role information presented by a requestor. This information is checked against an authorization repository and access is granted or refused. This mechanism is valid for implementing a coarse grained protection when accessing shared spaces because only those processes presenting valid certificates and roles are granted rights to run an XSQL page and as a result access a given shared space. However, this protection is not enough and a fine grained mechanism, where fields within a tuple can be accessed by a restricted number of processes, is needed. In order to achieve this goal we have followed the same approach that we defined in [9], i.e., use information contained in X509 certificates and roles to define access policies to fields within a tuple. This authorization information is stored in our authorization repository and retrieved when processes invoke *rd* or *in* operations.

Authorization information is defined whenever a tuple is presented and contains the distinguished names of X509 certificates and valid roles that are granted access to each field. In our previous example the following authorization policy could be defined:

```
<?xml version="1.0"?>
<TUPLE>
    <FIELD id="1">
        <LOCKSET>
            <Member   DN="/C=CH/O=CERN/OU=IT   Division   /CN=Javier   Jaen"   Role
"sysadmin"/>
            <Member DN="/C=ES/O=UPV/OU=DSIC/CN=Javier Jaen " Role "professor"/>
            ....
        </LOCKSET>
        <VALUE>
            <METADATA>
                <DESCRIPTION> http://data_repository /derived_data.dat</DESCRIPTION>
                <AUTHOR> Javier Jaen</AUTHOR>
                <TITLE> Calibration derived data </TITLE>
                <DATE>08/May/1970</DATE>
            </METADATA>
        </VALUE>
    </FIELD>
    <FIELD id="2">
        <LOCKSET>
            <Member DN="/C=ES/O=UPV/OU=DSIC/CN=Javier Jaen " Role "professor"/>
        </LOCKSET>
        <VALUE>23</VALUE>
    </FIELD>
    <FIELD id="3">
        <VALUE>This is just a string</VALUE>
    </FIELD>
</TUPLE>
```

In the example above the first field is visible to the list of processes that present a valid X509 certificate with the listed distinguished names and roles and the third field is visible to anybody. Of course this XML document is presented to the XSQL page responsible for the insertion through a secure HTTP connection and therefore all the contained authorization information is properly encrypted. Now the insertion process of a tuple with authorization information is a bit more complex because not only the fields but also the related security information should be stored. Our modified relational model consists now of four tables so that locks for each field of a tuple are adequately stored and users are mapped to the correct shared spaces.

```
TUPLES(URI,FIELDNUM,,XMLFIELD, LOCKSET),
LOCKSETS(LOCKSET,MEMBERID),
SPACES(MEMBERID,DBCONN),
MEMBERS(MEMBERID,DNAME,ROLE)
```

For simplicity we will not include here the XSQL and XSL code that converts the XML document shown above into relational tuples of this new model.

Having this authorization model in mind, it is also evident that the matching process that takes place whenever an *in* or *rd* operation is invoked is now more complex. If the following XSQL page is requested through a secure HTTP connection (note that database connections in this page are not explicit and <xsql-auth> tags are used instead [9])

```
<?xml version="1.0?>
/*XSQL page for reading from the shared space*/
<xsql:auth>
<xsql:rd expression=@rd-expr />
</xsql:auth>
```

and a valid XML document containing XPath expressions is presented (see example in previous section) the following process is triggered:

- The standard SSL handshake process takes place and a client X509 certificate is requested
- The XSQL page processor processes the requested XSQL page by looking for "Action Elements" from the XSQL namespace. The first action element to be processed being an authorization action element "<xsql:auth>"
- The page processor invokes the authorization action element handler class to process the element.
- The handler obtains all the client information from the SSL layer and the role based information in order to access the authorization repository.
- Based on the role and X509 information presented the handler decides whether access is granted or denied for the requested XSQL page and dynamically embeds within the XSQL page the appropriate database connection information (appropriate shared space).
- The XSQL page processor continues the parsing of the remaining XSQL tags and as a result of finding an <xsql-rd> its associated handler is invoked. This handler proceeds as before, evaluates the XPaths expressions against the fields stored in our database but it takes an additional step before returning any matching field. The field locking info is obtained and the DN and role presented by the requesting process is compared against the stored authorized identities. If there is a match or no locking information was found the field is included in the response XML document, otherwise it is hidden.

As an example, if a requestor presents a valid certificate with DN="/C=CH/O= CERN/OU=IT Division /CN=Javier Jaen " and role "sysadmin" and an XML document with XPath expressions like the ones shown in the previous section the following tuple would be delivered (locking information for the first field matched the identity of the requestor, the second field was locked, and the third field had no locks):

```
<?xml version="1.0"?>
<TUPLE>
    <FIELD id="1">
        <VALUE>
            <METADATA>
                <DESCRIPTION> http://data_repository /derived_data.dat</DESCRIPTION>
                <AUTHOR> Javier Jaen</AUTHOR>
                <TITLE> Calibration derived data </TITLE>
                <DATE>08/May/1970</DATE>
            </METADATA>
        </VALUE>
    </FIELD>
    <FIELD id="3">
        <VALUE>This is just a string</VALUE>
    </FIELD>
</TUPLE>
```

This process can be seen graphically in Fig. 2 where both dependencies and data flows are shown.

## Scalability

The mechanism described above is feasible and can be used to implement secure shared spaces where a limited number of users/processes are accessing the space. In this situation, locks can be defined by defining a complete list of the DNs of requestors that are granted access to the shared space or even fields within a tuple.

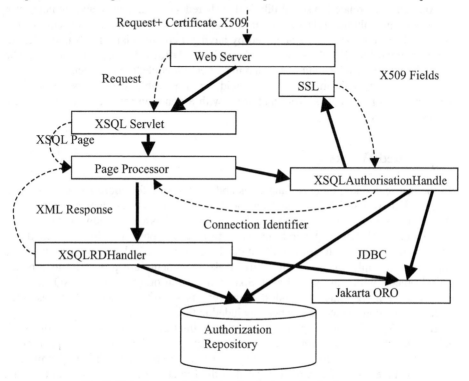

**Fig. 2.** Data flows and dependencies during authorization process

However, in a grid environment the number of potential users/processes that may request a tuple from a shared space is relatively large and fluctuates dynamically. In such a case, it is not practical to write down an exhaustive list of all authorized DNs and our mechanism would not scale well. Nevertheless, we have extended our authorization schema to support regular expressions over DNs so that more complex locks can be defined. For instance, assuming that we are building a shared space in a grid project like the one described in [6, 8, 9] and want to grant access to both all the members belonging to the IT Division of CERN and all Spanish members one just has to define the following lock set:

```
<LOCKSET>
  <Member DN="(/C=CH/O=CERN/OU=IT Division /*). " />
  <Member DN="(/C=ES/ *). " />
  ....
</LOCKSET>
```

This allows for scalable authorization policies that can be applied to a wide range of users/processes because any valid regular expression is supported. The only modification to the process described above is that handlers make use (figure 1) of a Java API for regular expressions (Jakarta ORO Matcher[10]) to compare the DN presented when requesting a tuple against the regular expressions stored in our database.

Another issue related to scalability is that shared spaces in a grid environment must scale with the volume of data stored in the space and with the number of requests per second. The first goal can be achieved by having a commercial DBMS under XSQL (let us remind that XSQL is compatible with any DBMS that supports JDBC). The second goal can also be achieved by having a tiered architecture in which a proxy web server (Apache with mod_jk [10] would be a possible choice) performs load balancing among XSQL servers that work with a common remote repository where tuples are stored.

# 4  Related Works

In the last few years, models, languages and middleware for coordination have been proposed in which XML-based technology or security issues play a central role. Nevertheless, not many proposals deal jointly with both issues as shown next.

TSpaces [24] defines general-purpose information repositories for networked and mobile applications with some built in XML support. XML documents are stored as tuples in the tuple space. Additionally, these documents are processed to produce DOM-objects which are stored as T Spaces tuples, in order to answer XQL queries with one or more matching nodes. However, its security model is very restricted because only control access has been included in this approach.

MARS-X[1] provides agents a JavaSpace interface to access a set of XML documents in terms of Java object tuples. These XML documents are specified in terms of unstructured sets of tuples which can be accessed and modified by exploiting the associative operation which is typical of the Linda model. Agents coordinate with each other by exchanging document tuples but with a restriction: being implemented as Java agents. This is an important problem when the coordinated processes are very heterogeneous as it may be the case in a grid environment where several stakeholders may form a virtual organization.

LIME offers strong support for coordination in ad-hoc networks, where computational units are mobile entities. This model addresses both logical and physical mobility, i.e. agents or physical devices. Each unit has its own tuple space whose behaviour can be programmed, similar to MARS-X but more restricted because it provides better control over the accesses. The coordination among co-located entities is allowed by automatically merging their tuple spaces, i.e., by temporal shared tuple spaces. Security enforcement is achieved by implementing authentication, cryptography, and access control in the underlying middleware. However, it disregards any interoperability issues, in a similar way to TuCSoN

TuCSoN[18] defines a coordination model based on logic tuple spaces, called *tuple centres*, associated and developed for the coordination of knowledge-oriented mobile agents. These tuple centres are programmable to provide a behaviour specified by the interaction rules. Furthermore, access control policies, such as authentication and authorization, have been implemented on these tuple centres [4]. However, some problems arise regarding interoperability. Although tuples can be translated into an XML format, because data is not typed, explicit translator reactions have to be programmed to face this problem.

Law Governed Linda [15] (LGL) was proposed to address Linda's inherent lack of safety that allows tuples to be anonymously passed between processes. In LGL, a set of rules, known as *laws*, restricts the reactions that may take place in the tuple space as a result of the events triggered by operations such as *in*, *out* or *rd*. It applies to any process wishing to participate in some exchange of data via the tuple space. Nevertheless, these laws are mainly intended to support the pair-wise communication, i.e. private channels, but they are not so appropriate for systems with a vast number of processes as it happens with grid systems. Furthermore, interoperability is not an issue in this approach.

The main advantage exhibited by our approach with respect to the others shown above is its ability to deal with interoperability by using standard protocols and services which makes it really simple to deploy a shared space. Since coordination is XML-based no special adding is needed to the involved nodes. Furthermore, security enforcement is accomplished by standard technologies that allow us not only to define authorization policies but also deal with authentication, privacy and integrity. Besides, the mechanism for defining access policies is scalable with the number of potential processes that may access a shared space.

## 5    Conclusions and Future Work

In this paper we have presented a powerful mechanism for implementing secure shared spaces in Grid-like environments. The main advantages of our approach are: tuples in shared spaces are represented as XML documents which enhances interoperability between different grid applications in need for coordination; issues like authentication, privacy, and integrity are covered by standard and well known technologies like SSL; authorization policies can be defined both at coarse (related to shared spaces) and fine-grained (related to fields within tuples) levels in terms of information contained in standard X509 certificates; scalability with the number of potential users/processes is achieved by supporting regular expressions over DNs and scalability with the number of requests is achieved by having in place web servers supporting load balancing. Finally, we also have to point out that all the technologies used in our approach will favour the use of our shared spaces for coordination of Web Services.

As future plans we want to provide support for revoked certificates so that access is not granted to shared spaces whenever such certificates are found and we also want to implement a linda-like Java API that uses our infrastructure so that developers do not have the burden of dealing with low level protocols like HTTP(S) and XML manipulation. Another interesting issue that we have not coped in this paper is delegation of certificates so that short-lived certificates may be automatically generated and used when accessing shared spaces and reduce the risk of certificates being stolen and used by non-authorized processes. In this context, we plan to investigate the work done in existing grid security infrastructures[21].

# References

[1]    Cabri, G., Leonardi, L., Zambonelli, F.: XML Dataspaces for Mobile Agent Coordination. 15th ACM Symposium on Applied Computing (2000).

[2]    Carriero, N. and Gelernter, D.: Linda in Context. Communications of the ACM, vol. 32, no. 4 (1989).

[3]    Ciancarini, P., Tolksdorf, R., Zambonelli, F.: A Survey on Coordination Middleware for XML-Centric Applications. The Knowledge Engineering Review, Vol. 17, No. 4, (2003).

[4]    Cremonini, M., Omicini, A., Zambonelli, F.: Multi-Agent Systems on the Internet: Extending the Scope of Coordination towards Security and Topology. Workshop on Modelling Autonomous Agents in a Multi-Agent Worlds (MAMAAW 1999), Valencia (E), LNAI n. 1647, Springer-Verlag (1999).

[5]    Düllmann, D., Hoschek, W., Jaen-Martinez, J., Samar, A., Segal, B., Stockinger, H. and Stockinger, K.:Models for Replica Synchronisation and Consistency in a Data Grid. 10th IEEE Symposium on High Performance and Distributed Computing (HPDC-10), San Francisco, California (2001).

[6]    Foster, I., Kesselman, C., Tuecke, S.: The Anatomy of the Grid: Enabling Scalable Virtual Organizations. International J. Supercomputer Applications, 3, Vol. 15 (2001).

[7]    Gelernter, D., Carriero, N.: Coordination languages and their significance. Communications of the ACM, Volume 35, Pages: 97 - 107, Issue 2 (1992).

[8]    Hoschek, W., Jaen-Martinez, J., Samar, A., Stockinger, H., Stockinger, K.. Data Management in an International Data Grid Project. In 1st IEEE/ACM International Workshop on Grid Computing (Grid'2000), Bangalore, India, December 17-20 (2000) Distinguished Paper Award.

[9]    Jaén-Martinez, J., Canós, J. H., An Advanced Security Infraestructure for Heterogeneous Relational Grid Data Sources, 1st European Across Grids Conference, Santiago de Compostela, Spain, February, (2003).

[10]   Jakarta ORO http://jakarta.apache.org/oro/

[11]   The Java Servlet Technology, http://java.sun.com/products/servlet/

[12]   JSR-000154 JavaTM Servlet 2.4 Specification, http://jcp.org/aboutJava/communityprocess/first/jsr154/index3.html

[13]   Kipp E.B. Hickman, The SSL Protocol, 1995 http://www.netscape.com/eng/security/SSL_2.html.

[14]   Lehman, T. J., McLaughey, S. W., Wyckoff, P.: T Spaces: The next Wave. Proceedings of the 32nd Hawaii International Conference on System Sciences, (1999).

[15]   Minsky, N., Leichter, J.: Law-Governed Linda as a Coordination Model. Object-Based Models and Languages for Concurrent Systems, LNCS, No. 924, pages 125-146, Springer-Verlag (1995).

[16]   Naming and Addressing (URIs, URLs, ... ), http://www.w3.org/Addressing/

[17]   Oracle9i XML Developer's Kits Guide – XDK Release 2 (9.2) Part Number A96621-0. Accessible at http://otn.oracle.com/tech/xml/xdkhome.htm.

[18]   Omicini, A., Zambonelli, F.: TuCSoN: a Coordination Model for Mobile Information Agents. 1st International Workshop on Innovative Internet Information Systems (IIIS'98), Pisa, Italy, June (1998).

[19]   Roman, G.-C., Handorean, R.: Secure Sharing of Tuple Spaces in Ad Hoc Settings. Proceedings of the 1st International Workshop on Security Issues in Coordination Models, Languages, and Systems, (SecCo 2003), Electronic Notes in Theoretical Computer Science Vol. 85, No. 3. (2003).

[20]   Roman, G.-C., Cunningham, H. C., Mixed Programming Metaphors in a Shared Dataspace Model of Concurrency. IEEE Transactions on Software Engineering, 12, Vol. 16 (1990) 1361-1373.

[21]    Rowstron, A.: Using asynchronous tuple space access primitives (BONITA primitives) for process coordination. Coordination Languages and Models (Coordination'97), editors D. Garlan and D. Le Métayer, pages 426-429. Published by Springer-Verlag, LNCS 1282, (1997).

[22]    Vitek, J., Bryce, C., Oriol, M., Coordinating Agents with Secure Spaces, Proceedings of Coordination '99, Amsterdam, The Nederlands, (1999)

[23]    Waldo, J. et al. Javaspace specification - 1.0. Technical report, Sun Microsystems, March (1998).

[24]    Wyckoff, P.: T Spaces. IBM Systems Journal, Vol 37 (3), (1998): 454–474.

[25]    XML Path Language V1.0 W3C Recommendation (1999), http://www.w3.org/TR/xpath

# Optimistic Concurrency Semantics
# for Transactions in Coordination Languages

Suresh Jagannathan and Jan Vitek

Department of Computer Sciences, Purdue University
West Lafayette, IN 47906
{suresh,jv}@cs.purdue.edu

**Abstract.** There has been significant recent interest in exploring the
role of coordination languages as middleware for distributed systems.
These languages provide operations that allow processes to dynamically
and atomically access and manipulate collections of shared data. The
need to impose discipline on the manner in which these operations occur becomes paramount if we wish to reason about correctness in the
presence of increased program complexity. Transactions provide strong
serialization guarantees that allow us to reason about programs in terms
of higher-level units of abstraction rather than lower-level data structures. In this paper, we explore the role of an optimistic transactional
facility for a Linda-like coordination language. We provide a semantics
for a transactional coordination calculus and state a soundness result
for this semantics. Our use of an optimistic concurrency protocol distinguishes this work from previous efforts such as Javaspaces, and enables
scalable, deadlock-free implementations.

## 1 Introduction

A transaction defines a locus of computation that adheres to well-known safety
and failure properties. To ensure these properties hold, the semantics of a transactional facility must guarantee that the effects of a transaction are not observable until a commit occurs; when a commit does occur, all effects are propagated
instantaneously to the enclosing parent transaction; once a transaction commits,
the global state records its effects, and forgets the association between the effect and the transaction; and, all data accesses performed by a transaction are
performed serially with respect to other concurrently executing transactions.
These four traits correspond to isolation, atomicity, durability, and consistency
properties respectively in classical transaction models.

There have been several attempts which explore the integration of transactional semantics within a coordination language framework. Most notably,
JavaSpaces [18] and TSpaces [27] combine Linda-like semantics augmented with
transactional features into Java. A formal treatment of JavaSpaces, along with
several important extensions, is given by Busi and Zavattaro [11, 12]. The Java-
Spaces implementation is based on a *pessimistic* concurrency control semantics:
locks are acquired when an entry is accessed, preventing other transactions from

R. de Nicola et al. (Eds.): COORDINATION 2004, LNCS 2949, pp. 183–198, 2004.
© Springer-Verlag Berlin Heidelberg 2004

witnessing that value until the owning transaction commits. An entry can be physically removed from the shared space only if the removing action is part of the same transaction as any uncommitted reads to that object. Writes to the space become visible to other transactions only when their initiator commits. Although relatively simple to describe, a pessimistic treatment of transactions for coordination languages has two notable disadvantages:

1. *Deadlock*: Since shared data are locked by reads, two transactions each of whom read distinct entries may deadlock depending upon the order in which the locks are acquired. Moreover, it is not possible to acquire locks prior to executing a transaction since determining whether an object will be read depends upon the transaction's dynamic control-flow. The ability to select entries based on pattern-matching further complicates the issue of deadlock detection and avoidance.

2. *Scalability*: Pessimistic concurrency control negatively impacts scalability of distributed implementations as read operations require the acquisition of global locks and thus increase synchronization between distributed nodes. Non-blocking operations, such as Linda's RDP and INP (which test for the presence of a tuple) further complicate the implementation of pessimistic concurrency control protocols as they require that every *potential* entry that may match the operation's template argument be locked for the duration of the transaction [11] to preserve desired serializability invariants.

In this paper, we explore an alternative treatment of transactions within a tuple space coordination framework that addresses these issues. We define a semantics for a transactional variant of Linda [19] based on the synchronous $\pi$-calculus [24]. This language can be viewed as the computational core of systems such as JavaSpaces (without some features such as leases and notification [18]) in which effects on the shared data space are controlled via a transactional mechanism based on an *optimistic* concurrency protocol. In this protocol, every transaction conceptually operates over its own local copy of the space and performs actions restricted to this copy. When a transaction is to commit, the state of the local copy is compared to the current state of the global space. If serializability invariants have been violated, the transaction aborts and its local copy is discarded. Otherwise, the changes can be propagated to the global space. The rate at which aborts occur in this scheme is closely correlated to the rate at which concurrent threads operate in incompatible ways over the same tuples.

Our work is distinguished from previous efforts in three main respects: (*a*) our transactional semantics is based on an *optimistic* concurrency model that eliminates issues of deadlock, and obviates scalability limitations which arise in more pessimistic lock-based transactional schemes; (*b*) our treatment of non-blocking operations that test for the presence or absence of tuples, allow us to reason about the validity of these operations using transaction-local, rather than global, judgments; and (*c*) the semantics naturally allows transactions to be arbitrarily nested. Taken together, these features suggest that expressive, scalable, and deadlock-free transactional implementations for coordination languages are feasible.

# 2    Coordination Languages and Transactions

We are interested in defining robust, scalable concurrent programs that use a Linda-style coordination framework to mediate access to shared data. Classical coordination models such as Linda allow atomic access and modification of content-addressable data. However, explicit support for treating a locus of computation and the collection of data the computation accesses as a single atomic unit is not provided. An atomic transaction is a control abstraction that provides such functionality. The transactional semantics of concurrent actions in the context of a coordination model ensures serializability and atomicity properties of operations that read, remove, write, and test for the presence of tuples in a global data space.

## 2.1    JavaSpaces

Sun Microsystem's JavaSpaces is a well-known attempt at integrating a Linda-like coordination language enriched with transactional support into a general purpose programming language. Although expressive, the JavaSpaces programming model is somewhat unintuitive and difficult to implement. We consider its main features here and refer interested readers to the specification [18] and related research papers [8, 11, 12, 9, 26] for further clarification. In particular, we do not consider leasing and event notification which are treated in detail by Busi and Zavattaro in [11, 12].

In JavaSpaces a shared data space is an object which supports at least the following operations: `write()`, `read()`, `take()`, `readIfExists()` and `takeIfExists()`. The first operation deposits an entry in the shared space. The operations `read( template)` and `take( template)` scan the shared space for an entry matching `template`, reading or removing a matching tuple, respectively, if one exists and blocking otherwise. Although the match operation in JavaSpaces is user-defined, we restrict ourselves in this paper to traditional value-based structural pattern matching familiar to pure Linda systems. If the template is the distinguished `null` value, any entry in the data space may match. `readIfExists()` and `takeIfExists()` are non-blocking equivalents of `read()` and `take()` respectively (similar to Linda's `rdp` and `inp`). If no value matching the template is currently in the shared space, these operations return `null`. Busi and Zavattaro have discussed in detail the implications of the ability to test for the presence of a value [11, 12]. We revisit these operations in later sections.

## 2.2    Transactions

In this paper, we consider a multi-threaded nested transactional model. When transactions are *nested* [25], each top-level transaction is divided into a number of child transactions; each of which can also have nested transactions. Nested transactions commit from the bottom up, and child transactions must always commit before their parent. A transaction abort at one level does not necessarily affect a transaction in progress at a higher level. The updates of committed

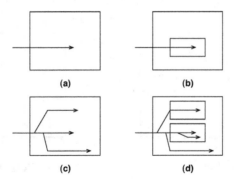

**Fig. 1.** Threads and transactions may be interleaved in various ways: (a) plain, (b) nested, (c) multi-threaded, (d) multi-threaded and nested

transactions at intermediate levels are visible only within the scope of their immediate predecessors. Support for nested transactions is an important feature of our semantics. A nested transaction defines a locus of computation whose effects are bounded by its parent. Thus, the effects of operations on shared data can be controlled by defining an appropriate transaction nesting structure, leading to improved modularity and scalability. Programs are more modular because the effects of a nested transaction are localized to its parent. Programs are scalable because effects are not propagated immediately as the nested transaction commits; instead, changes are aggregated and made globally visible only when the parent transaction commits.

In a multi-threaded transaction model, each transaction can have multiple concurrent threads operating on the same view of the shared state. In a nested transaction model, multiple threads can be executing in parent and child transaction concurrently. Fig. 1 summarizes the different interactions that arise between transactions and threads.

A transactional facility can be modeled by a simple API consisting of the operation start() and commit(). We assume an implicit transactional context so that start() initiates a new transaction. If the current thread is already running within a transaction, the new transaction is nested in the current one, otherwise the new transaction becomes a top-level transaction. The commit() operation attempts to finalize the changes made by the current transaction, propagating its results to the parent if one exists.

## 2.3   Motivating Examples

To illustrate some salient issues related to the incorporation of transactional semantics into a coordination language, consider the actions defined in Fig. 2. Transactions A and B perform read and write actions on a global data space which initially has two singleton tuples ⟨1⟩ and ⟨2⟩. Transaction A takes ⟨1⟩ and then writes it back. Once A is done, transaction B performs a non-destructive

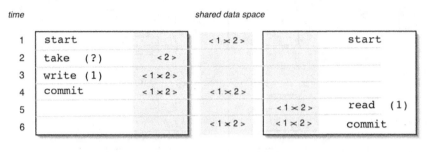

**Fig. 2.** Serialized execution of transaction A and B. The shared data space is only updated upon commit. Each transaction has its own view of the data space. The shared space starts out as { ⟨1⟩, ⟨2⟩ }. At time 2, transaction A performs a `take(?)` which removes entry ⟨1⟩ from the space. Thus from A's point of view the shared space contains a single entry (⟨2⟩). A commit reconciles a transaction's local view with the state of the shared space

read of ⟨1⟩ and commits. This is a valid interleaving as all actions of A precede the actions of B.

Figs. 3 and 4 illustrate possible interleavings if the actions performed by A and B are enclosed within transactions under different transactional semantics. In Fig. 3 transaction B reads ⟨1⟩ after it was taken by A. In a *pessimistic* model such as the one used by JavaSpaces [11], this interleaving is not valid as the `take()` performed by A locks ⟨1⟩ and prevents B from performing a read. In an *optimistic* semantics, transaction B can proceed and, in fact, both transactions can commit successfully.

Fig. 4 illustrates a case in which, under an *optimistic* semantics, transaction B has to abort. In this example, A reads ⟨1⟩ but writes back another copy of ⟨2⟩, while B still reads ⟨1⟩. Of course when B gets to the point of committing, it finds that the global space does not have tuple ⟨1⟩ and thus is forced to abort.

Fig. 5 illustrates a more serious problem with JavaSpaces. We use `inp` as a non-blocking take (*i.e.* `takeIfExists()`). Assume the global data space is initially empty. Transaction A checks if tuple ⟨2⟩ is present, and will take if it is, while transaction B attempts to take ⟨1⟩. Both operations fail as the space contains no matching value. A proceeds to write ⟨1⟩ and B to write ⟨2⟩, after which both transactions commit. In an *optimistic* semantics transaction B would abort because at time 6 the contents of the global space is {⟨1⟩ } while transaction B expect ⟨1⟩ *not* to be in the space (since it has checked this at time 2). In Sun's JavaSpace *implementation*, both transactions are allowed to commit successfully. This behavior is incorrect as noted by Busi and Zavattaro [11]. In a correct *pessimistic semantics* (*i.e.* [11]) this problem can be redressed by prohibiting other transactions from depositing any matching writes to the tuple-space once A performs its test. However, in this example, such a semantics would lock any

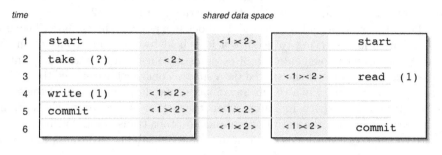

**Fig. 3.** Valid optimistic interleaving. In a pessimistic semantics transaction B would have to block until A commits, *i.e.* it would behave as illustrated in Fig. 2

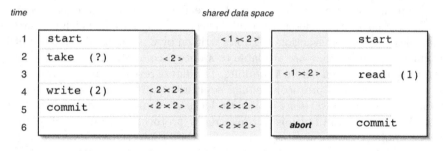

**Fig. 4.** Valid optimistic interleaving. Transaction B fails to commit due to a conflict in the global data space (entry ⟨1⟩ is absent)

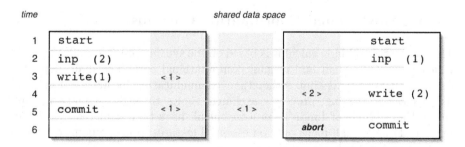

**Fig. 5.** Valid optimistic interleaving. Transaction B abort due to a conflict in the state of the shared space (⟨1⟩ is present). A pessimistic semantics would deadlock

transaction from depositing a single element tuple, and would thus prevent B from committing since it subsequently performs a `write` on ⟨2⟩.

Thus, the example of Fig. 5 would deadlock in a pessimistic semantics because each transaction is trying to acquire a lock held by the other transaction. In general, a correct implementation of pessimistic concurrency control may entail locking large portions of the shared data space. Consider for instance the action `readIfExists( null)` which, in JavaSpaces, matches *any* entry in the data space. If the data space is empty when the action is evaluated, the current transaction will lock the entire space and no other transaction will be able to write to the space until this one commits if serializability invariants are to be preserved.

Transaction protocols for coordination languages are further complicated when nested transactions are considered. The semantics of nested transactions permit child transactions to see the effects of their parents, even before the parent commits. Using pessimistic concurrency control, the rules governing when tuple operations become visible, and when read and write locks are released must be strengthened. Fig. 6 describes a valid execution sequence in which transaction A defines a nested transaction C. Tuples written by C are unavailable to B until A commits, although they are available to A once C commits. Tuples written by A are available to C even before A commits. This figure reveals that fine-grained pessimistic concurrency protocols require sophisticated lock management schemes to allow nested transactions to inherit locks on tuples owned by their ancestors. In constrast, an optimistic concurrency protocol maintains multiple local logs and directly incorporates notions of visibility into the log structure. When a nested transaction attempts to read a tuple, writes performed by its parent that match the tuple pattern are visible to the nested transaction. To ensure that writes performed in a nested transaction are propagated correctly, an optimistic concurrency mechanism need only guarantee that nesting of logs reflect transaction nesting. No special lock management protocol is required.

## 3    A Transactional Coordination Calculus

The transactional Linda calculus is based on the synchronous $\pi$ calculus [1, 4, 22] which provides a small and elegant computational core. The main departure from the $\pi$ calculus is that rather than communicating by means of channel-based message passing, processes exchange tuples through a common shared space. Embeddings of Linda in process calculi have been explored in previous work [6, 17]. We shall focus only on essential features from the point of view of the transactional behavior of the calculus.

### 3.1    Syntax

The syntax of the calculus is summarized in Fig. 7. We take an infinite set of names ranged over by meta-variable x. Tuples are sequences of formal and actual entries ranged over by meta-variable v. The empty tuple is denoted by ⟨⟩. The

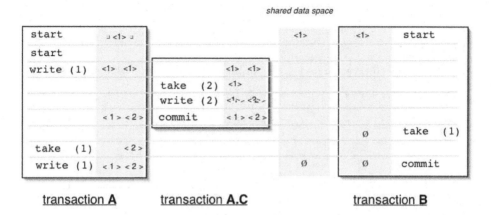

**Fig. 6.** Actions performed by a nested transaction are not visible to the parent until the inner transaction commits; the effects of a nested transaction are not visible to other transactions until its parent commits

expression x . v denotes the tuple resulting from concatenating an actual name x with tuple v, while $x^?$ . v denotes the concatenation of a formal variable x with v. Meta-variable t ranges over transaction identifiers, and $\ell$ over sequences of transaction identifiers.

The syntactic category of processes, ranged over by P and Q, includes the empty process **0** and parallel composition of processes P | Q. Synchronous output, written v.P, deposits the tuple denoted by v in the shared data space and proceeds to execute P. The input operation (v). P evaluates the template v against the shared space; if a matching value is found, the tuple is taken from the shared space and the process continues as P with the formals of v replaced by actuals from the tuple; the operation blocks if no matching value can be found. Guarded replication, written (v)! P, performs an input of v and, if a match is found, proceeds as P with (in parallel) a copy of the original process (v)! P. The test operation, (v)? P ; Q is a non-blocking test for presence which tries to find a tuple matching the template v, and if one is found, proceeds to evaluate P with the tuple; if no matching tuple is found in the space Q is evaluated. The restriction operator $(\nu x)$ P generates a fresh name x; the calculus is lexically scoped, so x is visible only in process P. Finally **trans** P and **commit** are used to, respectively, start and terminate a new transaction. The transaction **trans** P will execute the process P until a **commit** is evaluated, at which point all changes effected by the transaction will become visible to all other transactions. If a conflict is detected the transaction will not be able to commit and the evaluation of the thread will remain stuck. Note also that all other threads within the same transaction and nested transaction are terminated upon a commit. The calculus does not provide an explicit **abort** operation; we model aborted transactions as stuck terms on **commit** transitions.

**Syntax:**

$$P ::= 0 \mid P|Q \mid (\nu x)\,P \mid \textbf{trans}\,P \mid t[P] \mid \textbf{commit} \mid (v).P \mid v.P \mid (v)?P\,;Q \mid (v)!P$$

$$v ::= \langle\rangle \mid x.v \mid x^?.v \qquad \tau ::= v \mid {}^{v'}\!/_v \mid \neg v \mid \textbf{com} \mid \textbf{srt} \qquad \ell ::= \langle\rangle \mid \ell.t$$

$$\mathcal{E} ::= \langle\rangle \mid \mathcal{E}.\ell:\rho \qquad \rho ::= \langle\rangle \mid \rho.v \mid \rho.\neg v \mid \rho.v^?$$

---

$$(v).P \xrightarrow{{}^{v'}\!/_v}{}_{\langle\rangle} {}^{v'}\!/_v\,P \qquad \text{(L-INP)}$$

$$(v)?P\,;Q \xrightarrow{v}{}_{\langle\rangle} {}^{v'}\!/_v\,P \qquad \text{(L-POS)}$$

$$(v)?P\,;Q \xrightarrow{\neg v}{}_{\langle\rangle} Q \qquad \text{(L-NEG)}$$

$$(v)!P \xrightarrow{{}^{v'}\!/_v}{}_{\langle\rangle} {}^{v'}\!/_v\,P \mid (v)!P \quad \text{(L-LOOP)}$$

$$v.P \xrightarrow{v}{}_{\langle\rangle} P \qquad \text{(L-OUTP)}$$

$$\textbf{trans}\,P \xrightarrow{\textbf{srt}}{}_{t} t[P] \qquad \text{(L-START)}$$

$$t[\textbf{commit} \mid P] \xrightarrow{\textbf{com}}{}_{t} 0 \quad \text{(L-COMM)}$$

$$\frac{P \xrightarrow{\tau}{}_{\ell} P'}{t[P] \xrightarrow{\tau}{}_{t.\ell} t[P']} \qquad \text{(L-TRANS)}$$

$$\frac{P \xrightarrow{{}^{v'}\!/_v}{}_{\ell} P' \quad v',\mathcal{E}' = \mathsf{take}(\mathcal{E},\ell) \quad v \leq v'}{P\ \mathcal{E} \xRightarrow{\ell} P'\ \mathcal{E}'} \quad \text{(G-INP)}$$

$$\frac{P \xrightarrow{v}{}_{\ell} P' \quad \mathcal{E}' = \mathsf{put}(\mathcal{E},\ell,v)}{P\ \mathcal{E} \xRightarrow{\ell} P'\ \mathcal{E}'} \quad \text{(G-OUTP)}$$

$$\frac{P \xrightarrow{\neg v}{}_{\ell} P' \quad \mathcal{E}' = \mathsf{neg}(\mathcal{E},\ell,v)}{P\ \mathcal{E} \xRightarrow{\ell} P'\ \mathcal{E}'} \quad \text{(G-NEG)}$$

$$\frac{P \xrightarrow{\textbf{srt}}{}_{\ell} P' \quad \mathcal{E}' = \mathsf{start}(\mathcal{E},\ell)}{P\ \mathcal{E} \xRightarrow{\ell} P'\ \mathcal{E}'} \quad \text{(G-START)}$$

$$\frac{P \xrightarrow{\textbf{com}}{}_{\ell} P' \quad \mathcal{E}' = \mathsf{commit}(\mathcal{E},\ell)}{P\ \mathcal{E} \xRightarrow{\ell} P'\ \mathcal{E}'} \quad \text{(G-COMM)}$$

$$\frac{P\ \mathcal{E} \equiv P'\ \mathcal{E} \quad P'\ \mathcal{E} \xRightarrow{\ell} Q'\ \mathcal{E}' \quad Q' \equiv Q}{P\ \mathcal{E} \xRightarrow{\ell} Q\ \mathcal{E}'} \quad \text{(G-CONG)}$$

---

**Evaluation Contexts:**

$$E[\bullet] \mid E[\bullet] \mid P$$

$$\frac{P \xrightarrow{\tau}{}_{\ell} P'}{t[E[P]] \xrightarrow{\tau}{}_{t.\ell} t[E[P']]}$$

$$\frac{P \xrightarrow{\tau}{}_{\ell} P' \quad x \notin fn(\tau)}{(\nu x)\,P \xrightarrow{\tau}{}_{\ell} (\nu x)\,P'}$$

**Structural Congruence:**

$$P \mid Q \equiv Q \mid P \qquad (\nu x)\,(\nu y)\,P \equiv (\nu y)\,(\nu x)\,P$$

$$P \mid (\nu x)\,Q \equiv (\nu x)\,P \mid Q \quad \textit{if } x \notin fn(P)$$

$$t[(\nu x)\,P] \equiv (\nu x)\,t[P]$$

$$(\nu x)\,P\ \mathcal{E} \equiv P'\ \mathcal{E} \qquad \textit{if } x \notin fn(\mathcal{E}) \wedge P \equiv P'$$

**Fig. 7.** Syntax and Semantics

**Free Names:**

$$fn(0) = \{\} \qquad fn(\text{P} \mid \text{Q}) = fn(\text{P}) \cup fn(\text{Q}) \qquad fn((\nu\, x)\ \text{P}) = fn(\text{P}) - x \qquad fn(\text{t}[\,\text{P}\,]) = fn(\text{P})$$

$$fn(\textbf{commit}) = \{\} \qquad fn((\text{v}).\,\text{P}) = fn(\text{P}) \cup fn(\text{v}) - bn(\text{v}) \qquad fn(\text{v}.\,\text{P}) = fn(\text{P}) \cup fn(\text{v}) - bn(\text{v})$$

$$fn(\textbf{trans}\ \text{P}) = fn(\text{P}) \qquad fn((\text{v})?\,\text{P}\,;\,) = fn(\text{P}) \cup fn(\text{v}) - bn(\text{v}) \qquad fn((\text{v})!\,\text{P}) = fn(\text{P}) \cup fn(\text{v}) - bn(\text{v})$$

$$fn(\text{x}.\,\text{v}) = \{x\} \cup fn(\text{v}) \qquad fn(\text{x}^?.\,\text{v}) = fn(\text{v}) \qquad fn(\langle\,\rangle) = \{\}$$

$$bn(\text{x}.\,\text{v}) = bn(\text{v}) \qquad bn(\text{x}^?.\,\text{v}) = \{x\} \cup bn(\text{v}) \qquad bn(\langle\,\rangle) = \{\}$$

**Matching:**

$$\langle\,\rangle \leq \langle\,\rangle \qquad\quad \text{x}.\,\text{v} \leq \text{x}.\,\text{v}' \ \ \textit{if } \text{v} \leq \text{v}' \qquad\quad \text{x}^?.\,\text{v} \leq \text{x}.\,\text{v}' \ \ \textit{if } \text{v} \leq \text{v}'$$

**Fig. 8.** Free Names and Matching Rules

## 3.2 Semantics

The semantics of the calculus is shown in Figs. 7, 8, and 9. The semantics is stratified so that the local reduction relation P $\xrightarrow{\ \tau\ }_\ell$ Q defines that process P can reduce to Q in one step. The transition is labeled by an action $\tau$ and a trans-action $\ell$. The global relation P $\mathcal{E} \xRightarrow{\ \ell\ }$ Q $\mathcal{E}'$ defines the behavior of a program P in an environment $\mathcal{E}$. We assume congruence of environments under element reordering.

In the local reduction relation the tuple space remains implicit. Each reduction step is labeled by one of the following actions: v, $^\text{v}/_\text{v}$, ¬v, **srt**, and **com**, indicating a write of v, a take of v' matching v, a test for absence of v, the start of a transaction and a commit, respectively. Furthermore transitions are labeled by the issuing transaction name, $\ell$, composed of a sequence of transaction identifiers; the different identifiers correspond to the levels of nesting, thus $\text{t}.\text{t}'.\text{t}'''$ denotes an action performed by transaction $\text{t}'''$ nested in transactions $\text{t}'$ and $\text{t}$.

$$^{\text{x}.\text{v}}/_{\text{x}.\text{v}'}\,\text{P} = {}^\text{v}/_{\text{v}'}\,\text{P} \qquad {}^{\text{x}.\text{v}}/_{\text{y}^?.\text{v}'}\,\text{P} = {}^\text{v}/_{\text{v}'}\,{}^\text{x}/_\text{y}\,\text{P} \qquad {}^{\langle\rangle}/_{\langle\,\rangle}\,\text{P} = \text{P}$$

$$^\text{x}/_\text{y}\,0 = 0 \qquad {}^\text{x}/_\text{y}\,\text{P} \mid \text{Q} = {}^\text{x}/_\text{y}\,\text{P} \mid {}^\text{x}/_\text{y}\,\text{Q} \qquad {}^\text{x}/_\text{y}\,(\nu\, x)\ \text{P} = (\nu\, x)\ \text{P}$$

$$^\text{x}/_\text{y}\,(\nu\, x')\ \text{P} = (\nu\, x')\ {}^\text{x}/_\text{y}\,\text{P} \qquad {}^\text{x}/_\text{y}\,\text{t}[\,\text{P}\,] = \text{t}[{}^\text{x}/_\text{y}\,\text{P}\,] \qquad {}^\text{x}/_\text{y}\,\textbf{commit} = \textbf{commit}$$

$$^\text{x}/_\text{y}\,(\text{v}).\,\text{P} = ({}^\text{x}/_\text{y}\,\text{v}).\,{}^\text{x}/_\text{y}\,\text{P} \ \ \textit{if } x \notin fn(\text{v}) \qquad {}^\text{x}/_\text{y}\,(\text{v}).\,\text{P} = ({}^\text{x}/_\text{y}\,\text{v}).\,\text{P} \ \ \textit{if } x \in fn(\text{v})$$

$$^\text{x}/_\text{y}\,(\text{v})!\,\text{P} = ({}^\text{x}/_\text{y}\,\text{v})!\,{}^\text{x}/_\text{y}\,\text{P} \ \ \textit{if } x \notin fn(\text{v}) \qquad {}^\text{x}/_\text{y}\,(\text{v})!\,\text{P} = ({}^\text{x}/_\text{y}\,\text{v})!\,\text{P} \ \ \textit{if } x \in fn(\text{v})$$

$$^\text{x}/_\text{y}\,(\text{v})?\,\text{P}\,;\,\text{Q} = ({}^\text{x}/_\text{y}\,\text{v})?\,{}^\text{x}/_\text{y}\,\text{P}\,;\,{}^\text{x}/_\text{y}\,\text{Q} \ \ \textit{if } x \notin fn(\text{v}) \qquad {}^\text{x}/_\text{y}\,(\text{v})?\,\text{P}\,;\,\text{Q} = ({}^\text{x}/_\text{y}\,\text{v})?\,\text{P}\,;\ \ \textit{if } x \in fn(\text{v})$$

$$^\text{x}/_\text{y}\,\text{v}.\,\text{P} = ({}^\text{x}/_\text{y}\,\text{v}).\,{}^\text{x}/_\text{y}\,\text{P} \ \ \textit{if } x \notin fn(\text{v}) \qquad {}^\text{x}/_\text{y}\,\text{x}.\text{v} = \text{y}.{}^\text{x}/_\text{y}\,\text{v} \qquad {}^\text{x}/_\text{y}\,\text{x}^?.\text{v} = \text{x}^?.\text{v}$$

$$^\text{x}/_\text{y}\,\text{z}^?.\text{v} = \text{z}.{}^\text{x}/_\text{y}\,\text{v} \qquad {}^\text{x}/_\text{y}\,\langle\,\rangle = \langle\,\rangle$$

**Fig. 9.** Substitutions

Starting a transaction with **trans** P creates a process P running within some transaction t, and is denoted t[P]. We assume that each new transaction identifier t is chosen to be distinct. Transactions can be nested, for instance the expression t[t′[P] | Q] denotes two parallel processes P and Q such that Q is running within a top level transaction t and a process P in a transaction t′ nested within t. For example, the expression **trans** (**trans** v. 0) denotes a process that will spawn two transactions, the second nested within the first. Then the expression will reduce in one step to the inactive process:

$$t[\ t′[v.\mathbf{0}]\ ]\ \ \xrightarrow{\ v\ }_{t.t′}\ \ t[\ t′[\mathbf{0}]\ ]$$

Notice that in this configuration, the tuple v was output from transaction t . t′ and since there is no commit for that transaction that value will never become available to other processes.

The global reduction relation $\stackrel{\ell}{\Longrightarrow}$ manages the shared data space and defines the semantics of the transactional facility. The semantics does not fix a specific implementation or a particular transactional model as it is parameterized by an environment $\mathcal{E}$ which contains the tuple space and five operations over environments that implement the actual transactional model. Although we provide definitions for these operations that capture the essential traits of an optimistic concurrency protocol, other specifications that define alternative implementations of the protocol, or which express different transactional semantics (such as pessimistic concurrency) can be developed without modifying the global reduction relation.

The rule (G-INP) defines the behavior of a destructive read over the tuple space. Given an environment and a transaction, **take** returns a value available to that transaction; if that value matches the requested template, the transition proceeds with an updated environment. (G-OUTP) is similar in that it relies on the **put** operation to record that a transaction $\ell$ has output tuple v. (G-NEG) applies in case there is no tuple matching template v available to transaction $\ell$. When this occurs, the **neg** operation records this fact in the environment. (G-START) sets up the environment for a new transaction. (G-COM) attempts to commit a transaction. Finally, (G-CONG) allows reduction up to structural congruence of processes. Top level $\nu$-binders can be erased to allow names to flow into the environment.

### 3.3    Optimistic Transactional Facility

The implementation of an optimistic transactional model is shown in Figs. 10 and 11. In this scheme, the shared tuple space is represented by an environment $\mathcal{E} = \ell_1 : \rho_1 \dots \ell_n : \rho_n$ which contains per-transaction logs $\rho_1 \dots \rho_n$. Each of these logs is a sequence comprised of events, $v, v^?, \neg v$; these events denote an output of v, a removal of a tuple $v^?$ and an absence of a match for template $\neg v$, respectively.

The operations on the environment are **take, neg, put, commit** and **start**. Whenever a new transaction is created $\mathsf{start}(\mathcal{E}, \ell)$ is used to extend the environment with an empty log for transaction $\ell$. The operation $\mathsf{put}(\mathcal{E}, \ell, v)$ extends

$$v \in \mathtt{visible}(\mathcal{E}, \ell)$$
$$\mathcal{E}' = \mathcal{E} . (\ell : \rho . v^?)$$
$$\overline{v, \mathcal{E}' = \mathtt{take}(\mathcal{E}, \ell)}$$

$$\mathtt{match}(\mathtt{visible}(\mathcal{E}, \ell), v) = \{\}$$
$$\mathcal{E}' = \mathcal{E} . (\ell : \rho . \neg v)$$
$$\overline{\mathcal{E}' = \mathtt{neg}(\mathcal{E}, \ell, v)}$$

$$\mathcal{E}' = \mathcal{E} . (\ell : \rho . v)$$
$$\overline{\mathcal{E}' = \mathtt{put}(\mathcal{E}, \ell, v)}$$

$$\mathcal{E}' = \mathtt{reflect}(\mathcal{E}'', \rho, \ell)$$
$$\overline{\mathcal{E}' = \mathtt{commit}(\mathcal{E}'' . (\ell . \mathtt{t} : \rho), \ell)}$$

$$\mathcal{E} . (\ell : \langle \rangle) = \mathtt{start}(\mathcal{E}, \ell)$$

**Fig. 10.** Transactional semantics

$$\mathcal{E} = \mathtt{reflect}(\mathcal{E}, \langle \rangle, \ell)$$

$$\mathcal{E}' = \mathtt{reflect}(\mathcal{E} . (\ell : \rho' . v), \rho, \ell)$$
$$\overline{\mathcal{E}' = \mathtt{reflect}(\mathcal{E} . (\ell : \rho'), v . \rho, \ell)}$$

$$v \in \mathtt{visible}(\mathcal{E}, \ell)$$
$$\mathcal{E}' = \mathtt{reflect}(\mathcal{E} . (\ell : \rho' . v^?), \rho, \ell)$$
$$\overline{\mathcal{E}' = \mathtt{reflect}(\mathcal{E} . (\ell : \rho'), v^? . \rho, \ell)}$$

$$\mathtt{match}(\mathtt{visible}(\mathcal{E}, \ell), v) = \{\}$$
$$\mathcal{E}' = \mathtt{reflect}(\mathcal{E} . (\ell : \rho' . \neg v), \rho, \ell)$$
$$\overline{\mathcal{E}' = \mathtt{reflect}(\mathcal{E} . (\ell : \rho'), \neg v . \rho, \ell)}$$

$$\mathtt{visible}(\mathcal{E}, \ell) = \mathtt{find}(\mathtt{merge}(\mathcal{E}, \ell))$$

$$\mathtt{match}(\mathcal{V}, v) = \{v' \mid v' \in \mathcal{V} \wedge v \leq v'\}$$

$$\mathtt{find}(\rho . v) = \mathtt{find}(\rho \cup v)$$
$$\mathtt{find}(\rho . v^?) = \mathtt{find}(\rho - v)$$
$$\mathtt{find}(\rho . \neg v) = \mathtt{find}(\rho)$$

$$\mathtt{merge}(\mathcal{E}, \langle \rangle) = \langle \rangle$$
$$\mathtt{merge}(\mathcal{E} . (\ell . \mathtt{t} : \rho), \ell . \mathtt{t}) = \mathtt{merge}(\mathcal{E}, \ell) . \rho$$

**Fig. 11.** Auxiliary functions

the log of transaction $\ell$ with a tuple v. The operation $\mathtt{take}(\mathcal{E}, \ell)$ returns an arbitrary tuple visible by transaction $\ell$ and records in the log that the tuple has been removed. The operation $\mathtt{neg}(\mathcal{E}, \ell, v)$ records the fact no tuple matching template v is visible to the transaction $\ell$. Finally, operation $\mathtt{commit}(\mathcal{E}, \ell)$ attempts to commit the change performed by transaction $\ell$ to the log of the parent transaction. Commit operates by replaying the changes performed by transaction $\ell$. The commit fails if the environment for $\ell$'s parent is not in the expected state.

## 3.4 Soundness

Proving the correctness of the semantics requires that we show our treatment of transactions preserves desired isolation and atomicity properties. To do so, we first define a notion of a *well-defined* state. Intuitively, a state is well-defined if the contents of the logs associated with each transaction are such that no conflicts would arise. One way to manifest this idea is to compare the state of a transaction's parent with its child at the point the child attempts to commit. If the parent reflects commits from other transactions that violate invariants recorded in the log of the committing child, the child state is not considered well-defined. We formalize this intuition thus:

**Definition 1.** $\mathcal{E}$ *is well-defined if for any transaction* $\ell$ *such that* $\mathcal{E} \equiv \mathcal{E}' . (\ell : \rho)$ *and* $\ell = \ell' . \mathtt{t}$, *the function* $\mathtt{reflect}(\mathcal{E}', \ell', \rho)$ *is defined.*

Thus, the log of a child transaction is well-defined with respect to the parent if actions observed by the child are consistent with the actions seen by the parent. Satisfiability of this condition implies, that after a child commits, `write` and `take` operations performed by the child must be visible in the parent, and tuples that were observed to be absent by the child must still be so in the parent. Observe that the `reflect` operation propagates tuple events from a child transaction to a parent transaction provided these events do not violate natural visibility and serializability invariants.

**Definition 2.** *A trace* $tr(R) = \mathrm{P}_0 \mathcal{E}_0 \xrightarrow{\ell_0} \ldots \xrightarrow{\ell_n} \mathrm{P}_n \mathcal{E}_n$ *is serial iff* $\forall i, j, k$ *such that* $0 \leq i \leq j \leq k \leq n$, *and* $\ell_i = \ell_k$, $\ell_i \lhd \ell_j$ *(read "$\ell_i$ is a prefix of $\ell_j$).*

A serial trace is one in which for all pairs of reduction steps with the same transaction label $\ell$, all actions that occur between these two steps are taken on behalf of that transaction or its children. Given a notion of a serial trace, we can define a soundness theorem that captures our desired notion of serializability:

**Theorem 1.** *Let* $R$ *be a sequence of reductions* $\mathrm{P}_0 \mathcal{E}_0 \xrightarrow{\ell_0} \ldots \xrightarrow{\ell_n} \mathrm{P}_{n_1} \mathcal{E}_{n+1}$. *If* $\mathcal{E}_{n+1}$ *is well-defined, then there exists a sequence* $R' = \mathrm{P}_0 \mathcal{E}_0 \xrightarrow{\ell'_0} \ldots \xrightarrow{\ell'_n} \mathrm{P}_{n_1} \mathcal{E}_{n+1}$ *such that* $R'$ *is serial.*

The proof of this theorem appeals to notions of permutability on global actions. Informally, two actions $\alpha_1$ and $\alpha_2$ executed in transactions $\ell_1$ and $\ell_2$ are permutable if they have no data or control-dependency with each other. For example, a `take` operation performed by a transaction $\ell$ has a data dependency with any `write` operation performed by any of $\ell$'s parents that matches the read tuple. Simlarly, a `write` action logged in any parent transaction of $\ell$ has a data dependency with any $\neg v$ action recorded in $\ell$. This means that any valid serializable permutation cannot move a `write` action in a parent above a child action that successfully tested for the absence of the tuple being written.

## 4    Related Work and Conclusions

The Linda coordination model [19, 14] uses generative communication on anonymous structured data to facilitate interactions among concurrent programs. Its simplicity and generality make it a fertile vehicle in which to explore and formalize various concurrency abstractions [9, 17, 7, 13]. However, Linda does not directly support atomic operations on aggregate shared data. To alleviate this drawback, systems such as JavaSpaces [18] or TSpaces [27] allow operations on tuple-spaces to be encapsulated within transactions.

There is a large body of work that explores the formal specification of various flavors of transactions [23, 16, 20]. Most closely related to our work is that of Bussi, Gorrieri and Zavattaro [8] and Busi and Zavattaro [11] who formalize the semantics of JavaSpaces and discuss the semantics of important extensions such as leasing [10]. However, their work is presented in the context of a pessimistic concurrency control model. Our contribution is a formal characterization of transactions for Linda based on optimistic concurrency that provides scalable and deadlock-free execution.

Other related efforts include the work of Black *et. al.* [3] and Choithia and Duggan [15]. The former presents a theory of transactions that specify atomicity, isolation and durability properties in the form of an equivalence relation on processes. Choithia and Duggan present the pik-calculus and pike-calculus, extension of the pi-calculus that supports various abstractions for distributed transactions and optimistic concurrency. Their work is related to other efforts [11, 5] that encode transaction-style semantics into the pi-calculus and its variants. Our work is distinguished from these efforts in that it provides a simple operational characterization and proof of correctness of transactions that can be used to explore different trade-offs when designing a transaction facility for incorporation into a language. Haines *et. al.* [21] describe a composable transaction facility in ML that supports persistence, undoability, locking and threads. Their abstractions are very modular and first-class, although their implementation does not rely on optimistic concurrency mechanisms to handle commits. Berger and Honda [2] examine extensions to the pi-calculus to handle various forms of distributed computation include aspects of transactional processing such as two-phase commit protocols for handling commit actions in the presence of node failures.

While we have argued that Linda implementations that use optimistic concurrency protocols to subsume transactional behavior are likely to be more robust and exhibit better scalability than pessimistic variants, this argument depends on the way tuples are manipulated by transactions. If many transactions compete for a few tuples by attempting to update them in ways that cannot be expressed under a serializable schedule, aborts are likely to be high. Such applications are likely to exhibit better performance using a pessimistic protocol. Similarly, scalabilty limitations of pessimistic protocols that arise because of locking overheads incurred to support test-for-presence or absence operations are irrelevant if applications do not employ these actions. In an optimistic concurrency protocol, atomic propagation of updates from child to parent transactions when a commit action occurs incurs a cost proportional to the amount of work performed within the child transaction; we intend to explore implementation techniques to quantify these different overheads in scalable distributed environments.

# References

[1] Roberto M. Amadio, Ilaria Castellani, and Davide Sangiorgi. On Bisimulations for the Asynchronous π-Calculus. In Ugo Montanari and Vladimiro Sassone, editors, *CONCUR '96*, volume 1119 of *LNCS*, pages 147–162. Springer-Verlag, Berlin, 1996. 189

[2] Martin Berger and Kohei Honda. The Two-Phase Commitment Protocol in an Extended pi-Calculus. In Luca Aceto and Bjorn Victor, editors, *Electronic Notes in Theoretical Computer Science*, volume 39. Elsevier, 2003. 196

[3] Andrew Black, Vincent Cremet, Rachid Guerraoui, and Martin Odersky. An Equational Theory for Transactions. Technical Report CSE 03-007, Department of Computer Science, OGI School of Science and Engineering, 2003. 196

[4] Gérard Boudol. Asynchrony and the π-calculus (Note). Rapport de Recherche 1702, INRIA Sofia-Antipolis, May 1992. 189

[5] R. Bruni, C. Laneve, and U. Montanari. Orchestrating Transactions in the Join Calculus. In *13th International Conference on Concurrency Theory*, 2002. 196

[6] Nadia Busi, Roberto Gorrieri, and Gianluigi Zavattaro. A process algebraic view of Linda coordination primitives. *Theoretical Computer Science*, 192(2):167–199, February 1998. 189

[7] Nadia Busi, Roberto Gorrieri, and Gianluigi Zavattaro. A process algebraic view of linda coordination primitives. *Theoretical Computer Science*, 192(2):167–199, 1998. 195

[8] Nadia Busi, Roberto Gorrieri, and Gianluigi Zavattaro. On the Semantics of JavaSpaces. In *Formal Methods for Open Object-Based Distributed Systems IV*, volume 177. Kluwer, 2000. 185, 196

[9] Nadia Busi, Roberto Gorrieri, and Gianluigi Zavattaro. Process calculi for coordination: From Linda to JavaSpaces. *Lecture Notes in Computer Science*, 1816, 2000. 185, 195

[10] Nadia Busi, Roberto Gorrieri, and Gianluigi Zavattaro. Temporary Data in Shared Dataspace Coordination Languages. In *FOSSACS'01*, pages 121–136. Springer-Verlag, 2001. 196

[11] Nadia Busi and Gianluigi Zavattaro. On the serializability of transactions in JavaSpaces. In *Proc. of International Workshop on Concurrency and Coordination (CONCOORD'01)*. Electronic Notes in Theoretical Computer Science 54, Elsevier, 2001. 183, 184, 185, 187, 196

[12] Nadia Busi and Gianluigi Zavattaro. On the serializability of transactions in shared dataspaces with temporary data. In *Proc. of ACM Symposium on Applied Computing (SAC'02)*, pages 359–366. ACM Press, 2002. 183, 185

[13] N. Carriero, D. Gelernter, and L. Zuck. Bauhaus Linda. In P. Ciancarini, O. Nierstrasz, and A. Yonezawa, editors, *Object-Based Models and Languages for Concurrent Systems*, volume 924 of *LNCS*, pages 66–76. Springer-Verlag, Berlin, 1995. 195

[14] Nicholas Carriero and David Gelernter. Linda in Context. *Communications of the ACM*, 32(4):444–458, 1989. 195

[15] Tom Chothia and Dominic Duggan. Abstractions for Fault-Tolerant Computing. Technical Report 2003-3, Department of Computer Science, Stevens Institute of Technology, 2003. 196

[16] Panos Chrysanthis and Krithi Ramamritham. Synthesis of Extended Transaction Models Using ACTA. *ACM Transactions on Database Systems*, 19(3):450–491, 1994. 196

[17] R. DeNicola and R. Pugliese. A Process Algebra based on Linda. In P. Cian-
     carini and C. Hankin, editors, *Proc. 1st Int. Conf. on Coordination Models and
     Languages*, volume 1061 of *Lecture Notes in Computer Science*, pages 160–178.
     Springer-Verlag, Berlin, 1996. 189, 195

[18] Eric Freeman, Susanne Hupfer, and Ken Arnold. *JavaSpaces principles, patterns,
     and practice.* Addison-Wesley, Reading, MA, USA, 1999. 183, 184, 185, 196

[19] David Gelernter. Generative Communication in Linda. *ACM Transactions on
     Programming Languages and Systems*, 7(1):80–112, January 1985. 184, 195

[20] Jim Gray and Andreas Reuter. *Transaction Processing.* Morgan-Kaufmann, 1993.
     196

[21] Nicolas Haines, Darrell Kindred, Gregory Morrisett, Scott Nettles, and Jeannette
     Wing. Composing First-Class Transactions. *ACM Transactions on Programming
     Languages and Systems*, 16(6):1719–1736, 1994. 196

[22] Kohei Honda and Mario Tokoro. On Asynchronous Communication Semantics.
     In M. Tokoro, O. Nierstrasz, and P. Wegner, editors, *Object-Based Concurrent
     Computing. LNCS 612*, pages 21–51, 1992. 189

[23] Nancy Lynch, Michael Merritt, William Weihl, and Alan Fekete. *Atomic Trans-
     actions.* Morgan-Kaufmann, 1994. 196

[24] Robin Milner, Joachim Parrow, and David Walker. A calculus of mobile processes,
     Parts I and II. *Journal of Information and Computation*, 100, September 1992.
     184

[25] J. Eliot B. Moss. *Nested Transactions: An Approach to Reliable Distributed Com-
     puting.* MIT Press, Cambridge, Massachusetts, 1985. 185

[26] Jaco van de Pol and Miguel Valero Espada. Formal specification of JavaSpaces™
     Architecture using $\mu$CRL. *Lecture Notes in Computer Science*, 2315, 2002. 185

[27] P. Wyckoff, S. McLaughry, T. Lehman, and D. Ford. T Spaces. *IBM Systems
     Journal*, 37(3):454–474, 1998. 183, 196

# Active Coordination in Ad Hoc Networks

Christine Julien and Gruia-Catalin Roman

Department of Computer Science and Engineering, Washington University
Saint Louis, MO 63130
{julien,roman}@wustl.edu

**Abstract.** The increasing ubiquity of communicating mobile devices and vastly different mobile application needs have led to middleware models for ad hoc networks that simplify application programming. One such system, EgoSpaces, addresses the needs of individual applications, allowing them to define what data is included in their operating context using declarative specifications constraining properties of data, agents that own data, hosts where agents are running, and attributes of the network. In the resulting model, application agents interact with a dynamic environment through a set of views, or custom defined projections of the set of data present in the ad hoc network. This paper builds on EgoSpaces by allowing agents to assign *behaviors* to views. Behaviors consist of actions automatically performed in response to specified changes in a view. Behaviors discussed in this paper encompass reactive programming, transparent data migration, automatic data duplication, and event capture. Formal semantic definitions and programming examples are given for each behavior.

## 1 Introduction

In mobile ad hoc environments, the lack of an infrastructure necessitates new communication paradigms. Opportunistically formed ad hoc networks change rapidly in response to nodes entering and leaving communication range. Robots on an uninhabited planet explore the terrain and coordinate to assimilate collected information. Automobiles on a highway communicate to gather traffic information. Rescue workers in a disaster recovery scenario must coordinate to perform their tasks quickly and safely, but the communication infrastructure is often crippled or destroyed. These domains demonstrate a wealth of applications requiring coordination among mobile components.

Much research has developed protocols tailored to these networks. Ad hoc routing [2, 12, 14, 17] provides communication among groups of connected hosts, bringing the possibility of large scale ad hoc networks closer to reality. In such environments, the massive amounts of available information can overwhelm applications, yet this information serves as the context for an application operating in the network, and applications need to adapt to changes in this context.

An application's desire for adaptability manifests itself in the diversity of context-aware applications for traditional networks [8, 20]. FieldNote [18] allows

R. de Nicola et al. (Eds.): COORDINATION 2004, LNCS 2949, pp. 199–215, 2004.

researchers to implicitly attach context information to research notes, while tour guides [1, 5] display information based on the user's location. The radically different properties of ad hoc networks, however, require new context-awareness models tailored to the environment's specific complexities. The Context Toolkit [19] and Context Fabric [9] take steps to generalize context in various environments, but they do not address the need for a distributed coordination model.

Applications in this information-rich environment require coordination to manage, operate over, and react to context. As the demand for new applications grows, producing these applications places an increasingly heavy burden on programmers. Research has shown that providing coordination constructs in middleware can simplify programming. While early solutions focused on localizing reactions to individual hosts [3] or using symmetric communication [13], EgoSpaces [11] introduced asymmetric coordination, giving each application direct control over the size and scope of its personalized context. This approach is essential to accommodating programming for large, dense ad hoc networks.

Given the amount of data in an ad hoc environment and coordination constructs that have proven historically useful, the basic operations in EgoSpaces fall short of the requirements of rapid application development. This paper extends EgoSpaces to provide high-level coordination, including reactive programming, data migration, data duplication, and event capture. We demonstrate the ability to reduce the behaviors to a single construct, the reaction, giving promise for an efficient implementation that maximizes responsiveness and minimizes overhead without sacrificing simplicity. The next section reviews EgoSpaces. Section 3 presents the extensions. Section 4 addresses performance considerations in presenting the constructs' implementations. Conclusions appear in Section 5.

## 2    The EgoSpaces Coordination Model

EgoSpaces introduced an agent-centered context whose scope extends beyond the local host to contain data and resources associated with hosts and agents surrounding the agent of interest. This novel asymmetric coordination accommodates high-density and wide-coverage ad hoc networks.

### 2.1    Computational Model

EgoSpaces considers systems entailing logically mobile agents (units of modularity and execution) operating over physically mobile hosts. Communication among agents and agent migration can occur whenever the hosts involved are connected. A closed set of these connected hosts defines an ad hoc network.

EgoSpaces bases coordination on a Global Virtual Data Structure (GVDS) [15], in which all data distributed among agents in the network appears, to the programmer, to be stored in a single, common data structure. At any given time, the available data depends on connectivity. Each agent maintains a local data repository, and, when agents move within communication range, their data structures logically merge to form a single "global" structure.

## 2.2   View Concept

EgoSpaces structures data access in terms of *views*, projections of the GVDS. Since context is relative, the term *reference agent* denotes the agent whose context we are considering. Each agent defines its views using declarative specifications constraining properties of the network, hosts, agents, and data. Imagine a building with a fixed infrastructure of sensors and providing context information regarding the building's structural integrity, frequency of sounds, movement of occupants, etc. Engineers and inspectors carry PDAs that provide additional context and assimilate information. As an engineer moves through the building, he wishes to see structural information for only the floors adjacent to his current floor. His agent's view is:

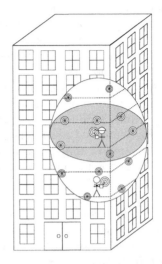

**Fig. 1.**  Example view definition

> *Data from the past hour (reference to data) gathered by structural agents (reference to agents) on sensors (reference to hosts) within one floor of my current location (property of reference host).*

Fig. 1 depicts this context, where the shaded area is the view of the engineer (in the hard hat). Because EgoSpaces automatically maintains views, as the engineer moves, his view updates in such a way that its contents remain consistent with his application's declaration.

In EgoSpaces, each agent specifies an *access control function* that limits the ability of other agents to access its data. When an agent specifies a view, it provides credentials that verify it to other agents and it also declares the operations it intends to perform on the view. To determine a view's contexts, EgoSpaces evaluates each contributing agent's access control function over the credentials and operations. The view contains only data that qualifies via the access control functions. More details on EgoSpaces' views can be found in [11] and [16].

## 2.3   Basic Data Access Operations

In EgoSpaces, each agent carries its own local tuple space, and, when connectivity is available, connected agents' tuple spaces merge into a GVDS. The operations provided over views are variations of the standard Linda [7] tuple space operations for tuple creation (**out**), tuple reading (**rd**), and tuple removal (**in**).

A tuple in EgoSpaces is a set of unordered triples of the form:

$$\langle (name, type, value), (name, type, value), \ldots \rangle.$$

where the *name* of each field in a tuple must be unique. The operations **rd** and **in** operate using a pattern that constrains a tuple's fields. To match a tuple, every constraint in the pattern must be satisfied by a corresponding field in the tuple.

Agents create tuples using **out** operations. A tuple in an agent's local tuple space is available in any view whose constraints it satisfies. To read and remove tuples, agents use **rd** and **in** operations restricted to a view. Because **in** operations remove tuples from the tuple space, they may affect other views if the tuple appears in multiple views. These two operations block the issuing agent until a match exists. If multiple tuples match, one is chosen non-deterministically. Variations of these operations include aggregate operations (**rdg** and **ing**) that return all matches and probing versions of both single (**rdp** and **inp**) and aggregate operations (**rdgp** and **ingp**) which return $\epsilon$ if no match exists. All operations listed thus far act over the view atomically, requiring a transaction over participants. Because this can become costly, EgoSpaces offers scattered probe operations (**rdsp**, **insp**, **rdgsp**, and **ingsp**) that do not lock the entire view and are allowed to miss a matching tuple. All operations and their semantics are provided in [11] with a formal description of tuples, patterns, and the matching function.

*Programming Example.* The engineer retrieves structural information about a floor, locally processes the data, and outputs a tuple with the floor's structural integrity. The following code accomplishes this in EgoSpaces:

```
ν = [data from structural agents on the current floor]
p = ⟨(strain, number, any), (acoustic emission, number, any),
       (time, time, [within 10 minutes])⟩
data[] = ν.rdgp(p)
[local processing using data]
result = [tuple containing result]
out(result)
```

The first line creates a view; view specification details are omitted. In the definition of the pattern p, the constraint any indicates that the tuple must contain a field with the indicated name and type but the value is unrestricted.

# 3   Extending EgoSpaces

Many applications require more sophisticated coordination mechanisms than those already presented. This section presents several additional constructs, including a powerful reactive mechanism, data migration, data duplication, and event capture and shows how these sophisticated constructs ease the programming task and increase code encapsulation and reusability.

## 3.1   Advanced Constructs

Using the previous constructs, to wait for a piece of data an agent must either block or poll, which can prevent it from performing other work. Furthermore, EgoSpaces primitives provide no mechanism for grouping operations transactionally. We introduce reactions and transactions to address these concerns.

**Reactions.** Like other mobile systems [3, 13], EgoSpaces allows agents to react to the presence of particular data. This style of interaction is also commonly found in publish-subscribe systems, e.g., [4] and [6]. An EgoSpaces reaction associates a pattern with actions to perform when a tuple matches the pattern. A reaction fires once for every matching tuple in the view. Disabling and re-enabling a reaction causes it to fire again for all matches. Similarly, disconnection followed by reconnection causes reactions to fire again. A reaction can delete its trigger and/or output the trigger modified in some way. This modification occurs through a *tuple_modifiers* operation that can add, remove, or change the tuple's fields. For example, if an agent with id ID1 retrieves the tuple:

$$\langle (ID, TupleID, 5), (dest, AgentID, \texttt{ID1}), (timestamp, time, 8\!:\!41), (temp, celsius, 28) \rangle$$

and wants to change the time stamp, remove the destination, and add an owner, it defines the following *tuple_modifiers*:

```
tuple_modifiers(t) =
        {t.changeField(timestamp, currentTime), t.removeField(dest),
         t.addField(owner, AgentID, ID1) t.newID()},
```

The **newID** method allows the tuple's new owner to give it a new, unique id. An example resulting tuple might be:

$$\langle (ID, TupleID, 12), (timestamp, time, 9\!:\!36), (temp, celsius, 28), (owner, AgentID, \texttt{ID1}) \rangle$$

If the *tuple_modifiers* add a field that already exists, the field's value is replaced. The tuple generated has the same id (unless it is changed by the *tuple_modifiers*), and therefore the reaction will not fire again for the tuple.

A reaction has one of two scheduling modalities, eager or lazy. Eager reactions occur immediately following the appearance of a matching tuple. Only other eager reactions can preempt them. A lazy modality brings a much weaker guarantee—the reaction eventually fires if the tuple remains in the view long enough. Other operations may occur in the meantime, possibly removing the tuple before the lazy reaction fires. Finally, reactions have a priority that arranges a hierarchy within each scheduling modality. Within each modality, reactions with higher priorities fire before reactions with lower priorities (the highest priority being 1). If more than one reaction with the same modality and same priority exists, the one to be fired first is chosen non-deterministically. If the first reaction removes the trigger, the second reaction will not fire. Reactions take the form:

$$\rho = \textbf{react to } p \, [\textbf{remove}] \, [\textbf{and out}(tuple\_modifiers(\tau))]$$

where the local name $\tau$ is bound to the trigger tuple; $p$ is the reactive pattern; the optional keyword **remove** causes tuple removal; and the optional **out**(*tuple_modifiers*($\tau$)) outputs the trigger tuple with the *tuple_modifiers* applied. A reference agent enables and disables reactions using:

> **enable** $\rho$ **with** *sched_modality, priority* **over** $\nu$
> **disable** $\rho$ **over** $\nu$

where *sched_modality* is either eager or lazy, and *priority* is an integer. Reactions affect contributing agents' access controls; when specifying a view, the reference agent indicates if it intends to register reactions on it. Triggering the reaction and executing the associated actions occur as a single atomic step. If used, the **out** places a tuple in the reference agent's local tuple space at the completion of the reaction's execution. This tuple may trigger additional reactions.

*Programming Example.* Consider a scenario in which the original sensors placed in the building generated Fahrenheit temperatures, but most have been replaced by Celsius sensors. For standardization, an agent in the Celsius sensors reacts to the Fahrenheit readings, converts the values, and replaces the readings. Without the reactive construct, a programmer could use code similar to:

```
ν = [temperature data on this floor and adjacent ones]
p = ⟨(tempType, string, = "Fahrenheit")⟩
while(true)
    sleep(time)
    data[] = ν.rdgp(p)
    if data ≠ null
        for i=1 to data.length
            ν.inp(data[i])
            data[i].changeField(tempType, "Celsius")
            data[i].changeField(tempValue, convert(oldT))
            out(data[i])
```

This code is slightly simplified because it refers to the Fahrenheit temperature as "oldT", but this value must really be retrieved from the tuple (`data[i]`). The programmer must manage this code independent of the agent's other operations. The agent creates and executes the thread to "enable" the reaction, and stops it to "disable" the reaction. In this example, the thread awakens periodically to check the reactive condition. The thread first reads all tuples matching $p$ from the tuple space and executes the actions for the tuple.

With the built-in reactive construct, the code becomes:

```
ν = [temperature data on this floor and adjacent ones]
p = ⟨(tempType, string, = "Fahrenheit")⟩
t_m(t) = {t.changeField(tempType, "Celsius"),
          t.changeField(tempValue, convert(oldT))}
ρ = react to p remove and out t_m(τ)
enable ρ with eager, 1 over ν
```

In this example, the programmer enables a high priority, eager reaction. Not only does this reactive construct simplify the code, it adds subtle, useful semantics. Instead of polling as in the example without a built-in construct, the implementation of this reactive behavior uses a style similar to a publish-subscribe system that evaluates the registration at each remote host, returning matches when they appear. As such, the reaction is guaranteed to fire immediately following the insertion of a matching tuple unless another eager reaction fires and removes the tuple. In the first example, tuples may be inserted and removed before the thread awakens to check for matches. Finally, the application programmer has encapsulated the reaction and can reuse it on other views if desired.

**Transactions.** For an agent, performing operations sequentially is not atomic because other operations can be interleaved. For example, if an agent performs a successful **rdp** operation and immediately attempts to **in** the same tuple, it may be unsuccessful if another agent has, in the meantime, removed the tuple. At times, an application may want a sequence of operations to be atomic with respect to other operations on the involved views. For example, if an application wants to replace a piece of data with an update, but does not want it to ever appear that the data is unavailable, it needs to group the removal and replacement as an atomic step. To support this, we introduce *transactions* to EgoSpaces.

A transaction is a named sequence of actions that can include plain code, probing operations, and tuple creation. Because transactions must complete, they cannot include blocking operations that could halt the transaction indefinitely. Transactions are atomic actions; their intermediate results are not visible. When creating a transaction, the reference agent provides a view restriction listing the involved views and serving as a contract between the agent and EgoSpaces. Any attempt by the transaction to perform operations outside the view restriction generates an exception. The view restriction makes a deadlock-free implementation possible (see Section 4). A transaction takes the form:

$$T = \textbf{transaction over } v_1, v_2, \ldots \textbf{begin } op_1, op_2, \ldots \textbf{ end}$$

where $T$ is the transaction's name; $v_1, v_2 \ldots$ is the view restriction; and $op_1$, $op_2, \ldots$ is the sequence of operations. An agent executes a transaction using:

$$\textbf{execute } T$$

**Augmenting Reactions.** In the previous reactive construct, an agent can only remove the trigger and output an modified trigger. We augment reactions to allow them to execute a transaction in response to a matching tuple. If the tuple triggering the reaction is local (i.e., in the reference agent's tuple space), the triggering of the reaction and the execution of the transaction can be grouped into a single atomic step. When the trigger tuple is local, we refer to the augmented reaction as an *extended reaction*, with the form:

$$\rho = \textbf{react to } p \; [\textbf{remove}] \; [\textbf{and out}(tuple\_modifiers(\tau))] \; \textbf{extended by } T(\tau)$$

An agent enables an extended reaction using:

$$\textbf{enable } \rho \textbf{ with } sched\_modality, priority \textbf{ over } \nu_l$$

EgoSpaces verifies that $\nu_l$ is restricted in scope to the reference agent.

When the trigger tuple is not local, trigger, removal, and notification are a single atomic action, while the execution of the associated transaction is a separate action. The most important ramification of this subtle difference is that the trigger might not be available when the transaction executes because other operations can interleave with the reaction's triggering and the transaction. The transaction does, however, receive a copy ($\tau$) of the trigger tuple. This type of reaction, a *followed reaction*, has the form:

$$\rho = \textbf{react to } p \; [\textbf{remove}] \; [\textbf{and out}(tuple\_modifiers(\tau))] \; \textbf{followed by } T(\tau)$$

The word **followed** indicates the separation of the transaction's execution. The enabling mechanism is the same as above but not limited to a local view.

*Programming Example.* Imagine an agent that replaces temperature readings generated on the current floor over the past hour with an average. Without reactions, a programmer writes something like:

```
ν = [Celsius temperature data on current floor]
p = ⟨(timestamp, time, minutes = :00)⟩
seenTuples = new Vector()
while(true)
    sleep(time)
    data = ν.rdp(p)
    if data ≠ null
        if !seenTuples.contains(data)
            p₁ = ⟨(tempValue, any, any), (timestamp, time, [within past hour])⟩
            temps[] = ν.inpg(p₁)
            avg = average(temps[])
            average = [tuple with average information]
            out(average)
            seenTuples.add(data)
```

With the built-in construct the code consists of defining a reaction:

```
ν = [Celsius temperature data on current floor]
p = ⟨(timestamp, time, minutes = :00)⟩
T(τ) = transaction over ν
          begin
              p₁ = ⟨(tempValue, any, any), (timestamp, time, [within past hour])⟩
              temps[] = ν.inpg(p₁)
              avg = average(temps[])
              average = [tuple with average information]
              out(average)
          end
ρ = react to p followed by T(τ)
enable ρ with eager, 1 over ν
```

The programmer's declaration of the views over which its transaction will act allows the system to provide atomicity guarantees associated with the execution of the operations; the transaction executes as a single atomic step, while in the hand-coded case, each operation may interleave with other operations.

## 3.2  Behavioral Extensions

The reactive constructs make programming with EgoSpaces more flexible and provide more powerful semantics. In some cases, applications exhibit common actions. We classify three such behaviors and express their semantics using reactions. Providing behaviors in the system reduces the programming burden in common cases. In this section, we describe data migration, duplication, and event capture. The system is also open to extension to include additional behaviors.

A reference agent attaches behaviors to views, and, as long as the behavior is enabled, encountering certain conditions triggers an automatic action. In general, a behavior responds to a trigger, identified via a pattern. Like reactions, behaviors respond once to each matching tuple. If tuples leave the view and return or the behavior is disabled and re-enabled, the behavior executes again.

Behaviors can be either eager or lazy. Eager behaviors execute as soon as the trigger is matched, and only other eager constructs can preempt them. Lazy behaviors eventually execute if the behavior remains enabled and the trigger stays present. Behaviors can also include tuple modifiers, which allow the reference agent to insert, change, or remove fields in resulting local tuples. How this is used will become apparent as we present the different behaviors. Finally, behaviors have an optional transaction executed at the behavior's completion:

$$\beta = \texttt{act}(p) \; [tuple\_modifiers(\tau)] \; [\textbf{followed by} \; T(\tau)]$$

In general, $\texttt{act}$ is the behavior's name (e.g., "migrate" or "duplicate"). The operation list in a view specification includes behaviors, and contributing agents consider this set when evaluating access control functions. Reference agents enable and disable behaviors using:

$$\textbf{enable} \; \beta \; \textbf{with} \; sched\_modality \; \textbf{over} \; \nu$$
$$\textbf{disable} \; \beta \; \textbf{over} \; \nu$$

We discuss each behavior individually, providing a brief description and syntax then show the behaviors' semantics. We also include programming examples.

**Data Migration.** Mobile agents encounter a lot of data, and an agent may want to collect certain data without explicitly reading each piece. When data consistency is important, a common solution is replica management, where copies of data items are kept consistent. This solution is impractical in ad hoc environments where agents carrying originals and duplicates meet unpredictably. Using transparent migration, only one copy of the data exists, and the migration behavior allows an agent to collect data matching a supplied pattern. For example, building engineers might respond to work orders generated by distributed components. A single engineer should take responsibility for each work order because work will be wasted if multiple engineers pick up the same job.

A migration behavior automatically moves all matching tuples in the view to the reference agent. Because EgoSpaces evaluates access control functions before determining which tuples belong to the view, contributing agents implicitly allow tuple transfer. Once migrated, the tuples become subject to the reference agent's access controls. If desired, a migration uses tuple modifiers to change migrated tuples. An engineer collecting work orders can mark the migrated tuples as "assigned" to prevent the work orders from migrating again.

*Semantics.* A migration reduces to a reaction that removes the trigger and generates a new tuple in the reference agent's tuple space:

$$\mathcal{M} = \texttt{migrate} \; p \; [tuple\_modifiers(\tau)]$$
$$\triangleq \rho_m = \textbf{react to} \; p \; \textbf{remove and out}(tuple\_modifiers(\tau)))$$

If the programmer supplies tuple modifiers, the tuple placed in the tuple space is the trigger tuple with the tuple modifiers applied. Otherwise, the tuple is exactly the trigger. Even though the migrated tuple is the same tuple (unless the tuple modifiers change the ID), tuple migration may trigger reactions in the new location that have already fired for the tuple in the previous location. Enabling a migration reduces to enabling the reaction using the migration's scheduling modality and a low priority (e.g., 10):

$$\textbf{enable } \mathcal{M} \textbf{ with } sched\_modality \textbf{ over } \nu$$
$$\triangleq \textbf{enable } \rho_m \textbf{ with } sched\_modality, 10 \textbf{ over } \nu_r$$

where $\nu_r$ is $\nu$ with the reference agent eliminated. This prevents EgoSpaces from "migrating" local tuples. The priority scheme maximizes the number of behaviors that execute, e.g., it ensures duplication occurs before migration. A migration's low priority allows other reactions and behaviors of the same modality to trigger first. If these actions remove the tuple, however, the migration will not occur.

*Programming Example.* The following code shows how a programmer would accomplish migration using only the basic EgoSpaces constructs. This code implements the work order collection application described above.

```
ν = [work orders on this floor and adjacent ones]
νr = [data in ν not owned by this agent]
p = ⟨(assigned, boolean, =false)⟩
while(true)
    sleep(time)
    data[] = νr.rdgp(p)
    if data ≠ null
        for i=1 to data.length
            ν.inp(data[i])
            data[i].changeField(assigned, true);
            out(data[i])
```

The tuple output has the same id as the one read, but the "assigned" field has been set to true. This implementation might miss matching tuples. To ensure tuples are not infinitely migrated, the programmer must explicitly define $\nu_r$, or the remote portion of a view $\nu$. The use of $\nu_r$ prevents tuples in the local tuple space (e.g., work orders created by this engineer that other engineers should perform) from being "migrated" to their current host.

The built-in migration behavior hides the declaration of $\nu_r$.

```
ν = [work orders on this floor and adjacent ones]
p = ⟨(taken, boolean, =false)⟩
t_m(t) = {t.changeField(taken, true)}
M = migrate p t_m(t)
enable M with eager over ν
```

Because this behavior is integrated with the system, we can guarantee, for eager migrations, that tuples are migrated if they appear in the reference agent's view, conditional on no other reactive constructs removing the tuple first.

**Data Duplication.** Under different circumstances, data availability is more important than consistency, and an application would rather duplicate data to make it available upon disconnection, with the knowledge that duplicates will not remain consistent with the originals. A duplication behavior copies tuples matching a pattern and leaves the originals unaffected. In our example application, the building engineer may collect sensor data for processing off-site. The engineer does not want to remove the data because others may need it.

Duplicated tuples may match the view specification and be infinitely duplicated. They may also appear in other agents' views. As with migration, applications deal with these concerns individually, e.g., by tagging all duplicates. Because replica management proves too costly, duplicates do not remain consistent with originals, even if both persist in the view.

*Semantics.* Duplication reduces to a reaction that does not remove the trigger and generates a new tuple (with a unique id).

$$\mathcal{D} = \textbf{duplicate}\, p\; tuple\_modifiers(\tau)$$
$$\triangleq tuple\_modifiers'(\tau) = \{\tau.\textbf{newID}()\}$$
$$\rho_d = \textbf{react to}\, p\, \textbf{and}\; \textbf{out}(tuple\_modifiers(\tau) \cup tuple\_modifiers'(\tau))$$

A duplication which specifies no tuple modifiers creates an exact copy (with a new tuple id), while one that adds a field "copied" marks all duplicates as such.

Enabling duplication reduces to enabling the reaction with the provided scheduling modality and a high priority (e.g., 1):

$$\textbf{enable}\,\mathcal{D}\,\textbf{with}\, sched\_modality\,\textbf{over}\,\nu$$
$$\triangleq \textbf{enable}\,\rho_d\,\textbf{with}\, sched\_modality, 1\,\textbf{over}\,\nu$$

A high priority ensures duplication occurs before other actions, e.g., migration.

*Programming Example.* Using only the EgoSpaces primitive operations, an engineer duplicating structural integrity data uses code similar to:

```
ν = [structural agent data on this floor and adjacent ones]
p = ⟨(strain, number, any), (acoustic emission, number, any),...⟩
seenTuples = new Vector()
while(true)
   sleep(time)
   data[] = ν.rdgp(p)
   if data ≠ null
      for i=1 to data.length
         data[i].newID()
         out(data[i])
         seenTuples.add(data[i])
```

Using `seenTuples` prevents the agent from re-duplicating the same data.

Using the built-in duplication behavior reduces to defining a view, creating a duplication behavior, and enabling it on the view:

```
ν = [structural agent data on this floor and adjacent ones]
p = ⟨(strain, number, any), (acoustic emission, number, any),...⟩
𝒟 = duplicate p
enable 𝒟 with eager over ν
```

This eager behavior is guaranteed to duplicate all matching tuples that appear in the view without missing any, while the hand-coded example may miss some. A lazy duplication has semantics identical to the hand-coded example.

**Event Capture.** The EgoSpaces primitives, reactions, and behaviors operate over the system's state. Many applications also benefit from reacting to events raised in the system. For example, an agent might want to be notified when another agent accesses a piece of data. In our system, events include an agent's arrival, another agent's data access operations, etc.

EgoSpaces events are special tuples. An agent registers its interest in an event via a pattern over such tuples. Once registered, event notifications matching the pattern propagate to the reference agent. To prevent superfluous event generation, EgoSpaces raises events only for specific registrations, and the event's callback execution consumes the event tuple created for it. This allows multiple registrations for the same event and guarantees that all registered parties receive notification. A reference agent uses a transaction to specify the event's callback.

*Semantics.* The event behavior reduces to a pair of reactions. The first generates a copy of the event tuple augmented with the event registration's id and places it in the reference agent's local tuple space. The second reacts to the generated tuple and executes the callback:

$$\mathcal{E} = \textbf{event}(p) \textbf{ followed by } T_e(\tau)$$
$$\triangleq eid = \textbf{new } event\ id$$
$$\rho_{e1} = \textbf{react to } p \textbf{ and out}(\tau \oplus \{(\texttt{eID}, event\ id, eid)\})$$
$$\rho_{e2} = \textbf{react to } (p \oplus \{(\texttt{eID}, event\ id, = eid)\} \textbf{ remove extended by } T_e(\tau)$$

The $\oplus$ indicates that the provided field, in this case the new event id, is added to the tuple. The generation of the event copy and the callback execution are not an atomic action. However, the reference agent can prevent other agents from stealing its event tuples using its access control function.

Enabling an event behavior reduces to enabling the two reactions:

$$\textbf{enable } \mathcal{E} \textbf{ with } sched\_modality \textbf{ over } \nu$$
$$\triangleq \textbf{enable } \rho_{e1} \textbf{ with eager}, 1 \textbf{ over } \nu$$
$$\textbf{enable } \rho_{e2} \textbf{ with } sched\_modality, 1 \textbf{ over } \nu_l$$

The first reaction has **eager** modality and high priority, guaranteeing the reference agent is notified. The second reaction's scheduling modality corresponds to the behavior's modality and also executes at high priority. This reaction is enabled on a local view ($\nu_l$) that contains only local event tuples.

This behavior's semantics differ slightly from the others. Every event behavior, eager or lazy, is guaranteed to be triggered because an event tuple is created specifically for each registration. In the lazy case, however, by the time the callback executes, the entity that caused the event may no longer be connected.

This reduction assumes mechanisms exist to generate events and clean up event tuples. The former is discussed in Section 4; the latter is accomplished by:

$$\rho_{gc} = \textbf{react to } p \textbf{ remove}$$

where $p$ matches any event tuple. This eager reaction with a priority of at least 2 executes after all event copies have been generated (at priority 1):

$$\textbf{enable } \rho_{gc} \textbf{ with eager}, 2 \textbf{ over } \nu_e$$

This reaction is defined and enabled on every agent's event view, so an agent need not define it each time it enables an event behavior.

*Programming Example.* Because event capture requires an event generation mechanism, there is no way to accomplish this behavior using the initial EgoSpaces operations. Assume that a tuple indicating a host's arrival is represented with an event tuple similar to the following:

$$\langle (eventType, string, hostArrival), (ID, HostID, newHost), \ldots \rangle$$

If the building engineer wants to receive notification of an inspector's arrival on adjacent floor, his application agent has the following code:

$$\nu = [\text{this floor and adjacent ones}]$$
$$\textbf{p} = \langle (eventType, string, =\text{hostArrival}) \rangle$$
$$T_e(\tau) = \textbf{transaction over null}$$
$$\qquad \textbf{begin}$$
$$\qquad\qquad [\text{display message to user}]$$
$$\qquad \textbf{end}$$
$$\mathcal{E} = \textbf{event}(\textbf{p}) \textbf{ followed by } T_e(\tau)$$
$$\textbf{enable } \mathcal{E} \textbf{ with eager over } \nu$$

The null view restriction indicates that the transaction does not use any views.

## 4   Design Strategies

The extensions presented build on the EgoSpaces middleware. In some cases (e.g., event generation, reaction registration), the new features are integrated into the core system, while others build on top of the system.

**View Construction and Maintenance.** View construction and maintenance directly influence implementation. Inefficient view building limits performance. We developed *network abstractions* that, given the reference agent's neighborhood restrictions maintains a tree of the qualifying agents. For details of this protocol, see [16].

**Basic Operations.** An efficient implementation of blocking operations uses reactions to prevent expensive polling. For example, an **ing** operation entails a (low priority) eager reaction that does not remove its trigger. When this reaction fires, its transaction attempts an **inpg**. If the **inpg** retrieves a tuple, it returns and disables its associated reaction. If the operation is unsuccessful, another operation removed the tuple first, which is within the operations' semantics.

Atomic probes are transactions on a single view. They require locking all view participants, performing the operation, and unlocking the participants. The locking mechanism is discussed below. Agents benefit from intelligent view definition, as transactions are costly on views involving large numbers of agents.

A variety of possible implementations for scattered probes exist. The simplest implementation polls the view's participants in order (by id). If all participants have been queried and no match found, the operation returns $\epsilon$. Group operations query all participants and return all matches. More sophisticated implementations of the single operations can take advantage of the environment; for example, one might query the physically closest agents first.

**Transactions.** A transaction operates over several views. As such, transactions are inherently costly. EgoSpaces reduces this cost by requiring a reference agent to explicitly declare what other agents need to be locked for the transaction by providing a list of views. Because the agents contributing to each view are known, EgoSpaces can lock the transaction's participants (including the reference agent) in order (by id). If any other agent also performs a transaction, it locks agents in the same order, avoiding deadlock. If a contributing agent moves out of the view while a transaction is locking agents, it is unlocked before departing. If the transaction's operations are already executing, the agent's departure must be delayed until the transaction completes. We guarantee enough time to complete the transaction before the agent disappears from communication range using *safe distance* [10]. If a new agent moves into the view while a transaction is in progress, its arrival is delayed until the transaction completes.

**Reactions.** Because reactions are the core of the EgoSpaces extensions, an efficient implementation is essential. Each agent keeps a reaction registry (containing all reactions it has registered) and a reaction list (containing all reactions this agent should fire on behalf of other agents, including itself). A reaction registry entry contains a reaction's id, the tuple to output when the reaction fires (if any), and the transaction that extends or follows this reaction (if any). A reaction list entry contains the reaction's id, the reaction issuer's id, the reaction's pattern, the view's data pattern, and a boolean indicating whether or not to remove the trigger. Upon registration, the reaction propagates to all view participants and is inserted in each participant's reaction list. For all matching tuples in the view, the reaction fires, sending a notification (containing a copy of the trigger) to the registering agent. If specified, the tuple is removed from the tuple space. While the reaction remains enabled, new tuples in the view are checked against the pattern. For each match, the registering agent receives a notification and locates the reaction in the reaction registry. If necessary, it performs the appropriate **out** operation and schedules any associated transaction.

In Fig. 2, agents B and C register reactions, which both match t. The reaction with the highest priority (B's reaction) fires first, generating notification n for B. Because this reaction removes t, C's lower priority reaction will not fire. B's

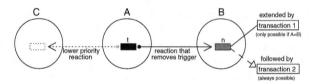

**Fig. 2.** The Reaction Mechanism

reaction can be extended or followed by a transaction. The former is only allowed when the trigger is local (i.e., A=B).

During the view's construction, new agents receive the reaction registration and add it to their reaction list. As new agents move into the view's scope, they receive any registered reactions. As agents move out of the view, they remove information regarding registered reactions. If these agents return, they receive the registrations and fire the associated reactions again for matching tuples.

**Behaviors.** Because the semantics of behaviors are written as reactions, their implementation relies on the reaction's implementation. We build these behaviors into the system to provide common actions as simple operations and to allow for code encapsulation and reuse.

**Event Generation.** To successfully implement event capture, we add an event raising mechanism to EgoSpaces. Some example event types include host arrival and departure, agent arrival and departure, and data access operations. Each type of operation has a defined type string (e.g., *hostArrival*) and some secondary information (e.g., the *HostID* for a host arrival or departure event). The event generation mechanism raises an event only if an agent has registered for the event. Upon generation, special event tuples are created for each registered agent, and these tuples are transmitted to the agent. The event's callback then executes according to the registration's modality (eager or lazy).

## 5   Conclusion

The success of a coordination middleware for ad hoc mobile environments lies in its ability to address the key issues of this constrained environment. First, the amount of information available necessitates mechanisms to easily and abstractly limit one's operating context. Second, the middleware must provide programming abstractions tailored to specific application domains while remaining general enough to maintain a small footprint on devices with constrained memory requirements. The original EgoSpaces model began to address the first of these three concerns. The additional constructs and behavioral extensions introduced in this paper complete this task and provide the needed high-level coordination mechanisms. The reduction of the behaviors to a unifying construct, the reaction, decreases the required middleware support. With such a direct attack on complexities specific to ad hoc mobile networks, EgoSpaces and its extensions promise to transform application development in this environment. Additionally, this paper shows how these behavioral extensions serve as a powerful abstraction for practical systems.

## Acknowledgements

This research was supported in part by the Office of Naval Research under ONR MURI research contract N00014-02-1-0715. Any opinions, findings, and conclusions or recommendations expressed in this paper are those of the authors and do not necessarily reflect the views of the sponsoring agencies.

## References

[1] G. Abowd, C. Atkeson, J. Hong, S. Long, R. Kooper, and M. Pinkerton. Cyberguide: A mobile context-aware tour guide. *ACM Wireless Networks*, 3:421–433, 1997. 200

[2] J. Broch, D. B. Johnson, and D. A. Maltz. The dynamic source routing protocol for mobile ad hoc networks. Internet Draft, March 1998. IETF MANET Working Group. 199

[3] G. Cabri, L. Leonardi, and F. Zambonelli. MARS: A programmable coordination architecture for mobile agents. *Internet Computing*, 4(4):26–35, 2000. 200, 203

[4] A. Carzaniga, D. S. Rosenblum, and A. L. Wolf. Design and evaluation of a wide-area even notification service. *ACM Trans. on Computer Systems*, 19(3):332–383, 2001. 203

[5] K. Cheverst, N. Davies, K. Mitchell, A. Friday, and C. Efstratiou. Experiences of developing and deploying a context-aware tourist guide: The GUIDE project. In *Proceedings of MobiCom*, pages 20–31. ACM Press, 2000. 200

[6] G. Cugola, E. Di Nitto, and A. Fuggetta. The JEDI event-based infrastructure and its application to the development of the OPSS WFMS. *IEEE Trans. on Software Engineering*, 27(9):827–850, 2001. 203

[7] D. Gelernter. Generative communication in Linda. *ACM Trans. on Prog. Lang. and Systems*, 7(1):80–112, 1985. 201

[8] A. Harter and A. Hopper. A distributed location system for the active office. *IEEE Networks*, 8(1):62–70, 1994. 199

[9] J. Hong and J. Landay. An infrastructure approach to context-aware computing. *Human Computer Interaction*, 16, 2001. 200

[10] Qingfeng Huang, Christine Julien, and Gruia-Catalin Roman. Relying on safe distance to achieve strong partitionable group membership in ad hoc networks. *IEEE Transactions on Mobile Computing*, 2003. (to appear). 212

[11] C. Julien and G.-C. Roman. Egocentric context-aware programming in ad hoc mobile environments. In *Proc. of the $10^{th}$ Int'l. Symp. on the Foundations of Software Engineering*, pages 21–30, 2002. 200, 201, 202

[12] Y. Ko and N. Vaidya. Location-aided routing (LAR) in mobile ad hoc networks. In *Proc. of MobiCom*, pages 66–75, 1998. 199

[13] A. L. Murphy, G. P. Picco, and G.-C. Roman. LIME: A middleware for physical and logical mobility. In *Proc. of the $21^{st}$ Int'l. Conf. on Distributed Computing Systems*, pages 524–533, 2001. 200, 203

[14] V. Park. and M. S. Corson. Temporally-ordered routing algorithm (TORA) version 1: functional specification. Internet Draft, August 1998. IETF MANET Working Group. 199

[15] G. P. Picco, A. L. Murphy, and G.-C. Roman. On global virtual data structures. In D. Marinescu and C. Lee, editors, *Process Coordination and Ubiquitous Computing*, pages 11–29, 2002. 200

[16] G.-C. Roman, C. Julien, and Q. Huang. Network abstractions for context-aware mobile computing. In *Proc. of the 24$^{th}$ Int'l. Conf. on Software Engineering*, pages 363–373, 2002. 201, 211

[17] E. Royer and C.-K. Toh. A review of current routing protocols for ad hoc mobile wireless networks. *IEEE Personal Communications*, pages 46–55, 1999. 199

[18] N. Ryan, J. Pascoe, and D. Morse. Fieldnote: A handheld information system for the field. In *1$^{st}$ International Workshop on TeloGeoProcessing*, 1999. 199

[19] D. Salber, A. Dey, and G. Abowd. The Context Toolkit: Aiding the development of context-enabled applications. In *Proc. of CHI'99*, pages 434–441, 1999. 200

[20] R. Want et al. An overview of the PARCTab ubiquitous computing environment. *IEEE Personal Communications*, 2(6):28–33, 1995. 199

# CoorSet: A Development Environment
# for Associatively Coordinated Components

Kevin Kane and James C. Browne

Department of Computer Sciences, The University of Texas at Austin
1 University Station C0500, Austin, TX 78712-0233 USA
{kane,browne}@cs.utexas.edu

**Abstract.** A development environment for applications specified in an extended version of a previously developed coordination model based on associatively broadcast interactions is presented. The previous associative broadcast coordination model is extended to incorporate more complex specifications for interactions including multiple message interactions and fault-tolerance by replication. The runtime system is extended to facilitate construction and application of distributed implementation of coordination systems. An interface definition language based on the extended coordination model and a compiler for the language are defined and described. Three example applications, a generalized readers/writers problem including replication, a "greedy reuse" algorithm and a distributed computation of Google pageranks are presented.

## 1   Introduction

There has been little research on coordination models and languages based on broadcast communication, despite the facts that many network intrinsically provide a physical broadcast capability including such widely available systems as Ethernet, FDDI, and wireless, and that broadcast enables consensus for asynchronous communication [2].

There has also been, except for Linda-based [5] coordination models and languages, relatively little experimental or systems-oriented research on application of coordination models and languages. Experimental research is needed to establish a basis for application of coordination models and languages and to add credibility to the utility value of coordination models and languages. This paper extends previous research on coordination models based on associative broadcast to a development environment for implementation of coordinating systems of processes, illustrates its applications and positions this research in the context of distributed and peer to peer systems research.

The goal for the development environment is to facilitate experimental research on broadcast-based coordination systems. The principal artifacts of the development environment are: extensions to the previous associatively broadcast programming model to facilitate experiments and applications, an interface definition language for expressing associative interactions, a compiler for this interface definition language and an environment for instantiating and executing coordinating systems of processes.

R. de Nicola, et al. (Eds.): COORDINATION 2004, LNCS 2949, pp. 216-231, 2004.
© Springer-Verlag Berlin Heidelberg 2004

Broadcast enables coordination based on every process in an interacting set locally maintaining common state necessary for collective decision procedures [1, 2]. Associative broadcast [3, 4] enables targeting of messages to processes in specific states and enables each process to select the properties of messages it will receive. Basing coordination on associative broadcast communication enables definition of multiple dynamic coordination subsets in a set of processes. Separation of message filtering from computation decreases the execution cost of coordination using broadcast and allows for specialization to specific algorithm requirements. Associative broadcast preserves anonymity similarly to tuple space based coordination [5]. It enables transparent distribution and replication for fault-tolerance. In summary, associative broadcast enables fully distributed and fully symmetric coordination over dynamic sets of processes.

The next section summarizes the results from previous research on definition and implementation of a coordination model based on associative broadcast. Section 3 sketches the extended coordination model.  Section 4 discusses formulation of algorithms as coordination systems in the extended coordination model.  Section 5 sketches the CoorSet interface definition language and illustrates formulation of algorithms and computations in the CoorSet coordination development environment including discussion of definition of algorithms.  Section 6 sketches the environment for instantiating and executing systems of coordinating processes. Section 7 discusses the implementation of our system.  Section 8 gives related research and section 9 gives a summary and conclusions.

## 2    Associative Broadcast Coordination Model

A previous paper [6] reported a coordination model based on extending communication by associative broadcast into a coordination model by extending associative communication to associative interactions.  This coordination model will be referred to as Associatively Specified Interactions (ASI). ASI is a model of coordination amongst a group of *components*.  A *component* is a logically distinct process executing on some host in a network.  Components may coexist with other components on the same physical host, or each may reside on a different host.  The ASI implementation of a component is one or more functions encapsulated by an interface which implements the ASI interaction protocols. In the ASI protocols, a target set specification travels with each message that is broadcast onto the network.  The target set is determined for each message by the recipients whose local state satisfies the target specification.  The sender does not know the membership of this set, and does not necessarily ever discover it.

The state of a component is specified in the interface as a "profile," which specifies the visible current state of the component.  Profiles are implemented as sets of attribute/value pairs taken from the attribute domain of the component set that specify a *descriptive name* [3] for the component. The target set for a message is determined by a conditional expression called a "selector," which is a predicate evaluated against the profile of each component.  The message is broadcast throughout the network, but is received only by those components for whose profiles the selector evaluates to true. This allows targeting of messages to subsets of components that have a desired state, without the sender knowing the membership of that set. All components in the system configure their profiles and broadcast messages with selectors according to a coordination protocol. Protocols implementing acknowledgements can be implemented if needed for a given coordination problem.

## 3    Extended Associative Broadcast Coordination Model and Programming Model

The previous associative broadcast coordination model has been extended into a programming model which enables direct representation of complex interactions with retention of separation of concerns. This model incorporates two additional features: complex conditions for enabling execution of a component and replication for both representation of SPMD parallelism and fault-tolerance.

The conditions for executing and action of a component commonly include receipt of multiple messages. To maintain separation of concerns it is necessary to incorporate this requirement into the coordination model.[1] We introduce the concept of a "firing rule" into the coordination model. A firing rule is a specification of the set of messages which must be received to initiate any action of a component. Additionally, since components may and often will have persistent state, there may be precedence relations among possible enabling message sequences. These extensions are accomplished by adding types to messages and incorporating a conditional expression over message types and local state into the associative interface.

The definition of firing rules used in the extended coordination model is taken from a data flow programming model [7], where rather than waiting on a single input, a node in a data flow graph waits on multiple inputs, possibly in a particular order, before becoming enabled for execution. Firing rules are specified with a Java-like logical syntax. Specifying reception of *either* of two message types $R, S$ is done with a rule "R || S". Reception of *both* of two message types is specified with a rule "R && S". Reception of *R followed by* $S$ is specified with a rule "R < S". These rules can be compounded and grouped with parentheses, such as "(R < S) || (R < T)". The '<' operator has the lowest precedence, followed by `||`, and `&&` has the highest precedence.

Replication is another feature that must be included in associative interaction specifications to enable facile specification of parallelism and fault-tolerance. SPMD parallelism can be readily implemented by replication of components. Replication of functionality for fault-tolerance can be made transparent and synchronization-free after initialization. If an initiating component starts several replicas of a given component to insure success in an unreliable environment and each of the replicated components responses by associative broadcast then the initiating component can safely proceed after the first successful result and set its profile to ignore the other completions. A component can be replicated by adding an index attribute to its profile and instantiating replicas in conformance to the index range. Once specified, a

---

[1]  In the previous coordination model, if multiple messages were required to enable an action by a component, the set of actions of the component had to include aggregation of these messages in effect breaking separation of concerns.

component can be started an arbitrary number of times. The runtime system will provide unique identifiers in a predictable way so replicas can alter their behavior, or they can all execute in the same way depending on the needs of the application.

A component in the extended model is a 5-tuple $(S, S_0, P, A, R)$ where $S$ is the state machine which implements the rules for the protocol specification, and the rules for profile and interface changes, $S_0$ is the initial state, $P$ is the profile of attributes and attribute-value pairs, $A$ is the list of accepted transactions $(T, T_A)$ where $T$ is a firing rule and $T_A$ is the argument signature, and $R$ is the list of requested transactions $(T, T_A)$ where $T$ is a transaction type and $T_A$ is the argument signature. Section 5 illustrates the concepts in the extended model in CoorSet language examples.

## 4    Algorithm Formulation

Most distributed algorithms explicitly or implicitly are formulated on the assumption of central control. Coordination models, on the other hand, do not assume central control. Development of algorithms and computations in coordination models therefore requires a shift in development paradigm. Use of a coordination model based on broadcast communication induces a further shift in development paradigm since most distributed computations and coordination models are based on point to point communication.[2]   There has been relatively little research in formulation of distributed/parallel algorithms in broadcast models of computation [8].

The development paradigm for distributed algorithms formulated in associative interactions is the integration of component composition and component interactions. An algorithm is specified as coordination among a set of components. Composition defines the structural relationships among components while coordination specifies the behavior of the composed system.   Associative interactions use the same mechanism to specify both coordination and composition.

A coordination system implementing an algorithm or computation is specified in terms of a set of attributes in which the profiles and selectors are specified, a set of components from which the algorithm or computation can be composed, a set of protocols in which interactions are specified including message types, the selectors to accompany each instance of a message type, the allowed sequences of messages and the responses to each instance of a message type which is received, and a state machine which implements the coordination protocols which are interfaced to each process or component.

## 5    CoorSet Interface Definition Language

CoorSet is an interface definition language for specification of the behaviors of components in terms of associative interactions.   The CoorSet compiler generates Java code to implement the coordination models for each component and a "main" component that starts the application in the runtime system described in Section 6. In the example that follows, components of the language that deal with details not

---

[2]   Linda-based coordination models [5] are the exceptions to this generalization.

directly related to the interface structure have been omitted for clarity; for complete details of the language, see [9].

```
component 5 {
  profile ("ReaderWriter", ("EID", 2),
        ("Status", "initializing"))

  execute startUp

  accepts "RequestToRead" processRead ()
  accepts "RequestToWrite" processWrite (Object)

  rule "update_value < (update_done || Collision)" processUpdate

  requests "ReplyFromData" sendReply "Client" (Object)
  requests "update_value" attemptUpdate "ReaderWriter" (Object, Integer)
  requests "update_done" completeUpdate "ReaderWriter" (Integer)
  requests "Collision" updateCollide "ReaderWriter" (Integer)
}
```

**Fig. 1.** CoorSet definition of a replicated data object store

### 5.1  Readers/Writers Algorithm In CoorSet

To demonstrate the language for describing components, we introduce a generalized distributed readers/writers system implemented in CoorSet. The data objects are replicated for fault-tolerance. Consistency is maintained across non-malicious failures of components and/or runtime creation of additional replicas. This generalized readers/writers problem is rather complex when programmed in conventional distributed/parallel programming languages but is quite simple in CoorSet. The readers/writers system consists of a set of reader/writer objects which store a data item that is replicated across multiple independent stores, and a set of client components which randomly invoke reads and writes of randomly selected data items. Each reader/writer is a single component in the system. Each encapsulates and stores a single replica of a single data item, provides reading and writing facilities to clients, and implements a coordination protocol amongst all the other replicas of that data item when a write is requested. Each replica's profile contains the unique identifier of the data object, and an index to indicate which replica it is. Each reader/writer component keeps track of the version number of its data item, increasing it each time an update is made. When two updates are attempted simultaneously, meaning they are sent out with the same sequence number, they are said to "collide." When they do, they are aborted. Each then executes an exponential backoff algorithm before attempting the update again with a new sequence number. A definition fragment for the reader/writer component is given in Fig. 1.

The "5" immediately following the "component" declaration specifies that five instances will be started of a component which has an initial profile of three entries. First, an ID attribute named ReaderWriter distinguishes it from other kinds of components in the system, such as clients. Second, a valued attribute EID (for entry identifier) indicates which data item this object contains. Here the entry identifier is declared in the configuration file, implying that each data object's replicas are declared separately. Third, a valued attribute named Status with the value initializing. This is the state of the component when it initially comes online, to show that it is not yet operational, and needs to synchronize with whatever other data stores are already in operation. This attribute later changes to values local processing, reading, and writing to reflect the various states it is in when processing requests.

This component type accepts two message types, RequestToRead and RequestToWrite. These requests are made by clients who want to read and write the data item, respectively. In each case, reception of these messages causes execution of the methods processRead and processWrite on the programmer-supplied computational code (not shown), each of which takes the given parameter types.

The readers/writers component also implements a firing rule which first receives an update_value message, and then an update_done message to indicate the update is successful, or a collision to indicate two writes were attempted at the same time and collided.

This component also requests four message types. ReplyFromData is the response sent to clients in response to a request to read or write. It carries a single Object parameter, which will contain a copy of the data item when read. Its default selector of "Client" will be received by all clients, but when such a response is actually sent, the selector will be refined to target only the requesting client. update_value, update_done, and Collision are all sent during the various stages of consensus to attempt an update of the data item, to signal the update is successful, or conversely, when two attempted updates collide and must be aborted. Each takes the new sequence number of the updated data, and for update_value, the new data value. Each of these are by default targeted to all other data stores by the default selector "ReaderWriter". The optional execute line specifies a method on the programmer-supplied class to execute immediately upon component start-up; if this line is absent, the component just waits for incoming transactions upon starting.

For a simple performance study the data objects were replicated 2 and 4 times. The number of processes reading and writing was varied up to 64, each on a separate workstation on a network. The average number of messages was about Nx2.5 where N is the number of *data object* replicas. Note that the performance of the algorithm is almost independent of the number of readers and writers.

## 5.2  Data Fitting Example

We now present a more complex example of distributed data fitting, motivated by the concept of "greedy reuse" [10]. "Greedy reuse" uses execution of multiple, perhaps redundant components, to ensure the success of a computation by simultaneously executing multiple implementations of a required functionality when it is not certain which implementation should be used. "Greedy reuse" is complex to program in conventional distributed programming systems but simple as a coordination language program. Consider an application that collects a set of data points, and requires approximating them by a curve. There are many possible approaches to data fitting. Consider for illustration a case where it is unclear simply from the data set what method will yield a fit with certain properties required by the application. Possible properties are a minimum of error, compactness of representation, and smoothness of curve. It may be that the requirement is satisfied only by a composition of fits.

Using associatively-coordinated components, several data fits can be executed simultaneously by addressing a data set with a selector that matches to true for the profiles of all data fitting components. The selector can be made more specific if only certain types of fits are desired. This application has more obvious connections between components as is common in more typical coordination models, and the component which initiates the computation is separate from the one that receives the result, to give a linear data flow as illustrated by Figure 2. There is no explicit link between these components, and each circle in fact represents any number of components of that type which may be operating when the request is made. These links should be seen as dynamic, existing only as long as they are required.

Transparent replication and fault-tolerance is obtained by having several copies of the same type of component running, and when the calling component receives all of the results, it can compare them to choose the ones which meet the requirements, or alternatively, those which are faulty. In an unreliable environment the initiating component might choose to simultaneously execute multiple copies of another component just to insure that a result is computed and successfully received with high probability.

We have, for this illustration of concepts, implemented components that provide an exact Lagrange interpolating polynomial fit, a least squares approximation, and a natural cubic spline fit. Each component maintains a profile that identifies it as a data fitting component for the purposes of addressing, as well as profile entries that allow it to be addressed more directly when an application wants only a particular kind of fitting.

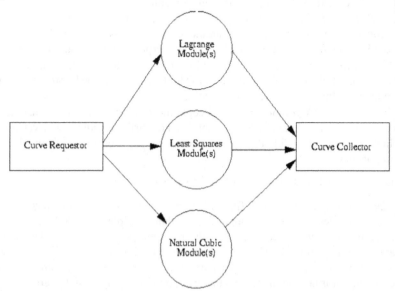

**Fig. 2.** Data flow between components of the data fitter application

The dynamic structure of associative broadcast allows an application to link to all components available at the time a request is made, and to do so without explicit knowledge of what components are available; simply the knowledge of the *accepts* interfaces used by data fitting components is sufficient.

There are two possible system configurations for the components. The components can be active as daemons on hosts in the broadcast network in which case the initiating component is invoked on some hosts and discovery, linking and execution proceeds as previously described. Alternatively, the components can be in a file with the initiating component or in a library. In these latter cases the runtime system will distribute the components to hosts in the broadcast network and start the associative interaction runtime system.

Figure 3 contains the definition fragments for each of the types of components in CoorSet. These interface definitions are used to create the initial configuration of the component network. Some details have been omitted due to space constraints.

In this example, we have five types of components. In this case, three of each of the fitter components is started, as indicated by the "3" after the "node" keyword, to create replicated instances. There is only a single instance of the other components, CurveRequestor and CurveCollector. The types of components are:

- *CurveRequestor*: A component that has collected some data set, and requires it be fit to a curve. It does not accept any transactions, but makes a "DataFit" request to all data fitting components by way of its selector.
- *LagrangeModule*: An exact Lagrange interpolating polynomial. Its initial profile has one attribute called "DataFitter" to indicate that it is a data fitting component, and a valued attribute called "Method" with a value of "Lagrange" to specify the particular kind of data fitter it is. It accepts the "FitData" request, and makes a "FitDataRespnse_Poly" request to send its result.
- *LeastSquaresModule*: A least squares polynomial fitter. Its interface is almost identical to that of the Lagrange module, except that its profile reflects its being a Least Squares fitter, rather than a Lagrange interpolating polynomial fitter.
- *NatCubicModule*: A natural cubic spline fitter. It accepts the same "FitData" transaction, but responds with a "FitDataResponse_Spline" transaction, which contains a spline rather than a single polynomial.
- *CurveCollector*: A component that accepts the resulting curve fits from the above components. Its default profile contains an attribute called "CurveCollector," which also is the default for selectors for the responses from the above components.

There are also three types of requests for service:

- *FitData*: A request for a data fit. This transaction has four parameters: the first, a String, specifies a transaction identifier, so that multiple fits may be requested and the responses can be connected with the appropriate request. The next two parameters are arrays of Double values, representing the X and Y coordinates of the data points. The final Integer parameter specifies the maximum order of the polynomial, for polynomial fitters that can bound the polynomial degree.

```
component 1 {
  class CurveRequestor
  execute start
  requests "FitData" Request "DataFitter" (String, Double[], Double[], Integer)
}
component 3 {
  class LagrangeModule
  profile ("DataFitter", ("Method", "Lagrange"))
  accepts "FitData" processRequest (String, Double[], Double[], Integer)
  requests "FitDataResponse_Poly" sendResponse "CurveCollector"
          (String, Double[])
}
component 3 {
  class LeastSquaresModule
  profile ("DataFitter", ("Method", "LeastSquares"))
  accepts "FitData" processRequest (String, Double[], Double[], Integer)
  requests "FitDataResponse_Poly" sendResponse "CurveCollector"
          (String, Double[])
}
component 3 {
  class NatCubicModule
  profile ("DataFitter", ("Method", "NatCubicSpline"))
  accepts "FitData" processRequest (String, Double[], Double[], Integer)
  requests "FitDataResponse_Spline" sendResponse "CurveCollector"
          (String, Cubic[], Cubic[])
}
component 1 {
  class CurveCollector
  profile ("CurveCollector")
  accepts "FitDataResponse_Poly" processPoly (String, Double[])
  accepts "FitDataResponse_Spline" processSpline (String, Cubic[], Cubic[])
}
```

**Fig. 3.**  Initial configuration of data fitting in *CoorSet*

- *FitDataResponse_Poly*: A response to a data fitting request, containing a polynomial fitting to the data. It carries a String with the transaction identifier for which this is a fit, and an array of Double values representing the polynomial coefficients.
- *FitDataResponse_Spline*: A response to a data fitting request, containing a natural cubic spline fitting to the data. It also carries a String transaction identifier, as well as two arrays of Cubic polynomials. The first is a piecewise parameterized representation of the X coordinates of the spline, and the second is a piecewise parameterized representation of the Y coordinates.

### 5.3 Distributed Computation of Google Pageranks

The Google PageRank algorithm [31] is the computation of the eigenvectors of the lowest eigenvalue of a matrix defined by the link structure of web pages. This computation is readily formulated in asynchronous iteration [32]. We have implemented a distributed, dynamic computation [27] of pageranks in CoorSet. Documents which have url-like links are distributed across a set of hosts (which model web servers.) coupled by a broadcast capability. The pageranks are computed in place in the hosts. Pageranks are incrementally computed as documents are added or deleted. A detailed discussion of the implementation of this algorithm (See [27]) is beyond the scope of this paper. On a data set of 1000 documents running on eight processors on a 100-megabit local area network, an average of 1846 messages were required to converge, with an average running time of 68.6 seconds.

## 6   Runtime Functionality for CoorSet

The requirements for experimental research on distributed coordination systems in CoorSet are: implementation of timed reliable asynchronous broadcast, configuration and realization of coordination systems on distributed resources and a runtime system which supports the extended associative interactions coordination model specified in Section 3.   This section defines and describes the capabilities for these three requirements currently implemented for the CoorSet development environment.

A system for supporting experimental research on distributed systems needs the following capabilities:

**Discovery of Available Hosts.** A distributed launching system must be able to find out what hosts are available to participate in the experiment.

**Request Authentication.** Any system of this type must ensure that only requests with the proper security credentials are honored.

**Filesystem Independence.** A distributed system should not assume a shared file system. Therefore it is its responsibility to see that binaries are transported to the execution sites when launching.

**Host Independence.** The system should handle the loading and execution of code on a variety of architectures.

**Dynamic System Structure.** Such a system should allow dynamic structuring of experiments, as these experiments will often involve joining and leaving protocols, and fault tolerance.

The CoorSet development environment uses the "Component Starting Component" (CSC) [14], an environment for launching Java components to configure and instantiate coordination systems for execution on distributed resources. The CSC is deployed on participating systems in a network. Once installed on a host in a network it can stay resident indefinitely. A coordination system is initialized by multicasting a solicitation for available hosts to discover CSCs without *a priori* knowledge of their locations. After receiving service offers, the program initializing the coordination system connects to an appropriate set of responding hosts, and then sends Java bytecode data and startup instructions. The CSC loads the component and starts the component in a different thread in its local Java Virtual Machine (JVM). Communication is guarded by cryptographic signatures to prevent unauthorized use. The CSC provides automated support for distributed systems research that does away with the necessity of manually logging into a number of remote workstations to launch the components of a system. The "main program" generated by the CoorSet compiler consists of instructions to a network of participating CSC units to launch the components of the application across available hosts.

Once the CSC is installed on a network connected by timed asynchronous reliable broadcast then distributed coordination systems can be instantiated in minutes or even seconds. This allows a CoorSet program to be launched from a single point. The runtime system assigns a unique index to each component, which allows components of a like type to differentiate themselves. The runtime system assigns these in a predictable manner based on the format of the configuration file. This allows components running the same code to behave differently if so desired by choosing a control path based on that identifier. This identifier can also be used in interactions where a unique identifier is desired, such as for point-to-point communications, or identities in an election, just to name a few.

The Associative Interactions runtime listens to broadcast messages on the underlying network substrate, evaluates selectors, and forwards matching messages upwards to the application. Data flow semantics are now supported with a component of the run-time system that implements firing rules. Firing rule components inherit standard code that listens to messages and waits for the rule to be satisfied. The computational code connected to that rule is then executed.

Compound nodes inherit code that provides an event dispatcher for the accepts interface, and a standard application programming interface (API) for runtime modification of the profile, accepts and requests interfaces.

# 7    Implementation

The CoorSet language compiler, runtime system, and Component Starting Component are implemented in Java. CoorSet executes either with an implementation based on the Light-weight Reliable Multicast Protocol [11] that operates on top of IP Multicast, or Scribe [12], a multicast overlay that runs on top of the peer-to-peer Pastry [13] protocol. The latter implementation allows for implementation over wide area distributed systems. The Associative Interface, a class which mediates communication between the application and the network, listens on the multicast socket and evaluates the selectors of incoming broadcasts as the application invokes the message reception API. Matching messages are delivered, and the rest are discarded.

The CoorSet compiler generates Java classes for each defined component type, and a main program invoked to start the system. These generated classes use methods provided by the programmer for the computational part of the component as well as the CoorSet library.

The Component Starting Component is also written entirely in Java. When it receives components to launch, they are launched in independent threads in the same virtual machine. The Java Cryptographic Extensions (JCE), now a standard part of the Java SDK, provide the cryptographic primitives for secure key generation, signature generation, and signature verification for code bundles.

The broadcast model of communication allows greater efficiency of communication on systems like Ethernet where broadcast is the norm, requiring small numbers of messages to reach large numbers of recipients. In the data fitting example in section 5.2, a single message is all that is required to request processing by all available fitter units, instead of dispatching a separate message to each one. This represents a savings when some or all of the units are in the same broadcast domain, and invokes all units that are available, allowing for transparent replication of fitter units. The invoker can compare results for consistency to guard against faulty units, and choose the one that best satisfies a chosen metric amongst the various kinds of fits available.

# 8   Related Research

The previous paper [6] positioned the associative broadcast based coordination model in classification proposed by Papadopoulos and Arbab [15] and related it to other coordination models and languages. Since this paper focuses on a development environment for coordination systems in associative broadcast the related research is that which enables development of applications as coordination systems including languages, runtime systems and graphical specification environments.

## 8.1  Runtime Systems

Runtime implementations of coordination models and peer to peer systems are essential for experimental research on distributed implementations of coordination systems. The most closely related research to the runtime system described herein is Klava [16], which implements the Linda [5] model on top of an infrastructure that supports mobile code in a distributed tuple space, including a facility for transporting Java code across a network and starting it in a remote location.

Picco and Buschini [17] describe Linda in a Mobile Environment (LIME) that uses the Linda tuple-space model, dividing the tuple-space amongst a number of mobile agents. They extend the model by allowing the tuple space to contain classes, and using it as the code basis for a class loading mechanism, instead of the local disk.

SPACETUB [18] is a simulation environment for Linda-style languages, rather than an actual production environment. Each language is modeled in UML, and interpreted by the modeled class whose methods are the primitives of the language under consideration. Although intended to evaluate Linda-like languages, SPACETUB itself could be used as a coordination language by agents directly invoking SPACETUB's primitives.

Peer-to-peer networks can be viewed as a special case of a coordination model, where coordination is accomplished entirely on a set of agreed upon protocols for interaction. In this way each has a well-defined interface and a method for interacting with peers to request and provide services. The associative broadcast coordination model can be viewed as a peer to peer system with protocols for discovery of services and remote procedure calls. In peer-to-peer and associatively coordinated systems, connections are ephemeral, and exist only so long as two components are actually interacting. Although coordination models are commonly more structured than this, those particular models are part of a subclass of all coordination models. In general, a coordination model makes no such assumptions of communications medium, or the nature of connections between components.

## 8.2  Coordination Languages

HOBS [28], a higher-order calculus for broadcasting systems, models many of the important features of the bare Ethernet. It gives a calculus for reasoning about broadcast systems, including using "filters" on incoming broadcasts. This system has been implemented in the ML-descended language OCaml.

PiLar [19] is an architecture description language that uses the $\pi$-calculus to describe its semantics. Each component is also abstracted with a series of exported ports which can be connected to other ports in a strictly point-to-point fashion. PiLar was originally created to describe software architectures, but it is shown that it can be used as a coordination language, and an example of implementation of the Linda [5] model is given.

Manifold [20] is a language which collects groups of components into *manifolds* and encapsulates them into an independent process with its own virtual processor, having its own set of external ports and interconnections amongst the encapsulated members, and reactions to events and other changes in state of the members. Components and manifolds are connected explicitly point-to-point, and once constructed, the system remains static.

Law-Governed Linda (LGL) [25] extends Linda by introducing a *controller* for each entity in the Linda network which mediates communication between the entity and the shared tuplespace. It enforces a set of rules called the *law* of the system on how entities read and write tuples. These rules are expressed in a predicate calculus such as Prolog.

Coordination Contracts [26] express relationships between objects in a business model. A *contract* between a number of *partners* represents an agreement that certain invariants will always be maintained, and that actions of partners will be coordinated with local actions. These actions are in the language itself, specifying what an object will do when a guard condition is satisfied.

CoML [21] is an XML-based language that describes the interconnections between a group of components implemented in a general-purpose language, for components that operate in an interconnection platform such as CORBA, JavaBeans, or .NET. It uses an event-driven model for communication, where there are event sources that fire events when conditions are met, such as during state changes, event sinks that react upon them, and event data. Components are composed by describing their interfaces and explicit connections to other components. Connections are changeable during runtime.

Linear Objects [29] are an integration of logic and object programming where the "facts" in a knowledge base include methods defined by classes. Program clauses may have multiple "heads" including references to these methods connected by an operator closely related to logical disjunction. Generation of a search tree creates references to the method signatures. Each step in generation of a search tree corresponds to a restricted form of broadcasting an associatively addressed message.

A CoorSet program is equivalent to a parallel production rule program [30] where both the rules and the object store are distributed. There are two object types: a rule object type has some member variables and three methods, a condition evaluation method, a conflict resolution method and an action execution method, a data object type has some member variables and two methods, an access method and a distribution method.

Web Services Flow Language (WSFL) [22] describes interactions amongst web services in either a flow model, which illustrates a particular business process, or a global model which describes how a set of web services interact without regard to a particular application, but this language is geared specifically towards web services specified in the Web Services Description Language (WSDL). Explicit connections are made between service instances, and using web service interfaces. Grid services [24] address the same idea as web services, but in the context of the computational grid. Services here also use WSDL, but extend it to allow stateful services, discovery, and use of the standard authorization mechanisms present in a grid.

WSFL's successor, Business Process Execution Language for Web Services (BPEL4WS) [23] describes relationships between business entities which use web services for all interaction. It also allows the separate specification of public protocols from private, internal protocols, further underscoring the need for components to be viewed as black boxes with a well-defined observable behavior, irrespective of how the internals work. This allows internal processes to be modified as needed, while still maintaining the same public behavior and protocols. It abstracts web services-style interactions into "partner links."

## 9    Summary and Future Research

The CoorSet development environment appears to provide a capability for readily constructing applications in the extended associative interactions coordination model. The CSC provides a capability for easily constructing and executing experiments.

Future research will focus on formulation and evaluation of algorithms and applications in the CoorSet coordination model, development of an interactive interface for composition of CoorSet programs, and upon providing a more flexible and powerful security mechanism for the CSC.

## Acknowledgements

This research was supported by the National Science Foundation under grant number 0103725, "Performance-Driven Adaptive Software Design and Control." We also wish to express our gratitude to the reviewers who suggested additional related work for our consideration, as well as future lines of research.

# References

[1]    Dolev, D., Dwork, C., and Stockmeyer, L.: On the minimal synchronism needed for distributed consensus. Journal of the ACM (1987) 34(1):77-97.

[2]    Turek, J. and Shasha, D.: The Many Faces of Consensus in Distributed Systems. Computer (1992) 25(6):8-17.

[3]    Bayerdorffer, B.: Associative broadcast and the communication semantics of naming in concurrent systems.   Ph.D. dissertation, Department of Computer Sciences, The University of Texas at Austin (1993).

[4]    Bayerdorffer, B.: Distributed computing with associative broadcast. Proceedings of the Twenty-Eighth Hawaii International Conference on System Sciences (1995).

[5]    Gelertner, D.: Generative communication in Linda.   ACM Trans. Prog. Lang. Sys., (1985) 7(1):80-112.

[6]    Browne, J. C., Kane, K. and Tian, H.: An associative broadcast based coordination model for distributed processes.  Proceedings of COORDINATION 2002, LNCS 2315, Springer-Verlag (2002) 96-110.

[7]    Newton, P. and Browne, J. C.: The CODE 2.0 Graphical Parallel Programming Language. Proceedings of the ACM International Conference on Supercomputing (1992) 167-177.

[8]    Dolev, D. and Malki, D.:  On distributed algorithms in a broadcast domain.  Proceedings of ICALP (1993) 371-387.

[9]    Kane, K. "The CoorSet Interface Definition Language." Preprint.

[10]   Mittermeir, R. and Wurfl, L.: Greedy Reuse: Architectural Considerations for Extending the Reusability of Components."  Proceedings of SEKE'96, the Eighth International Conference on Software Engineering and Knowledge Engineering  (1996).

[11]   Liao, T.: Light-weight Reliable Multicast Protocol. INRIA Technical Report (1998), http://webcanal.inria.fr/lrmp/lrmp_paper.ps

[12]   Rowstron, A., Kermarrec, A-M., Castro, M., and Druschel, P.: SCRIBE: The design of a large-scale event notification infrastructure. NGC2001, UCL, London (2001).

[13]   Rowstron, A. and Druschel, P.: Pastry: Scalable, distributed object location and routing for large-scale peer-to-peer systems. IFIP/ACM International Conference on Distributed Systems Platforms (Middleware), Heidelberg, Germany (2001) 329-350.

[14]   Kane, K. and Browne, J.C.: The Component Starting Component: an environment for distributed systems and peer to peer research.   Department of Computer Sciences Technical Report TR-03-42, University of Texas at Austin (2003).

[15]   Papadopoulos, G. A. and Arbab, F.: Coordination Models and Languages. Advances in Computers, v. 46, Academic Press, August 1998.

[16]   Bettini, L., De Nicola, R., and Pugliese, R.: Klava: a Java Framework for Distributed and Mobile Applications. Software – Practice and Experience (2002) 32:1365-1394.

[17]   Picco, G. and Buschini, M.: Exploiting Transiently Shared Tuple Spaces for Location Transparent Code Mobility. Proceedings of COORDINATION 2002, LNCS 2315, Springer-Verlag (2002) 258-271.

[18]   Tolksdorf, R. and Rojec-Goldmann, G.: The SPACETUB Models and Framework. Proceedings of COORDINATION 2002, LNCS 2315, Springer-Verlag (2002) 348-363.

[19]   Cuesta, C., de la Fuente, P., Barrio-Solórzano, M., and Beato, E.: Coordination in a Reflective Architecture Description Language. Proceedings of COORDINATION 2002, LNCS 2315, Springer-Verlag (2002) 141-148.

[20]   20.Arbab, F., Herman, I. and Spilling, P.: An overview of Manifold and its implementation. Concurrency: Practice and Experience (1993) 5(1):23-70.

[21]   Birngruber, D.: CoML: Yet Another, But Simple Component Composition Language. Proceedings of Workshop on Composition Languages (2001).

[22]    22.Leymann, F.: Web Services Flow Language (WSFL 1.0). http://www-3.ibm.com/software/solutions/webservices/pdf/WSFL.pdf

[23]    23.Thatte, S. (ed.): Specification: Business Process Execution Language for Web Services Version 1.1. http://www-106.ibm.com/developerworks/webservices/library/ws-bpel/

[24]    24.The Globus Alliance: Open Grid Services Architecture. http://www.globus.org/ogsa/

[25]    Minsky, N. and Leichter, J.: Law-Governed Linda as a Coordination Model. Object-Based Models and Languages for Concurrent Systems, LNCS 924, Springer-Verlag (1995) 125-146.

[26]    Andrade, L. and Fiadeiro, J.: Interconnecting objects via contracts. UML'99 -- Beyond the Standard, R.France and B.Rumpe (eds), LNCS 1723, Springer-Verlag (1999) 566-583.

[27]    Sankaralingam, K., Sethumadhavan, S. and Browne, J.C.: Distributed Pageranks for P2P Systems" Proceedings of the Twelfth IEEE International Symposium on High Performance Parallel and Distributed Systems (2003) 58-69.

[28]    Ostrovský, K.: Higher Order Broadcasting Systems. Thesis for the Degree of Licentiate of Philosophy, Göteborg University (2002).

[29]    Andreoli, J-M. and Pareschi, R.: Linear Objects: Logical Processes with built-in Inheritance Proceedings of 7th ICLP (1990) 495-510.

[30]    30.Wu, S. Y., Miranker, D. P., and Browne, J. C.: Decomposition Abstraction in Parallel Rule Languages. IEEE Transactions on Parallel and Distributed Systems (1996) 7(11):1164-1184.

[31]    Page, L., Brin, S., Motwani, R., and Winograd, T.: The pagerank citation ranking: Bringing order to the web. Technical report, Stanford Digital Library Technologies Project, 1998.

[32]    Chazan, D. and Miranker, W.: Chaotic relaxation. Linear Algebra Applications, 2 (1969) 199-222.

# On the Expressiveness
# of Absolute-Time Coordination Languages

I. Linden and J.-M. Jacquet

Institute of Informatics, University of Namur, Belgium

**Abstract.** Although very simple and elegant, Linda-style coordination
models lack the notion of time, and are therefore not able to precisely
model real-life coordination applications. Nevertheless, industrial proposals such as TSpaces and JavaSpaces, inspired from Linda, have incorporated time constructs.
This paper aims at a systematic study of the introduction of absolute
time in coordination models. It builds upon previous work to study the
expressiveness of Linda extended with a wait mechanism and Linda primitives extended to support the duration of tuples and the duration of the
suspension of communication operations.

## 1   Introduction

As motivated by the constant expansion of computer networks and illustrated
by the development of distributed applications, the design of modern software
systems centers on re-using and integrating software components. This induces
a paradigm shift from stand-alone applications to interacting distributed systems, which, in turn, naturally calls for well-defined methodologies and tools
aiming at integrating heterogeneous software components.

In order to tackle properly the development of modern software, a clear
separation between the *interactional* and the *computational* aspects of software
components has been advocated by Gelernter and Carriero in [15]. Their claim
has been supported by the design of a model, Linda ([9]), originally presented as
a set of inter-agent communication primitives which may be added to almost any
programming language. Besides process creation, this set includes primitives for
adding, deleting, and testing the presence/absence of data in a shared dataspace.

A number of other models, now referred to as coordination models, have
been proposed afterwards. Some of them extend Linda in different ways, for
instance by introducing multiple dataspaces and meta-level control rules (e.g.,
Bauhaus Linda [23], Bonita [27], $\mu Log$ [19], PoliS [11], Shared Prolog [6]), by
addressing open distributed systems (e.g., Laura [34]), middleware web-based
environments (e.g., Jada [12]), or mobility (e.g., KLAIM [24]). A number of
other coordination models rely on a notion of shared dataspace, e.g., Concurrent
Constraint Programming [30], Gamma [3], Linear Objects [1] and Manifold [2], to
cite only a few. A comprehensive survey of these and other coordination models
and languages has been reported in [26].

R. de Nicola et al. (Eds.): COORDINATION 2004, LNCS 2949, pp. 232–247, 2004.

However, the coding of applications evidences the fact that data rarely has an eternal life and that services have to be provided in a bounded amount of time. For instance, a request for information on the web has to be satisfied in a reasonable amount of time. More crucial is even the request for an ambulance which, not only has to be answered eventually but within a critical period of time. The list could also be continued with software in the areas of air-traffic control, manufacturing plants and telecommunication switches, which are inherently reactive and, for which, interaction must occur in "real-time".

Although there is an obvious application need, the introduction of time has not been deeply studied in the context of coordination languages and models, the notable exceptions being [5, 25, 28, 29], yet proposed in the context of concurrent constraint programming, and [7, 8].

Our recent work has aimed at contributing to the study of time in coordination languages and models. In [20], we have described four ways of introducing time in Linda-like languages. They rely on two notions of time, relative time and absolute time, and, for each notion, on two types of features: delay mechanism and explicit deadlines on the validity of tuples and on the duration of suspension of communication operations. In addition to the description of the language primitives, elementary expressiveness results have been presented and implementation techniques have been detailed. In [18], a systematic study of relative time coordination languages has been performed. We turn in this paper to a systematic study of absolute time coordination languages. In addition to their scientific interest, the results presented in the paper are of great importance for implementation issues. Indeed, the implementation techniques described in [20] are based on the existence of a global clock and on mechanisms using absolute time. Moreover, in contrast to our previous work, we use here a new notion of embedding making explicit use of the global clock.

Following previous work, we shall use the so-called *two-phase functioning* approach to real-time systems illustrated by languages such as Lustre ([10]), Esterel ([4]) and Statecharts ([16]). This approach may be described as follows. In a first phase, elementary actions of statements are executed. They are assumed to be atomic in the sense that they take no time. Similarly, composition operators are assumed to be executed at no cost. In a second phase, when no actions can be reduced or when all the components encounter a special timed action, time progresses by one unit. Although simple, this approach has been proved to be effective for modelling reactive systems.

Related proposals for the introduction of time in coordination-like languages mainly fall in the category of relative time languages, namely languages where time is not considered with respect to time instants of a clock but rather with respect to durations. For instance, [28] introduces time in the concurrent constraint setting[1] ([30]) by identifying quiescent points in the computation where no new information is introduced and by providing an operator for delaying

---

[1] Concurrent constraint languages may be viewed as a variant of Linda restricted to two communication primitives putting information of a dataspace and checking the presence of information on it.

computations by one unit. At each quiescent point of time, the dataspace is reinitialized to an empty content. The paper [29] extends this framework, on the one hand, by introducing a primitive for checking the absence of information and reacting on this absence during the same unit of time and, on the other hand, by generalizing the delay mechanism in an *hence A* construct which states that *A* holds at every instant after the considered time. The resulting languages are called *tcc* and *tdcc*.

The paper [33] has shown that the language *tcc* can embed one classical representative of the state oriented synchronous languages, namely Argos ([22]), and one representative of the declarative class of dataflow synchronous languages, namely Lustre ([10]).

De Boer, Gabbrielli, and Meo have presented in [5] a timed interpretation of concurrent languages by fixing the time needed for the execution of parallel tell and ask operations as one unit and by interpreting action prefixing as the next operator. A delay mechanism is presented in Oz ([32]), a language which combines object oriented features with symbolic computation and constraints, and, (relative) time-outs have been introduced in TSpaces ([35]) and JavaSpaces ([14]). A formal semantics of these time-outs and other mechanisms, different from our expressiveness study, is presented in [7].

Another piece of work on the expressiveness of timed constraint system is [25]. There, various extensions of the *tcc* languages have been studied: extension with replication and recursion static scoping. Decidability results are proved as well as several encodings, which are however not of the form of modular phased embeddings studied in this paper.

Finally, [8] investigates the impact of various mechanisms for expired data collection on the expressiveness of coordination systems. However, the study is based on Random Access Machines, on ordered and unordered tells of timed data and on decidability results.

As may be appreciated from the above description, our work is quite different. We shall study absolute time instead of relative time. We shall also study a richer class of languages and will use to that end a new form of embedding.

The rest of this paper is structured as follows. Section 2 introduces the families of languages under study in the paper. All of them rest on common sequential, parallel and choice operators. The Linda-like languages are first modelled as the $\mathcal{L}$ family. Wait mechanims are then introduced and absolute timing primitives are defined thereafter. The expressiveness hierarchy of each families of languages, considered in isolation, is studied in section 3 together with the intercomparison of the families. Finally, section 4 draws our conclusion and discusses related work.

# 2 The Families of Languages

## 2.1 Common Syntax and Rules

All the languages considered in this paper contain sequential, parallel and choice operators. They only differ in the set of communication primitives they embody.

$$
\begin{array}{ll}
\text{GENERAL RULE} & \mathcal{L} \text{ RULE} \\[4pt]
A ::= C \mid A \; ; \; A \mid A \parallel A \mid A + A & C ::= tell(t) \mid ask(t) \mid get(t) \mid nask(t) \\[12pt]
\mathcal{W} \text{ RULE} & \mathcal{I} \text{ RULE} \\[4pt]
C ::= tell(t) \mid ask(t) \mid get(t) \mid & C ::= tell_{[b:e]}(t) \mid ask_{[b:e]}(t) \mid \\
\quad\quad nask(t) \mid wait(m) & \quad\quad get_{[b:e]}(t) \mid nask_{[b:e]}(t)
\end{array}
$$

**Fig. 1.** Comparative syntax of the languages

As a result, assuming such a set, the syntax of a statement, called agent subsequently, is defined by the "general rule" of figure 1 and its semantics is provided by rules (S), (P), and (C) of figure 2. There, configurations are of the form $\langle A \mid \sigma \rangle$ where $A$ represents the agent under consideration and $\sigma$ represents a memory, subsequently called dataspace or store, to be specified for each family of languages.

Note that, for simplicity of the presentation, only finite processes are treated here, under the observation that infinite processes can be handled by extending the results of this paper in the classical way, as exemplified for instance in [17].

### 2.2   The Family of Linda-Like Concurrent Languages

To start with, let us consider the family of languages $\mathcal{L}(\mathcal{X})$, parameterized on the set of Linda-like communication primitives $\mathcal{X}$. This set $\mathcal{X}$ consists of the basic Linda primitives out, in, and rd primitives, for putting an object in a shared dataspace, getting it and checking for its presence, respectively, together with a primitive testing the absence of an object from the dataspace. Formally, the language is defined as follows.

**Definition 1.** *Let Stoken be a denumerable set, the elements of which are subsequently called tokens and are typically represented by the letters $t$ and $u$. Define the set of communication actions Scom as the set generated by the $\mathcal{L}$ rule of figure 1. Moreover, for any subset $\mathcal{X}$ of Scom, define the language $\mathcal{L}(\mathcal{X})$ as the set of agents $A$ generated by the general rule of figure 1.*

For any $\mathcal{X}$, computations in $\mathcal{L}(\mathcal{X})$ may be modelled by a transition system written in Plotkin's style. Following the intuition, most of the configurations consist of an agent together with a multi-set of tokens denoting the tokens currently available for the computation. To easily express termination, we shall introduce particular configurations composed of a special terminating symbol $E$ together with a multi-set of tokens. For uniformity purposes, we shall abuse language and qualify $E$ as an agent. However, to meet the intuition, we shall always rewrite agents of the form $(E \; ; \; A)$, $(E \parallel A)$, and $(A \parallel E)$ as $A$. This is technically

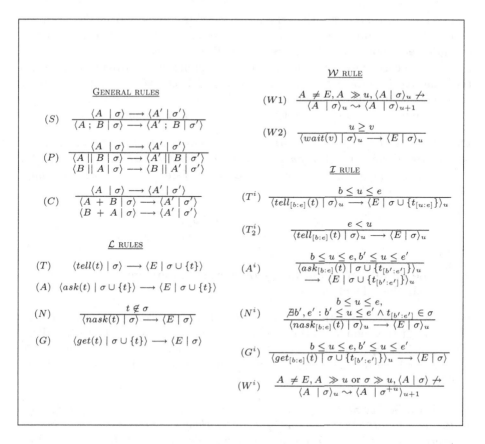

**Fig. 2.** Comparative semantics of the languages

achieved by defining the extended set of agents as follows, and by operating simplifications by imposing a bimonoid structure.

**Definition 2.** *Define the extended set of agents Seagent by the following grammar Ae ::= E | C | A ; A | A || A | A + A. Moreover, we shall subsequently assert that the structure (Seagent, E, ; , || ) is a bimonoid and simplify elements of Seagent accordingly.*

**Definition 3.** *Define the set of stores Sstore as the set of finite multisets with elements from Stoken.*

*Define the set of configurations Sconf as Seagent × Sstore. Configurations are denoted as $\langle A \mid \sigma \rangle$, where A is an (extended) agent and $\sigma$ is a multi-set of tokens.*

*The transition rules for the $\mathcal{L}$ agents are the general ones of figure 2 together with rules (T), (A), (N), (G) of that figure, where $\sigma$ denotes a multi-set of tokens.*

Rule (T) states that an atomic agent $tell(t)$ can be executed in any store $\sigma$, and that its execution results in adding the token $t$ to the store $\sigma$. Rules (A) and (N) state respectively that the atomic agents $ask(t)$ and $nask(t)$ can be executed in any store containing the token $t$ and not containing $t$, and that their execution does not modify the current store. Rule (G) also states that an atomic agent $get(t)$ can be executed in any store containing an occurrence of $t$, but in the resulting store the occurrence of $t$ has been deleted. Note that the symbol $\cup$ actually denotes multiset union.

We are now in a position to define the operational semantics.

**Definition 4.** *Let $\delta^+$ and $\delta^-$ be two fresh symbols denoting respectively success and failure. Define the set of final states $Sfstate$ as the set $Sstore \times \{\delta^+, \delta^-\}$.*

*Define the* operational semantics $\mathcal{O} : \mathcal{L} \rightarrow \mathcal{P}(Sfstate)$ *as the following function: For any agent $A$,*

$$\mathcal{O}(A) = \{(\sigma, \delta^+) : \langle A \mid \emptyset \rangle \rightarrow^* \langle E \mid \sigma \rangle\}$$
$$\cup \{(\sigma, \delta^-) : \langle A \mid \emptyset \rangle \rightarrow^* \langle B \mid \sigma \rangle \not\rightarrow, B \neq E\}$$

## 2.3   The Family of Linda-Like Concurrent Languages with Wait Declarations

One way of introducing time in coordination languages consists of delaying the execution of the communication primitives after a precise point of time. This is obtained by introducing a primitive $wait(m)$ which forces suspension until time $m$ has been reached. Formally, the resulting family of languages is defined as follows.

**Definition 5.** *Let $Stime$ be the set of positive integers. Define the set $Swcom$ as the set generated by the $\mathcal{W}$ rule of figure 1, where $t \in Stoken$ and $m \in Stime$. Moreover, for any subset $\mathcal{X}$ of $Swcom$, define the language $\mathcal{W}(\mathcal{X})$ as the set of agents generated by the general rule of figure 1 for $C \in \mathcal{X} \cup \{wait\}$.*

The configurations to be used here are similar to those used for the $\mathcal{L}$ family of languages. Time introduced in an absolute way induces just one adaptation: to explicitly introduce time in the configurations. We are thus lead to configurations of the form $\langle A \mid \sigma \rangle_u$ where $u$ represents the current time. The general rules (S), (P), (C) need then to be rephrased to this new notation. Of course, they leave the $u$ subscript unchanged. Rule (W1) is introduced to make time progress and rule (W2) is used to reduce a wait declaration. Note that time is allowed to progress only if the new situation differs from the old one. This is expressed by the relation $A \gg u$, which states that $A$ contains a $wait(m)$ operation with $m > u$.

**Definition 6.** *Define $\mathcal{F} : \mathcal{W}(Swcom) \rightarrow \mathcal{P}(Swcom)$ as follows: for any communication primitive $p$ and agents $A$ and $B$, $\mathcal{F}(p) = \{p\}$, $\mathcal{F}(A \; ; \; B) = \mathcal{F}(A)$, $\mathcal{F}(A + B) = \mathcal{F}(A) \cup \mathcal{F}(B)$, $\mathcal{F}(A \parallel B) = \mathcal{F}(A) \cup \mathcal{F}(B)$.*

*For any agent $A$ and time $u$, $A \gg u$ holds iff there is some $m > u$ such that $wait(m) \in \mathcal{F}(A)$.*

*Define the set of configurations Swconf as the set* $(\mathcal{W}(Swcom) \cup \{E\}) \times$ *Sstore $\times$ Stime. Define the transition rules for the $\mathcal{W}$ agents as the general ones of figure 2 and rules (T), (A), (N), (G), (W1) and (W2) of that figure.*

*Define the operational semantics $\mathcal{O}_w : \mathcal{W}(Swcom) \to \mathcal{P}(Sfstate)$ as the following function: for any agent A*

$$\mathcal{O}_w(A) = \{(\sigma, \delta^+) : \langle A \mid \emptyset \rangle_1 \mapsto^* \langle E \mid \sigma \rangle_u\}$$
$$\cup \{(\sigma, \delta^-) : \langle A \mid \emptyset \rangle_1 \mapsto^* \langle B \mid \sigma \rangle_u \not\mapsto, B \neq E\}$$

*where $\mapsto$ denote the relation defined by $\langle A \mid \emptyset \rangle_t \mapsto \langle B \mid \sigma \rangle_u$ iff $\langle A \mid \emptyset \rangle_t \to \langle B \mid \sigma \rangle_u$ or $\langle A \mid \emptyset \rangle_t \rightsquigarrow \langle B \mid \sigma \rangle_u$*

## 2.4 The Family of Linda-Like Concurrent Languages with Time Intervals

Time may also be introduced by extending the Linda primitives with time intervals during which the reduction should take. We are thus lead to communication primitives of the form $tell_{[b:e]}(t)$, $ask_{[b:e]}(t)$, $nask_{[b:e]}(t)$, $get_{[b:e]}(t)$, where we assume that $0 \leq b \leq e$. The resulting family of languages is referred to as $\mathcal{I}(\mathcal{X})$.

**Definition 7.** *Define Sicom as the set generated by the $\mathcal{I}$ rule of figure 1, where $t \in Stoken$ and $b \in Stime$, $e \in Stime \cup \{\infty\}$ with $b \leq e$. Moreover, for any subset $\mathcal{X}$ of Sicom, define $\mathcal{I}(\mathcal{X})$ as the set of agents generated from Sicom by the general rule of figure 1.*

*Define the set of interval stores Sistore as the set of multisets of elements of the form $t_{[b:e]}$ where $t \in Stoken$, $b \in Stime$, $e \in Stime \cup \{\infty\}$ are such that $b \leq e$.*

*Define the set of configuration Siconf as the set $(\mathcal{I}(Sicom) \cup \{E\}) \times Sistore \times Stime$.*

*For any agent A of $\mathcal{I}(Sicom)$ and time u, define $A \gg u$ to hold if $\mathcal{F}(A)$, defined in a way similar to definition 6, contains at least one primitive $tell_{[b:e]}(t)$, $ask_{[b:e]}(t)$, $nask_{[b:e]}(t)$, $get_{[b:e]}(t)$, with $b > u$.*

*For any interval store $\sigma$ and time u, define $\sigma \gg u$ to hold if there is $t_{[b:e]} \in \sigma$ such that $e \neq \infty$ and $e > u$. Moreover, define $\sigma^{+u}$ as*

$$\sigma^{+u} = \{t_{[max\{b,u+1\}:e]} : t_{[b:e]} \in \sigma, u + 1 \leq e\}.$$

*Define the set of transition rules for the $\mathcal{I}$ agents as rules (S), (P), (C) rewritten so as to include the u subscript and rules (Ta), (Aa), (Na), (Ga), and (Wa) of figure 2.*

The operational semantics is adapted from that of the previous section. It is subsequently written as $\mathcal{O}_i$.

# 3   Language Comparison

## 3.1   Introduction

A natural question to ask is whether the time extensions we just introduced strictly increase the expressivity of the Linda language and, if so, whether some of the timed primitives may be expressed in terms of others.

A basic approach to answer that question has been given by Shapiro in [31] as follows. Consider two languages $L$ and $L'$. Assume given the semantics mappings (*observation criteria*) $S : L \rightarrow Obs$ and $S' : L' \rightarrow Obs'$, where $Obs$ and $Obs'$ are some suitable domains. Then, according to [31], $L$ can *embed* $L'$ if there exists a mapping $C$ (*coder*) from the statements of $L'$ to the statements of $L$, and a mapping $D$ (*decoder*) from $Obs$ to $Obs'$, such that $D(S(C(A))) = S'(A)$, for every statement $A \in L'$. This approach is however too weak since, for instance, the above equation is satisfied by any pair of Turing-complete languages. To circumvent this problem, De Boer and Palamidessi have proposed in [13] to add three constraints on the coder $C$ and on the decoder $D$. First, $D$ should be defined in an element-wise way w.r.t. $Obs$:

$$\forall X \in Obs : \ D(X) = \{D_{el}(x) \mid x \in X\} \qquad (P_1)$$

for some appropriate mapping $D_{el}$. Second, the coder $C$ should be defined in a compositional way w.r.t. the sequential, parallel and choice operators:[2]

$$C(A \ ; \ B) = C(A) \ ; \ C(B)$$
$$C(A \parallel B) = C(A) \parallel C(B) \qquad (P_2)$$
$$C(A \ + \ B) = C(A) \ + \ C(B)$$

Finally, the embedding should preserve the behavior of the original processes w.r.t. deadlock, failure and success (*termination invariance*):

$$\forall X \in Obs, \forall x \in X : \ tm'(D_{el}(x)) = tm(x) \qquad (P_3)$$

where $tm$ and $tm'$ extract the information on termination from the observables of $L$ and $L'$, respectively. An embedding satisfying these properties ($P_1$, $P_2$, $P_3$) is said to be *modular*.

## 3.2   Phased Embedding

In our time context, we introduce an additional requirement associated with time. Intuitively, we require that statements and their codings obey the commuting equation $D(S(C(A))) = S'(A)$ after each phase, thus giving rise to the situation depicted in figure 3. A modular embedding satisfying this constraint is called modular phased embedding. The formal definition is as follows. It is phrased directly in our time coordination setting.

---

[2] Actually, this is only required for the parallel and choice operators in [13].

$$\langle A \mid \emptyset \rangle \to^* \langle A_1 \mid \alpha_1 \rangle \rightsquigarrow \langle A_1 \mid \alpha_1^+ \rangle \to^* \ldots \to^* \langle A_n \mid \alpha_n \rangle \not\rightarrow$$

$$\mathcal{C} \downarrow \qquad\qquad \uparrow \mathcal{D} \quad \mathcal{C} \downarrow \qquad\qquad\qquad\qquad \uparrow \mathcal{D}$$

$$\langle B \mid \emptyset \rangle \to^* \langle B_1 \mid \beta_1 \rangle \rightsquigarrow \langle B_1 \mid \beta_1^+ \rangle \to^* \ldots \to^* \langle B_n \mid \beta_n \rangle \not\rightarrow$$

**Fig. 3.** Phased embedding

**Definition 8.** *Define the semantics $\mathcal{O}^*$ as a generalisation of the semantics $\mathcal{O}$, $\mathcal{O}_w$ and $\mathcal{O}_i$ to arbitrary starting store but restricted to one phase: for any agent $A$ and any store $\alpha$,*

$$\mathcal{O}^*(A)(\alpha) = \{(\sigma, \delta^+) : \langle A \mid \alpha \rangle \to^* \langle E \mid \sigma \rangle\}$$
$$\cup \{(\sigma, \delta^-) : \langle A \mid \alpha \rangle \to^* \langle A' \mid \sigma \rangle \not\rightarrow, A' \neq E\}$$

**Definition 9.** *Assume a coder $\mathcal{C}$ and a decoder $\mathcal{D}$. For any agents $A$, $B$, any store $\alpha$, $\beta$, $(A, \alpha)$ is* phase-simulable *in $(B, \beta)$ iff the following properties hold:*

1. *$B = \mathcal{C}(A)$*
2. *$\mathcal{O}^*(A)(\alpha) = \mathcal{D}(\mathcal{O}^*(B)(\beta))$*
3. *for any agents $A'$, $B'$ and any stores $\alpha'$, $\beta'$, $\sigma$ if $\langle A \mid \alpha \rangle \longrightarrow^* \langle A' \mid \alpha' \rangle \rightsquigarrow$*
   *$\langle A' \mid \sigma \rangle$ and $\langle B \mid \beta \rangle \longrightarrow^* \langle B' \mid \beta' \rangle \not\rightarrow$ then there is a store $\tau$ such that*
   *$\langle B' \mid \beta' \rangle \rightsquigarrow \langle B' \mid \tau \rangle$ and such that $(A', \sigma)$ is phase-simulable in $(B', \tau)$.*

**Definition 10 (Modular phased embedding).** *Let $L$ and $L'$ be two languages of the families $\mathcal{L}$, $\mathcal{W}$ and $\mathcal{I}$ and let $\mathcal{O}_x$ and $\mathcal{O}'_x$ denote their corresponding operational semantics. The language $L$ can embed $L'$ in a modular and phased manner iff there exists a coder $\mathcal{C}$ (coder) from the statements of $L'$ to the statements of $L$, and a decoder $\mathcal{D}$ (decoder) from $\mathcal{O}_x$ to $\mathcal{O}'_x$ such that properties $(P_1)$, $(P_2)$, $(P_3)$ hold and such that for any agent $A$ of $L'$, $(A, \emptyset)$ is phase-simulable in $(\mathcal{C}(A), \emptyset)$.*

The existence of a modular phased embedding from $L'$ into $L$ is subsequently denoted by $L' \leq L$. It is easy to see that $\leq$ is a pre-order relation. Moreover if $L' \subseteq L$ then $L' \leq L$, that is, any language embeds all its sublanguages. This property descends immediately from the definition of modular phased embedding, by setting $\mathcal{C}$ and $\mathcal{D}$ equal to the identity function.

With the help of modular phased embedding, let us now turn to the comparison of the languages. This is subsequently achieved in three steps. The languages are first compared inside their families. The inter-family comparison is then done.

In order to keep the paper in reasonable size, the most interesting proofs are given and, yet, the major arguments in them are given. Nevertheless, the reader may refer to the full version of this paper [21] where all the results are established with details.

### 3.3   The Hierarchy of the Languages with Wait

Let us first turn to the $\mathcal{W}$ family of languages. A first result is that any language embeds all its sublanguages. One may also establish that the primitive $nask$ alone has no more power than $wait$ and that, while $\mathcal{W}(tell)$ and $\mathcal{W}(ask)$ are both strictly more powerful than $\mathcal{W}(\emptyset)$, they are not comparable one another. Moreover, without the $tell$ primitive, the store stays empty and the $get$ and $nask$ do not provide more power than the $ask$ and $wait$ primitives. This leads to the equivalence between the languages composed of the primitives $ask$, $nask$, $get$.

**Proposition 1.**

1. $\mathcal{W}(\emptyset) \equiv \mathcal{W}(nask)$, $\mathcal{W}(ask) \not\leq \mathcal{W}(tell) \not\leq \mathcal{W}(\emptyset)$, $\mathcal{W}(tell) \not\leq \mathcal{W}(ask) \not\leq \mathcal{W}(\emptyset)$
2. $\mathcal{W}(ask) \equiv \mathcal{W}(get) \equiv \mathcal{W}(ask, get) \equiv \mathcal{W}(ask, nask) \equiv \mathcal{W}(nask, get) \equiv \mathcal{W}(ask, nask, get)$

Let us now consider the languages $\mathcal{W}(ask, tell)$ and $\mathcal{W}(nask, tell)$ obtained by extending $\mathcal{W}(tell)$ with the ability of checking the presence and the absence of data, respectively, in the dataspace. It may be established that both $\mathcal{W}(ask, tell)$ and $\mathcal{W}(nask, tell)$ are strictly more expressive than $\mathcal{W}(tell)$.

**Proposition 2.** $\mathcal{W}(ask, tell) \not\leq \mathcal{W}(tell)$ and $\mathcal{W}(nask, tell) \not\leq \mathcal{W}(tell)$.

While $\mathcal{W}(ask, tell)$ extends stricly $\mathcal{W}(ask)$, $\mathcal{W}(nask, tell)$ is uncomparable with $\mathcal{W}(ask)$.

**Proposition 3.** For any $X \subseteq \{nask, get, tell\}$, $Y \subseteq \{ask, get\}$ one has

(i)   $\mathcal{W}(ask, tell) \not\leq \mathcal{W}(ask)$          (iii)     $\mathcal{W}(ask, X) \not\leq \mathcal{W}(nask, tell)$
(ii) $\mathcal{W}(nask, tell) \not\leq \mathcal{W}(ask)$          (iv) $\mathcal{W}(nask, tell, Y) \not\leq \mathcal{W}(ask, tell)$

In the presence of $tell$ and $get$ primitives, the $ask$ primitive is redundant. Moreover, $\mathcal{W}(get, tell)$ appears to be strictly is more expressive than $\mathcal{W}(ask, tell)$.

**Proposition 4.**

(i)        $\mathcal{W}(get, tell) \equiv \mathcal{W}(ask, get, tell)$        (iii) $\mathcal{W}(ask, tell) \leq \mathcal{W}(get, tell)$
(ii) $\mathcal{W}(nask, get, tell) \equiv \mathcal{W}(ask, nask, get, tell)$  (iv) $\mathcal{W}(get, tell) \not\leq \mathcal{W}(ask, tell)$

Finally, in the presence of the $tell$ primitive, $nask$ and $get$ are incomparable.

**Proposition 5.** $\mathcal{W}(nask, tell, X) \not\leq \mathcal{W}(get, tell)$ and $\mathcal{W}(get, tell, Y) \not\leq \mathcal{W}(ask, nask, tell)$, for any $X \subseteq \{ask, get\}$ and $Y \subseteq \{ask, nask\}$.

## 3.4   The Hierarchy of the Languages with Time Intervals

Immediate results for languages with time intervals are that sublanguages are embedded in superlanguages and that the empty language is strictly less powerful than any non-empty languages. Moreover, on the empty store, the *ask*, *nask*, and *get* primitives have the same behavior. However, except in the case of *ask* and *get* on the empty store, none of the primitives can be expressed by combining the others.

**Proposition 6.**

(i) $\mathcal{I}(ask) \equiv \mathcal{I}(get) \equiv \mathcal{I}(ask, get)$    (iv) $\mathcal{I}(ask) \not\leq \mathcal{I}(nask, tell)$

(ii) $\mathcal{I}(nask) \not\leq \mathcal{I}(ask, get, tell)$    (v) $\mathcal{I}(tell) \not\leq \mathcal{I}(ask, nask, get)$

(iii) $\mathcal{I}(ask, nask) \equiv \mathcal{I}(nask, get) \equiv \mathcal{I}(ask, nask, get)$

In the $\mathcal{I}(tell, X)$ family of languages the embedding relation is equivalent to the inclusion one. This is shown by the three following propositions.

**Proposition 7.** $\mathcal{I}(nask, tell) \not\leq \mathcal{I}(ask, get, tell)$, $\mathcal{I}(get, tell) \not\leq \mathcal{I}(ask, nask, tell)$.

**Proposition 8.** $\mathcal{I}(ask, tell) \not\leq \mathcal{I}(nask, get, tell)$.

*Proof.* Let us proceed by contradiction. Assume $\mathcal{I}(ask, tell) \leq \mathcal{I}(nask, get, tell)$ and the existence of a coder $\mathcal{C}$ and a decoder $\mathcal{D}$.

At first, let us observe $\mathcal{C}(ask_{[0:\infty]}(t))$. It is possible to prove that its normal form cannot contain a choice starting with a *nask* or *tell* primitive. It is thus of the following type $(get_{[b_1:e_1]}(t_1) ; A_1) + \ldots + (get_{[b_n:e_n]}(t_n) ; A_n)$. Let $M$ be the biggest finite upper bound of the *tell* primitives occuring in the $A_i$'s.

Secondly, let us consider the agent $tell_{[0:M+1]}(t)$. By the phase-simulable property, its coder admits the following computation $\langle \mathcal{C}(tell_{[0:M+1]}(t) \mid \emptyset \rangle_1 \rightarrow^*$ $\langle E \mid \sigma t \rangle_1$, for some store $\sigma t$. Let us denote $\tau$ the submultiset composed of the $t_i$'s included in $\sigma t$ and $K$ the number of tokens of this multiset.

Let us now consider a computation of an agent that will take all those $t_i$'s out of the store. For this, we take the coder of the agent $tell_{[0:M+1]}(t)$ ; $( \parallel_{i=1}^{K} ask_{[0:\infty]}(t))$, where $\parallel_{i=1}^{K} ask_{[0:\infty]}(t)$ denotes $K$ parallel execution of $ask_{[0:\infty]}(t)$. Its coder admits the following computation

$$\langle \mathcal{C}(tell_{[0:M+1]}(t) ; \parallel_{i=1}^{K} ask_{[0:\infty]}(t)) \mid \emptyset \rangle_1 \rightarrow^* \langle \mathcal{C}( \parallel_{i=1}^{K} ask_{[0:\infty]}(t)) \mid \sigma t \rangle_1$$
$$\rightarrow^* \langle \parallel_{i=1}^{K} A_{j(i)} \mid \sigma t \setminus \tau \rangle_1$$
$$\rightarrow^* \langle E \mid \sigma \rangle_1$$

for some store $\sigma$ where $j(i)$ denotes the alternative selected in the $i^{th}$ parallel execution of $\mathcal{C}(ask_{[0:\infty]}(t))$.

The store $\sigma t \setminus \tau$ contains no token $t_i$. Moreover, the $t_i$'s occuring in $\sigma$ follow from the execution of one of the $A_i$'s agents.

We have three cases to consider according to the presence of the $t_i$'s in $\sigma$.

*Case 1. There is no* $t_i$ *in* $\sigma$. In that case, the contradiction occurs by considering the agent $tell_{[0:M+1]}(t)$ ; $( \parallel_{i=1}^{K} ask_{[0:\infty]}(t))$ ; $ask_{[0:\infty]}(t)$.

*Case 2. All the $t_i$'s occuring in $\sigma$ have a finite duration.* Here we consider the agent $tell_{[M+1:\infty]}(u)$ for some token $u$ different of $t$. By the phase-simulable property, its coder accepts the following computation

$$\langle \mathcal{C}(tell_{[M+1:\infty]}(u)) \mid \emptyset \rangle_1 \leadsto^M \langle \mathcal{C}(tell_{[M+1:\infty]}(u)) \mid \emptyset \rangle_{M+1} \to^* \langle E \mid \sigma u \rangle_{M+1}$$

for some store $\sigma u$. This store contains none of the tokens $t_i$'s. Consider now the agent $tell_{[0:M+1]}(t)$ ; ( $\|_{i=1}^{K} ask_{[0:\infty]}(t)$) ; $tell_{[M+1:\infty]}(u)$ ; $ask_{[0:\infty]}(t)$. It accepts only successful computations. Its coder accepts the following computation

$$\begin{aligned}
&\langle \mathcal{C}(tell_{[0:M+1]}(t) \; ; \; ( \|_{i=1}^{K} ask_{[0:\infty]}(t)) \; ; \; tell_{[M+1:\infty]}(u) \; ; \; ask_{[0:\infty]}(t)) \mid \emptyset \rangle_1 \\
&\to^* \langle \mathcal{C}(tell_{[M+1:\infty]}(u) \; ; \; ask_{[0:\infty]}(t)) \mid \sigma \rangle_1 \\
&\leadsto^M \langle \mathcal{C}(tell_{[M+1:\infty]}(u) \; ; \; ask_{[0:\infty]}(t)) \mid \sigma^{[+M]} \rangle_{M+1} \\
&\to^* \langle \mathcal{C}(ask_{[0:\infty]}(t)) \mid \sigma^{[+M]} \cup \sigma u \rangle_{M+1}
\end{aligned}$$

where $\sigma^{[+M]}$ denotes the store $\sigma$ after $M$ temporal steps. This is a valid prefix for a failing computation of the coder, which, by $P3$, contradicts the fact that the agent accepts only successful computation.

*Case 3. There is one $(t_i)_{[1:\infty]}$ in $\sigma$.* Similarly to case 2, the proof consider the agent $tell_{[M+2:\infty]}(v)$ for some token $v$ different from $t$ and the coding of the agent

$$tell_{[0:M+1]}(t) \; ; \; ( \|_{i=1}^{K} ask_{[0:\infty]}(t)) \; ; \; tell_{[M+2:\infty]}(v) \; ; \; (ask_{[0:\infty]}(t) + tell_{[0:\infty]}(t)).$$

## 3.5   Comparing the L, W and I Families

A first observation is that introducing time is a safe and necessary extension to the Linda family. Rephrased in more formal terms, the $\mathcal{L}$ family of languages can be embedded in the $\mathcal{W}$ and $\mathcal{I}$ families. The converse properties do not hold except for the trivial languages.

**Proposition 9.** *For any $X, Y, Z \subseteq \{ask, nask, get, tell\}$ such that $X \neq \emptyset$*
   (i) $\mathcal{L}(\emptyset) \equiv \mathcal{I}(\emptyset)$
   (ii) $\mathcal{L}(X) \leq \mathcal{I}(X)$ and $\mathcal{I}(X) \nleq \mathcal{L}(Y)$
   (iii) $\mathcal{L}(Y) \leq \mathcal{W}(Y)$ and $\mathcal{W}(Y) \nleq \mathcal{L}(Z)$

Let us now turn to the comparison between the $\mathcal{W}$ and $\mathcal{I}$ families of languages. An immediate result is that the $ask$ and $get$ primitives are not sufficient to express the $wait$ primitive. In contrast, the $nask$ and $tell$ primitives are sufficient to express the $wait$ primitive. Moreover, the $tell$ primitive is not powerful enough to distinguish the two families.

**Proposition 10.** $\mathcal{I}(\emptyset) < \mathcal{W}(\emptyset)$, $\mathcal{W}(ask) \nleq \mathcal{I}(ask)$, $\mathcal{W}(get) \nleq \mathcal{I}(get)$, $\mathcal{I}(tell) \leq \mathcal{W}(tell)$, $\mathcal{W}(ask, get) \nleq \mathcal{I}(ask, get)$, $\mathcal{W}(X) \leq \mathcal{I}(X)$ *for any set of primitives $X$ such that $X \cap \{nask, tell\} \neq \emptyset$.*

The $ask$ and $nask$ primitives of the $\mathcal{I}(X)$ family cannot be expressed in the $\mathcal{W}(X)$ family.

**Proposition 11.** $\mathcal{I}(ask) \not\leq \mathcal{W}(Y)$, for any $Y \subseteq \{ask, nask, get, tell\}$.

*Proof.* By contradiction, assume that $\mathcal{I}(ask) \leq \mathcal{W}(ask, nask, get, tell)$. The proof is based on the examination of the behaviours of the agent $ask_{[2:2]}(t)$ and its coder. The only valid computation of this agent is the following failing computation.

$$\langle ask_{[2:2]}(t) \mid \emptyset \rangle_1 \rightsquigarrow \langle ask_{[2:2]}(t) \mid \emptyset \rangle_2 \not\rightarrow$$

By the phase-simulable property, any execution of its coder finishes at time 2.

Our first observation is that the coder can not contain any choice starting with a $nask$, $tell$, $wait(0)$ or $wait(1)$ primitive. Indeed, if it is the case, by property $P3$ and the phase-simulable property, the agent $\mathcal{C}(nask_{[2:2]})$ accepts a derivation failing at time 2 of the following type

$$\langle \mathcal{C}(ask_{[2:2]}(t)) \mid \emptyset \rangle_1 \rightarrow \langle C \mid \emptyset \rangle_1 \mapsto^* \langle C' \mid \sigma \rangle_2 \not\rightarrow$$

This is also a valid computation finishing at time 2 for the coder of the agent $ask_{[2:2]} + ask_{[3:3]}$. This contradicts the fact that, by the phase-simulable property, all the computations of this agent finish at time 3.

Consequently, the agent $\mathcal{C}(ask_{[2:2]})$ has a normal form of the following type

$$\begin{aligned}
\mathcal{C}(ask_{[2:2]}(t))) = {}& (wait(j_1) \; ; \; A_1) + \ldots + (wait(j_n) \; ; \; A_n) \\
& + (ask(t_1) \; ; \; B_1) + \ldots + (ask(t_m) \; ; \; B_m) \\
& + (get(u_1) \; ; \; D_1) + \ldots + (get(u_o) \; ; \; D_o)
\end{aligned}$$

for some tokens $j_i$'s, $t_i$'s and $u_i$'s, with $j_i > 1$ and $n, m, o \geq 0$.

The second observation is that none of the $j_i$'s is 2. An argument similar to the first observation ensures that the coder of $ask_{[3:3]}$ has the same normal form than $\mathcal{C}(ask_{[2:2]}(t)))$. Assume $j_I = 2$, the coder admits the following computation

$$\langle \mathcal{C}(ask_{[2:2]}(t)) \mid \emptyset \rangle_1 \rightsquigarrow \langle \mathcal{C}(ask_{[2:2]}(t)) \mid \emptyset \rangle_2 \rightarrow \langle A_I \mid \emptyset \rangle_2 \rightarrow^* \langle A' \mid \sigma \rangle_2 \not\rightarrow$$

This provides a valid computation for $\mathcal{C}(ask_{[2:2]}(t)) + \mathcal{C}(ask_{[3:3]}(t))$ finishing at time 2. This contradicts, by the phase-simulable property, the fact that the only computation of $ask_{[2:2]}(t) + ask_{[3:3]}(t)$ is

$$\begin{aligned}
\langle ask_{[2:2]}(t) + ask_{[3:3]}(t) \mid \emptyset \rangle_1 &\rightsquigarrow \langle ask_{[2:2]}(t) + ask_{[3:3]}(t) \mid \emptyset \rangle_2 \\
&\rightsquigarrow \langle ask_{[2:2]}(t) + ask_{[3:3]}(t) \mid \emptyset \rangle_3 \not\rightarrow
\end{aligned}$$

The final contradiction results from the two following facts. On the one hand, if the smallest of the $j_i$'s is greater than 3, computations of the coder finish at times greater than 3. On the other hand, if there is no $j_i$, i.e. if $n = 0$, computations fail at time 1. These two situations contradict, by the phase-simulable property, the fact that the only computation of $ask_{[2:2]}(t)$ finishes at time 2.

**Proposition 12.** $\mathcal{I}(nask) \not\leq \mathcal{W}(Y)$, for any $Y \subseteq \{ask, nask, get, tell\}$.

*Proof.* Similar by examining the agent $nask_{[2:2]}(t)$.

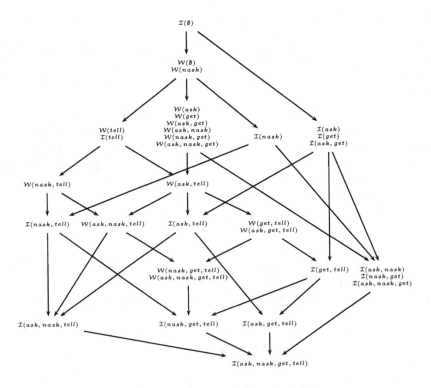

**Fig. 4.** Comparison of the $\mathcal{W}(X)$ and $\mathcal{I}(X)$ languages

## 4   Conclusion

The paper has studied two extensions of Linda in order to introduce absolute time in coordination languages. Both are based on the two-phase functioning approach to real-time systems already employed by languages such as Lustre ([10]) and Esterel ([4]).

The resulting families of languages have been described by means of transition systems written in Plotkin's style. Their expressiveness has been studied by means of a new concept of embedding, called modular phased embedding. The complete expressiveness hierarchy of each family has been examined. We have also compared the expressiveness of languages of the different families. All these results are summed up in figure 4. On the point of notations, an arrow from a language $\mathcal{L}_1$ to a language $\mathcal{L}_2$ means that $\mathcal{L}_2$ strictly embeds $\mathcal{L}_1$, that is $\mathcal{L}_1 < \mathcal{L}_2$.

Future work will be concerned with extending the results of the paper in the case of infinite processes as well as with exploring other phase-similation definitions more in the lines of the simulation and bisimulation properties used in concurrency theory.

# References

[1] J.-M. Andreoli and R. Pareschi. Linear Objects: Logical Processes with Built-in Inheritance. *New Generation Computing*, 9(3-4):445–473, 1991. 232

[2] F. Arbab, I. Herman, and P. Spilling. An Overview of Manifold and its Implementation. *Concurrency: practice and experience*, 5(1):23–70, 1993. 232

[3] J. Banatre and D. LeMetayer. Programming by Multiset Transformation. *Communications of the ACM*, 36(1):98–111, 1991. 232

[4] G. Berry and G. Gonthier. The Esterel Synchronous Programming Language: Design, Semantics, Implementation. *Science of Computer Programming*, 19, 1992. 233, 245

[5] F.S. De Boer, M. Gabbrielli, and M.C. Meo. A Timed Concurrent Constraint Language. *Information and Computation*, 161(1):45–83, 2000. 233, 234

[6] A. Brogi and P. Ciancarini. The Concurrent Language Shared Prolog. *ACM Transactions on Programming Languages and Systems*, 13(1):99–123, January 1991. 232

[7] N. Busi, R. Gorrieri, and G. Zavattaro. Process Calculi for Coordination: from Linda to JavaSpaces. In *Proc. AMAST*, Lecture Notes in Computer Science. Springer Verlag, 2000. 233, 234

[8] N. Busi and G. Zavattaro. Expired Data Collection in Shared Dataspaces. *Theoretical Computer Science*, 298:529–556, 2003. 233, 234

[9] N. Carriero and D. Gelernter. Linda in Context. *Communications of the ACM*, 32(4):444–458, 1989. 232

[10] P. Caspi, N. Halbwachs, P. Pilaud, and J. Plaice. Lustre: a Declarative Language for Programming Synchronous Systems. In *Proc. POPL'87*. ACM Press, 1987. 233, 234, 245

[11] P. Ciancarini. Distributed Programming with Logic Tuple Spaces. *New Generation Computing*, 12(3):251–284, 1994. 232

[12] P. Ciancarini and D. Rossi. Jada: Coordination and Communication for Java Agents. In *Proc. $2^{nd}$ International Workshop on Mobile Object Systems*, volume 1222 of *Lecture Notes in Computer Science*, pages 213–228. Springer-Verlag, 1996. 232

[13] F.S. de Boer and C. Palamidessi. Embedding as a Tool for Language Comparison. *Information and Computation*, 108(1):128–157, 1994. 239

[14] E. Freeman, S. Hupfer, and K. Arnold. *JavaSpaces: Principles, Patterns, and Practice*. Addison-Wesley, 1999. 234

[15] D. Gelernter and N. Carriero. Coordination Languages and Their Significance. *Communications of the ACM*, 35(2):97–107, 1992. 232

[16] D. Harel. Statecharts: a Visual Formalism for Complex Systems. *Science of Computer Programming*, 8, 1987. 233

[17] E. Horita, J.W. de Bakker, and J.J.M.M. Rutten. Fully abstract denotational models for nonuniform concurrent languages. *Information and computation*, 115(1):125–178, 1994. 235

[18] K. De Bosschere I. Linden, J.-M. Jacquet and A. Brogi. On the Expressiveness of Relative-timed Coordination Models. *Electronic Notes in Theoretical Computer Science*, 2003. To appear. 233

[19] J.-M. Jacquet and K. De Bosschere. On the Semantics of $\mu$Log. *Future Generation Computer Systems*, 10:93–135, 1994. 232

[20] J.-M. Jacquet, K. De Bosschere, and A. Brogi. On Timed Coordination Languages. In A. Porto and G.-C. Roman, editors, *Proc. 4th International Conference on Coordination Languages and Models*, volume 1906 of *Lecture Notes in Computer Science*. Springer, 2000. 233

[21] I. Linden and J.-M. Jacquet. On the Expressiveness of Absolute-time Coordination Languages. Technical report, Institute of Informatics, University of Namur, 2003. 240

[22] F. Maraninchi. Operational and Compositional Semantics of Synchronous Automaton Composition. In *Proc. Concur'92*, volume 630 of *Lecture Notes in Computer Science*. Springer, 1992. 234

[23] D. Gelernter N. Carriero and L. Zuck. Bauhaus Linda. In In P. Ciancarini, O. Nierstrasz, and A. Yonezawa, editors, *Object based models and languages for concurrent systems*, volume 924 of *Lecture Notes in Computer Science*, pages 66–76. Springer-Verlag, 1994. 232

[24] R. De Nicola, G. Ferrari, and R. Pugliese. KLAIM: a Kernel Language for Agents Interaction and Mobility. *IEEE Transactions on Software Engineering*, 1998. 232

[25] M. Nielsen, C. Palamidessi, and F. D. Valencia. On the Expressive Power of Temporal Concurrent Constraint Programming Languages. In *Proceedings of the 4th international ACM SIGPLAN conference on Principles and practice of declarative programming*, pages 156–167. ACM, 2002. 233, 234

[26] G. A. Papadopolous and F. Arbab. Coordination Models and Languages. *Advances in Computers*, 48, 1998. 232

[27] A. Rowstron and A. Wood. A Set of Tuple Space Primitives for Distributed Coordination. In *Proc. 30th Hawaii International Conference on System Sciences*, volume 1, pages 379–388. IEEE Press, 1997. 232

[28] V. Saraswat, R. Jagadeesan, and V. Gupta. Programming in Timed Concurrent Constraint Languages. In B. Mayoh, E. Tougu, and J. Penjam, editors, *Computer and System Sciences*, volume ASI-131 of *NATO*. Springer Verlag, 1994. 233

[29] V. Saraswat, R. Jagadeesan, and V. Gupta. Timed Default Concurrent Constraint Programming. *Journal of Symbolic Computation*, 11, 1996. 233, 234

[30] V. A. Saraswat. *Concurrent Constraint Programming Languages*. The MIT Press, 1993. 232, 233

[31] E. Y. Shapiro. Embeddings among Concurrent Programming Languages. In W. R. Cleaveland, editor, *Proceedings of CONCUR'92*, pages 486–503. Springer-Verlag, 1992. 239

[32] G. Smolka. The Oz Programming Model. In J. Van Leuwen, editor, *Computer Science Today*, volume 1000 of *Lecture Notes in Computer Science*, pages 324–343. Springer Verlag, 1995. 234

[33] S. Tini. On the Expressiveness of Timed Concurrent Constraint Programming. *Electronics Notes in Theoretical Computer Science*, 1999. 234

[34] R. Tolksdorf. Coordinating Services in Open Distributed Systems with LAURA. In P. Ciancarini and C. Hankin, editors, *Coordination'96: First International Conference on Coordination Models and Languages*, volume 1061 of *Lecture Notes in Computer Science*. Springer-Verlag, 1996. 232

[35] P. Wyckoff, S. W. McLaughry, T. J. Lehman, and D. A. Ford. TSpaces. *IBM Systems Journal*, 37(3), 1998. 234

# Logic Based Coordination for Event–Driven Self–healing Distributed Systems

Carlo Montangero, Laura Semini, and Simone Semprini

Dipartimento di Informatica, Università di Pisa

**Abstract.** The ability to deal with events explicitly may enhance the expressivity and simplicity of logical specifications. To this purpose, we explore the use of events in the context of DSTL, a logic tailored for the description and verification of distributed systems in a setting based on asynchronous communications. We define an extension that allows the engineer to mix conditions and events in the specification formulae. To validate our approach we formalize a complex coordination pattern where the events play a central role. The pattern describes the rules a set of components must follow to self–organize in a token–ring.

## 1 Introduction

Our long term research goal is logical reasoning on systems based on asynchronous communication [10, 6]. Recently, we defined DSL (Distributed States Logic) [11] and DSTL (T stays for temporal) [9]. The pragmatic reason for these new logics is to ease the expression of properties in a setting of growing interest. They permit to name system components and to causally relate properties which might hold in distinguished components, in an asynchronous setting. A typical DSTL formula is:

$$\mathsf{m}\,p \ \text{LEADS\_TO} \ \mathsf{n}\,q \wedge \mathsf{m}\,r \tag{1}$$

where the operator LEADS_TO is similar to Unity's $\mapsto$ (leads to) [3], and m, n express locality. Formula (1) says that a property $p$ holding in component $m$, causes properties $q$ and $r$ to hold in future states of components $n$ and $m$, respectively. Future has to be intended as the partial order relationship defined by state transitions and communications. An example is the computation below. Horizontal arrows denote the sequence of states of a component, oblique arrows denote the communications.

We build on the Unity logic since it is only a subset of linear time temporal logic, with a limited number of operators, which are rather easy to understand intuitively, and cannot be nested. However, the logic permits to express most of the important properties of a system, exploiting the simplicity and proof straightforwardness which makes Unity more appealing for the designers than linear time temporal logic.

R. de Nicola et al. (Eds.): COORDINATION 2004, LNCS 2949, pp. 248–263, 2004.
© Springer-Verlag Berlin Heidelberg 2004

The key characteristic of DSL and DSTL is a novel semantic domain: the Kripke models are built on worlds that are arbitrary sets of computation states, rather than single states or tuples of them (one for each component), as it is normally proposed.

DSL carries over $1^{st}$ order logic rules, like *and* simplification, so that they can be exploited orthogonally to any temporal operator. A major consequence of the introduction of DSL is that the exploitation of the local theories in the proofs of the distributed properties becomes smooth and robust. In DSTL we add the temporal operators, and the corresponding derivation rules. The semantic domain of DSL, the power–set of the set of all system states, even if chosen for technical reasons, makes the full logic DSTL a very expressive language, that meets the pragmatic expectations of a designer fully.

The achievement is that it is possible to reason about properties that involve several components, even in the absence of a global clock, the typical assumption in an asynchronous setting.

In this paper we explore the introduction of a primitive operator, $\Delta$, to specify events: $\Delta p$ occurs when property $p$ is established, i.e. $p$ *becomes* true in a state.

The interest for event description is growing in the literature. Andrade and Fiadeiro propose a set of semantic primitives to model event–based systems, and argue that event–based interconnections better permit to separate inter-action from computation than explicit invocation mechanisms, accordingly to coordination principles [1]. The main difference with our approach is that they assume a synchronous communication model.

Dias and Richardson discuss the importance of event description when defin-ing the architecture of dependable systems, and introduce, to this purpose, an XML–based language [5].

ForSpec is a temporal logic used in Intel [2]. It includes event specification via the formula $\sim p \wedge future(p)$, where $future(p)$ is essentially the $p'$ of TLA [8]. It is interesting to notice the change of perspective: we predicate on the states where the event occurs, while ForSpec and TLA predicate on the states where it is about to occur. Besides, due to the different setting of interest, ForSpec and TLA do not include any location concept.

The use of events proves particularly useful in distributed systems. For instance, formula m$p$ LEADS_TO n$q$ says that a property $p$ holding in component $m$ implies that property $q$ must hold in a future state of component $n$. This means that if $p$ is stable in $m$, not only $q$ has to be true infinitely often as it would be the case in a non–distributed setting, but also that infinitely many communications must occur between $m$ and $n$. In the practice, it is convenient to let the specifier state a weaker assertion, m$\Delta p$ LEADS_TO n$q$, where the premise is restricted to the states where the condition is established, and a single communication from $m$ to $n$ is sufficient to establish the consequence.

Finally, the use of a mix of events and conditions as in m($\Delta p \wedge q$), offers a straightforward way to express the premises of event–condition rules.

Technically, the introduction of events raises two problems. The first one is how to define the semantics of an event in the initial state; our solution is to consider any litteral holding in the initial state as an event. The second problem is whether constraining the argument of the $\Delta$ operator to be an atom or permitting the specification of more complex events, like $\Delta(p \wedge q)$. Complex events enhance the expressive power and simplify the axiom system (which would include a lot of *special case* axioms in the case of atomic events), while the semantics definition might become elaborated. However, the models we introduce to solve the problem of the initial state events, also permit to easily accommodate complex events in the logic. Notice that these questions could have been skipped with the syntax used by ForSpec or TLA. However, we claim that our $\Delta$ operator allows writing specifications in a more natural way, in particular with regard to conditioned events and reactions to events.

To validate our approach, we specify a coordination pattern that allows a set of components to form a token ring. Asynchronous communications and the absence of a global clock characterize the reference setting. Moreover, participants may join the ring, even once a token is already traveling around. One can think of the components as of independent computational entities, each one knowing the identity of the others, that need to coordinate in order to access a shared resource orderly and sequentially. A bunch of roaming robots, communicating with each other using high frequency radio channels and sharing a single low frequency channel to communicate with a home station, would be the case.

The coordination pattern presented here is characterized by the ability of a set of components to organize in a token ring starting from a chaotic situation where the only knowledge is a set of radio frequencies. Since this is the typical situation that can arise after a major accident, we consider the pattern a promising illustration of how our logic can deal with the essential features of the dynamic adaptive behaviour of self–healing systems.

In Section 2 we formally define the logic $\Delta$DSTL(x), and explain the semantics on a large example. In Section 3 we specify the token–ring coordination pattern, and derive its most important properties.

## 2    $\Delta$DSTL(x)

$\Delta$DSTL(x) is an asynchronous, distributed, temporal, first order logic. It includes a primitive operator ($\Delta$) to specify events. Foundational works towards the definition of $\Delta$DSTL(x) include a logic for distributed states, DSL [11], and a temporal logic for distributed states, DSTL [9], which includes temporal operators à la Unity [3]. The following presentation does not assume any prior knowledge.

We assume a denumerable set of component names $\{m, n, m_1, m_2, \ldots\}$, and that the variables set includes a denumerable set of component variables $\{M, N, M_1, M_2, \ldots\}$.

We introduce location modalities for each component in a system: we use component names, with a different font. For instance, $\mathsf{m_1}$ is the location modality corresponding to component $m_1$, and $\mathsf{m_1} Iam(m_1)$ stays for "in component $m_1$, $Iam(m_1)$ holds". We let quantifiers range over modalities, and $\mathsf{M}$, $\mathsf{N}$, $\mathsf{M_i}$ ... are location modality variables. Binding between location variables and regular variables is possible. For example, $\forall M. \, M Iam(M)$ means that for all components $m_i$, $\mathsf{m_i} Iam(m_i)$ holds. Quantification over modality variables is done in a standard way, following, for instance [4].

## 2.1  Syntax

$$
\begin{aligned}
F \;&::=\; A \;\mid\; \bot \;\mid\; \sim F \;\mid\; F \wedge F' \;\mid\; \varDelta F \;\mid\; \mathsf{M_i} F \\
\phi \;&::=\; \forall \exists F \;\mid\; \textsc{init}\; F \;\mid\; \textsc{stable}\; F \;\mid \\
&\quad\;\; F \;\textsc{leads\_to}\; F' \;\mid\; F \;\textsc{leads\_to\_c}\; F' \;\mid \\
&\quad\;\; F \;\textsc{because}\; F' \;\mid\; F \;\textsc{because\_c}\; F'
\end{aligned}
$$

The first equation defines $\varDelta\mathrm{DSL}(\mathrm{x})$ formulae: $A$ is an atom, $\bot$ is the propositional constant *false*, $\varDelta F$ is an event. With $\bar{\mathsf{M}}_{\mathsf{i}}$ we denote the dual of $\mathsf{M_i}$, i.e., $\bar{\mathsf{M}}_{\mathsf{i}} F \equiv\; \sim \mathsf{M_i} \sim F$. With $\top$ we denote *true*, i.e. $\top \equiv\; \sim \bot$.

The second equation defines $\varDelta\mathrm{DSTL}(\mathrm{x})$ formulae: a $\varDelta\mathrm{DSL}(\mathrm{x})$ formula is also a $\varDelta\mathrm{DSTL}(\mathrm{x})$ formula, provided it is a closed sentence, in prenex normal form. For the sake of readability, we leave universal quantification implicit, and make explicit, when needed, existential quantifiers. For instance, $\exists y. \, M\varDelta p(x) \to q(x, y)$, is implicitly prefixed by $\forall M, x$. Conversely, quantification of temporal formulae is always implicit, as discussed below.

Operator LEADS\_TO expresses a liveness condition, and is similar to Unity's $\mapsto$ (leads to): $F$ is always followed by $F'$; BECAUSE expresses a safety condition, and says that $F$ must be preceded by $F'$; STABLE extends Unity's STABLE to the distributed case; INIT permits to describe the initial state. Temporal operators are suffixed with _C when the consequence has to hold in a state *close* to the state satisfying the premise: $F$ LEADS\_TO\_C $F'$ requires $F'$ to occur in the same state in which $F$ occurs, or in the next one; $F$ BECAUSE\_C $F'$ requires $F'$ to occur in the same state of $F$ or in the previous one.

Temporal formulae are written without explicit quantification. The intended meaning is that a formula $F$ is universally quantified over all values of the variables appearing in the premises of $F$, and existentially quantified on the remaining variables. For example $M\,p(x) \wedge q(y)$ LEADS\_TO $N\,r(x, M, z)$ should be understood as prefixed by $\forall M, x, y \;\exists N, z$. The variables in the formulae with INIT and STABLE are all universally quantified.

The domain over which a variable is quantified (i.e. its sort) can be understood from the context or explicitly defined. We assume that these domains are invariant during time and in space.

## 2.2  Semantics

The models for $\Delta$DSTL(x) formulae are built on structures like the one in the following figure, which describes the computation of a system with two components. Here, $p$, $q$, ... are the properties holding in the states.

We call $S_i$ the set of states of component $m_i$, and $S$ the set of all the states of the computation. A distributed state $ds$ is any subset of $S$, and $ds^0$ is the set of the initial states. We consider also extra states, represented with $\circ$ in the figure, that precede the initial states. We assume they belong to $S$, and use them to give semantics to the events in the initial state.

Let $\mathcal{M}$ be a model, the semantics of $\Delta$DSTL(x) formulae is given by structural induction in Table 1.

Note that a distributed state is any set of states. This means that when we have to check a condition like $\forall ds \geq ds^0 \ldots \exists ds' \ldots$, we need to consider all possible subsets of $S$. This may lead to counter–intuitive choices, like taking larger states than needed. However, the specifier can be safely guided by the natural interpretation of the operators. Anyhow, our definition of distributed state is exactly what was needed to overcome the problems with the existing logics for distributed systems, which do not have the right expressive power to reason on the systems behaviour, when the communication is based on asynchronous message passing. A discussion on these issues follows (see Section 2.3).

*Example 1.*
We discuss the satisfiability of some formulae with respect to the computation above.

$\mathcal{M} \models_T n u$ LEADS_TO $m u \wedge n t$.
$\mathcal{M} \models_T n \Delta u$ LEADS_TO $m u \wedge n t$.
  Consider the first formula: a distributed state satisfies the premise if it contains, for instance, the second state of component $n$, where $u$ holds, call it $s$. It is immediate to find a distributed state following $\{s\}$ and satisfying the consequence, e.g. the first pair of states where $u$ holds in $m$ and $t$ holds in $n$ (related by a communication in the figure), call this pair $P$. Any larger distributed state $ds$ including $s$ satisfies the premise and is followed, for instance by $ds \cup P$, which satisfies $m u \wedge n t$. The same considerations hold for the second formula, since $\{s\}$ satisfies $\Delta u$ as well.

$\mathcal{M} \models_T n \Delta w$ LEADS_TO_C $m u$.
$\mathcal{M} \not\models_T n w$ LEADS_TO_C $m u$.
  Only the ($5^{th}$) state of $n$, where $w$ becomes true, is followed by a state of $m$ where property $u$ holds.

$\mathcal{M} \models_T n w$ BECAUSE $n p \wedge n u$.

**Table 1.**   Semantics of $\Delta$DSTL(x)

| | | |
|---|---|---|
| $\mathcal{M} \models_T F$ | iff | $\forall ds \geq ds^0.\, ds \models F$ |
| $\mathcal{M} \models_T F \text{ LEADS\_TO } F'$ | iff | $\forall ds \geq ds^0.\, ds \models F$ implies $\exists\, ds' \geq ds.\, ds' \models F'$ |
| $\mathcal{M} \models_T F \text{ LEADS\_TO\_C } F'$ | iff | $\forall ds \geq ds^0.\, ds \models F$ implies $\exists\, ds' \geq_c ds.\, ds' \models F'$ |
| $\mathcal{M} \models_T F \text{ BECAUSE } F'$ | iff | $\forall ds > ds^0.\, ds \models F$ implies |
| | | $\exists\, ds'.\, ds^0 \leq ds' \leq ds$ and $ds' \models F'$ |
| $\mathcal{M} \models_T F \text{ BECAUSE\_C } F'$ | iff | $\forall ds > ds^0.\, ds \models F$ implies |
| | | $\exists\, ds'.\, ds^0 \leq ds' \leq_c ds$ and $ds' \models F'$ |
| $\mathcal{M} \models_T \text{STABLE } F$ | iff | $\forall ds \geq ds^0.\, ds \models F$ implies $\exists ds' >_c ds.\, ds' \models F$ |
| $\mathcal{M} \models_T \text{INIT } F$ | iff | $ds^0 \models F$ |

**where:**

| | | |
|---|---|---|
| $ds \models \top$ | | |
| $ds \models A$ | iff | $A$  holds in $s$ for all $s \in ds$ |
| $ds \models\, \sim F$ | iff | not $ds \models F$ |
| $ds \models F \wedge F'$ | iff | $ds \models F$ and $ds \models F'$ |
| $ds \models \Delta F$ | iff | $ds \models F$ and |
| | | $\exists ds'.\, ds' <_l ds$ implies $ds' \models\, \sim F$ |
| $ds \models \mathsf{m}_{\mathsf{i}} F$ | iff | $\exists s \in ds \cap S_i$ and $\{s\} \models F$ |

**and:**

| | | |
|---|---|---|
| $\{s_i^{-1}\} \models L$ | iff | $\{s_i^0\} \not\models L$ |
| | | A literal holding in an initial state does not hold in the extra state preceding it. |

**and:**

| | | |
|---|---|---|
| $ds > ds'$ | iff | each state in $ds'$ is followed by a state in $ds$, and each state in $ds$ is preceded by a state in $ds'$. |
| $ds \geq ds'$ | iff | each state in $ds'$ is either in $ds$ or followed by a state in $ds$, and each state in $ds$ is either in $ds'$ or preceded by a state in $ds'$. |
| $ds \geq_c ds'$ | iff | each state in $ds'$ in either in $ds$ or immediately followed by a state in $ds$, and and each state in $ds$ is either in $ds'$ or immediately preceded by a state in $ds'$. |
| $ds >_c ds'$ | iff | $ds \geq_c ds'$ and $ds$ does not include $ds'$. |
| $ds >_l ds'$ | iff | all the states in $ds'$ have a local immediate successor in $ds$, and viceversa, all the states in $ds$ have a local immediate predecessor in $ds'$. Formally a state $s$ is a local successor of a state $s'$ iff $\{s\} >_c \{s'\}$ and $s \in S_i$ implies $s' \in S_i$. When $ds$ includes some initial states, $ds'$ includes the extra states preceding them. Note that each distributed state has a unique local predecessor. |

We recall that a $\Delta$DSTL(x) formula is a closed sentence, shaping (implicitly or explicitely) $\forall \ldots \exists \ldots \phi$. Hence, we restrict the semantic definitions to the (ground) subformula $\phi$.

$\mathcal{M} \not\models_T$ n$w$ BECAUSE n$(p \wedge u)$.

Consider, for instance, the first state, say $s$, of $n$ where $w$ holds. Set $\{s\}$ is preceded by the pair $P$ composed of the initial and the second state of $n$. Set $P$ satisfies the consequence of the first formula. Any superset $ds$ of $\{s\}$ is preceded by $ds \cup P$. On the contrary, to satisfy the second formula, we would need a singleton state of $n$ satisfying both $p$ and $u$.

$\mathcal{M} \models_T$ STABLE n$(w \wedge t)$.

Any distributed state including a state of $n$ satisfying $w \wedge t$, is immediately followed by a distributed state including a state of $n$ satisfying $w \wedge t$.

$\mathcal{M} \models_T \exists M. \bar{\mathsf{M}}(u \rightarrow z)$.

There exists a component, $m$ in our example, where each state satisfies: $u \rightarrow z$.

$\mathcal{M} \models_T$ INIT $\Delta p$.

In both initial states property $p$ holds. A litteral holding in the initial state implies the corresponding event to hold as well.

Axioms and rules of the logic are presented in Tables 4 and 5 in the appendix.

### 2.3   Discussion

We discuss here the choice of defining, as semantic domains, Kripke models built on worlds that are arbitrary sets of computation states, rather than single states or tuples of them.

The choice of taking as a world a singleton state was adopted in Oikos–*adtl* [10] and has shown some problems. For instance, consequence weakening, or, more in general, the possibility of reasoning on logical relations between formulae like the premises or the consequences of a temporal formula is not part of the logic. For instance, a formula like $(n\,q \wedge m\,r) \rightarrow n\,q$, which would permit to weaken the consequences of m$p$ LEADS_TO n$q \wedge$ m$r$, would not be a legal formula, since no world can satisfy the conjunction n$q \wedge$ m$r$.

Most logics for distributed systems let worlds be tuples of states, one for each component (see [9] for references). This choice would infer a form of remote knowledge which is meaningless in an asynchronous setting. For instance, assume a pair of worlds $w$ and $w'$ with $w'$ following $w$, with $p$ holding in the $n$ state of $w$ and $q$ holding in the $m$ state of $w'$. Then, one can assert that n$p$ LEADS_TO m$q$ holds, even in the absence of any communication between these two states.

## 3   Case Study: Establishing a Token Ring

We start with an informal description of how things evolve. To build the ring we need a consistent successor relation between the participants. Hence, the first task the components must accomplish is to give themselves an ordering, which can then be used to build the successor relation. We reduce the ordering task to a sequence of distributed leader elections: when a leader is found it is assigned the number of its election turn. Each election turn starts only once the previous one has been completed, i.e. a leader has been elected[1].

Once there is a leader, the token ring begins operating. The leader creates a token and passes it to itself until the second leader is elected. At this point the ring is enlarged and the first leader passes the token to the newcomer, which will pass the token to the first leader until a third leader is elected, and so forth. In general, once in the ring any leader passes the token to its successor; if no successor can be found, the token is passed to the first leader, thus giving place to another round.

In the following, we give the complete specification of this coordination pattern, i.e. the establishment of an ordering and the concurrent building of a growing token ring, together with interesting properties the pattern exhibits. The formal proofs of these properties are not reported for lack of space, but we provide hints on how they have been carried out. The complete proofs are available at www.di.unipi.it/~semprini/tokenring.htm. At the same page, the reader can find the proofs as performed using the proof assistant Mark [6], in the case of a fixed number of participants.

To ease the understanding, we present separately the tasks of ordering the components and that of building and maintaining a dynamically growing token ring based on the ordering. Anyway, it is important, to appreciate the high level of complexity of the coordination, to remember that the two tasks interact and are actually performed in parallel since the token ring evolves from the election of the first leader incorporating new leaders as they are elected.

### 3.1   Ordering the Components

We reduce the ordering of $n$ components to the election of $n$ leaders. As a reference election leader algorithm in an asynchronous setting, we take the one presented in [9]. A proper parameterization allows to introduce the notion of election turn and to axiomatize the behaviour of each component during a turn. A few axioms provide the proper glue to put together different elections turns. The resulting axioms are in Table 2.

At the beginning of each turn all the components are eligible (axiom 10, where $e(M, X)$ says that component $M$ is eligible in turn $X$). Each component repeatedly tosses a coin: if it gets a head, it immediately records its own non-eligibility and communicates it to the other components (axioms 1, 5 and 6). A component stops tossing in a turn when it realizes that all the other components are no longer eligible (axiom 2). If no component is eligible in a turn, there is no leader for that turn (axiom 3).

The only reason for a component to become not eligible is that it tossed a head, and once a component becomes not eligible for a turn it will stay so

---

[1] In principle, we can only require that each component is assigned at most one natural number. We cannot guarantee components to be assigned a number because it is known [7] that in our reference setting we could not be able to elect a leader. In practice, the problem can be alleviated by a more complex solution envisaging several attempts per turn.

**Table 2.** Axioms of the leader election protocol

---

1. $\mathsf{M}\,\Delta t(X)$ LEADS_TO $\mathsf{M}\,(stop(X) \vee h(X))$
2. $\bar{\mathsf{M}}(stop(X) \leftrightarrow \bigwedge_{N \neq M} \sim e(N, X))$
3. $no\_leader(X) \leftrightarrow \bigwedge_{N} \sim e(N, X)$
4. $leader(M, X) \leftrightarrow (e(M, X) \wedge stop(X))$
5. $\mathsf{M}\,h(X)$ LEADS_TO $\bigwedge_{N} \mathsf{N} \sim e(M, X))$
6. $\mathsf{M}\,h(X)$ LEADS_TO_C $\mathsf{M} \sim e(M, X)$
7. $\mathsf{M} \sim e(N, X)$ BECAUSE $\mathsf{N}\,h(X)$
8. STABLE $\mathsf{M}\,t(X)$
9. STABLE $\mathsf{M} \sim e(N, X)$
10. INIT $\mathsf{M}\,e(N, X)$
11. INIT $\mathsf{M}\,t(0)$
12. INIT $\mathsf{M}\,(t(X) \to X = 0)$
13. $\bar{\mathsf{M}}(leader(M, X) \to\sim h(X))$
14. STABLE $\mathsf{M}\,leader(M, X)$
15. $\mathsf{M}\,\Delta leader(M, X)$ LEADS_TO $\bigwedge_{N \neq M} \mathsf{N}\,t(X + 1) \wedge \bigwedge_{Y > X} \sim e(M, Y)$
16. $\mathsf{M}\,(t(X) \wedge X \neq 0)$ BECAUSE $\mathsf{N}\,leader(N, X - 1)$
17. $\mathsf{M}\,leader(N, X)$ BECAUSE $\mathsf{M}\,t(X)$

---

for that turn (axioms 7 and 9). When a component knows that there is just one participant to a turn, it records that participant as the leader for that turn (axiom 4). The knowledge about being the leader of a turn is stable (axiom 14). Once a component knows to be the leader it stops tossing thus preventing head outcomes (axiom 13). Each turn starts only once, and turn 0 starts initially (axioms 8, 11 and 12). From these axioms we can derive that each turn leads to the agreement on the identity of a leader or on the lack of one:

**Election1.** $\bigwedge_{M} \mathsf{M}\Delta t(X)$ LEADS_TO $\bigwedge_{M} \mathsf{M}\,no\_leader(X) \vee \bigvee_{M} \bigwedge_{N} \mathsf{N}\,leader(M, X)$

Variables $M$ an $N$ range over the set of component names. Property Election1 is a generalization of the one proved in [9] and can be proved following the same procedure.

When a component realizes to be turn leader, it makes the others components start a new turn, in which it is not eligible. No turn starts if a leader for the previous turn has not been elected and no leader is elected for a turn that is not yet started (axioms 15, 16, and 17).

Let $n$ be the number of the components. Axiom 15 and Election1 allow to prove the following property as the result of a chain of transitivity steps built using rule LTR.

**Election2.** $\bigwedge_{M} \mathsf{M}\Delta t(0)$ LEADS_TO $\bigvee_{X} \bigwedge_{N} \mathsf{N}\,no\_leader(X) \vee \bigvee_{N} \bigwedge_{M} \mathsf{M}$

$$leader(N, n - 1)$$

Variable $X$ ranges in the interval $[0, n)$. Election2 says that once the first turn begins, all the components will agree on the leader of the last turn $(n\text{-}1)$, if there has not been a turn without leader elected. This property guarantees that once the first turn begins, a state will be reached in which all the components either agree that at least a turn has failed electing a leader, or recognize the same component as their leader of the last turn.

Since no leader is elected if the previous one was not elected and no component is chosen as the leader of a turn if the turn did not start, we can prove repeatedly using axioms 15, 16 and 17 that the following property holds.

$$\textbf{Election3.} \bigwedge_M M \Delta t(0) \text{ LEADS\_TO } \bigvee_X \bigwedge_N N\, no\_leader(X) \vee \bigwedge_X \bigvee_N \bigwedge_M$$

$$M\, leader(N, X)$$

From here, it is easy to verify that leaders are elected in sequence and that any number of leaders less or equal to the number of components involved can be elected as the result of the election mechanism. Since we inherit the limits of the single turn leader election, we cannot guarantee that all leaders will be elected, but, if the $i^{th}$ leader is elected, all the previous leaders have been elected too.

## 3.2  Building the Token Ring

We use the order defined in the previous section to define the successor of each component and build the ring. The axioms 1–5 of Table 3 are the interface between the leader election mechanism and the token ring protocol.

Being the leader of a turn means having as order number in the ring the number of that turn. A new leader communicates its number to the other components (axioms 1 and 2). Initially, no component has an order number; order numbers cannot be forgotten and are not assigned arbitrarily (axioms 3, 4 and 5). Exploiting these axioms, Election3 and the transitivity of LEADS\_TO, it is possible to prove a result similar to Election3, but predicating on the ordering of the components.

$$\textbf{Ring1.} \bigwedge_M M \Delta t(0) \text{ LEADS\_TO } \bigvee_X \bigwedge_N N\, no\_leader(X) \vee \bigwedge_X \bigvee_N \bigwedge_M M\, ord(N, X)$$

Another interesting property exhibited by the interface axioms is that once a component gets an ordering assignment, a state will be reached in which all the components know all the ordering assignments up to that one.

$$\textbf{Ring2.} \; M \Delta ord(M, X) \wedge \bigwedge_N N \top \text{ LEADS\_TO } \bigwedge_N N\, (ord(M, X) \wedge \bigwedge_{Y < X} ord(O, Y)$$

This property can be proved by cases on the value of X. For X=0, we exploit a generalized version of Notif and axioms 1, 2, 3 and 5. If X≠0, the proof starts

**Table 3.** Token ring axioms

---

1. $\bar{\mathsf{M}}(leader(M,X) \leftrightarrow ord(M,X))$
2. $\mathsf{M} \,\Delta ord(M,X)$ LEADS_TO $\bigwedge_N \mathsf{N}\, ord(M,X)$
3. STABLE $\mathsf{M}\, ord(N,X)$
4. INIT $\mathsf{M} \sim ord(N,X)$
5. $\mathsf{M} \,\Delta ord(N,X)$ BECAUSE $\mathsf{N} \,\Delta ord(N,X)$
6. $\bar{\mathsf{M}}(succ(N) \leftrightarrow (ord(M,X) \wedge ord(N,X+1)) \;\vee\; (\sim ord(P,X+1) \wedge ord(N,0)))$
7. $\mathsf{M} \,\Delta ord(M,0)$ LEADS_TO $\mathsf{M}\, token(0)$
8. $\bar{\mathsf{M}}(token(0) \rightarrow ord(M,0))$
9. $\mathsf{M} \,\Delta token(X)$ LEADS_TO $\mathsf{M} \,\Delta completed\_task(X)$
10. $\mathsf{M} \,\Delta completed\_task(X)$ BECAUSE $\mathsf{M} \,\Delta token(X)$
11. $\mathsf{M} \,(\Delta completed\_task(X) \wedge succ(N))$ LEADS_TO $\mathsf{N} \,\Delta token(X+1)$
12. $\mathsf{M} \,\Delta token(X) \wedge X > 0$ BECAUSE $\mathsf{N} \,(\Delta completed\_task(X-1) \wedge succ(M))$
13. INIT $\mathsf{M} \,(\sim token(X) \wedge \sim completed\_task(X))$
14. STABLE $\mathsf{M}\, token(X)$
15. STABLE $\mathsf{M}\, completed\_task(X)$

---

by using LCC and LSW to split the two conjuncts of the consequences of the main property. One of the subgoals is the generalization of the case X=0 and can be proved in the same way. To solve the remaining subgoal, we use again LCC and LSW producing one new subgoal for each value of Y from 0 to X-1, these can be proved exploiting Notif and a chain of BTR that allows to subdue the assignment of an order number to the election of any of the previous leaders.

Each component gets connected to its successor, if any, or to the first component in the ring if a successor cannot be found. This allows the ring to work even when not all components have received an ordering, and to dynamically accommodate newcomers (axiom 6)[2].

Axioms 7–15 of Table 3 describe how the participants of a token ring behave, that is, how they handle the token passing. In the axioms, X is used to qualify the token and the tasks that are performed on its receipt.

---

[2] Asynchronous communication does not allow to assume any temporal ordering on the arrival of messages. This implies in particular that even if numbers are assigned in the right order, and a common knowledge will be reached between all the components, it may be the case that for a while two components have different partial knowledge of the ordering results. E.g., let's assume that $M$ has been chosen as the first leader and has been assigned 0 as order number. If $M$ does not know which component has the order number 1 it will chose itself as its own successor, thus forming a singleton ring, even if it already knows the component with order number 2. The ring is enlarged when $M$ gets to know the component with order number 1. The ring is always built starting from the component with order number 0 and grows by including newcomers strictly following the ordering.

Axioms 7 and 8 state that the component having 0 as order number, and only that component, will create the token. A component accomplishes a task if and only if it received the related token (axioms 9 and 10). Apart from the initial situation (axiom 8), a component $M$ receives a token only if a component completed a task when considering $M$ its successor (axiom 12). Together with axiom 11, that says that on completion of a task a component passes the token to its successor, this defines a correct handling of the token. Conditions on the initial values of the token, the related tasks and their stability complete the axiomatization.

Three interesting properties hold:

**Ring3.** $M\Delta token(X) \rightarrow ord(M,Y)$

a component receives a token only if it is in the ring;

**Ring4.** $\bigwedge_N N(\bigwedge_{Y<Z} ord(M,Y) \wedge ord(O,Z)) \wedge O(\Delta token(X) \wedge \sim ord(M, Z+1))$ LEADS_TO $O\Delta token(X+Z+1)$

if a component receives a token when it is the last in the ring, the token will come back to it incremented by the current size of the ring;

**Ring5.** $P\, ord(P, Z+1) \wedge \bigwedge_N N(\bigwedge_{Y<Z} ord(M,Y) \wedge ord(O,Z)) \wedge O\Delta token(X)$ LEADS_TO $P\Delta token(W)$

if a component enters the ring, becoming its new last participant, it will receive a token.

The proof of Ring3 proceeds by cases on the value of X. If X is 0, then Ring3 reduces to axioms 9. If X is not 0 we use rule BSE and axioms 3, 5: if a component $M$ receives a token it is because someone sent it when considering $M$ its successor: to consider $M$ its successor, this component needed to know $M$'s order number, but for axiom 5 this means that $M$ already knew its own position in the ring and this completes the proof.

Ring4 can be proved by a repeated use of rule LTR and axioms 9–12: if a component $M$ receives a token when believing to be the last in the ring, it will pass the token to the component having order number 0, if such component is $M$ itself, the property is easily proved since $M$ will receive, by itself, the token incremented by 1. If component 0 is not $M$, then it will receive the token and pass it along the ring as stated by the axioms. Since ring participants from 0 to $M$ are fixed, the token will eventually reach $M$ again. The token is incremented by 1 at each step, and will reach $M$ incremented by the size of the ring.

The proof of Ring5 is based on Ring4 and LTR. Let's call $M$ the new component and O the component that was previously the last in the ring. $M$ enters the ring, at this point O can get to know this before receiving a new token or not. In the first case O will pass the token to $M$ and the property is proved. In the second case, O will pass the token to the first component in the ring. For Ring4, O will eventually receive a new token and the reasoning applies again as before. Ring1 guarantees that sooner or later O will get to know that the new last participants in the ring is $M$ and will pass it the token. To sum up: the first participant in the ring will create a token and all new participants will receive a token. Moreover, once a component receives a token it will receive all the following tokens it is supposed to receive, i.e. with the right number.

## 4   Conclusions

We have introduced an operator, $\Delta$, to specify events logically, and provided a first validation by describing a coordination pattern.

From a theoretical point of view, the introduction of operator $\Delta$ has required the definition of a new semantic domain, to deal with events in the initial state, and the extension of the axiom system. A practical consequence has been the update of Mark [6], a support tool to mechanize the proofs in the logic.

The coordination pattern is characterized by the ability of a set of components to organize in a token ring starting from a chaotic situation. Since this is the typical situation that can arise after a major accident, we consider the pattern a promising illustration of how our logic can deal with the essential features of the dynamic adaptive behaviour of self–healing systems.

## Acknowledgements

The work was supported by the MIUR Cofin project on Software Architectures for Heterogeneous Access Networks Infrastructure (SAHARA).

## References

[1] L. Andrade and J. L. Fiadeiro. Coordination primitives for event-based systems. In *In Proceedings of the $1^{st}$ Int. Workshop on Distributed Event-Based Systems (DEBS'02)*, 2002.  249

[2] R. Armoni, L. Fix, A. Flaisher, R. Gerth, B. Ginsburg, T. Kanza, A. Landver, S. Mador-Haim, E. Singerman, A. Tiemeyer, M. Y. Vardi, and Y. Zbar. The forspec temporal logic: A new temporal property-specification language. In *Tools and Algorithms for Construction and Analysis of Systems (TACAS'02)*, volume 2280 of *Lecture Notes in Computer Science*, pages 296–211, Grenoble, 2002. Springer-Verlag.  249

[3] K. M. Chandy and J. Misra. *Parallel Program Design: A Foundation*. Addison-Wesley, Reading Mass., 1988.  248, 250

[4] T. Costello and A. Patterson. Quantifiers and operations on modalities and contexts. In A. G. Cohn, L. Schubert, and S. C. Shapiro, editors, *KR'98: Principles of Knowledge Representation and Reasoning*, pages 270–281. Morgan Kaufmann, San Francisco, 1998. 251

[5] M. S. Dias and D. J. Richardson. The role of event description in architecting dependable systems. In 1$^{st}$ *Workshop on Architecting Dependable Systems (WADS'02)*, Orlando, May 2002. 249

[6] G. Ferrari, C. Montangero, L. Semini, and S. Semprini. Mark, a reasoning kit for mobility. *Automated Software Engineering*, 9(2):137–150, Apr 2002. 248, 255, 260

[7] M. J. Fischer and N. A. Lynch. Impossibility of distributed consensus with one faulty process. *Journal of the ACM*, 32(2):374–382, Apr. 1985. 255

[8] L. Lamport. The Temporal Logic of Actions. *ACM Transactions on Programming Languages and Systems*, 16(3):872–923, May 1994. 249

[9] C. Montangero and L. Semini. Distributed states temporal logic. The Computing Research Repository (CoRR): cs.LO/0304046. (Submitted for pubblication) 2003. 248, 250, 254, 255, 256

[10] C. Montangero and L. Semini. Composing Specifications for Coordination. In P. Ciancarini and A. Wolf, editors, *Proc. 3nd Int. Conf. on Coordination Models and Languages*, volume 1594 of *Lecture Notes in Computer Science*, pages 118–133, Amsterdam, April 1999. Springer-Verlag. 248, 254

[11] C. Montangero and L. Semini. Distributed states logic. In 9$^{th}$ *International Symposium on Temporal Representation and Reasoning (TIME'02)*, Manchester, UK, July 2002. IEEE CS Press. 248, 250

# Appendix

We present in Table 4 the axioms and rules of the spatial logic DSL(x). Axioms and rules of the temporal logic with events $\Delta$DSTL(x) are listed in Table 5.

**Table 4.**    Axioms and rules of DSL(x)

---

| | | | |
|---|---|---|---|
| **FOL** | axioms of the $1^{st}$ order logic | **K** | $\bar{\mathsf{M}}(F \rightarrow F') \; \rightarrow \; (\bar{\mathsf{M}}F \rightarrow \bar{\mathsf{M}}F')$ |
| **DSL1** | $\bar{\mathsf{M}}(\bar{\mathsf{M}}F \leftrightarrow F)$ | **DSL2** | $\mathsf{M} \neq \mathsf{N} \rightarrow \bar{\mathsf{M}}\bar{\mathsf{N}}\bot$ |
| **MP** | $\dfrac{F \quad F \rightarrow F'}{F'}$ | **Nec** | $\dfrac{F}{\bar{\mathsf{M}}F}$ |

---

**Table 5.**   Axioms and Rules of $\Delta$DSTL(x)

- **Necessitation.** (We use $\vdash_{\Delta DSL(x)}$ and $\vdash_{\Delta DSTL(x)}$ for the sake of comprehension).

$$\frac{\text{for all } x_1 \ldots x_n \text{ exists } y_1 \ldots y_n \ \vdash_{\Delta DSL(x)} F}{\vdash_{\Delta DSTL(x)} \ \exists y_1 \ldots y_n F} \ \textbf{Nec}$$

- **Introduction and Elimination.**

$$\textbf{LcI} \ \ F \ \text{leads\_to\_c} \ F \qquad\qquad \textbf{BcI} \ \ F \ \text{because\_c} \ F \qquad\qquad \Delta\textbf{E} \ \ \ \Delta F \to F$$

$$\frac{F \ \text{leads\_to\_c} \ G}{F \ \text{leads\_to} \ G} \ \textbf{LI} \qquad \frac{F \ \text{because\_c} \ G}{F \ \text{because} \ G} \ \textbf{BI} \qquad \frac{F}{\text{stable} \ F} \ \textbf{SI}$$

$$\frac{F \ \text{leads\_to} \ \perp}{\sim F} \ \textbf{LE} \qquad \frac{\text{init} \sim F \ \ F \ \text{because} \ \perp}{\sim F} \ \textbf{BE} \qquad \frac{\text{init} \ \mathsf{M} F \ \ \text{stable} \ \mathsf{M} F}{\bar{\mathsf{M}} F} \ \textbf{SE}$$

$$\frac{F \ \text{leads\_to} \ G}{F \wedge \sim G \ \text{leads\_to} \ \Delta G} \ \Delta\textbf{I} \qquad \frac{\mathsf{M} F \ \text{because} \ \mathsf{M} G \ \ \ \text{stable} \ \mathsf{M} G}{\bar{\mathsf{M}}(F \to G)} \ \textbf{BSE}$$

- **Transitivity.**

$$\frac{F \ \text{leads\_to} \ F' \ \ \ F' \ \text{leads\_to} \ G}{F \ \text{leads\_to} \ G} \ \textbf{LTR} \qquad \frac{F \ \text{because} \ F' \ \ \ F' \ \text{because} \ G}{F \ \text{because} \ G} \ \textbf{BTR}$$

- **Premises and consequences strengthening and weakening.** Similar rules hold for BECAUSE, LEADS\_TO\_C, and BECAUSE\_C.

$$\frac{\exists_{\mathsf{F}} \ G \to F \ \ \ F \ \text{leads\_to} \ F' \ \ \ \exists_{\mathsf{G}'} \ F' \to G'}{G \ \text{leads\_to} \ G'} \ \textbf{LSW}$$

$$\frac{F \ \text{leads\_to} \ G \ \ \ F' \ \text{leads\_to} \ G}{F \vee F' \ \text{leads\_to} \ G} \ \textbf{LPD} \ \frac{G \ \text{leads\_to} \ F \ \ \ G \ \text{leads\_to} \ F'}{G \ \text{leads\_to} \ F \wedge F'} \ \textbf{LCC}$$

- **Notification and Confluence.**

$$\frac{F \ \text{because} \ G \ \ G \ \text{leads\_to} \ \mathsf{M} G' \ \ \text{stable} \ \mathsf{M} G'}{F \wedge \mathsf{M}\top \ \text{leads\_to} \ \mathsf{M} G'} \ \textbf{Nf} \ \frac{\text{stable} \ \mathsf{M} F \ \ \text{stable} \ \mathsf{M} F'}{\mathsf{M} F \wedge \mathsf{M} F' \to \mathsf{M}(F \wedge F')} \ \textbf{Cf}$$

- **Properties of the initial state.**

$$\textbf{I1} \ \ \text{init} \ \mathsf{m}\top \ \ \ \frac{\text{init} \ \mathsf{m} F}{\text{init} \ \bar{\mathsf{m}} F} \ \textbf{I2} \ \ \frac{\text{init} \ \bar{\mathsf{m}} F}{\text{init} \ \mathsf{m} F} \ \textbf{I3} \ \ \frac{\text{init} \ F \ \ F \to G}{\text{init} \ G} \ \textbf{IW} \ \ \frac{\text{init} \ F \ \ \text{init} \ F'}{\text{init} \ F \wedge F'} \ \textbf{IC}$$

We recall that non temporal $\Delta$DSTL(x) formulae are implicitly universally quantified in all variables with the exception of those explicitly bound by existential quantification. Here, in the case of implication, with $\exists_{\mathsf{G}} \ F \to G$ we denote a formula universally quantified in all the variables of premise $F$, and existentially quantified in all the free variables of the consequence $G$.

# Using Coordination Middleware
# for Location-Aware Computing:
# A LIME Case Study

Amy L. Murphy[1,2] and Gian Pietro Picco[2]

[1] Dipartimento di Elettronica e Informazione, Politecnico di Milano, Italy
picco@elet.polimi.it
[2] Department of Computer Science, University of Rochester, NY, USA
murphy@cs.rochester.edu

**Abstract.** The decoupling between behavior and communication fostered by coordination becomes of paramount importance in mobile computing. In this scenario, however, coordination technology typically deals only with the application data necessary to orchestrate the process activities. In this paper, we argue instead that the very same coordination abstractions can be used effectively to deal also with information coming from the physical *context*–a fundamental aspect of mobile computing applications.

We cast our considerations in LIME, a coordination model and middleware designed for mobile computing. To support our arguments with concrete examples, we report about the development of TULING, a proof-of-concept application enabling the tracking of mobile users. The lessons learned during development enable us to assess the feasibility of the approach and identify new research opportunities.

## 1  Introduction

Mobile computing defines a challenging environment for software development. Communication is enabled by wireless links, which are less reliable and intrinsically dependent on the relative positions of the mobile parties. Similarly, location affects the overall *context* perceived by a mobile unit, by constraining not only the available communication parties, but also the data available for computation, the set of accessible services, and in general the resources available to a component.

It has been observed [13] that software development in the mobile environment can be tackled successfully by exploiting a coordination perspective. The decoupling between behavior and communication fostered by coordination enables one to separate the applicative behavior of components from the continuously changing context in which they are immersed. Examples of systems that have applied this intuition to deal with physical mobility of hosts or logical mobility of agents include Klaim [10], XMIDDLE [7], Tucson [12], Mars [2], and LIME [8]. In all of these systems, a shared data structure–typically a tuple space– is used to store the data available to mobile units and to represent naturally the

R. de Nicola et al. (Eds.): COORDINATION 2004, LNCS 2949, pp. 263–278, 2004.
© Springer-Verlag Berlin Heidelberg 2004

context available to them. Nevertheless, all of these systems focus on providing support for coordination through a context consisting essentially of application data. Little or no support is provided for constraining the application behavior based also on the physical context.

Clearly, this is a limitation. Dealing with a changing physical context is fundamental in many mobile applications. Physical context information can be very diverse, and can include local system information such as battery level or signal-noise ratio, or environmental information such as light intensity, temperature, or ambient noise. Among all, *location* is possibly the most relevant context element, in that it often *qualifies* the values of the others. For example, a temperature reading becomes more meaningful when accompanied by the identity of the room where it was sensed. The point, however, is that the actions of an application component in a mobile environment may depend on one or more of these context information values and modeling physical context becomes a necessity.

At the opposite extreme of coordination approaches, several middleware systems have been proposed that explicitly tackle the problem of managing a dynamically changing context. Relevant examples include the Context Toolkit [3], Odyssey [11], Aura [5], Gaia [14], and Owl [4]. The focus of these systems is on allowing applications to retrieve information about context, either proactively (by directly querying some context representation) or reactively (by subscribing to changes in the context information). The middleware takes care of properly disseminating the context information to the involved parties, and hence greatly simplifies the management of physical context used in mobile applications. On the other hand, these systems provide little or no support for representing and managing the data context, used for coordinating the behavior of the application components.

In this paper, we argue that the gap between the two aforementioned perspectives can be reduced, if not eliminated, by exploiting coordination abstractions also for the management of the physical context. Once acquired by appropriate sensors, context information is essentially like any other data, and hence can be treated as such in a data-centric coordination approach. The very same primitives used to manipulate, retrieve, or react to available data for the sake of coordination can now be used for dealing with physical context information. These two traditionally separate dimensions are unified under a common set of abstractions, simplifying considerably the design and implementation of mobile applications.

Although our considerations are in principle applicable to any data-centric coordination approach, in this paper they are cast in LIME [8], a coordination model and middleware expressly designed for mobile computing. A concise overview of LIME is provided in Section 2. Section 3 illustrates the premise of our approach, and describes how a coordination middleware can be used to disseminate physical context information. The implications of our design approach can be understood and assessed only through the reality check provided by application development. Hence, to support our arguments with concrete examples, in Section 4 we report about the design and implementation of TULING, a proof-of-concept application providing location tracking of mobile users. The lessons learned from this experience enable us to assess, in Section 5, the feasibility of the approach and identify new research opportunities. Finally, Section 6 ends the paper with brief concluding remarks.

## 2 LIME: Linda in a Mobile Environment

The LIME model [8] defines a coordination layer for applications that exhibit logical and/or physical mobility. It has been embodied in a middleware available as open source at http://lime.sourceforge.net and a formal semantics is available in [9]. LIME borrows and adapts the communication model made popular by Linda [6].

In Linda, processes communicate through a shared *tuple space*, a multiset of tuples accessed concurrently by several processes. Each tuple is a sequence of typed parameters, such as <"foo",9,27.5>, and contains the actual information being communicated. Tuples are added to a tuple space by performing an **out**($t$) operation. Tuples are anonymous, thus their removal by **in**($p$), or read by **rd**($p$), takes place through pattern matching on the tuple content. The argument $p$ is often called a *template*, and its fields contain either *actuals* or *formals*. Actuals are values; the parameters of the previous tuple are all actuals, while the last two parameters of <"foo",?integer,?float> are formals. Formals act like "wild cards" and are matched against actuals when selecting a tuple from the tuple space. For instance, the template above matches the tuple defined earlier. If multiple tuples match a template, selection is non-deterministic.

Linda characteristics resonate with the mobile setting. Communication is implicit, and decoupled in *time* and *space*. This decoupling is of paramount importance in a mobile setting, where the parties involved in communication change dynamically due to migration, and hence the global context for operations is continuously redefined. LIME accomplishes the shift from a fixed context to a dynamically changing one by breaking up the Linda tuple space into many tuple spaces, each permanently associated to a mobile unit, and by introducing rules for transient sharing of the individual tuple spaces based on connectivity.

*Transiently Shared Tuple Spaces.* In LIME, a mobile unit accesses the global data context only through a so-called *interface tuple space* (ITS), permanently and exclusively attached to the unit itself. The ITS, accessed using Linda primitives, contains tuples that are physically co-located with the unit and defines the only data available to a lone unit. Nevertheless, this tuple space is also *transiently shared* with the ITSs belonging to the mobile units currently accessible. Upon arrival of a new unit, the tuples in its ITS are merged with those already shared, belonging to the other mobile units, and the result is made accessible through the ITS of each of the units. This sequence of operations, called *engagement*, is performed as a single atomic operation. Similarly, the departure of a mobile unit results in the *disengagement* of the corresponding tuple space, whose tuples are no longer available through the ITS of the other units.

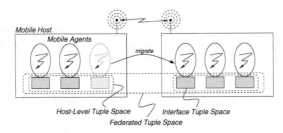

**Fig. 1.** Transiently shared tuple spaces encompass physical and logical mobility

Transient sharing of the ITS is a very powerful abstraction, providing a mobile unit with the illusion of a local tuple space containing tuples coming from all the units currently accessible, without any need to know them explicitly. Moreover, the content perceived through this tuple space changes dynamically according to changes in the system configuration.

The LIME notion of a transiently shared tuple space is applicable to a mobile unit regardless of its nature, as long as a notion of connectivity ruling engagement and disengagement is properly defined. Figure 1 shows how transient sharing may take place among mobile agents co-located on a given host, and among hosts in communication range. Mobile agents are the only active components, and the ones carrying a "concrete" tuple space; mobile hosts are just roaming containers providing connectivity and execution support for agents.

Operations on the transiently shared tuple space of LIME include those already mentioned for Linda, namely **out**, **rd**, and **in**, as well as the probing operations **rdp** and **inp** whose semantics is to return a matching tuple or return null if no matching tuple exists at the time the query is issued. For convenience LIME also provides the bulk operations **rdg** and **ing** that return a set of tuples that match the given pattern. If no matching tuples exist, the set is empty.

*Restricting Operation Scope.* The idea of a transiently shared tuple space reduces the details of distribution and mobility to changes in what is perceived as a local tuple space. This view is powerful as it relieves the designer from specifically addressing configuration changes, but sometimes applications may need to address explicitly the distributed nature of data for performance or optimization reasons. For this reason, LIME extends Linda operations with scoping parameters, expressed in terms of agent or host identifiers, that restrict operations to a given projection of the transiently shared tuple space.

The **out**$[\lambda](t)$ operation extends **out** by allowing the programmer to specify that the tuple $t$ must be placed within the tuple space of agent $\lambda$. This way, the default policy of keeping the tuple in the caller's context until it is withdrawn can be overridden, and more elaborate schemes for transient communication can be developed. Location parameters are also used to annotate the other operations to allow access to a slice of the current context. For instance, **rd**$[\omega, \lambda](p)$ looks for tuples matching $p$ that are currently located at $\omega$ but destined to $\lambda$. LIME allows

$\omega$ to be either a host or an agent, enabling queries over the entire host-level tuple space or only over the subset pertaining to a specific user.

*Reacting to Changes.* In the dynamic environment defined by mobility, reacting to changes constitutes a large fraction of application design. Therefore, LIME extends the basic Linda tuple space with a notion of *reaction*. A reaction $\mathcal{R}(s,p)$ is defined by a code fragment $s$ specifying the actions to be performed when a tuple matching the pattern $p$ is found in the tuple space. A notion of *mode* is also provided to control the extent to which a reaction is allowed to execute. A reaction registered with mode ONCE is allowed to fire only one time, i.e., it becomes automatically deregistered after its execution. Instead, a reaction registered with mode ONCEPERTUPLE is allowed to fire an arbitrary number of times, but never twice for the same tuple. Details about the semantics of reactions can be found in [8]. Here, it is sufficient to note that two kinds of reactions are provided. *Strong reactions* couple in a single atomic step the detection of a tuple matching $p$ and the execution of $s$. Instead, *weak reactions* decouple the two by allowing execution to take place eventually after detection. Strong reactions are useful to react locally to a host, while weak reactions are suitable for use across hosts, and hence on the entire transiently shared tuple space.

*Exposing System Configuration.* In the perspective presented thus far, applications are aware only of changes in the portion of context concerned with application data. Although this is enough for many mobile applications, in others knowing which hosts are connected also plays a key role. For instance, a typical problem is to react to departure of a mobile unit, or to determine the set of units currently belonging to a LIME group. LIME provides this form of awareness of the system configuration by using the same abstraction already discussed: a transiently shared tuple space conventionally named LimeSystem to which all agents are permanently bound. The tuples in this tuple space contain information about the mobile units present and their relationship, e.g., which tuple spaces they are sharing or, for mobile agents, which host they reside on. Insertion and withdrawal of tuples in the LimeSystem is the prerogative of the run-time support. Nevertheless, applications can read tuples and register reactions to respond to changes in the configuration of the system.

## 3   Representing Physical Context in LIME

Applications written for the mobile environment must have access to their own data as well as data of the other components within range. Providing this access while ignoring the details of communication is the primary goal of LIME and of other coordination systems targeting the mobile environment. In addition to application data, many mobile applications are characterized by their need to respond to the environment in which they find themselves, adapting application behavior as their location, bandwidth, or environmental parameters change. In other words, they must be able to react to changes in the physical context.

The LimeSystem tuple space described previously shows that the transiently shared tuple space style of coordination promoted by LIME can be used successfully to provide mobile applications access to one form of context, namely the identity of accessible hosts and agents. Our goal here is to show that LIME can similarly be used to represent, share, and interact with other aspects of context as well. We further show that by placing context information into a transiently shared tuple space applications obtain easy access to what we refer to as the *distributed context*, or the context of all components within range.

At its core, our idea is simple: insert context information into a transiently shared tuple space thus allowing all connected components to access it through the proactive and reactive constructs of LIME. In this section we describe the representation of context information in the tuple space, the primary access mechanisms, and the benefits provided to the application programmer.

*Making Context Accessible.* Our work focuses on the sharing of and interaction with context data through tuple spaces, intentionally leaving aside the issues related to detecting context information as well as the format of that information. Therefore, we focus neither on specific sensing technologies, nor on a specific type of context information. Instead, we provide a general, adaptable infrastructure to exploit and *disseminate* context. The key component of our infrastructure providing this isolation is a context agent that interacts with the sensors and with LIME.

The context information to be made available is represented as tuples, identical in all respects to traditional application data tuples. Interestingly, this can be exploited to represent single values as well as sequences of temporally related values to maintain history or for aggregation of context information. In principle, it is therefore possible to mix data and context tuples in a single tuple space. This, however, leads to a cumbersome design that imposes restrictions on applications (such as requiring that no application tuple use the same pattern as any context tuple) and mixes the interaction with the two types of data. Therefore, ideally the two kinds of data should be insulated from one another. LIME supports this separation with a mechanism for creating multiple tuple spaces, uniquely identified by name, and whose contents are independent. By creating a separate *context tuple space* (e.g., named CONTEXT), application tuple formats remain unrestricted and interaction with context information is made explicit by issuing operations on the context tuple space.

For applications residing on the same host as the context agent, the context information is accessible locally by issuing the normal LIME operations on a CONTEXT tuple space. Such interaction enables an application to query for the current context, and attach this to generated data. For example, a video player can adjust its buffer size based on the currently available local memory. This memory level information is retrieved from the local context tuple space.

Because LIME tuple spaces are transiently shared, the information in the context tuple space is also available to all connected components, yielding what we refer to as the *distributed context*. For example, firefighting equipment can leverage off location-enabled temperature sensors spread throughout a forest by generating a map with the temperature gradient from the information available in the distributed context. Even if only a limited number of sensors are within range, those connected provide the context for the area immediately surrounding the firefighter requesting the map generation.

*Interacting with Context.* Middleware, and in general systems targeted toward the mobile environment, have demonstrated that access to context information should be both proactive and reactive, meaning that a program should be able to *pull* the information on demand or have it *pushed* whenever it changes. By representing the context information inside a LIME tuple space, both styles of operation are available. Proactive operations map to the query operations of LIME (e.g., **rdp**) while reactive mechanisms are enabled by strong and weak reactive statements. Furthermore, the LIME extensions to control scope enable operations over the entire distributed context or over a projection of the context tuple space, therefore tailoring operations to apply to all hosts in range or only a single host.

For applications such as the video player described previously, the query operation **rdp**, restricted in scope to the application's own host-level tuple space, returns the needed current available memory. The same operation can be used to retrieve the context of a remote host simply by changing the scope parameters. LIME bulk operations, such as **rdg**, are especially useful to retrieve historical context. For example, an application validating the functioning of the air conditioning in a building can query for the history of temperatures in a given room.

In our previous LIME programming efforts, we found that although query operations are useful, the core application functionality often utilizes reactive constructs. With respect to context information, reactions are most useful for monitoring and immediately adapting to changes. For example, a reaction over the host's own context tuple space can notify an application when its battery power is low. Changing the scope of the reaction to monitor a remote host's battery can trigger a modification in the mode of interaction between the two hosts. Alternately, to keep the aforementioned temperature map up to date, a (weak) reaction over the distributed context can be registered to fire every time any sensor's temperature value changes.

Finally, the distributed context can easily be searched, providing a dimension of accessibility not present in most context systems. For example, a query can be formed to find one or all components at a specific location in space. This powerful operation uses the same LIME primitives as before, **rdp** in this case, and does not require any kind of server support–a solution commonly found in other context-aware systems. Such serverless operation makes our solution for managing context particularly amenable to mobile ad hoc networks, and other highly dynamic scenarios.

*Benefits to the Application.* The ideas presented here unveil how a variety of context information can be represented in the context tuple space and accessed by connected components using the usual LIME primitives. This approach has two main benefits. First, the management of context is decoupled from the applications that use it. This implies that the context maintenance mechanisms can easily be substituted or extended to present more context information from additional sensors. For example, if an application is designed to use location information to build a map of connected users, the location context information can be changed from GPS to an indoor infrared or radio tracking system without changes to the application, as long as the tuple format does not change.

Second, placing context information into a tuple space unifies the management of application data exploited for coordination, and of the physical context perceived by the application. This allows programmers to deal with both using the same interface, with evident benefits in terms of ease of development and understanding of the resulting implementation.

## 4   TULING: Tracking Users in LIME with GPS

To further explore and validate our ideas about representing context in LIME, we chose to focus on a single aspect of context, namely location in physical space. This choice is motivated by the observation that location is critical to many mobile applications. Often, context information is dependent on the particular location where it is sensed. Moreover, location has a value *per se*, in that it provides a direct and intuitive way to express mobility of users.

In this section, we discuss the design and implementation of TULING, an application for collaborative exploration of a space. Although we have already discussed the main idea for representing and interacting with context in LIME, it is only through the elaboration of these ideas in a real application that they can be fully appreciated and that we can report about the ease of incorporating location context into an application.

TULING is intended to be used by multiple individuals moving through a common environment, each equipped with a GPS- and wireless-enabled PDA. While the immediate goal of this application is to provide a proof-of-concept for our approach, we can envision the functionality provided as useful in several real-world scenarios, e.g., coordination of a rescue team deployed in a disaster scenario. The major portion of the display of each user, as seen on the left of Figure 2, is a representation of the user's current location in space, where a sequence of dots indicates her past movement itinerary. When a new user comes within range, his name is displayed in the box on the top right of the display. To allow users to coordinate their actions as they move, each user can specify a monitoring mode for viewing the movement of the others by first selecting the user, then pressing one of the buttons to the top right.

By pressing the *monitor* button, the selected user's movements are marked on the screen as long as he is connected. When the user disconnects, his name disappears from the list, but the dots remain on the screen. In monitor mode, the user's displayed location is kept as up to date as possible, but only the itinerary during connection is tracked. To retrieve the history of movement that occurred before connection, a user must press the *getItinerary* button. Instead of being

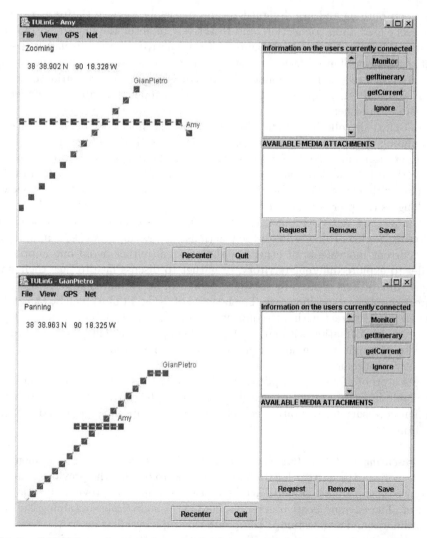

**Fig. 2.** Screenshot of two TULING users, Amy (the top image) and GianPietro, after disconnection. Before the two users were disconnected, each was monitoring the location of the other, but only Amy had retrieved the itinerary of GianPietro. After disconnection, the movements of the users are not visible to one another, but only to themselves

a continuous operation such as monitoring, this is a one-time operation that displays the entire history of movement (up to that moment) for the selected user. Another one-time operation is to display the current location of a user by pressing the *getCurrent* button. The final mode is simply to ignore a user.

In addition to these monitoring modes, TULING provides two others that apply globally to all users that come within range. These modes are available as menu options and are designed to automatically retrieve the past itinerary for every user upon connection, and to actively monitor the movement of every user within range. When both these modes are active, a user's display shows the entire itinerary of every user she has encountered, i.e., including movements that occurred before and during connection. In a disaster recovery scenario, this mode can be useful for a supervisor to monitor the movements of all the members of a team around her.

TULING also allows users to add annotations, such as a textual note or a digital photograph, to their own current location. For instance, after an earthquake, annotations could take the form of photographs of damaged walls or descriptions of work to be completed at a location. These annotations are indicated on the display with a special icon: by clicking on the icon, the annotation can be viewed as long as the user is connected.[1]

As already noted, TULING can be useful in disaster recovery scenarios for allowing workers to coordinate their actions. For example, workers monitoring the current movements of others in the area can either avoid one another in order to explore different territory, or gather to discuss face to face their findings. Annotations created by survey workers can be evaluated by aid workers to direct supplies to specific areas. The benefits of using TULING include the ability for users to interact without requiring line-of-sight, the enabling of impromptu sharing of information without the required support of a central server, and the variety of monitoring modes to adjust the communication overhead, and thus battery requirements, on a per-user basis.

As a proof-of-concept application, TULING demonstrates how the operations available in LIME are both natural and sufficient to provide the range of interaction necessary for exploiting context, as we illustrate in the remainder of this section.

*Representing and Updating Location Context.* The combined requirements to both monitor the current location of a user and to display the previous itinerary require that TULING provide access to the current and previous locations of a user. The *current location* is represented by a single tuple containing the GPS coordinates and a timestamp. To update this tuple, we first insert the new location tuple, then remove the old. The motivation for this sequence of operations is to ensure that a location is always accessible to a probe operation. It is true that the old value may be returned instead of the new, but the two values are unlikely to be significantly different, and furthermore the timestamp can be examined for freshness.

Because a host has only one current location, we needed a separate tuple representation for the location *history*, i.e., the user itinerary. We explored the idea of having one tuple for each previous location, simply changing the pattern to include a new field with the label HISTORY. This solution turns out to be

---

[1] The choice of making annotations inaccessible while users are disconnected was motivated by the performance considerations discussed later. If needed by an application, this choice can be easily reversed, but with an accompanied increase in overhead.

unreasonable because the overhead necessary to retrieve the entire history of a user is proportional to the number of tuples retrieved. Therefore, we opted for grouping multiple locations together into a single *stride* tuple that contains a sequence number and a list of locations. The number of locations in the stride list is tunable. We chose a value that balances the overhead of retrieving all the stride tuples to build a history with the overhead of updating the stride tuple with each new location. In other words, to keep the entire history in the tuple space, each time a new location is generated the most recent stride tuple, identified by a sequence number, is removed, updated, and reinserted into the tuple space. This solution also opens up opportunities for implementing "garbage collection" of old stride tuples.

It is worth noting that the updating of both the current and stride tuples are operations entirely local to the agent performing them. Therefore they generate low system overhead.

*Accessing Location Context.* To implement the functionality of the buttons on the top right of the display as well as the global options found in the menus, TULING uses a combination of reactions and probe operations. Changes in the scope of the operations affect whether the information retrieved is from one or all users.

To our surprise, the LimeSystem continued to be an integral part of the operation of TULING. For example, to display the name of each user within range, TULING employs a reaction on the LimeSystem tuple space. By exploiting the fact that LIME keeps this list up to date, users are able to select monitoring modes on a per user basis, as well as see, at a glance, which users are connected.

As already mentioned, the *monitor* mode allows a user to be tracked while she is connected. This essentially involves reacting to a change in the user location and updating the display–an operation that naturally calls for a LIME reaction. Therefore, the tracking functionality is implemented with the installation of a ONCEPERTUPLE weak reaction restricted to the projection of the tuple space of the selected user. The pattern of the reaction is that of current location tuples.

The functionality of both the *getItinerary* and *getCurrent* buttons are implemented with probe operations over the projection of the tuple space of the selected user. The first exploits a **rdg** operation for stride tuples to retrieve *all* of the tuples of the itinerary. The latter uses a similarly scoped **rdp** for retrieving the current location tuple.

These explicitly selected modes offer the ability to tailor monitoring on a per-user basis, therefore constructing a user's view of the environment and controlling the amount of system resources dedicated to monitoring each of the other users. If such tight controls are not necessary, the two options for monitoring all users and automatically downloading the histories of all users can be enabled. Monitoring all users in LIME is accomplished with a single ONCEPERTUPLE weak reaction registered on the transiently shared tuple space, with the pattern of the current location tuples. The reaction fires each time any user's location changes, updating the display accordingly.

As mentioned previously, the bulk operation **rdg** is used to retrieve a specific user's itinerary. In order to retrieve the itineraries of *all* users when they come within range, TULING registers a reaction on the LimeSystem tuple space to fire each time a host arrives. This, in turn, causes a **rdg** to be invoked to return the stride tuples of the newly arrived user.

*Exploiting Location.* While the previously described functionality is designed to show how context information can be shared and visualized, the annotation feature of TULING demonstrates how applications can attach location context to application data.

Annotations can be either simple text, or a file containing, for example, an image. After the annotation has been created, TULING associates it with the user's most recent location. To find it, TULING queries the local context tuple space using a probing read, **rdp**. This returns a tuple containing the timestamp and the current location coordinates. These are combined, along with the annotation, into a single annotation tuple, which is inserted into a regular LIME tuple space, making it accessible to other users.

One of the requirements of TULING is to display the existence of an annotation as an icon on top of the normal location icon. With the implementation of annotations just described, the only way to do this is to query for the actual annotation tuples at the same time that the itinerary tuples are retrieved, or to react to annotations when a host is being monitored. If the annotations themselves are large, this creates an unreasonable amount of overhead, especially wasteful if the annotations are not viewed eventually by the user. Therefore, we modified the representation of annotations in the tuple space, effectively creating two tuples representing the same information as the original tuple. The first tuple contains only the location and an annotation identifier. It is this tuple that is retrieved and monitored in the cases above, reducing the overhead because the identifier is small in comparison to a typical annotation. The second tuple contains the annotation identifier and the actual annotation. This tuple is retrieved on demand when a user opts to view the annotation. The result, however, is the restriction that annotations can only be viewed while users are connected, a reasonable compromise for effectively managing overhead.

## 5   Discussion and Lessons Learned

Experience with TULING provides evidence to support our argument for placing context information into the tuple space. In this section we discuss the relationship between our work and others and discuss extensions to LIME that would better support context.

*Related Work.* The unification of access to both data and context is the distinguishing factor of our work with respect to other context accessing systems. For example, the Context Toolkit [3] wraps context providers with a standard interface that provides query and notification access. In LIME, these two modes of interaction are naturally provided by the query and reaction operations, the same operations used for application data access.

Furthermore, the Context Toolkit provides a separate service discovery server that identifies context providers to which the programmer can explicitly bind to receive context information. By using LIME, this type of centralized service discovery, which is impractical in mobile scenarios, is not necessary. Instead, the currently available components are identified from the fully distributed LimeSystem tuple space, which is also accessed by the same tuple space operations. Finally, in LIME, while it is possible to access specific context providers by limiting the scope of the operations, it is also possible to access the entire distributed context with the LIME primitives. Although this is possible in some other systems, it would require additional, non-trivial programming effort.

Placing context information in a LIME tuple space also simplifies access and reaction to the context of remote components. This is fundamentally different from the context reaction mechanisms provided by Odyssey [11]. In Odyssey, a component can register to be notified when the local context changes, allowing, for example, a server to detect a bandwidth reduction. However, Odyssey is not designed for servers to monitor context changes at the mobile client. In LIME, instead, registering for remote changes is as straightforward as registering for local changes. Furthermore, the implementation of weak reactions ensures reasonable performance.

The work presented here is also related to the many other coordination approaches designed to address the concerns of the mobile environment. We chose LIME as our foundation both because we are most familiar with it, and because it is well suited to the needs of interacting with context in a mobile environment. In principle, it should be possible to apply our idea of representing context as data in other coordination systems, although we are not aware of any work from the coordination community in this direction.

LIME *Extensions.* While the current implementation of TULING well serves as a proof-of-concept that the coordination model provided by LIME is well suited to providing context interaction, the development process illuminated several directions for extending the implementation of LIME. These extensions would allow for easier manipulation of context information and would most likely aid typical application development as well. They include the ability to atomically change the contents of a tuple, to sequentially order a set of tuples, to replicate data, and to search for tuples based on a range. These features were initially left out of LIME, in an effort to strive for a minimal and yet expressive application programming interface. In the light of their relevance for improving handling of the physical context, however, we are currently reconsidering this decision and planning to include these features in the next release of our middleware.

As explained in Section 4, the updating of the current location field is accomplished by first outputting the new tuple, then removing the old tuple. The result is that in the short interval between the two operations, the component has *two* current locations, and a probe operation such as **rdp** is just as likely to return the old tuple as it is the actual current tuple. Reversing the operations, however, leaves an interval where a component has no location and **rdp** may return **null**. Both of these conditions could be avoided if LIME provided either an atomic "change" operation, performing **in** and **out** in the same atomic step, or a generic transaction construct for grouping arbitrary LIME operations.

When TULING retrieves itinerary tuples to display the history of movement of a user, the LIME bulk operation **rdg** returns the set of all stride tuples. Although this set does not have an inherent ordering according to LIME and Linda semantics, in TULING an order is implied by the stride sequence number. Currently, the application uses this value to sort the stride tuples before visualizing them. It would be convenient if LIME bulk operations were extended to allow the specification of a field over which an ordering is automatically imposed, thus releasing the programmer from the burden of coding sorting explicitly.

Another feature to consider adding to LIME is replication. In TULING, the previous locations of the other components are effectively replicated at the application level, to enable their visualization. Location information, however, is not duplicated within the tuple space. Therefore, if $A$ copies $B$'s history, and then later meets $C$, the information about $B$ is outside the tuple space and therefore not accessible to $C$. Several efforts in the mobile ad hoc community have looked at the issue of replication [1, 7, 15], but none of the solutions is immediately applicable to the tuple space environment.

Finally, a useful operation to add to TULING is to support a query such as "find all resources within a radius $r$ from point $(x, y)$." Such a query requires a range search inside the tuple space, while LIME provides only value matching. Supporting this functionality requires a change in the tuple space implementation underlying LIME, as well as a change in the interface to the tuple space. Nevertheless, this would provide a great improvement in the expressiveness of the system. In TULING, the user could monitor an area around herself, or even request information in an area away from her current position.

## 6    Conclusions and Future Work

In this paper, we argued that applications requiring explicit access to the physical context where they execute, notably mobile computing ones, can do so effectively by exploiting the same coordination abstractions available for distributing application data. Our statements have been illustrated with reference to LIME, a coordination middleware designed for mobile computing, and concretely exemplified through TULING, an application whose design and implementation showed that location context can be disseminated effectively using LIME.

Although the focus of our evaluation has been location, the approach can be applied to other contextual information. For instance, if the available bandwidth or storage space are exposed to applications, the latter can adjust their use of the tuple space, e.g., by querying for large tuples only when the bandwidth and storage are plentiful. Given our coordination approach, it is our contention that most (if not all) of the effort involved in extending an application with a new kind of contextual information goes into the design and implementation of the interface to the corresponding sensing device: the additional effort required to make the contextual information available both locally and remotely is negligible, since this problem is already solved by the underlying coordination infrastructure.

Our work fills a gap between coordination systems that focus on providing access to application data and context-aware toolkits that concentrate only on enabling interactions with context. Furthermore, it effectively demonstrates that context information and application data can be treated in a unified manner and accessed with the same coordination operations. The result is a significant reduction in the programming effort to develop mobile applications that require access to physical context.

## Acknowledgements

The work described in this paper was partially supported by the Italian Ministry of Education, University, and Research (MIUR) under the VICOM project, and by the National Research Council (CNR) under the IS-MANET project. The authors wish to thank Emanuele Cordone and Thomas Pengo for their work on the implementation of TULING.

## References

[1] M. Boulkenafed and V. Issarny. A middleware service for mobile ad hoc data sharing, enhancing data availability. In *Proceedings of the ACM/IFIP/USENIX International Middleware Conference*, Rio de Janeiro (Brazil), June 2003. 276

[2] G. Cabri, L. Leonardi, and F. Zambonelli. Reactive Tuple Spaces for Mobile Agent Coordination. In *Proc. of the $2^{nd}$ Int. Workshop on Mobile Agents*, LNCS 1477. Springer, 1998. 263

[3] A. K. Dey, D. Salber, and G. D. Abowd. A conceptual framework and a toolkit for supporting the rapid prototyping of context-aware applications. *Human-Computer Interaction (HCI) Journal, special issue on Context-Aware Computing*, 16(2-4):97–166, 2001. 264, 274

[4] M. R. Ebling, G. D. H. Hunt, and H. Lei. Issues for context services for pervasive computing. In *Proceedings of the Workshop on Middleware for Mobile Computing*. IFIP/ACM, 2001. 264

[5] D. Garlan, D. Siewiorek, A. Smailagic, and P. Steenkiste. Project aura: Toward distraction-free pervasive computing. *IEEE Pervasive Computing*, April-June 2002. 264

[6] D. Gelernter. Generative Communication in Linda. *ACM Computing Surveys*, 7(1):80–112, Jan. 1985. 265

[7] C. Mascolo, L. Capra, S. Zachariadis, and W. Emmerich. XMIDDLE: A data-sharing middleware for mobile computing. *Kluwer Personal and Wireless Communications Journal*, 21(1), April 2002. 263, 276

[8] A. L. Murphy, G. P. Picco, and G.-C. Roman. LIME: A Middleware for Physical and Logical Mobility. In F. Golshani, P. Dasgupta, and W. Zhao, editors, *Proc. of the $21^{st}$ Int. Conf. on Distributed Computing Systems (ICDCS-21)*, pages 524–533, May 2001. 263, 264, 265, 267

[9] A. L. Murphy, G. P. Picco, and G.-C. Romjan. LIME: A coordination middleware supporting mobility of hosts and agents. Technical Report WUCSE-03-21, Washington University, Department of Computer Science, St. Louis, MO (USA), 2003. 265

[10] R. De Nicola, G. Ferrari, and R. Pugliese. KLAIM: A Kernel Language for Agents Interaction and Mobility. *IEEE Trans. on Software Engineering*, 24(5):315–330, 1998. 263

[11] B. D. Noble and M. Satyanarayanan. Experience with adaptive mobile applications in odyssey. *Mobile Networks and Applications*, 4, 1999. 264, 275

[12] A. Omicini and F. Zambonelli. Tuple Centres for the Coordination of Internet Agents. In *Proc. of the 1999 ACM Symp. on Applied Computing (SAC'00)*, February 1999. 263

[13] G.-C. Roman, A. L. Murphy, and G. P. Picco. Coordination and Mobility. In A. Omicini, F. Zambonelli, M. Klusch, and R. Tolksdorf, editors, *Coordination of Internet Agents: Models, Technologies, and Applications*, pages 254–273. Springer, 2000. 263

[14] M. Román, C. Hess, R. Cerqueira, A. Ranganathan, R. H. Campbell, and K. Nahrstedt. Gaia: a middleware platform for active spaces. *ACM SIGMOBILE Mobile Computing and Communications Review*, 6(4):65–67, 2002. 264

[15] D. Terry, M. Theimer, K. Petersen, A. Demers, M. Spreitzer, and C. Hauser. Managing Update Conflicts in Bayou, a Weakly Connected Replicated Storage System. *Operating Systems Review*, 29(5):172–183, 1995. 276

# VIPER: A VIsual Protocol EditoR

C. F. B. Rooney, R. W. Collier, and G. M. P. O'Hare

Department of Computer Science, University College Dublin, Belfield, Dublin 4, Ireland
{colm.rooney,rem.collier,gregory.ohare}@ucd.ie
http://www.cs.ucd.ie/

**Abstract.** Agent interactions play a crucial role in Multi-Agent Systems. Consequently graphical formalisms, such as Agent UML, have been adopted that allow agent developers to abstract away from implementation details and focus on the core aspects of such interactions. Agent Factory (AF) is a cohesive framework that supports the development and deployment of agent-oriented applications. This paper introduces the Visual Protocol Editor (VIPER), a graphical tool that allows users to diagrammatically construct agent interaction protocols. These protocols are subsequently realised through AF-APL, the purpose-built Agent-Oriented Programming language that sits at the heart of AF. In particular, we focus upon the design of interaction protocols using a subset of Agent UML. To this end, we specify a number of tools and an associated process through which developers can supplement these protocols with application- and domain-dependant AF-APL rules to create useful agents that adhere to the protocol constraints.

## 1 Introduction

Agent UML (AUML) is a language and set of graphical formalisms geared towards the design of agent oriented systems. It takes its primary inspiration from UML, a de facto standard for object-oriented design, but also draws from other agent design frameworks, e.g. MESSAGE [1], Gaia [17], Tropos [5]. One of the first areas of focus of the AUML community was the specification of graphical conventions for describing agent interaction protocols, i.e. sequence diagrams [10]. Due to the newness of the AUML effort however there is still little in the way of actual agent development tools that utilise AUML for specifying agent interactions. In [1] the authors of the MESSAGE system propose its use to enhance their interaction modelling phase and this is again reiterated in [12] which describes its extension IGENIAS. [8] describes a system that will generate code from AUML sequence diagrams. However, the code generated is pure Java and, as the author admits, is not well equipped to capture certain semantic elements of agent interactions and communication performatives. One approach to capturing such semantics, which we advocate in this paper, is through the use of an Agent-Oriented Programming (AOP) language. An additional issue with the above solutions is that the source for the code

R. de Nicola, et al. (Eds.): COORDINATION 2004, LNCS 2949, pp. 279-293, 2004.

generation process is a textual description of a protocol in a pre-defined notation and as such no graphical assistance is provided to the user. [15] has an early prototype of an AUML sequence diagramming tool that will take a textual description of a sequence diagram and display a graphical version. However once again the diagram may only be edited at the textual level. There are other agent development systems that actually provide diagramming tools for agent interactions that then link to code generators, e.g. AGIP [9], JiVE [4]. These however do not employ AUML and also generally produce code in common programming languages rather that more specialised AOP languages.

Therefore, this research aims to fill this gap by producing a suite of graphical tools that allow users to develop agent interaction protocols using the AUML conventions, which may then be realised as agent programs in an actual AOP language through a process of user-driven code generation. While a number of AOP languages exist, e.g. 3APL [6] and AgentSpeak(L) [14], we focus upon generating code for the Agent Factory Agent Programming Language (AF-APL), an AOP language that sits at the heart of the Agent Factory (AF) framework [2, 3, 11].

This framework delivers structured support for the development and deployment of applications comprised of agents that are: autonomous, situated, socially able, intentional, rational, and mobile [2]. To achieve this, AF combines: the AF-APL programming language; a distributed FIPA-compliant Run-Time Environment; an integrated development environment; and an associated software engineering methodology. A detailed explanation of AF is beyond the scope of this paper. Instead, we focus upon two aspects: AF-APL and the visual agent programming tools that are delivered as part of the Development Environment.

## 2    Agent Programming with AF-APL

AF-APL is a purpose-built AOP language that has been developed to support the fabrication of agents. As is usual for AOP languages, AF-APL agent programs combine an initial mental state (comprised of *beliefs* and *commitments*), with a set of rules that define the dynamics of that mental state (known as *commitment rules*). These are joined by a *plan library* that may be populated with a number of partial plans describing potential courses of action. The syntax and semantics of AF-APL is based on a logic of commitment, details of which may be found in [2].

Beliefs represent the current state of both the agent and its environment. In AF-APL, this state is realised as a set of facts that describe atomic information about the environment, and which are encoded as first-order structures wrapped within a belief operator (**BELIEF**). For example, in a mobile computing application an agent may be asked to monitor the users current position using a Global Positioning System (GPS) device. The agent may generate a belief about this position that takes the form: "**BELIEF**(userPosition(Lat, Long))" where Lat and Long are replaced by values for the users latitude and longitude respectively. In AF, the actual values for the latitude and longitude are retrieved directly from the GPS device by a *perceptor unit,* which converts the raw sensor data into corresponding beliefs. The triggering of this perceptor unit is part of a perception process, which is central to our strategy for updating the beliefs of agents and is realised by triggering a pre-selected set of perceptor units at regular intervals. The specific set of perceptor units to be used by an agent is specified as part of the agent program through the **PERCEPTOR** keyword.

Commitments represent the courses of action that the agent has chosen to perform. That is, they represent the results of some reasoning process in which the agent makes a decision about how best to act. From this perspective, commitment implicitly represents the intentions of the agent. This contrasts with more traditional Belief Desire Intention approaches [14,16] in which intention is represented explicitly and commitment is an implicit feature of the agents' underlying reasoning process. This alternative treatment of commitment is motivated by our goal of explicitly representing the level of commitment the agent has to a chosen course of action. In AF-APL a commitment is comprised of: an agent identifier (the agent for whom the commitment has been made), a start time (before which the commitment should not be considered), a maintenance condition (which defines the conditions under which the commitment should not be dropped), and an activity (the course of action that the agent is committed to). Currently, an activity may take one of three forms: (1) an action identifier (i.e. some primitive action that the agent must perform), (2) a plan identifier (i.e. an identifier that can be used to retrieve a partial plan from the agents plan library), and (3) an explicit partial plan (i.e. partial plans can be directly encoded into a commitment).

Action identifiers are modelled as first-order structures where the parameters may be used to customise the action. For example, the activity of one agent informing another agent of something is realised through the "inform(?agent, ?content)" action. Here, the ?agent parameter refers to the agent to whom the message is to be sent (their identifier), and the ?content parameter refers to the content of the message. An example of an inform message can be seen in figure 1 below. Within AF-APL, actions are realised through the triggering of an associated *actuator unit*. As with perceptor units, actuator units are associated with specific agents as part of the agent program through the **ACTUATOR** keyword. Actions can be combined into plans that form more complex behaviours using one or more plan operators - currently there are four plan operators: sequence (**SEQ**), parallel (**PAR**), unordered choice (**OR**), and ordered choice (**XOR**). Plans can be stored within an agents internal plan library, where they are distinguished from one another by a unique plan identifier.

Finally, commitment rules describe the situations, encoded as a conjunction of positive and negative belief literals, under which the agent should adopt a given commitment. An implication operator (**=>**) delimits the situation and the commitment.

AF-APL agent programs (actuators + perceptors + plans + initial mental state + commitment rules) are executed upon a purpose-built agent interpreter. Specifically, the agent program is loaded into appropriate data structures inside the agent interpreter. The interpreter then manipulates these data structures through a simple control cycle that encapsulates various axioms defined in the associated logic of commitment. This cycle is comprised of three steps: (1) update the agents' beliefs, (2) manage the agents' commitments, and (3) check whether or not to migrate. It is invoked repeatedly for the lifetime of the agent (at least whenever the agent is active).

```
// Perceptor & Actuator Configuration
PERCEPTOR ie.ucd.core.fipa.perceptor.MessagePerceptor;
ACTUATOR ie.ucd.core.fipa.actuator.InformActuator;
ACTUATOR ie.ucd.aflite.actuator.AdoptBeliefActuator;

// Initial Mental State
ALWAYS(BELIEF(providesService(docRelease)));

// Commitment Rules for DocService
BELIEF(fipaMessage(request, sender(?agt, ?addr), subscribe(?svc))) &
BELIEF(providesService(?svc)) =>
COMMIT(Self, Now, BELIEF(true), PAR(inform(?agt, subscribed(?svc)),
               adoptBelief(ALWAYS(BELIEF(subscribed(?svc, ?agt)))))));

BELIEF(newDocument(?doc)) & BELIEF(subscribed(docRelease, ?agt)) =>
COMMIT(Self, Now, BELIEF(true), inform(?agt, newDocument(?doc)));
```

**Fig. 1.** An Example AF-APL program for a World Wide Web (WWW) spider agent

By way of illustration, Fig. 1. presents a fragment of AF-APL code from a WWW spider agent that provides a service in which it informs subscribed agents of any new documents it finds. This is realised through two commitment rules and one initial belief. The first commitment rule states that if the agent receives a request to subscribe to a service (identified by the variable "?svc"), and the agent believes that it provides the service, then it should commit to performing two actions in parallel (specified by the **PAR** plan operator). The first action involves the agent informing the requester that they have successfully subscribed to the service, and the second action involves that adoption of a belief by the agent that the requester has been subscribed to the service. The second commitment rule states that if the agent believes that it has found a new document, and the agent believes that another agent (?agt) has subscribed to the "docRelease" service, then it should commit to informing that agent of the existence of the new document. Finally, the initial belief that the agent adopts on start up allows the agent to believe that it can provide the service "docRelease".

## 3  Applying AUML

A benefit of using a formal graphical language such as AUML for specifying agent interactions is that there is a solid underlying formal model that may be used to analyse and validate the interactions developed. This formal model also serves to constrain and guide any visual tools that support the language. As shall be seen in section 4, the system described in this paper uses such a model to manage how protocols are constructed. Each VIPER protocol diagram has an associated protocol model that stores the details of that protocol. The formal model serves to constrain what may be included in the protocol and thus we will refer to it as the *meta-model*.

In the terms of this work an interaction protocol diagram is regarded as comprising a set of visual components linked together by associations. For example in an AUML sequence diagram a lifeline is associated with an agent role [10]. Therefore, a meta-model in this context is comprised of a set of component types, a set of association types and a set of constraints on how these components and associations relate. The following meta-model is used to provide a subset of Agent UML.

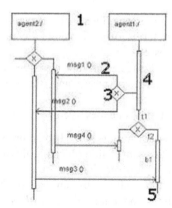

**Fig 2.** Dependant components

## Components:

- **Roles**. These are used to specify a particular agent instance, class or role acting within a protocol. They are represented graphically as rectangles containing text, see 1 in figure 2.

- **Threads**. These represent the thread of control for particular roles within a protocol. Each thread corresponds to a section of an AUML sequence diagram lifeline and is represented as a vertical line, see 5 in figure 2.

- **Messages**. These represent the asynchronous messages that make up the interaction protocols. They are sent as a result of and result in processing in Blocks. A message is described by a horizontal arrow (2 in figure 2).

- **Concurrent Guards**. These are used to represent a conditional guard on either a set of concurrent messages or concurrent lifelines. Three classes of guard are allowed: AND, OR and XOR. The component 3 in figure 2 illustrates an XOR guard.

- **Blocks**. These represent the actual processing that takes place when sending and receiving messages in the protocol and are represented as rectangular blocks (see 4 in figure 2). When compiling agent designs from published protocols, it became apparent that there might need to be some constraints upon the associations between blocks and messages. For example, there was the issue of whether a block should be viewed externally as the change in state caused by sending a message, or internally as the processing that results in such. If we take the internal perspective, then any change in the ordering of messages within a block will have substantial consequences on any processing within that block, e.g. invalidating pre-conditions. Therefore, to facilitate agent code generation it was decided that the tool would implement a subset of AUML that enforced certain constraints on the associations between messages and blocks. The constraints were as follows:

- If a block receives a message, then that message is received at the top of the block. That is, in terms of processing, the message receipt is the first act/event to be processed.
- If a block sends a message, then that message is sent at the bottom of the block. That is, in terms of processing, the message sending is the final act/event to be processed.
- A block may send at most one message and receive at most one message.

- **Sub-blocks.** While block constraints solved some problems, they raised the issue of how to handle messages sent within blocks in the traditional AUML notation. One such example is a request for clarification of an order as in figure 3. This convention was simply too useful to be omitted for the sake of implementation efficacy. This led to the introduction of the *sub-block* class of component. The sub-block is identical in almost every respect to a block with the exception that it may not be associated with any thread but rather is encapsulated within another block (or another sub-block). Furthermore the relationship between sub-blocks and messages is identical to that of blocks and messages. As such the insertion sequence example mentioned above could be represented using two sub-blocks: one to send the request for clarification (s1) and another to receive it (s2).
- **Null.** Another decision made with this version of the tool was that there be no un-associated components within the model. In order to capture the notion of floating fragments a *null component* has been introduced. Therefore, when a component is dis-associated from its parent component the newly un-associated component is associated with the null component instead.
- **Root.** This is the parent component (in essence the canvas).

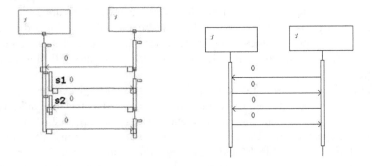

**Fig 3.** Use of sub-blocks

**Associations:**

- **Dependency.** A dependant component is one that is related (directly or indirectly) to another component further down (temporally) that component's thread of control. For example, in Fig. 2., the block b2 is directly dependent on the thread t2 and they are both indirectly dependent on the thread t1. The SCA only keeps explicit track of associations between directly dependent components.

- **Anchored.**  When developing the meta-model it was decided that allowing components to be dependent on more than one parent component was unsuitable. As a result a message sent from a block in one role to a block in a different role is a dependant of the sending block alone and forms an anchored association with the receiving block. This captures the idea that the message belongs to the sender but also has some relationship with the receiver.  Anchored associations are weaker than dependant associations and this is represented in the interface also. If a message is moved so that it is no longer in contact (or anchored) with the receiving block then the association is dissolved.
- **Encapsulation.**  A third class of association allowed by the meta-model is encapsulation.  This captures the relationship between blocks and sub-blocks.

### Constraints

The meta-model also defines the constraints that describe how the components are associated. For example, a component may only be dependant upon one other component, or a block may only receive one message.  By altering these constraints the meta-model and hence the type of protocols it can represent can be customised.

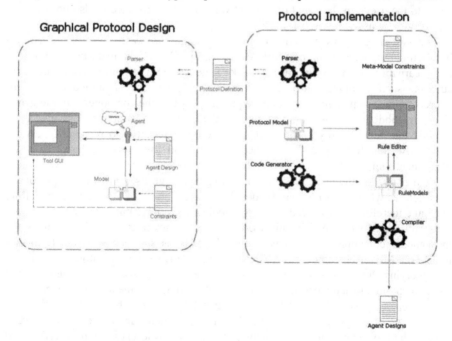

**Fig 4.**  VIPER Agent Interaction Protocol Development Processes

## 4   Visual Development of Agent Interaction Protocols

Visual development of agent interaction protocols within VIPER may be divided into two distinct processes as illustrated in figure 4.  Firstly there is the design phase where a user graphically constructs a protocol diagram using the AUML sequence diagram. The second phase is implementation and involves the user populating the protocol with customised agent code, which together with code automatically generated to reflect the protocol semantics is compiled into useable agent designs.

## 4.1  Visual Design

The VIPER Protocol Editor (PE) is composed of three loosely coupled components: the Model, the GUI and the Semantic Checker Agent. This is analogous to a Model View Controller (MVC) architecture common in software engineering. The GUI is of course the front-end that the user sees and interacts with (see figure 6), the Model acts as the data store and the Semantic Checker Agent (SCA) implements the business logic. The flow of control is as follows: Any non-cosmetic user updates to the protocol (i.e. those that effect the Model) are forwarded from the Interface to the SCA. The SCA then queries the current state of the Model and evaluates the user's request in the light of this information and the constraints set down in the meta-model. If the request is successful the Model is updated accordingly and the updated details are communicated to the Interface component, which in turn displays the result to the user. In the event of a rejected request the Interface is also notified and can inform the user.

The system employs a component-based architecture with the flow of control between components being primarily event-based. One of the main design goals of this incarnation of the system was to make it generic and easy to re-configure[1]. By adopting such a component-based model the system is not as limited in terms of interchanging components. The only requirement is that the components implement a single method that allows them to receive the events. A wrapper class may even provide this functionality. The components are not required to respond to events, only those that hold special relevance to them and these can be handled at the component's leisure.

At the core of the system is the modelling language used to develop protocols. This defines what protocols may be developed and how. For a particular modelling language therefore the PE needs a meta-model (see section 3) in order to manage and constrain the Model. Within this work, an agent known as the SCA enforces the meta-model constraints. To achieve this the SCA is supplied with the following tools: (i) a Model Perceptor; (ii) a Tool Perceptor; (iii) various actuators for updating and querying the model, e.g. addAssociation, requestOptions, saveProtocol, and (iv) perceptors and actuators for parsing and interacting with the tool interface.

At every time step the model perceptor generates a set of beliefs that reflect the current state of the protocol model, i.e. the current elements and associations between them. The tool perceptor receives any user-requests made via the tool interface and translates them into beliefs that can then (in conjunction with the model beliefs) be used by the agent to decide the appropriate course of action. These decisions are guided by commitment rules (see figure 5) that have been written to enforce the semantic constraints laid down in the meta-model.

---

[1]    Inspired in part by the nascent state of the Agent UML specification.

```
BELIEF(associate(?c1type,?c1,?c2type,?c2,?class)) &
BELIEF(comp(?c2,?c2type)) & !BELIEF(assocCount(?c2,?Assoc,?M)) &
BELIEF(legal(?Assoc,?c2type,?c1type,?N,?class))         =>
COMMIT(Self,Now,adoptBelief(BELIEF(addAssociation(?c1type,?c1,?c2,?class))))
```

**Fig 5.** Example Semantic Constraint Commitment Rule

Therefore, a developer would also be able to influence the tool behaviour and meta-model semantics by editing the agent definition, i.e. through their choice of perceptors, actuators and commitment rules.

### 4.2    Realising the Protocol: User-Driven Agent Code Generation

While a tool for the graphical design of protocols is useful as a visual aid, what the developer really needs in the end is agent code. The purpose therefore of the VIPER Rule Editor (RE) (see figure 7) is for the user to graphically associate rules with the various stages of a protocol. In order to achieve this they firstly need to be presented with a graphical representation of the protocol. To this end the RE has a canvas that displays the protocol diagram much as the PE has. As the user needs to interact with some of the protocol diagram elements, these too are stored in the canvas in the same fashion as the PE, with the exception that the protocol diagram is no longer editable.

The implementation process involves the following steps:

1. The protocol is loaded into the protocol model and an appropriate RuleSet subclass is instantiated for each editable component, e.g. blocks. The particular RuleSet subclass is defined in the RE configuration file. This file is analogous to the PE configuration file (section 6) and for every permitted component specifies the RuleSet subclass and an associated EditorPanel subclass.
2. The protocol model information is used to generate skeleton code (see figure 7) for the RuleSets.
3. The user fills in the blanks in this skeleton code. When a user selects a component, its associated EditorPanel is displayed. This is a view on the underlying RuleSet and allows the user to review and manipulate any skeleton and/or user-generated code stored in the RuleSet.
4. When the user has finished editing the code they choose the *compile* option. The RE then divides the protocol into the various roles and each role is compiled from those RuleSets associated with its dependent components.

The following mappings are used in the skeleton code generation process:

- **Blocks** are mapped to Agent Factory plans. The user fills in the blanks by entering actions or other plan names combined using the plan operators (section 2).
- **Messages** are in essence the pre- and post-conditions for the Block RuleSets. However, in order to remove agents from the burden of storing every message received and sent, the code generation process translates a message received/sent event to a unique landmark. As these landmarks are updated by each event, the

agent need only retain the most recent landmark as that adequately reflects the current state of the protocol. Note that as these landmarks act as the link between protocol RuleSets the user is responsible for ensuring that any code they add does not interfere with landmarks or their ordering. This may involve the user having to add their own intermediate landmarks and suitable bridging code.

- *Guards* for concurrent messages or threads are mapped to a set of commitment rules, one for each subsequent branch. These rules take the form of a pre-condition with the previous landmark and a commitment to generate a landmark that uniquely identifies the branch. For each rule, the user then adds any other pre-condition terms needed to represent the guard.

## 5    Case Study

In order to highlight the operation and usage of VIPER we commission a simplified FIPA query-if protocol as illustrated in figure 6. As the user edits the protocol diagram the SCA constantly monitors their progress and guides them through the process. For example, whenever the user selects a component the SCA is notified and uses the information to provide an *adaptive interface* via contextualised menus. In terms of this example therefore, when the user starts with a blank canvas (i.e. the current component is the root component) the SCA updates the menus so that the user is only presented with the option to add a role component.

When a user chooses to add a role (or any component) the following steps take place. Firstly, the interface generates an event that the user wishes to associate a new role with the current component (i.e. the root canvas). Note that from the interface perspective all updates on the model take the form of adding, updating or removing associations. If the component to be associated does not yet exist then it is created by the SCA. Once the event has been generated it is picked up by the SCA Tool Perceptor, which adds it to the SCA's belief set. At the next deliberation cycle this belief about the association request fires commitment rules that have the effect of checking the feasibility of the user's request against the current state of the protocol model. Factors taken into account are: the type of association; the type of components; any existing associations involving either component; and the maximum associations of the requested type allowed for these components. As a result of this deliberation the user's request is either permitted or rejected and the SCA's belief set is updated to reflect this. In the case where the request is granted then the resulting belief causes the agent to fire commitment rules that update the model and notify the tool interface (via events) of the update in the protocol. The interface then uses this information to update the graphical display, i.e. in this case adding the new role to the canvas. If however, the user's request is refused, then the SCA sends a corresponding error event to the interface. This event can be used by the interface to display a contextualised error message to the user.

Once a role component has been added the user can then edit its details by selecting it and entering details in the panel (specified in the configuration file) that appears at the side of the GUI see figure 6. If the user then reselects the canvas they are presented with the option to add additional roles. In this way we can insert the roles needed for our example protocol as in figure 6.

Having established our roles the next step is to add lifelines and start to build the protocol in earnest. When a user selects a role once again the SCA uses that knowledge to contextualise the GUI. In this case the user is presented with the option to add a thread to the role. Once a lifeline is in place the user can add a block. As described in section 3, blocks represent computation within the protocol and result from and/or result in the sending of a message. Therefore, when a block has been added the user is free to add a message sent from that block, or to associate a message received with the block. The latter is achieved by dragging the arrow of an existing message sent from another block so that it intersects the block the user wishes to receive the message. This triggers an association event and a process analogous to the one described above. As a result the SCA either permits or denies the association formation. In either case the interface displays the result to the user.

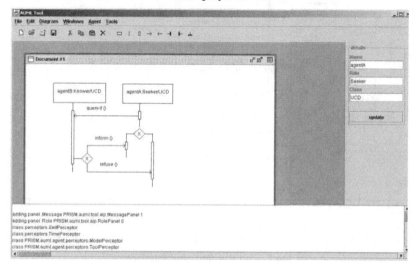

**Fig 6.** Protocol Design Interface

To continue the protocol and begin a new block of computation the user selects the final block along the given lifeline and adds a new thread after it and then a new block to that thread. The tool also incorporates features for deleting and dis-/re-associating (groups of) components. In this way diagrams can be chopped up and re-organised as needed, as long as the result is deemed semantically consistent by the SCA. (Groups of) Dis-associated components are referred to as *floating fragments* and are associated with the null component by the SCA so as not to corrupt the model.

When the protocol diagram is finished the user must save it before proceeding to the next phase of development. This involves the interface notifying the SCA of the filename chosen by the user and the SCA then using this to fire an actuator that outputs the model data to the appropriate file. In actuality there are two files created. It was decided that rather than a single file with semantic and display information combined, a better solution would be to decouple the graphical display information from the actual protocol representation. This separation of concerns means that if the format of one changes it does not affect the other. While protocol diagrams are graphical in nature, this is really just a convenience to assist developers. The real power of them is the actual protocol being represented, i.e. what messages are sent by and to whom and when. This information should be independent of how exactly it is visually represented. The first of these files is the Protocol Diagram Definition file that contains the information needed to build up the protocol model, i.e. components and associations. The second file is the coordinates file. This file stores the coordinates and dimensions of each component in the diagram and is used to position them when the protocol is reloaded.

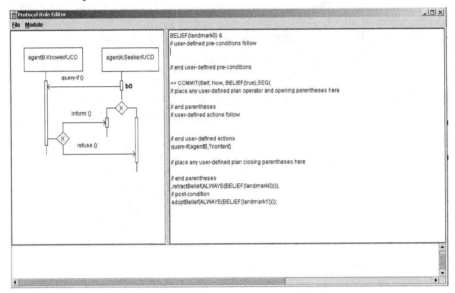

**Fig 7.** VIPER Rule Editor Interface

Once the user has saved a version of the protocol diagram they are happy with they can begin the next phase of the development process. As described in section 4.2, the RE is used to graphically associate rule sets with the blocks of computation in a protocol diagram. The code generator utilises the meta-model mappings detailed in section 3 and the protocol model information to generation the agent skeleton code. This code is stored in the RuleSets and is used to frame the user-defined rules within the constraints of the protocol diagram. Whenever a component is selected in the RE, the information in the corresponding RuleSet is loaded and displayed. Continuing with our example, the block of computation (b0) represented in figure 7 would result in the illustrated skeleton code.

The user is now free to add their agent code to the designs. In order to do so they select the component they wish to ascribe functionality to and use the displayed EditorPanel to edit the code. For example, in figure 7 block b0 has an associated EditorPanel subclass that displays the agent code using a text-editor interface. A user could add additional pre-conditions to determine when to send the query-if or include additional activities to be achieved before the message is sent. The pre-conditions are specified using the AF-APL **BELIEF** construct. Activities are either primitive actions or plans as described in section 2. The user also needs to explicitly specify a message content for the placeholder ?content or include pre-conditions that bind a value to it.

When the user is ready, the final stage of the process is the compilation of the actual agent definition files. The compiler splits the combines the RuleModels into files based on the roles they belong to in the protocol. Agent Factory users may then compose these files into workable agent designs.

## 6    Discussion and Conclusions

In an attempt to increase system flexibility we utilize configuration files, rather than hard-coding features and functionality. Two files are used to initialise the protocol design system: the *VIPER PE configuration file* and the *agent design*. The latter contains an AF-APL agent program (as specified in section 2), which is used to instantiate the SCA. The former is used in configuring both the tool interface and the model. It details in XML the types of components that may be added to the model and consequently displayed by the interface. The following information is detailed for each component type: (i) the name used to represent this type of component; (ii) the Java class that implements the graphical component - this must be sub-classed from the ModelElement class; (iii) any Java methods (and their corresponding arguments) that are needed to initialise the component; (iv) the icon file (if any) to be used for menus and buttons in the tool; (v) the event string to be fired when a new component of that type is requested; (vi) the Java panel class (if any) that is used in the tool to display and edit any component specific information, e.g. message string and performative; (vii) and any triggers that the component will need.

Using this information the tool can load component classes (using Java Reflection API) and recognise the component events without them having to be hard-coded. In this way simply editing the configuration file can change the type of diagram that may be edited. The XML fragment below illustrates how a component is represented in the constraints definition file.

```
<COMPONENT name='Message'>
          <CLASS name='MessageComponent' package='PRISM.auml.tool.aip'>
             <INIT><METHOD name='setType'><ARG value='Message'/></METHOD></INIT>
     </CLASS>
     <ICON name='arrow1.gif' path='classes\\images\\'/>
     <EVENT type='dependency'/>
     <PANEL><CLASS name='MessagePanel' package='PRISM.auml.tool.aip'/></PANEL>
     <TRIGGER><CLASS name='DependantMessageTrigger' package='PRISM.auml.tool'/></TRIGGER>
     <TRIGGER><CLASS name='AnchoredMessageTrigger' package='PRISM.auml.tool'/></TRIGGER>
</COMPONENT>
```

Upon parsing some of the details from this file is also fed in to the SCA. The SCA makes use of this information to build up the list of the components it can support and any constraints related to them, e.g. the number of messages a control block can send. In addition to component information, the configuration file also defines the types of associations permissible by the meta-model. This (in conjunction with the component information) allows a designer to alter the semantics of the model by simply editing the configuration file. A typical association would be represented in XML as below.

```
<ASSOCIATION class='dependency' type='output' comp1='Block' comp2='Thread' max='1'/>
```

This configurability will play a large part in the evolution of the tool. The iteration of the tool described here is based upon AUML sequence diagrams as they are presented in [10] and as such does not incorporate the newer features proposed in [7]. In addition, as mentioned above, the meta-model only supports a subset of AUML. Certain features were omitted in this prototype in order to simplify the meta-model, ensuring a focus could be placed on determining the links between firstly the meta-model and the graphical model and secondly the protocol model and the agent design. So, for example, features such as synchronous messages while supported graphically are not supported by the meta-model as yet.

The next step in the development of the tool will involve augmenting the meta-model to incorporate a fuller range of AUML features e.g. some of the newer features proposed in [7] could play a very important role in the process of implementing protocols using the RE. In particular, AUML sequence diagram constraints and actions would allow protocol designers to include more implementation information within protocol diagrams. However, it should be noted that in [7] there is no fixed format in which these constraints and actions are to be specified. Therefore, automatically generating skeleton code would be impossible unless we constrained the VIPER Design Tool to only accept certain supported formats. If another format were used then the onus would be on the developer to fill in the blanks.

This paper has introduced VIPER, a visual protocol editor, which has been successfully integrated into Agent Factory (AF). It provides partial tool support for the design phase of the AF Development Methodology. While VIPER automatically generates agent code skeletons, necessarily, the designer will need to customise fragments within these. Notwithstanding this, VIPER surpasses previous visual tools for protocol editing in that code generation is more complete; it provides for richer expression of semantic elements of agent interactions; it enforces a separation of concerns between the editing tool, the underlying semantic model, and the agent implementation framework; and finally, it provides an adaptive user interface. VIPER currently provides the most complete AUML sequence diagram editing and code generation tool.

# References

[1]    Caire, G., Leal, F., Chainho, P., Evans, R., Garijo, F., Gomez, J., Pavon, G., Kearney, P., Stark, J. & Massonet, P., Agent Oriented Analysis using MESSAGE/UML, in proceedings of the International Workshop Series on Agent-Oriented Software Engineering (AOSE), (2001).

[2]    Collier, R.: Agent Factory: A Framework for the Engineering of Agent-Oriented Applications, Ph.D. Thesis, Department of Computer Science, University College Dublin, Ireland (2001).

[3]    Collier, R.W., O'Hare G.M.P., Lowen, T., Rooney, C.F.B., Beyond Prototyping in the Factory of the Agents, 3rd Central and Eastern European Conference on Multi-Agent Systems (CEEMAS'03), Prague, Czech Republic (2003).

[4]    Galan, A.K., JiVE: JAFMAS integrated Visual Environment, MSc Thesis, Department of Electrical and Computer Engineering and Computer Science of the College of Engineering, University of Cincinnati, (2000).

[5]     Giorgini, P., Kolp, M., Mylopoulos, J., and Pistore M., The Tropos Methodology: an overview, in F. Bergenti, M.-P. Gleizes and F. Zambonelli (Eds) Methodologies And Software Engineering For Agent Systems, Kluwer Academic Publishing (New York), December (2003).

[6]     Hindriks, K.V., de Boer, F.S., van der Hoek, W., and Meyer, J-J., Agent programming in 3APL. Autonomous Agents and Multi-Agent Systems, 2(4):357-401, (1999).

[7]     Huget, M-P., Bauer, B., Odell, J., Levy, R., Turci, P., Cervenka, R., and Zhu, H., FIPA Modelling; Interaction Diagrams, FIPA Working Draft, (2002).

[8]     Huget, M-P, Generating Code for Agent UML Protocol Diagrams, In Proceedings of Agent Technology and Software Engineering (AgeS), Bernhard Bauer, Klaus Fischer, Jorg Muller and Bernhard Rumpe (eds.), Erfurt, Germany, October (2002).

[9]     Koning, J-L, AGIP: a tool for automating the generation of conversation policies, in Z. Shi, editor, Proceedings of 16th IFIP World Computer Congress, Intelligent Information Processing (IIP-00), Beijing, China, August. (2000).

[10]    Odell, J., Van Dyke Parunak, H., Bauer, B., Representing Agent Interaction Protocols in UML, Agent-Oriented Software Engineering, Paolo Ciancarini and Michael Wooldridge eds., Springer, Berlin, pp. 121-140, (2001).

[11]    O'Hare, G.M.P.: Agent Factory: An Environment for the Fabrication of Distributed Artificial Systems, in O'Hare, G.M.P. and Jennings, N.R.(Eds.), Foundations of Distributed Artificial Intelligence, Sixth Generation Computer Series, Wiley Interscience Pubs, New York (1996).

[12]    Pavon, J., Gomez-Sanz, J., Agent Oriented Software Engineering with INGENIAS, 3rd Central and Eastern European Conference on Multi-Agent Systems (CEEMAS'03), Prague, Czech Republic (2003).

[13]    Rao, A.S. and Georgeff, M.P., Modeling Rational Agents within a BDI Architecture, in Proceedings of Second International Conference on Principles of Knowledge Representation and Reasoning, (J.Allen, R.Fikes, and E.Sandwall eds) pp 473-484, Morgan-Kaufmann, San Mateo, CA, (1991).

[14]    Rao, A., AgentSpeak(L): BDI Agents speak out in a logical computable language, in Proceeding of the 7th International Workshop on Modelling Autonomous Agents in a Multi-Agent World (de Velde, W. Va;Perram, J. W eds) , Eindhoven, The Netherlands, January 22-25 1996. LNAI 1038. Springer Verlag, (1996).

[15]    Winkoff, M., http://goanna.cs.rmit.edu.au/~winikoff/auml/index.html, (2003)

[16]    Wooldridge, M., Practical Reasoning with Procedural Knowledge: A Logic of BDI Agents with Know-How, in Proceedings of the International Conference on Formal and Applied Practical Reasoning, (D. M. Gabbay and H.-J. Ohlbach, eds), Springer-Verlag, (1996).

[17]    Wooldridge, M., Jennings, N.R., and Kinny, D., The Gaia Methodology for Agent-Oriented Analysis and Design, in Journal of Autonomous Agents and Multi-Agent Systems 3 (3) 285-312, (2000).

# Social Control Mechanisms to Coordinate an Unreliable Agent Society

Hamid Haidarian Shahri and M. Reza Meybodi

Faculty of Computer Engineering and Information Technology
Amirkabir University of Technology (Tehran Polytechnic), Tehran, Iran
hhaidarian@aut.ac.ir

**Abstract.** In multiagent systems a common problem is how to assign tasks to other agents. It is very desirable to be able to guarantee the error rate of a solution in a multiagent system's society. In this paper, a novel approach for this problem has been introduced by devising social control mechanisms, analyzing their mathematical models and simulating and comparing them. It is also shown that the open multiagent society is modeled and coordinated in this way and is able to achieve any desired and predetermined threshold of correctness for the final solution, regardless of the performance of selfish and unreliable agents in the society or any stipulation about their honesty. This is extremely critical and problematic in the design of coordinated multiagent societies, today.

## 1 Introduction

In today's complex and distributed systems, the fitting solution for the development of a practical application is to effectively utilize a flexible multiagent system (MAS), in which a large number of *self-interested* autonomous agents with different design objectives take advantage of other agents' skills, to solve a problem. There are many issues involved in the engineering of an agent society and coordination and integration of separately designed agents. Negotiation mechanisms for solving agent's goals assume that the agents are honest about what they claim. Hence, there is a need for mechanisms to encourage agents to be honest.

Many factors come into consideration in the design and implementation of a distributed problem strategy, and its formulation has more complexities than, what we would like to see in an engineering discipline. One of the important points that must be considered in a large agent society is, how to choose between a huge number of options available in the allocation of tasks to agents. This is of particular interest in an environment, where the agents are totally unknown and there is no information about the *reliability* and *characteristics* of agents in the system. To date, this case has not been addressed thoroughly, because in most of the real-world applications, the agents in a MAS had been designed and implemented by the same group of people. For example in the production of a multiagent system for discovering an unknown planet, the designers are aware of the capabilities and the reliability and honesty of agents, which are working in the system. However, with the growth of geographically distributed agents in open environments, which are communicating through WANs (e.g. many e-commerce applications), there is a very urgent demand for building a mutual *trust* between agents in a coordinated agent society.

R. de Nicola, et al. (Eds.): COORDINATION 2004, LNCS 2949, pp. 294-306, 2004.

A variety of fault tolerance mechanisms have previously been suggested for reducing hardware and software errors in legacy computing systems and specially distributed systems [4], but usually, they are not quite applicable in the agent context because of their overhead and inefficiency, as well as not accounting for an agent society. So, we prefer to propose the more descriptive term of "social control mechanisms" instead. In this paper, three different social control mechanisms have been devised for assuring correctness of a solution in a multiagent system [12]. The task allocating agent is totally *unaware* of the society that he is living in. It assigns the tasks to other agents and gathers the results. It will gradually learn about the honesty of his partners. Nevertheless, he can *guarantee* any level of accuracy for the final solution, which consists of accumulating intermediate results from untrustable and self-interested agents in the environment. The goal is to make socially desirable decisions using rational agents that only care about their own and may act insincerely. Before going further, it should be mentioned that in this paper, the term *error* is used for an incorrect result for a task and *error rate* is the ratio of the incorrect results accepted to the total number of accepted results.

In the next section, the related work on ensuring correctness is presented. Section three provides the mathematical model used for creating a coordinated agent society. Section four is a detailed analysis of three different social control mechanisms, which the last one provides a general and flexible framework for modeling agent behavior. Simulation and evaluation of these mechanisms are described in section five. The last part is the conclusion and some directions for future work are also suggested in this section.

## 2    Related Work

Indeed the conceptual and practical tools needed for building dependable agent systems, resilient to errors and other unexpected situations, are still at an early stage of research. Better methods are needed to develop multiagent systems that can guarantee correctness, reliability, and robustness in an agent society. This fact has given rise to the arrangement of specialized agent conferences with the theme of agent societies, e.g. [1], [2].

Turner and Jennings have very recently started a project on agents for mobile communication environments and are currently exploring integrity and correctness issues [3]. Using formal transformation systems for multiagent system synthesis is one way, to meet this growing need [14]. Defining boundaries in the behavior space by leveraging the goal hierarchy has also been used for validating complex agent behavior [15]. [9] discusses the development of an agent system having a computational model with correctness criteria. Notions of correctness are embedded at a higher level, without any coding for fault tolerant behavior in the plans of individual agents. Verification can then be undertaken at the higher level of abstraction. [8] describes a design for the integration of AgentScape, a multi-agent system support environment, and DARX, a framework for providing fault tolerance in large scale agent systems. Although, all these works are somehow related to fault tolerance or action validation, they have used different approaches for achieving it. They do not capture the spirit of a real multiagent community, i.e. modeling of a coordinated agent society for guaranteeing the correctness of a solution, while tackling the problem of insincere agents at the same time.

Social laws and dependencies may govern the behaviors of a large number of agents in a society [6]. Different types of protocols and settings have been discussed for motivating self-interested agents to follow the designer's strategy and many impossibility results and constructive demonstrations exist [5], [10]. For example, work on auctions, bargaining and market mechanisms from microeconomics and especially game theory, try to make socially desirable decisions using self-interested agents. In this paper, in contrast to the works mentioned above, no rules/protocols have been set from the beginning, and a practical approach is utilized for solving the problem.

[13] suggests that when allocating tasks to agents, the agents form coalitions to perform the tasks or to improve the efficiency. That is with the assumption that group's performance is more efficient than the performance of single agents. Shehory assigns a vector of non-negative capabilities to each agent, in which, each capability quantifies agent's ability to perform a specific action. In our work, there is no coalition and emphasize is on the computational power of agents and not on capabilities of performing various actions. [7] describes task allocation in the RoboCup Rescue Simulation Environment where the tasks arrive dynamically and the arrival intensity can change. It explains the need for exploration, to discover new tasks and discusses the centralized combinatorial auction approach and the distributed approach to solve the task allocation problem.

## 3    Mathematical Model

Consider that the master agent is going to solve a large *problem*. The problem is made up of *tasks* which are executed in *batches*. A new batch begins only after the termination of the previous batch. Each task has a *result*. The final *solution* of the large problem consists of the accumulation of these results. The problem solving agent starts to distribute the tasks of one batch from the pool of tasks, between untrusted agents in the environment, until there are no more tasks in the batch. When the results of tasks in the batch are gathered, the agent starts distributing the next batch of tasks.

As mentioned previously, *error rate*, $e$, is the ratio of the incorrect results accepted to the total number of accepted results. For simplicity, it is assumed that batches are independent and the results of one batch do not affect the next one, unless explicitly mentioned as otherwise. The aim is to design a mechanism to ensure a pre-determined non-zero acceptable error rate, $e$, for the solution of the large problem. This rate is very dependent on the type of application in which the multiagent system is used. For example, in a large scale and complex simulation application, different tasks are allocated to the agents. There is no information on how well the agents will solve the tasks; nevertheless, we can guarantee the probability of the final solution of the simulation to be correct. Assume that acceptable error rate for a large problem is $e=0.01$, i.e. it would only be acceptable, if the solution of the problem is wrong in 1% of the cases, and the problem consists of 10 batches with 10 tasks each. If tasks are dependent and a failure in one task causes the whole problem to fail, then the probability of one task failing must be less than $e/(10*10) = 0.0001$. Although this number might seem small, in section four, it is shown that it can be achieved with a small increase in redundancy.

A fraction of malicious agents, $m$, of the total agents' population returns wrong results, without actually doing the assigned tasks or maybe doing it incorrectly for some reason. In some instances of the problem, the master agent, which allocates the tasks, knows $m$, otherwise the master can always assume an upper bound for it. If $m$ is higher than the assumed upper bound, then the master does not guarantee any degree of correctness for the final problem. Since there is no assumption about the speed or computational power of other agents, each result can arrive from any of the agents with equal probability. Therefore, without using any error preventative mechanism, the probability of error for the result of a task would be $m$.

The malicious agents are modeled as Bernoulli processes having a probability of $s$ (sabotage rate), for producing a bad result, which is constant in time and the same for all malicious agents. It is assumed that the worker agents do not communicate with each other and can not agree on when to give a bad result. However, when malicious agents return wrong results, they agree on the wrong result to allow voting for malicious agents, i.e. they produce the same but incorrect result for a task. If this assumption does not hold, we would expect more correct results than the guaranteed rate.

The criteria, which are used for comparing the efficiency of different preventative mechanisms, are *redundancy* and *slowdown*, while meeting the pre-determined desired threshold for error rate. Redundancy is the ratio of the total number of tasks assigned, to the original number of tasks. In an analogous manner, slowdown is defined as the ratio of the execution time using the mechanism, to without using it. Although the two criteria are related, if agents can leave the computation or become blacklisted in the middle of a batch, the slowdown would increase but the redundancy would be the same. Social control mechanisms should generally minimize or reduce the final error rate to an acceptable level and at the same time, minimize slowdown and redundancy.

# 4    Analysis of Social Control Mechanisms

The master agent decomposes a big problem into a pool of tasks. Then it allocates tasks from the pool using eager scheduling in a round robin fashion, and a task could be reallocated to different agents in a *redundant* fashion. Since one task is done by several agents, any agent in the society can leave the computation *without* previous notice, without effecting the whole computation. The slow agents are overtaken by faster ones, because when the required results for one task are collected from faster agents, the task is marked as done and no further computation is required for it.

## 4.1 Voting

The master agent allocates tasks to different worker agents redundantly. As soon as $v$ equal results (votes) from a total of $2v-1$ allocations, for the same task are returned, the task is marked as done. When all the tasks in a batch are done, the master accumulates the results and starts distributing the next batch. The redundancy in this method is $v/(1-m)$, where $m$ is the fraction of malicious agents. The final error rate in voting is due to wrong results forming a majority which is:

$$e(m,v) = \sum_{i=v}^{2v-1} \binom{2v-1}{i} m^i (1-m)^{2v-1-i} \approx cm^v \qquad (1)$$

As proven in [17] this error rate shrinks *exponentially* with $v$, as shown in figure 1.

This method performs well, if the fraction of malicious agents, $m$, is low such that they can not easily form a majority. With this assumption, the error rate can be reduced to very low levels with a small increase in redundancy. The weakness of this method is its large overhead, when $m$ is large, because $v$ has to be higher, to meet the acceptable error threshold. Having a large $m$ is a probable situation in an open agent society. More importantly, redundancy can not be reduced to less than two, even when $m$ is zero (no malicious agents). Therefore, it can only be used in cases where, we have an honest society and the population is very large, i.e. we have lots of trustable resources.

## 4.2 Verification

In the method that we call verification, instead of asking for the result of a task from at least two agents, as we need to do in voting, we might sometimes allocate a task with a known result to an agent, to verify its reliability. It is not assumed that the faulty agents consistently produce wrong results, i.e. a sabotage rate ($s$) is assumed for the agents as explained later. The agents are not aware of when they are going to be tested, with a task that the result of it is already known to the master. It is like scaring students into taking an unplanned quiz, while actually, not always planning to do so. This way the teacher ensures that the students are working correctly, without incurring too much slowdown in class progress. If a malicious agent replies with a wrong result to a known task, its results would be *backtracked* to the beginning of the batch. The agent could also be *blacklisted* and no more tasks would be assigned to it. In this case, if the probability of verifying an arbitrary agent is $p$, redundancy will be $1/(1-p)$, which has a lower bound of one instead of two for the previous method.

By utilizing *blacklisting*, the errors could only be caused by agents, which survive until the end of the batch, and the error rate is:

$$e(p,n,m,s) = \frac{sm(1-ps)^n}{(1-m)+m(1-ps)^n} \qquad (2)$$

where $p$ is the probability of verifying an agent, $n$ is the number of tasks assigned to an agent from a batch, $m$ is the malicious fraction of an agent population, and $s$ is the sabotage rate of an agent. See figure 2, which demonstrates the error rate for various values of $s$. By approximation [11], the above function has an upper bound of:

$$e^*(p,m,n,s) = \frac{m}{(1-m)} \cdot \frac{1}{pne} \qquad (3)$$

where $e$ is the base of the natural logarithm, and the maximum is at:

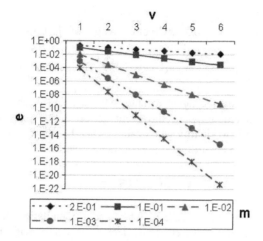

**Fig. 1.** Error rate of voting for different values of $v$ and $m$

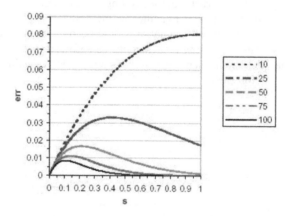

**Fig. 2.** Verification with blacklisting: theoretical error rate ($e$) at $p = 0.1$ and $m = 20\%$ for various values of $s$ and $n$

$$s^* = \min(1, \frac{1}{m(n+1)}).\tag{4}$$

If the agent can change its sabotage rate ($s$) and set it to the optimal value, the error rate would decrease *linearly* with the length of the batch, i.e. $n$, and in time. Hence, it is advantageous for the master to make the batches longer. Nevertheless, that is in the worst case only and the malicious agent does not have the required information to set $s$ in such a way.

It is not always possible to enforce *blacklisting*, since the malicious agent might hide or forge its identity and IP in a network. In this situation, the error rate is:

$$e(p,n,m,s) = m.\frac{1}{n}.s. \text{ Average length of "last run"}$$

$$= \frac{ms}{n}\left[ n(1-ps)^n + \sum_{i=0}^{n-1} i(1-ps)^i.ps \right] \tag{5}$$

Assuming that enforcing the agent to stay, until the end of the computation is not done, and if the agent stays in the computation for $l$ tasks ($l<n$) and rejoins immediately under a new identity when caught, then by approximation [11], the error rate has an upper bound according to the following relation:

$$e^*(p,l,m,s) < \frac{m}{pl} \tag{6}$$

which is much worse than the case of when using blacklisting. See figure 3, for an illustration of the error rate. The error rate decreases *linearly* with the length of run ($l$) that, the agent participates in the computation. Here, error rate is significantly higher than with blacklisting. This is caused by unreliable agents, contributing to the results and leaving the computation early, before getting caught. Therefore they increase the error rate and it would be desirable to somehow increase $l$. Since malicious agents can return again in the same batch, the situation would become worsened. To prevent the return of malicious agents, sign-in delays could be enforced. If the sign-in process is delayed until the next batch, then the malicious agents do not gain any benefit from leaving the computation early.

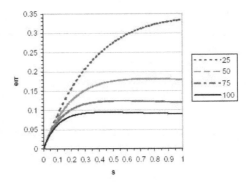

**Fig. 3.** Verification without blacklisting: theoretical error rate ($e$) at $p = 0.1$ and $m = 20\%$ for various values of $s$ and $n$

## 4.3 Honesty

Now, the notion that comes to mind is to use voting on top of verification to exponentially reduce the already linearly reduced error rate and to achieve better result correctness for the same redundancy. This section culminates with an effective framework for *combining* any social control mechanism similar to the two, mentioned above, or any other possible future mechanism. Hence, this method is open to *variations*.

A parameter that, we call honesty is assigned to every agent in the society, in analogy to our own *human society*. If the result of a task is only accepted when the conditional probability of that result being correct is higher than a threshold $p$, then the probability of accepting a correct result, averaged over all tasks is at least $p$. This principle is critical in ensuring the correctness. Meaning that, by accepting results from agents which are honest enough, the correctness of the final *solution* can be ensured, for any *desired non-zero error rate*. The honesty of an agent is determined by monitoring his behavior and testing him. Obviously the newly arriving agents are unreliable and have a low degree of honesty. Honesty might also depend on the agent society and the master's prediction about the fraction of malicious agents in the population.

There are four types of objects in the system: *agent, result* coming from an agent, *result group* and *task*. Fig. 4. is a visualization of this method, showing the four types of objects, the round-robin allocation of tasks from a pool to agents, and how the probability of correctness is computed as later explained. The honesty of an agent determines the probability of correctness for the result, passed by him. The master might receive different results from agents in the society, and a result group consists of all *matching* results for the same task. Each task could have several result groups. The probability of correctness for the results in a result group, determine the conditional probability of correctness for the result group for a particular task, as explained in equation 8. The probability of correctness of the *best* result group is assigned to its task. The task will be accepted and marked as done, only when it has reached the desired probability of correctness for the task, which is equal to the determined threshold for the final solution.

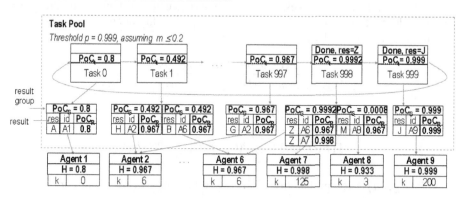

**Fig. 4.** Honesty framework and assignment of a pool of tasks to agents

While the master is assigning tasks from a batch, the probability of correctness for a result group in the system increases, if the agent passes verification tests, or a matching result arrives from another agent (vote), or both. By time, the probability of correctness for a result group will reach the desired threshold. The task related to that result group will be marked as done and it will not be reassigned by the master. This method is very efficient, because if the result is arriving from an honest agent, then it will not require voting and it reduces redundancy.

To assign the initial honesty value to agents, if verification is not used, the honesty can be set to $H=1-m$ ($m$: the fraction of malicious agents). By using the verification method, the more tests the agent passes, the better his honesty would be. With blacklisting, the only bad results are from agents which survive the verification test. The probability of receiving a bad result from an agent, after surviving $k$ verification tests is (similar to equation 2):

P (result from Agent is bad | Agent survived $k$ verification tests)

$$= \frac{sm(1-s)^k}{(1-m)+m(1-s)^k} \tag{7}$$

$$< \frac{m}{(1-m)} \cdot \frac{1}{ke}$$

where $m$ is the fraction of malicious agents and $e$ is the base of the natural logarithm. Therefore, with blacklisting, the strict lower bound for honesty (probability of receiving a good result) would be $H=1-(m/(1-m)ke)$. This can be used for computing the honesty of an agent.

Without blacklisting, the probability of a result being bad would be higher than the previous case. It would be $m.s$ ($s$: sabotage rate). But $s$ is not known and has to be estimated. $\hat{s}=1/k$ seems to be a good estimate for $s$, considering that a malicious agent would be detected after $k$ verifications. Hence, honesty of an agent will be set to $H=1-m/k$. When using verification, with or without blacklisting, if $k$ is equal to zero, honesty should be set to $1-m$, instead of using the previous formulae.

The probability of correctness for a result is equal to the honesty of the agent which produces it. If there are $g$ result groups, the probability of correctness ($PoC$) for a result group $G_a$, where $1 < a < g$, is:

$$PoC(G_a) = \frac{P(G_a \ good).P(all \ others \ bad)}{P(get \ g \ groups, where \ each \ G_a \ has \ m_a \ members)}$$

$$= \frac{P(G_a good).\prod\limits_{i \neq a} P(G_i bad)}{\prod\limits_{j=1}^{g} P(G_i bad) + \sum\limits_{j=1}^{g} \left[ P(G_i good)\prod\limits_{i \neq j} P(G_i bad)\right]} \tag{8}$$

Here, $P(G_a good)$ is the probability of all the results in $G_a$ being good, computed as $\prod_{i=1}^{m_a} H(R_{ai})$ for all results $R_{ai}$ in the group $G_a$. Correspondingly, $P(G_a bad)$ is the probability of all the results in $G_a$ being bad, computed as $\prod_{i=1}^{m_a} (1 - H(R_{ai}))$.

When applying the honesty mechanism, both voting and verification can be combined to reduce the error rate to any desired threshold. Voting does not increase the honesty of an agent, but increases the $PoC$ of a result group according to equation 8. Verification increases the honesty of the agents. As shown later, by using the mechanism and combining the two methods, extremely high *accuracies* can be reached with an acceptable amount of redundancy and slowdown. It also guarantees a limit on error by watching the conditional probabilities.

For verification, the assumption was that the correct result for the computation was known or one of the few trusted agents must do the task. This limits the probability of verification ($p$) and reduces the performance and speed of increase of $PoC$ for a result. Honesty alleviates the problem by using voting *for* verification, i.e. whenever one of the task's result groups reaches the threshold (such that the task is considered as done), $k$ which is the number of verifications passed, is incremented for the agents which contributed to that result group. The agents contributing to the loser result groups are considered as caught and their results are backtracked.

The other advantage of honesty is that by using honesty without blacklisting and $H=1-m/k$, there is no benefit for a malicious agent to forge its identity or leaving the computation early and returning again. This also fixes the problem of blacklisting. Therefore using honesty provides a very flexible framework for assuring the correctness of a solution without any previous stipulation on the reliability of agents in a society.

## 5   Simulation and Evaluation

To implement the above mathematical model, the Java programming language was used. Although in our implementation agents and other objects in the model were all simulated on one computer, this language can flexibly meet the requirements of writing a distributed agent application working over a network like real software agents. This way the agents can communicate with each other and work towards solving a big problem, even though they do not trust each other in terms of reliability and correctness of the returned results.

The main program breaks down the problem into tasks, which are grouped into batches. The tasks of a batch are assigned to agents in a round-robin fashion. When a result is returned, the honesty of the agent is taken as the probability of correctness of the result. As different results arrive for one task, different result groups are gradually formed, and the $PoC$ of each result group is computed. When one of the result groups reaches the acceptable threshold, it is accepted immediately and the task is done. This threshold is equal to the probability of correctness of the final solution which has been guaranteed by the multiagent system. In the setup of the simulation 10 batches of 10000 tasks each, were allocated to 200 agents, which randomly contained a malicious fraction $m$, in the agent population. The experiment was repeated for different values of $m$.

Different social control mechanisms can be used in combination with various $m$ values and the incurred slowdowns, for several predetermined final error rates are calculated. The results [11] are summarized in table 1. In table 1a, when m is larger the slope of the line is steeper, which demonstrates the weak performance of voting in a society with many malicious agents. Here, slowdown is always above 2 as well. Note that in table 1c, at $m=0.2$ an error rate of $1\times10^{-6}$ is achieved using honesty with voting and verification with blacklisting with a slowdown of 3, while in table 1a the same error rate would be achieved with a slowdown of more than 30. Table 1d even exhibits a better performance than 1c, which has blacklisting. In table 1d, honesty with voting for verification without blacklisting achieves an error rate of $1\times10^{-6}$, which shows 100,000 times better performance than voting alone in table 1a, for the same slowdown of 2.5. Best results are achieved by honesty with voting for verification.

## 6    Conclusion and Future Work

In an open and geographically distributed multiagent system, malicious agents might exist. There is no way of guaranteeing that they actually do the tasks that are allocated to them, since the agents have made no stipulation regarding this issue. They are usually autonomous, self-interested and selfish, or even worse, could have spiteful intensions. It is very critical to utilize social control mechanisms and interaction protocols to make the error rate tractable. In this way the unreliable agent society is coordinated by using the above mechanisms. The contributions of this paper are: setting up the assumption for producing an open multiagent system, modeling the society of agents without any stipulation on agent reliability, presenting an analysis of mechanisms for assurance of solution correctness in such a society, comparing their performance by simulation and introducing the generic and effective honesty framework for modeling a coordinated agent society.

**Table 1.** (a) voting alone, (b) honesty with verification without blacklisting, (c) honesty with voting and verification with blacklisting and (d) honesty with voting for verification without blacklisting (for different m: malicious fraction)

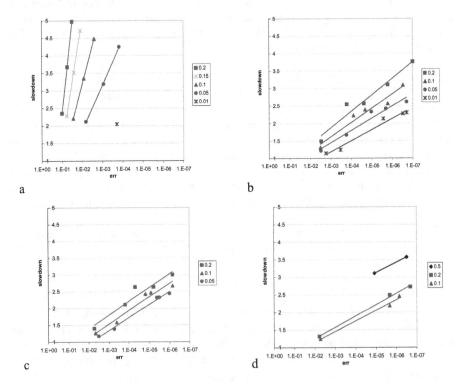

The first mechanism introduced is voting. After all, the more agents return the same result, the more likely it is to be true, assuming that the good agents form a majority. The assumption limits the use of this mechanism and it is highly redundant and inefficient. The second mechanism is verification. The agents are sometimes tested to see that, they are working properly. This way redundancy is mitigated and in effect, agents are scared off into doing the right thing. The human society acts in an analogous fashion.

Finally the honesty mechanism is proposed to create the required infrastructure in a society, for agents to act legitimately. The honesty attribute is not stipulated in advance, nor is it a characteristic of the agent. Instead it is computed gradually, based on the agent's own behavior in the society. It represents the faith of others towards the agent. The generic approach of solving this problem culminated to, acquiring a better understanding of the agents' interactions in an inaccessible environment. Best results were achieved by honesty with voting for verification.

The application domain of these mechanisms includes software agents, living in a *competitive* society like the web environment; agent-based simulation applications [16] for research related to sociology, political science, economics, business, and ecology; and coordinating agents' behavior using negotiation and collaboration. Considering the many possible real-world applications, which can harvest these mechanisms and the comparative mathematical and simulation analysis that is presented here, the next logical step and future direction for research is, to deploy the mechanisms in a real-world MAS application similar to the ones mentioned above.

Future computational systems will increasingly be designed and built in a distributed fashion. A larger number of systems will be used by multiple real-world parties. The problem of coordinating, manipulating and controlling these parties is not possible with technological or economic methods alone. Hence, a successful approach requires a hybridization of both [10].

# References

[1]     Agent 2003 Conference on Challenges in Social Simulation, Chicago, IL, USA, October 3-4, (2003)

[2]     Fourth International Workshop on Engineering Societies in the Agents World, Imperial College, London, UK, October 29-31, (2003)

[3]     Jennings, N.R.: http://www.ecs.soton.ac.uk/~nrj/mobilevce.html

[4]     Lynch, N. A.: Distributed Algorithms. Morgan Kauffman Publishers, Inc., (1996)

[5]     Mas-Colell, A., Whinston, M., Green, J.R.: Microeconomic Theory. Oxford University Press, (1995)

[6]     Moses, Y., Tenenholtz, M.: On Computational Aspects of Artificial Social Systems. In Proc. 11$^{th}$ DAI Workshop, Glen Arbor, MI, USA, (1992)

[7]     Nair, R., Ito, T., Tambe, M., Marsella, S.: Task Allocation in the RoboCup Rescue Simulation Domain: A Short Note. RoboCup 2001: Robot Soccer World Cup V. Lecture Notes in Computer Science, Vol. 2377, Springer (2002)

[8]     Overeinder, B., Brazier, F., Marin, O.: Fault Tolerance in Scalable Agent Support Systems: Integrating DARX in the AgentScape Framework. 3rd International Symposium on Cluster Computing and the Grid, Tokyo, Japan, May 12 - 15, (2003)

[9]     Ramamohanarao, K. and Bailey, J.: Transaction Oriented Computational Models for Multi-Agent Systems. 13th IEEE International Conference on Tools with Artificial Intelligence (ICTAI'01), Dallas, Texas, USA, November 07 - 09, (2001)

[10]  Sandholm, T.W.: Negotiation among Self-Interested Computationally Limited Agents. Ph.D. thesis, University of Massachusetts, Amherst, (1996), http://www.cs.wustl.edu/~sandholm/dissetation.ps

[11]  Sarmenta, L.F.G.: Volunteer Computing. Ph.D. thesis, Dept. of Electrical Engineering and Computer Science, MIT, Cambridge, MA, Dec., (2000)

[12]  Shahri, H.H.: Assurance of Solution Correctness in Task Allocation without Stipulation in an Agent Society. Proceedings of the Agent 2003 Conference on Challenges in Social Simulation, Chicago, IL, USA, Oct (2003)

[13]  Shehory, O., Kraus, S.: Task Allocation via Coalition Formation among Autonomous Agents. Proceedings of the Fourteenth International Joint Conference on Artificial Intelligence (IJCAI 95), Montreal, Quebec, Canada, August (1995)

[14]  Sparkman, C.H., DeLoach, S.A., Self, A.L.: Automated Derivation of Complex Agent Architectures from Analysis Specifications. Second International Workshop on Agent-Oriented Software Engineering (AOSE-2001), Montreal, Canada, May (2001)

[15]  Wallace, S.: Validating Agent Behavior. 23rd Soar Workshop, Ann Arbor, Michigan, USA, June 23-27, (2003)

[16]  Winoto, P.: A Multi-Agent Based Simulation of the Market for Offenses. AAAI-02 Workshop on Multi-Agent Modeling and Simulation of Economic Systems (MAMSES-02), Edmonton, Canada, July 29, (2002)

[17]  Zuev, Y.A.: The Estimation of Efficiency of Voting Procedures. In: Theory of Probability and its Applications, Vol. 42, No. 1, March, (1997), http://www.siam.org/journals/tvp/42-1/97594.html

# A Component-Based Parallel Constraint Solver

Peter Zoeteweij* and Farhad Arbab

CWI, P.O. Box 94079, 1090 GB Amsterdam, the Netherlands
{P.Zoeteweij,Farhad.Arbab}@cwi.nl

**Abstract.** As a case study that illustrates our view on coordination and component-based software engineering, we present the design and implementation of a parallel constraint solver. The parallel solver coordinates autonomous instances of a sequential constraint solver, which is used as a software component. The component solvers achieve load balancing of tree search through a time-out mechanism. Experiments show that the purely exogenous mode of coordination employed here yields a viable parallel solver that effectively reduces turn-around time for constraint solving on a broad range of hardware platforms.

**Keywords:** component-based software engineering, coordination, parallelization, constraint solving.

## 1 Introduction

Over the past years, constraint solving has been a useful test case for coordination techniques. [3, 8, 9, 14]. One of the reasons is that because of the general nature of the constraint programming paradigm, any constraint solver inevitably supports only a specific class of constraint satisfaction problems (CSP's). By having different solvers, supporting different classes of specialized problems cooperate to solve a more general problem, a broader range of problems can be addressed. The goal of having stand-alone constraint solvers cooperate in a uniform and structured way brings solver cooperation into the area of coordination programming and component-based software engineering.

Constraint solving is an NP-complete problem. Efficient algorithms exist for some classes of CSP's, and when completeness is not important we may be able to find a solution to a CSP quickly by using local search techniques. Nevertheless, generally constraint solving comes down to tree search. In this paper, we deal with a specific mode of solver cooperation that aims at reducing the turn-around time of constraint solving through parallelization of tree search. Contrary to other modes of solver cooperation, parallel constraint solving has received little attention from a coordination point of view.

The primary aspect of our approach is to equip a tree search based constraint solver with a time-out mechanism. When a CSP can be solved before the elapse

---

* Supported by NWO, the Netherlands Organization for Scientific Research, under project number 612.069.003.

R. de Nicola et al. (Eds.): COORDINATION 2004, LNCS 2949, pp. 307–322, 2004.
© Springer-Verlag Berlin Heidelberg 2004

of a given time-out, such a solver simply produces all solutions that it has found (or *the* solution that it has found, if we are not interested in all solutions). Otherwise it also produces some representation of the work that still needs to be done. For tree search, this is a collection of (disjunct) subproblems that must still be explored: the search frontier. These subproblems are then re-distributed among a set of identical solvers that run in parallel. The initial solver is part of this set, and each solver in the set may split its input into further subproblems, when its time-out elapses. The aim of the time-out mechanism is to provide an implicit load balancing: when a solver is idle, and there are currently no subproblems available for it to work on, another solver is likely to produce new subproblems when its time-out elapses. We expect to be able to tune the time-out value such that it is both sufficiently small to ensure that enough subproblems are available to keep all solvers busy, and sufficiently large to ensure that the overhead of communicating the subproblems is negligible. The idea of using time-outs is quite intuitive, but to our knowledge, its application to parallel search is novel.

Rather than a parallel algorithm, we present this scheme as a pattern for constructing a parallel constraint solver from component solvers. The only requirement is that these components can publish their search frontiers. We believe that this requirement is modest compared to building a parallel constraint solver from scratch. Our presentation of the scheme in Section 3 uses the notion of abstract behavior types, and the Reo coordination model. These, and the relevant aspects of constraint solving are introduced in Section 2. To test the concept, we equipped a constraint solver with the time-out mechanism, and implemented the coordination pattern as a stand-alone distributed program. In Section 4 we give an account of this implementation, and in Section 5 we describe the experiments that were performed to test the parallel solver. Compared to parallelizing an existing constraint solver, the component-based approach has further benefits. These are discussed in Section 6, together with related work and directions for future research.

## 2    Preliminaries

To make the paper self-contained, in this section we provide the necessary background on constraint solving (2.1), abstract behavior types, and Reo (2.2).

### 2.1    Constraint Solving

Constraint solving deals with finding solutions to constraint satisfaction problems. A CSP consists of a number of variables and their associated domains (sets of possible values), and a set of constraints. A constraint is defined on a subset of the variables, and restricts the combinations of values that these variables may assume. A solution to a CSP is an assignment of values to variables that satisfies all constraints. Tree search in constraint solving performs a systematic exploration of assignments of values to variables: at every node of the search tree, the descendant nodes are generated by assigning different subdomains to some variable.

The search tree is expanded as a part of the traversal of the tree, but before generating a next level of nodes, we try to limit the number of possible alternatives. This is called pruning the search tree, and for constraint solving, this is done by *constraint propagation*. The purpose of constraint propagation is to remove from the variable domains the values that do not contribute to any solution. For example if two integer variables $x, y \in [0..10]$ are constrained by $x < y$, we may remove 10 from the domain of $x$, and 0 from the domain of $y$. Constraint propagation is usually implemented by computing the fixpoint of a number of reduction operators [1]. These operators are functions (domain reduction functions, DRF's) that apply to the variable domains, and enforce the constraints. If the domains of one or more variables become empty as a result of constraint propagation, the node of the search tree for which this happens is a failure. If, on the other hand, after constraint propagation all domains are singleton sets, these domains constitute a solution to the CSP. In all other cases, the node of the search tree is an internal node, and constraint solving proceeds by branching.

Important concerns in this branch-and-prune approach to constraint solving are the choice of the variable for branching, and how to construct the subdomains for that variable. In this paper we assume a *fail-first* variable selection strategy, where a variable is selected for which the number of possible assignments is minimal. Subdomains are constructed by *enumeration*: they are singleton sets, one for every value in the original domain.

Branching adds new nodes of the search tree to the set of nodes where search may continue. This set is called the *search frontier* [10]. Managing the search frontier as a stack effectively implements a depth-first traversal. Other traversal strategies exist, but depth-first keeps the search frontier small. Apart from memory requirements this is especially important for our application, because the size of the search frontier determines the communication volume of the parallel solver.

## 2.2    Coordination and Abstract Behavior Types

In our view, coordination programming deals with building complex software systems from largely autonomous component systems. The more autonomous these components are, the more it becomes justified to refer to their composition as coordination. Contrary to modules and objects, which are the counterparts of components in the classical software engineering paradigms of modular and object-oriented programming, an instance of a prospective software component has at least one thread of control. For the purpose of composition, the component is a black box, that communicates with its environment through a set of ports. Coordination programming involves writing the "glue code" to actually make the component instances cooperate. Depending on the complexity of the interaction, it may make sense to use a dedicated coordination language. For example if the population of processes is highly dynamic, the Manifold coordination language [2] may be a logical choice.

A software system that complies with the above notion of a component can be specified conveniently by an abstract behavior type (ABT) [4]. ABT's are the coordination counterpart of abstract data types, as used in classical software engineering. Before we can introduce ABT's we first need to recall the definition of timed data streams from [5].

A *stream* over some set $A$ is an infinite sequence of elements of $A$. Zero-based indices are used to denote the individual elements of a stream, e.g., $\alpha(0)$, $\alpha(1)$, $\alpha(2)$, ... denote the first, second, third, etc. elements of the stream $\alpha$. Also $\alpha^{(k)}$ denotes the stream that is obtained by removing the first $k$ values from stream $\alpha$ (so $\alpha(0)$ is the head of the stream, and $\alpha^{(1)}$ is its tail). Relational operators on streams apply pairwise to their respective elements, e.g., $\alpha < \beta$ means $\alpha(0) < \beta(0)$, $\alpha(1) < \beta(1)$, $\alpha(2) < \beta(2)$, ...

A *timed data stream* over some set $D$ is a pair of streams $\langle \alpha, a \rangle$, consisting of a data stream $\alpha$ over $D$, and a time stream $a$ over the set of positive real numbers, and having $a(i) < a(j)$, for $0 \leq i < j$. The interpretation of a timed data stream $\langle \alpha, a \rangle$ is that for all $i \geq 0$, the input/output of data item $\alpha(i)$ occurs at "time moment" $a(i)$.

An *abstract behavior type* is a (maximal) relation over timed data streams. Every timed data stream involved in an ABT is tagged either as its input or output. For an ABT $R$ with one input timed data stream $I$ and one output timed data stream $O$ we use the infix notation $I \; R \; O$. Also for two such ABT's $R_1$ and $R_2$, let the composition $R_1 \circ R_2$ denote the relation $\{\langle \langle \alpha, a \rangle, \langle \beta, b \rangle \rangle \mid \exists \langle \gamma, c \rangle \cdot \langle \alpha, a \rangle R_1 \langle \gamma, c \rangle \wedge \langle \gamma, c \rangle R_2 \langle \beta, b \rangle\}$.

ABT's specify only the black box behavior of components. For a model of their implementation, other specification methods are likely to be more appropriate, but that information is irrelevant from a coordination point of view.

Reo [4, 6] is a channel-based exogenous coordination model wherein complex coordinators, called *connectors* are compositionally built out of simpler ones. The simplest connectors in Reo are a set of *channels* with well defined behavior. In Section 3.2 we use Reo connectors to specify the coordination of our component solvers.

## 3   Specification

### 3.1   Component Solver

In this section we define an ABT for a constraint solver with the time-out mechanism. First we need some formal notion of a CSP:

Let $P$ be a finite set of *problems* and let $(P \cup \{\top\}, \sqsubseteq)$ be a partial order such that for all $p \in P$, $\top \not\sqsubseteq p$. For a problem $p \in P$, we define the sets $sub(p) = \{q \in P \cup \{\top\} \mid p \sqsubseteq q\}$ and $sol(p) = \{s \in sub(p) \mid \forall q \in sub(p) \setminus \{s\} \cdot s \not\sqsubseteq q\} \setminus \{\top\}$. Intuitively, $sub(p)$ represents the set of subproblems of a problem $p$, possibly including $\top$, which represents the deduction of a failure. The set of maximal subproblems excluding $\top$, $sol(p)$, represents the set of solutions of $p$.

Next we specify that a constraint solver transforms a problem into a set of mutually disjunct problems. Let $D$ denote the data domain $P \cup 2^P \cup \{\tau\}$, where $\tau \notin P$ is an arbitrary data element that serves as a *token*. In the following, let $\langle \alpha, a \rangle$ and $\langle \beta, b \rangle$ be timed data streams over $D$. Now the behavior of a *basic solver* is captured by the *BSol* ABT, defined as

$$\langle \alpha, a \rangle \; BSol \; \langle \beta, b \rangle \equiv a < b \wedge S(\alpha, \beta)$$

where $S$ is a relation on $P$ and $2^P$, such that for all $p \in P$ and $R \in 2^P$, $S(p, R)$ iff

- $\forall r \in R, p \sqsubseteq r$,
- $\forall r, s \in R, r \sqsubseteq s$ implies $r = s$, and
- $sol(p) = \cup_{r \in R} sol(r)$

The *Str* (streamer) ABT specifies that stream of sets of problems, as produced by a basic solver, is transformed into a stream of problems, where the sequence of problems for each input set is delimited by a token:

$$\begin{aligned} \langle \alpha, a \rangle \; Str \; \langle \beta, b \rangle \equiv \; & a(0) = b(0) \\ & \wedge \; \beta(k) = \tau \\ & \wedge \; \alpha(0) = \{\beta(0), \ldots, \beta(k-1)\} \\ & \wedge \; \langle \alpha^{(1)}, a^{(1)} \rangle \; Str \; \langle \beta^{(k+1)}, b^{(k+1)} \rangle \end{aligned}$$

where for all $i \in \mathbb{N}$, $\alpha(i) \in 2^P$ and $\beta(i) \in P \cup \{\tau\}$, and $k$ denotes $|\alpha(0)|$, the cardinality of the set of problems at the head of stream $\alpha$. Now the behavior of a constraint solver component is captured by the *Sol* ABT, defined as

$$Sol = BSol \circ Str$$

Our top-level model of a solver component is the composition of a basic solver and a streamer. The token $\tau$ can be thought of as the notification "no" that a PROLOG interpreter would produce to indicate that no (more) solutions have been found. If we model a typical constraint solver as a basic solver, then for any given input problem the output set corresponds to the set of solutions for that problem, i.e. $\beta(i) = sol(\alpha(i))$, and there is no upper bound on the time $b(i) - a(i)$ needed to produce this set.

In contrast, the load-balancing solver component that we propose here stops searching for solutions after the elapse of a time-out $t$. At that moment, it generates a subproblem for every solution that it has found, plus one for every node of the search tree that must still be explored. For $t \in \mathbb{R}^+$, the *Sol$_t$* ABT defines this behavior:

$$\begin{aligned} \langle \alpha, a \rangle \; BSol_t \; \langle \beta, b \rangle \equiv \; & \langle \alpha, a \rangle \; BSol \; \langle \beta, b \rangle \\ & \wedge \; \forall i \in \mathbb{N} \cdot b(i) - a(i) < t \end{aligned}$$

$$Sol_t = BSol_t \circ Str$$

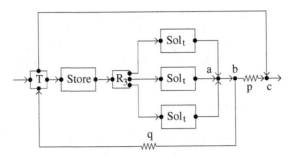

**Fig. 1.** 3-way parallel solver

## 3.2   Parallel Solver

Figure 1 shows a channel-based design for a (3-way) parallel solver. All channels in this design are synchronous: read and write operations block until a matching operation is performed on the opposite channel end. The "resistors" depict Reo filters: synchronous channels that accept data items that match a certain pattern (set of allowable data items) and discard data items that do not match this pattern. At node b in Figure 1, all output of the solvers is replicated onto two filters. Channel bc filters out solutions. Its pattern (p) is $\texttt{Filter}(\{p \in P \mid sol(p) = \{p\}\})$. The channel from b to T discards all solutions. Its pattern (q) is $\texttt{Filter}(\{p \in P \mid sol(p) \neq \{p\}\} \cup \{\tau\})$. The ABT's of the channels are specified in [4].

Apart from the channels and the three load-balancing solvers $Sol_t$, there are three elements of the design that require further clarification: the special-purpose connector T, the 3-ary exclusive router $R_3$, and the Store. We do not give full ABT's, but an intuitive description.

The special purpose connector T implements termination detection. Initially, it reads a problem from its left-hand side input port. All problem descriptions entering T, through either input port, are forwarded immediately through its right-hand side output port to the Store. Also T counts the number of problems forwarded to the Store, and the number of tokens $\tau$ received through its bottom port (from node b). While these numbers do not match, the parallel solver is busy, and T will accept new (sub)problems from its bottom input port (connected to node b) only. As soon as the number of problems is canceled out by the number of tokens, T sends a token $\tau$ through its top port (to node c), indicating that the parallel solver has finished working on its current problem. Then it will return to its initial state, and accept a new problem from its left-hand side input port.

Connector $R_3$ is a general-purpose 3-ary exclusive router. It operates synchronously, and every data item on its input port is forwarded on exactly one of its output ports. If none of the channels connected to the output ports is able to forward a data item, the router blocks. If a data item item can be forwarded on more than one output port, a non-deterministic choice is made. Construction of the exclusive router from Reo primitives is shown in [6].

The Store is a channel-like connector that is specific to this application. Its operation is asynchronous: it buffers incoming problems, and interprets these problems to determine the level of the corresponding node of the search tree. This information can be used to enforce a global traversal strategy. When $R_3$ is ready to accept data (i.e., when one of the load-balancing solvers has become idle) it forwards a problem according to this strategy. For example, it may forward a node of the deepest available level in an attempt to implement depth-first search globally. This effectively drains the Store. Forwarding a node of the shallowest available level implements breadth-first search, filling up the Store with more subproblems.

## 4    Implementation

To test the proposed implementation of parallel search, we equipped our Open-Solver constraint solver with the time-out mechanism, and developed a distributed program to combine several such solvers into a parallel constraint solver.

### 4.1    Component Solver

OpenSolver is an experimental constraint solver that implements a branch-and-prune tree search algorithm. This algorithm is abstract in the sense that its actual functionality is determined by software plug-ins in a number of predefined categories, corresponding to different aspects of the model of constraint solving outlined in Section 2.1. For example, there are categories for variable domain types and domain reduction functions. OpenSolver has been developed with coordination in mind: a special category of plug-ins covers the *coordination layer* of the solver (Figure 2). Through a plug-in in this category, the execution of the solving algorithm can be controlled, and data can be shared with the environment. In addition to the coordination layer plug-in described below, a plug-in exists that implements a simple user interface, and a plug-in is being developed that will allow an OpenSolver to participate in a general framework for distributed constraint solving [15].

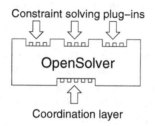

**Fig. 2.** Plug-ins determine the actual functionality of the OpenSolver

```
VARIABLE q1 IS DiscreteDomain {1..4};
VARIABLE q2 IS DiscreteDomain {1..4};
VARIABLE q3 IS DiscreteDomain {1..4};
VARIABLE q4 IS DiscreteDomain {1..4};
DRF DDNEQ { q1-q2 <> 0 }; DRF DDNEQ { q1-q2 <>-1 };
                         DRF DDNEQ { q1-q2 <> 1 };
DRF DDNEQ { q1-q3 <> 0 }; DRF DDNEQ { q1-q3 <>-2 };
                         DRF DDNEQ { q1-q3 <> 2 };
...
DRF DDNEQ { q3-q4 <> 0 }; DRF DDNEQ { q3-q4 <>-1 };
                         DRF DDNEQ { q3-q4 <> 1 };
```

**Fig. 3.** Part of a problem description for the 4-queens puzzle

The plug-in mechanism is implemented by inheriting from C++ abstract classes for each of the categories. It is explained in more detail in [14]. The coordination layer is implemented by having the solver execute a command loop, where it continually asks the coordination layer plug-in what to do next. Examples of commands that can be given by the coordination layer plug-in are:

– from the search frontier, select a set of nodes for further exploration,
– perform constraint propagation in the nodes of the search tree that have been selected for further exploration,
– apply the branching strategy plug-in to the nodes where constraint propagation has finished, in order to expand the search tree,
– flush the nodes of the search tree: this generates a textual representation of the search frontier and of all solutions that are available. The data structures for these nodes are then deallocated.

The latter command is important for implementing the time-out mechanism. A special coordination layer plug-in StreamingIO has been developed, that turns an OpenSolver into a load-balancing solver, as specified in Section 3. When it is equipped with this plug-in, an OpenSolver instance keeps reading problem descriptions from its standard input. These problem descriptions are coded as sequences of ASCII characters where the individual problem descriptions are delimited by brackets. An example of a problem description is shown in Figure 3.

The problem descriptions themselves contain instructions for the solver to activate plug-ins for variables, DRF's, etc. When a problem description has been read from standard input, the coordination layer plug-in instructs the solver to parse it, and subsequently starts the search for solutions. When the time-out elapses, or when the search frontier becomes empty, the StreamingIO plug-in stops issuing commands that drive the search for solutions. Instead it issues the command to flush the nodes of the search tree. Our implementation is an approximation of the $Sol_t$ ABT of Section 3.1 in the sense that the subproblems appear on the output stream just *after* the time-out elapses. In theory this could take unacceptably long, for example if suddenly the workload of the system increases. In practice the approximation is realistic.

Every plug-in implements a method to write itself into a character string. When executing the command to flush the search tree, this method is called for all plug-ins that define a particular node of the search tree, notably the variable domains and the DRF's. These strings are then passed to the coordination layer. Normally this mechanism is used to produce the solutions of a CSP, but because we don't perform an exhaustive search, in this case it also produces the search frontier. This information is used by the StreamingIO coordination layer plug-in to construct new problem descriptions, that are written to standard output. After the flushing operation is complete, the coordination layer plug-in generates a character-encoded token $\tau$, and proceeds by reading a new problem specification from standard input. Except for the token, the output of this coordination layer plug-in can be directly fed into another solver as a stream of problem descriptions.

The component solvers are configured to perform a depth-first traversal of the search tree, but through a special category of plug-ins, problem descriptions are annotated with the level of the corresponding node in the search tree. This allows the master process, implementing the Store of Section 3.2, to impose a high-level traversal strategy on top of the depth-first traversal of the solvers.

An important aspect of a constraint solver implementation is the construction of the data structures, notably the variable domains, that define the node of the search tree where search continues. While hybrid methods have been studied, the main options are [11]:

**Copying** When the search tree is expanded by branching, the data structures that define the current node are copied for all new nodes. These copies are then modified to construct subproblems. At potentially high memory costs, every node of the search frontier is immediately available for further exploration.

**Trailing** Only the current node of the traversal is maintained, but all changes (deletions of values) to the domains of variables leading up to this node are registered. Backtracking is implemented by undoing changes to reach an internal node of the search tree, from which search can progress along an alternative branch. Trailing is the predominant method used in current constraint solvers.

**Recomputation** Internal nodes are represented by the branching choices that were made in order to arrive at that node. Instead of unwinding a trail of changes, the internal nodes are reconstructed from a shallower internal node by repeating a part of the traversal of the search tree.

OpenSolver is based on copying, so the search frontier is maintained explicitly (but plug-ins in the variable domain type category can implement a copy-on-write policy). Admittedly, this is a great convenience for publishing the search frontier, but we are convinced that our method extends to solvers that use trailing or recomputation. Especially when searching for all solutions, every node of

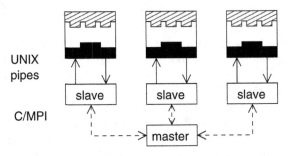

**Fig. 4.** Software architecture of the parallel solver

the search tree must be generated eventually, so no extra work is involved if this is done for the current search frontier when the time-out elapses.

## 4.2   Glue Code

We implemented the coordination protocol of Section 3.2 as a master-slave distributed program coded in C using the MPI message passing interface. Without the facilities for gathering statistics, the size of this glue code is just a little more than 600 lines. The slave processes fork a new UNIX process to start the component solvers, and a pair of pipes is connected to the standard input and output of these processes to facilitate the character-based implementation of the timed data streams.

The channels of the coordination model are implemented by directed send and receive MPI calls. Upon reception of a token $\tau$, a new subproblem is sent to the solver that generated the token. For this purpose, the character-based encoding of the token contains the identity of this solver. Also the number of solutions counted for each subproblem is piggybacked on the token.

When reading from the pipe that is connected to the standard output of a solver, the slave processes perform some parsing to recognize the beginning of a new problem description. At this point, an entire problem is sent to the master process as a character string. The master process implements the distribution and gathering of the problems. Figure 4 illustrates this software architecture.

Note that the component solvers are still stand-alone applications that rely on character-based standard I/O only. Our primary goal was a performance evaluation of the time-out mechanism, and from that perspective, a master-slave implementation is acceptable. However, the channel-based design of section 3.2 has many advantages over this rigid scheme. In particular, the decision where to send the next subproblem is now taken on the basis of solver output, whereas a true implementation of the exclusive router would be able to detect that a solver is idle when the channel connecting to that solver is ready to accept new data. This has the benefit of a better separation of concerns and of a reusable solution.

## 5   Experiments

The parallel solver was tested on three combinatorial problems:

*Queens* An instance of the $n$-queens problem, where $n$ queens must be placed on an $n \times n$ chess board, such that no two queens attack each other. Figure 3 shows a problems description for $n = 4$. The results reported here are for $n = 15$, for which there are 2279184 solutions.

*Sat* The problem is to find an assignment of truth values to propositional variables such that a given propositional formula in conjunctive normal form is satisfied. Such a formula is a conjunction of clauses, where a clause is a disjunction of literals (a propositional variable or its negation). In our model for this problem we use a constraint for every clause of the formula, which states that at least one of the literals of that clause must be true. A special-purpose DRF plug-in has been developed, which is initialized by a sequence of positive literals and a sequence of negative literals. When all except one literal have been assigned the value false, this DRF plug-in removes the value that would render the last literal false from the domain of that literal's variable. For these experiments we used formula par16-2-c from the dimacs test set[1]. This formula has 1392 clauses on 349 variables.

*Coloring* This is a graph coloring problem. In general, the problem is to find an assignment of colors to the vertices of a graph, such that two vertices that are connected by an edge have different colors. Here we verify that no 9 coloring exists for graph DSJC125.5[2] from the dimacs test set, having 125 nodes and 3891 edges. In our model we use a variable for every node, and a disequality constraint for every edge. The disequalities are implemented using the DDNEQ DRF plug-in of Figure 3.

In all cases, we used a fail-first variable selection strategy, selecting a variable with the smallest number of alternative values. As a second criterion for *Coloring*, variables are ordered according to the degree of their corresponding nodes of the graph. The component solvers perform a depth-first traversal, but using the level annotation of the problem descriptions generated by the solvers, the master switches between breadth-first and depth-first traversal, depending on the number of available subproblems. If this number is below a certain threshold value (512, for these experiments) priority is given to the shallowest available nodes. These are least likely to complete within the time-out, and can thus be expected to increase the number of problems available to the master, making it easier to keep all solvers busy. Also, when the full problem is first submitted to the first solver, this solver uses a very small time-out in order to generate

---

[1] available from e.g. `http://www.lri.fr/~simon/satex` (the Sat-Ex website).

[2] available from e.g. `http://mat.gsia.cmu.edu/` (Michael Trick's Operations Research Page.)

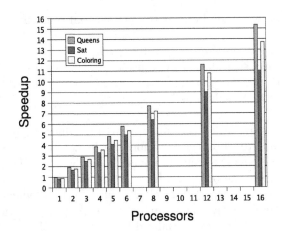

**Fig. 5.** Speedup figures

work for the other solvers quickly. Finally it should be mentioned that in our test runs, solutions are only counted, not stored or communicated.

Table 1 shows the sequential and parallel runtimes (elapsed time) for our test problems, as well as the parallel efficiency, which is the actual speedup divided by the number of processors. As an indication that our solver is a realistic implementation, depending on the search strategy, the standard example for 15-queens in ECLiPSe [3] 5.5 completes in 900 - 1500 sec. on the same hardware. The speedup figures (sequential runtime divided by parallel runtime) are shown in Figure 5. All elapsed times shown are averages of 10 repeated runs on a Beowulf cluster built from 1200 MHz Athlon nodes. The entries for parallel runs on 1 processor are an indication of the overhead of the time-out mechanism. For *Queens* and *Sat* we used a time-out value of 3200ms. For *Coloring* we used 9600ms. The master process always runs on the same node as one of the component solvers.

As can be seen from Figure 5, our parallel solver scales well. For *Queens* and *Coloring*, the parallel efficiency remains practically constant for the numbers of processors that we have tested with, and the scalability can be expected to extend to higher numbers of processors. The difference in efficiency for these two series of runs, and for the *Sat* runs on lower numbers of processors can be explained by the different sizes of the problem representations, and their associated communication costs.

For *Sat*, parallel efficiency drops after 8 processors. The reason is that because the variable domains are binary, the search frontiers are smaller than for the other two problems, and the master has difficulty keeping all solvers busy. Also the problem seems to have a less balanced search space: submitting a shallow

---

[3] ECLiPSe Constraint Logic Programming System. See
http://www-icparc.doc.ic.ac.uk/eclipse

**Table 1.** Elapsed times (sec.) and parallel efficiency

|          | Seq     | 1       | 2      | 3      | 4      | 5      | 6      | 8      | 12     | 16     |
|----------|---------|---------|--------|--------|--------|--------|--------|--------|--------|--------|
| *Queens* | 734.16  | 760.79  | 380.85 | 253.41 | 190.04 | 152.01 | 126.67 | 95.18  | 63.32  | 47.86  |
| eff.     |         | 0.96    | 0.96   | 0.97   | 0.97   | 0.97   | 0.97   | 0.96   | 0.97   | 0.96   |
| *Sat*    | 1541.12 | 1842.55 | 931.26 | 619.65 | 466.08 | 378.14 | 313.91 | 240.91 | 171.43 | 140.02 |
| eff.     |         | 0.84    | 0.83   | 0.83   | 0.83   | 0.82   | 0.82   | 0.80   | 0.75   | 0.69   |
| *Coloring* | 419.29 | 475.92 | 236.50 | 156.47 | 117.70 | 94.31  | 78.11  | 58.23  | 38.92  | 30.56  |
| eff.     |         | 0.88    | 0.89   | 0.89   | 0.89   | 0.89   | 0.89   | 0.90   | 0.90   | 0.86   |

subproblem to one of the solvers is less likely to generate new nodes than for *Queens* and *Coloring*. We hope to remedy the problem of the binary search trees by using a special-purpose branching strategy plug-in, which instantiates several variables at the same time, thus generating larger search frontiers. However, this strategy will also generate assignments that would otherwise have been prevented by constraint propagation, so it is hard to predict the overall effect.

The *Queens* experiments have also been run overnight on several (mostly idle) workstations connected by a local area network. While a detailed analysis of these experiments has not been made, here too we saw good speedup and scalability. Our approach seems well suited for such an environment: because no solver will work longer than the specified time-out before sharing work with other solvers, the proposed implementation of parallel search will likely be insensitive to the existing load and heterogeneity of the hardware. Because good results were obtained on a cluster (distributed memory), the parallel solver can also be expected to perform well on shared memory machines.

# 6   Discussion and Directions for Future Work

In [14] we described a constraint solver based on the coordination protocols of [8, 3]. This solver implements distributed constraint propagation using channel-based communication. In [15] we presented a design for extending this system to support a large variety of solver cooperation schemes, including parallel search for which we suggested the time-out mechanism that is evaluated in the present paper. OpenSolver is intended to play the role of the main component solver in this extended system. In addition to the coordination protocol of [8], [9] describes an IWIM implementation of a system for the coordination of heterogeneous solvers.

Other approaches to parallel constraint solving often use a scheme where the parallel solvers exchange nodes of the search tree only when one of them becomes idle, see for example [10, 12]. For such schemes, solvers can potentially run for a long time without having to respond to a request for work from other solvers, but once a solver becomes idle, it may be more difficult to find another solver that is willing to share part of its search frontier. In contrast, our approach aims at having a large repository of work, assuming that the time-out can be tuned such that publishing the search frontier is relatively cheap. From a software engineering point of view it is simpler, and better suited for a component-based implementation, but from a user's point of view, our scheme is more complicated because it introduces a tuning factor.

In [7] a shared-memory scheme is described where first the original CSP is split by assigning values to variables in a generate and test phase, in order that a large set of subproblems is available. These problems are then solved in a data-parallel way, using either a static or dynamic partitioning. We expect that scheme to be more sensitive to load imbalance because it is possible that most of the work is concentrated in only a few of the generated subproblems. For all alternatives discussed here, a comparison of reported efficiency results is difficult, because the hardware platforms and the benchmark problems used in each case are simply too diverse.

As an alternative to implementing the time-out mechanism in the component solver, we could move this mechanism into the glue code. It would be equally easy to modify a constraint solver to respond to some interrupt, and somehow an interrupt mechanism seems less alien to constraint solving than a time-out mechanism. In both cases the solver must be able to publish the state of its search algorithm, for which we use a character-based encoding. There are other advantages to enabling a solver to publish its search frontier. For instance, it allows user interaction in constraint solving, e.g. for computational steering, and supports a mechanism for checkpoints. When the set of subproblems held by the master process is saved to disk at regular intervals, and subproblems are not discarded until their results have been processed, the solver can restart from the last saved set of subproblems after, for example, a power failure has occurred.

Constraint solving was used as an example application, but our method can probably be applied to other problems that involve tree search. This is not surprising, because for many such problems, there exists a more or less efficient encoding as a constraint satisfaction problem. However, some problems that involve tree search have special requirements. For example in optimization we try to minimize some cost function during search. This can be implemented as a branch-and-bound algorithm, to prevent the exploration of subtrees that cannot improve the current best value found for the cost function. Our first goal is to adopt our method for branch-and-bound. Such an algorithm has been studied from a coordination point of view in [13], but in our work, the emphasis is on the component side rather than on the coordination framework, and on the demonstration of a realistic implementation. We expect that our parallel solver can be adapted for branch-and-bound by inserting a dedicated solver into the loop of Figure 1, to record the best value for the cost function found for a solution, and to filter out any nodes produced by the other solvers that will not improve on this bound. Some special care should be taken to communicate new bounds to other solvers.

As a further example, specialized solvers for the propositional satisfiability problem rely on so called learning search algorithms, that derive new constraints during the traversal of the search tree. These constraints are redundant, but when they are made explicit they achieve a stronger pruning of the search tree. It is not directly clear how our method should be extended to facilitate learning solvers, and this is a subject for future research.

# 7    Conclusion

In this paper we proposed an implementation of parallel tree search in constraint solving based on time-outs. Instead of a parallel algorithm, we presented and implemented the method as a protocol for the coordination of multiple instances of a component solver. After equipping a constraint solver with the time-out mechanism, some 600 lines of C/MPI code were sufficient to coordinate several of these component solvers to perform parallel search. Experiments showed that a good speedup is obtained on 2 to 16 CPU's, which indicates a good load balance. We conclude that:

- The time-out mechanism is an effective way to implement parallel search in constraint solving.
- Once a solver is able to publish its search frontier, building a parallel constraint solver becomes a matter of component-based software engineering.
- The OpenSolver plug-in mechanism made it very easy to meet this requirement.

# References

[1] K. R. Apt. The Rough Guide to Constraint Propagation. In Jaffar (ed.) *Proceedings of the 5th International Conference on Principles and Practice of Constraint Programming (CP'99)*, LNCS 1713, pp. 1–23, Springer-Verlag, 1999. 309

[2] F. Arbab. The IWIM Model for Coordination of Concurrent Activities. In Ciancarini, Hankin (eds.) *Coordination Languages and Models*, LNCS 1061, pp. 34–56, Springer-Verlag, April 1996. 310

[3] F. Arbab, E. Monfroy. Distributed Splitting of Constraint Satisfaction Problems. In Porto, Roman (eds.) *Coordination Languages and Models*, LNCS 1906, pp. 115–132, Springer-Verlag, 2000. 307, 319

[4] F. Arbab. Abstract Behavior Types: A Foundation Model for Components and Their Composition. In De Boer, Bonsangue, Graf, De Roever (eds.) *Formal Methods for Components and Objects*, LNCS 2852, Springer-Verlag, 2003. 310, 312

[5] F. Arbab, J. J. M. M. Rutten. *A Coinductive Calculus of Component Connectors*. Technical report SEN-R0216, Centrum voor Wiskunde en Informatica, Amsterdam, The Netherlands, September 2002. 310

[6] F. Arbab, C. Baier, J. J. M. M. Rutten, M. Sirjani. Modeling Component Connectors in Reo by Constraint Automata (extended abstract). In *Proceedings of the 2nd International Workshop on Foundations of Coordination Languages and Software Architectures (FOCLASA 2003)*, to appear on ENTCS. 310, 312

[7] Z. Habbas, M. Krajecki, D. Singer. *Shared Memory Implementation of Constraint Satisfaction Problem Resolution*. Parallel Processing Letters, Vol. 11, No. 4 (2001), pp. 487–501. 320

[8]  E. Monfroy. A Coordination-based Chaotic Iteration Algorithm for Constraint Propagation. In Carroll, Damiani, Haddad, Oppenheim (eds.) *Proceedings of the 2000 ACM Symposium on Applied Computing*, pp. 262–269, ACM Press. 307, 319

[9]  E. Monfroy, F. Arbab. Constraints Solving as the Coordination of Inference Engines. In Omicini, Zambonelli, Klusch, Tolksdorf (eds.) *Coordination of Internet Agents: Models, Technologies and Applications*, Springer-Verlag, 2001. 307, 319

[10] L. Perron. Search Procedures and Parallelism in Constraint Programming. In Jaffar (ed.) *Proceedings of the 5th International Conference on Principles and Practice of Constraint Programming (CP'99)*, LNCS 1713, pp. 346–360, Springer-Verlag, 1999. 309, 319

[11] C. Schulte. Comparing Trailing and Copying for Constraint Programming. In De Schreye (ed.) *Proceedings of the Sixteenth International Conference on Logic Programming*, Las Cruces, NM, USA, pp. 275–289, The MIT Press, November 1999. 315

[12] C. Schulte. Parallel Search Made Simple. In Beldiceanu et al. (eds.) *Proceedings of TRICS: Techniques foR Implementing Constraint programming Systems, a post-conference workshop of CP 2000*, September 2000. 319

[13] A. Stam. A Framework for Coordinating Parallel Branch and Bound Algorithms. In Arbab, Talcott (eds.) *Coordination Models and Languages*, LNCS 2315, pp. 332–339, Springer-Verlag, 2002. 320

[14] P. Zoeteweij. A Coordination-Based Framework for Distributed Constraint Solving. In O'Sullivan (ed.) *Recent Advances in Constraints*, LNAI 2736, Springer-Verlag, 2003. 307, 314, 319

[15] P. Zoeteweij. Coordination-Based Distributed Constraint Solving in DICE. In *Proceedings of the 2003 ACM Symposium on Applied Computing (SAC)*, Melbourne, FL, USA, pp. 360–366, ACM, 2003. 313, 319

# Lecture Notes in Computer Science

For information about Vols. 1–2834

please contact your bookseller or Springer-Verlag